T0319754

Bioregionalism and Civil Society

The Sustainability and the Environment series provides a comprehensive, independent, and critical evaluation of environmental and sustainability issues affecting Canada and the world today.

SUSTAINABILITY
AND THE
ENVIRONMENT

Mike Carr

Bioregionalism and Civil Society: Democratic Challenges to Corporate Globalism

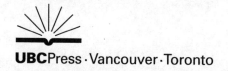

UBCPress · Vancouver · Toronto

15 14 13 12 11 10 09 08 07 06 05 04   5 4 3 2 1

Printed in Canada on acid-free paper that is 100% post-consumer recycled,
processed chlorine-free, and printed with vegetable-based, low-VOC inks.

Library and Archives Canada Cataloguing in Publication

Carr, Mike, 1942-
   Bioregionalism and civil society : democratic challenges to corporate globalism /
Mike Carr.

   (Sustainability and the environment; ISSN 1196-8575)
   Includes bibliographical references and index.
   ISBN 0-7748-0944-2

   1. Bioregionalism. 2. Civil society. 3. Sustainable development. I. Title. II. Series.

GE43.C37 2004   333.72   C2004-904775-2

Canadä

UBC Press gratefully acknowledges the financial support for our publishing
program of the Government of Canada through the Book Publishing Industry
Development Program (BPIDP), and of the Canada Council for the Arts, and the
British Columbia Arts Council.

This book has been published with the help of a grant from the Canadian Federation for the Humanities and Social Sciences, through the Aid to Scholarly Publications Programme, using funds provided by the Social Sciences and Humanities
Research Council of Canada, and with the help of the K.D. Srivastava Fund.

A reasonable attempt has been made to secure permission to reproduce all material
used. If there are errors or omissions, they are wholly unintentional and the
publisher would be grateful to learn of them.

UBC Press
The University of British Columbia
2029 West Mall
Vancouver, BC V6T 1Z2
604-822-5959 / Fax: 604-822-6083
www.ubcpress.ca

Contents

Acknowledgments

I would like to acknowledge the following people:

Doug Aberley for uncounted hours of discussion on bioregionalism, its philosophy, history, and actuality; for many useful references, especially on bioregionalism but also on methodology and postmodernism; for teaching me bioregional mapping methods; and for the mutual support we give each other as two unlikely bioregional actors in academia, both struggling with writing critically about our movement.

John Bacher for his informed and stimulating discussions with me on Earth-centred philosophy, radical politics, Native philosophy and history, and for suggesting excellent works on colonial and Native peoples history, including works by William Cronon and Paula Gunn Allen.

Priscilla Boucher for many engaging and critical exchanges on ecofeminism, ecology, culture, First Nations, paradigm shifts, methodology, and indeed a huge range of topics over the entire period of my time at York University in the Faculty of Environmental Studies, as well as at the School of Community and Regional Planning at UBC. Thanks for helping me to cope with and sort my way through the diverse and abundant literature on qualitative research. Thanks also for moral support in the struggle between the dominant modernist paradigm and the emergent ecologically centred worldview.

David Bouvier for many hours of informative discussion and mutual philosophical exploration of social, cultural, political, economic, scientific, and ecological revolutions, and of Marxism and Buddhism, and for suggesting several critically important books to me.

Don Carr, my brother, for his helpful comments on my section on ritual and for the many deep discussions on art, philosophy, and Western civilization that we have had over three decades.

Kathryn Cholette for encouraging me to keep working on my dissertation and reminding me that it is important to have radicals in academia.

Bob Everton for informing me about the theoretical work of Jean Cohen and Andrew Arato and for our subsequent engaging discussions on civil society theory, the International of Hope and the Zapatista movement, and ecological and social transformation.

Professor John Friedmann for a long, engaging exchange one rainy day exploring our respective frameworks on civil society theory and for his encouragement to publish this book.

Caterina Geuer for spiritual support for and encouragement of my effort to broaden the circle of rational inquiry into the spiritual dimension of existence, for her wisdom and joyful spirit, for turning me on to important books by wise medicine women, and for intelligent and supportive feedback over the fall, winter, and spring as I moved through the final effort to finish the thesis from which this book emerged.

Krisztina Hernadi, always my strongest supporter throughout the entire process of both my academic and my creative lives after I went back to school but especially when I was down or ready to quit. I could always bounce ideas, even the most outlandish ones, off Kriszta. In the end, it was one such session that helped me to break through to my conclusions.

Dolores LaChapelle for publishing an earlier "work in progress" that I wrote while completing my MES at York University and for encouraging me to persist in Earth-centred thinking in the face of much academic and political resistance to the rising paradigm.

Least Livingston for his phenomenological insights; his amazing abilities at birding, which I have witnessed directly on field trips and outings; and his jocular camaraderie.

Steve Lloyd for his research on Huehuecoyotl that contributed to this book and for our many critical discussions on the history and philosophy of Western civilization.

Arne Naess for encouraging me, as a bioregional and social movement activist in academia, to write about the movement in a grounded way that dispels some of the misconceived claims of certain academic writings about bioregionalism.

William Rees, the supervisor of the thesis on which this book is based, who supported me with his incisive, critical comments and suggestions and his abiding faith in the quality and importance of my work.

Randy Schmidt, my editor at UBC Press, who believed in this book from the outset and supported me with many helpful suggestions during the rigorous work of rewriting and editing it.

The Zapatista movement in Mexico for its enormous contribution to organizing a liberated, indigenous civil society in Chiapas and for its role in inspiring and helping to organize an emergent planetary peoples movement against the neoliberal capitalist order, all of which provided huge inspiration for this book.

And, finally, my many sisters and brothers who participated in the Barefoot Cartographers group and more broadly in the bioregional movement in the United States, Mexico, and Canada and who have all inspired me not only to write this book but also to join in their very brave and loving efforts toward sustainable, just, and bioregional societies.

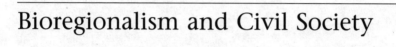

Bioregionalism and Civil Society

Introduction:
Corporate Globalism, Civil Society, and Bioregionalism

Before 11 September 2001, globalization and the global marketplace were already rapidly becoming household words in the advanced industrial consumer societies so often characterized as the "Western world." Then, on that fateful day, low technology (plastic knives) combined with fanatical human determination struck deadly blows at symbolic (and actual) centres of economic and military power in the most technologically advanced and powerful nation on Earth. Before that horrific 9/11 tragedy, globalization appeared to many as an unstoppable juggernaut. Since that terrible day, which some have named Black Tuesday, the global juggernaut now shows a more vulnerable face. Many fears have surfaced publicly, fears about personal safety, impending social chaos, systematic crackdowns on civil and political rights. Among the deepest fears is perhaps one that has for some time now been nagging us in the dark recesses of our minds: a deep recognition that the singular system of global corporate power and multiple technological wonders is, in fact, very fragile – a house of cards – and strategically dependent on centralized military-industrial organization, Middle Eastern oil, and many other nonrenewable critical mineral resources far distant from major centres of industry and consumption in the Western world.

Does the Western capitalist system as we knew it in the late twentieth century have a viable future? In some ways, 9/11 is a reminder that the dominant global economic order has many vulnerabilities – nuclear war, widespread pollution of air, soil, and water, global warming, ozone layer holes, accelerating loss of habitat, increasing desertification, depletion of groundwater, growing inequality and poverty, abuse of political and economic power, et cetera. Yet, in the face of these and many other severe problems of ecological and social sustainability, world leaders of economic globalism and their neoclassical economic theorists present us with no choice but to continue with globalization. For the World Bank, the International Monetary Fund (IMF), the World Trade Organization (WTO), the G-8, the Organisation for Economic Co-operation and Development (OECD), the

North American Free Trade Agreement (NAFTA), the European Union (EU), the Asia Pacific Economic Council (APEC), the Free Trade Area of the Americas (FTAA), and other elite institutions and movers and shakers of global capitalism, there is only one possible future: a worldwide order of market-set prices, liberalized trade and finance, privatization, and limited and decentralized government power. This is a program originally inspired by the economics of one of its leading "gurus," Milton Friedman (1962, 1-6). Whether one supports or opposes this one-world program for the future, one can no longer deny its present reality, a point made in great detail with many examples by William Greider in *One World, Ready or Not: The Manic Logic of Global Capitalism* (1997).

In contrast, the principal subject of this book is a little-known social and cultural movement that promises to contribute vitally to civil society-based regional alternatives to that "manic logic." This social movement is known by the unlikely and somewhat awkward name of bioregionalism. The bioregional movement has been growing slowly but steadily over the past thirty years in the United States and Canada, over the past fifteen years in Mexico, and more recently in Central and South America. There are also expressions of bioregionalism in Europe, Japan, and Australia. This movement of small communities and groups has been quietly growing in spite of the expanding capitalist juggernaut, and it has been unnoticed or ignored in the cultural mainstream (informed by the corporate-controlled media). Although bioregionalism as a movement of people is small and largely unnoticed, bioregional ideas have been adopted in varying degrees by certain jurisdictions from national to regional and municipal such as New Zealand, the State of California, and the City of Toronto.

In the following chapters, one of my goals is to contribute to an understanding that bioregionalism, based on locally and regionally integrated, self-reliant, holistic economies networked through communication and limited trade linkages, offers a crucial contribution toward sustainable, healthy, and sane alternatives to an increasingly unhealthy, unsustainable, and fragile global capitalist monoculture. Over the past twenty years, my own experience has been that, when people first hear about bioregional ideas, a common response is that they make a lot of sense but that they will never work in practice. So my purpose is also to show how the bioregional movement is beginning to carry out its long-term vision through short- and medium-term projects and processes in civil society and public life and in certain lifelong, committed experiments in cultural and social change in both urban and rural settings. An essential aspect of my approach is to show that these projects and processes engender immediate rewards for the participants in the short term as well. By rewards, I mean profound emotional and spiritual experiences that defy the narrow economistic vision of globalism centred on its abstract, neoclassical concept of the economic human being (this concept is explored in Chapter 1).

Globalization and bioregionalism offer two very opposed views of what a sustainable human future might look like, so globalization provides a logical context in which to explore bioregional alternatives. Globalization is now so geographically pervasive that it is inevitably a real-world context for local and regional efforts to build or enhance alternative approaches. Given the immense importance of corporate globalism, the breadth of discourse about it, and the deep opposition between the vision of globalism as a single system on the one hand and place-based bioregional diversity on the other, it is essential to present a clear analytical picture of what I understand by globalization.

In simple terms, globalization centres on the concept of a single global economy in which each region produces only one commodity or a few specialized commodities for the global market. In that sense, it is almost the opposite of a fully developed bioregionalism, which favours a planetary diversity of place-based bioregional economies conservatively and carefully producing and consuming primarily for their own populations' needs and only secondarily for interbioregional trade. Global trade is, of course, a key mechanism for globalization, but trade is only one of many aspects of the process of globalization. Today we hear of global corporations, global cities, global networks and forums, global TV, global monoculture, and even global malls where "global teens" shop for global brand name consumer products such as Nike, Calvin Klein, Tommy Hilfiger, Benetton, et cetera. As Naomi Klein (2000) has effectively pointed out, such global commodities are increasingly produced in developing countries in "global sweatshops."

So what do I understand as globalization? My understanding of corporate globalization is informed by a range of important critical thinkers within and beyond academic circles. Some have compared the process of globalization to a global machine: "Imagine a wondrous new machine, strong and supple, a machine that reaps as it destroys. It is huge and mobile, something like the machines of modern agriculture but vastly more complicated and powerful – as it goes, the machine throws off enormous mows of wealth and bounty, while it leaves behind great furrows of wreckage" (Greider 1997, 11). Greider's metaphor of a great machine is not new. Over thirty years ago, American man of letters and generalist thinker Lewis Mumford (1970) used the term "the new megamachine" to describe the concentration of industrial and military power that developed during World War II in the United States and then used nuclear weapons on civilian populations. For Greider, the machine metaphor offers a simplified way to visualize the process of globalization. The global megamachine translates as none other than "modern capitalism driven by the imperatives of global industrial revolution – the drama of a free-running economic system that is reordering the world" (1997, 11). While the megamachine provides a useful and vivid metaphor, I think that a more substantial and structural analysis is necessary to deal with such a huge and daunting phenomenon.

There are those (usually more traditional Marxists) who argue that the term "globalization" is, at best, confusing. The argument is that the process of globalization is not new but merely a continuation of the process of imperialism and capital accumulation on a world scale in the nineteenth and twentieth centuries as analyzed by figures such as Lenin and Rosa Luxemburg in the early twentieth century and later updated by Samir Amin and others (see Amin 1974; Galtung 1971; Mies 1986; and Wallerstein 1979). Others, such as Noam Chomsky (1999) and geographer David Harvey (1989, 2000), while certainly not denying earlier imperialist development and a globalized, historical process of capital accumulation, argue that there is something new in the current phase of globalization that merits new analysis. There is also a growing critical discourse among political economists, political scientists, ecological economists, planners, and others involved with rethinking globalization that contributes to this spreading discourse (Aulakh and Schecter 2000; Douglas and Friedmann 1998; Lipschutz 1996; Rees 2002; Schecter 1999).

As someone who has been a longtime radical activist and thinker, as well as a more recently minted critical academic, I share the view that the contemporary process of globalization is rooted in a long period of capitalist development. For this view, I draw especially on the work of Harvey, whose analysis of the historical development of capitalism integrates a strong geographical dimension, one not developed by Marx. Harvey, in contrast, focuses on the uneven geographical dimension of the process of capital accumulation and development and the related process of "creative destruction."

Throughout his work, Harvey returns to the process of creative destruction engendered by capital accumulation. On the one hand, capitalism is about an extremely powerful, creative process "particularly with respect to technology, organization and the ability to transform material nature into social wealth" (1989, 53). This very success produces huge surpluses that must be consumed if the process of capital accumulation and growth is to continue. Historically (and geographically), this process of consumption occurs in real places – cities and urban regions: "Urbanization has always been about the mobilization, production, appropriation, and adsorption of economic surpluses" (53). Over the past few decades, this drive for consumption has been reflected, in part, in the widespread phenomenon of local "growth machines" that take the form of urban pro-growth coalitions and urban boosterism (Davis 1992; Harvey 1989; Molotch 1976, 1993). In this view, urban growth machines have become an integral part of the global megamachine, essential to the continued process of capital accumulation and adsorption of surpluses.

Of course, the process of capital accumulation didn't happen in a day. Harvey (1989) takes pains to describe three major periods in the long historical process of capital accumulation leading to the present period at the outset of a new millennium. In the first period, there was primitive and violent accumulation of capital under colonialism, the trade in slaves, and the initial concentration of capital in the mercantile city in the eighteenth century.

In the second period, the capitalist production of surpluses in early-nineteenth-century industrial cities such as Manchester, Birmingham, and Leeds represented a shift from the mercantile appropriation of surpluses through trade, monopoly, and military control to the production of surpluses through the command over labour processes. This was, of course, the industrial revolution. It took place in or very near cities. In this period, overaccumulation of surpluses eventually became a serious problem for capitalism until it was partially resolved by geographical expansion and the shift from the industrial city to the imperialist city, which, in the last half of the nineteenth century, poured surplus capital into the colonies searching for further opportunities. Harvey points out that this development was an "unstable mix" of intense interurban competition, spiralling technological innovation, and imperialist geographical expansionism, which produced national geopolitical rivalries and two world wars, "the second of which inflicted enormous and uneven geographical destruction on urban assets – a neat but hideously violent resolution to capitalism's over accumulation problem" (34).

The third period, following World War II, is characterized by Harvey as the adsorption of surpluses accomplished by the shift from the Fordist industrial city to the Keynesian city, the expansion of consumption through Keynesian demand-side economic policies such as the expansion of the credit system, and unlimited debt creation (a perversion of Keynes's original concept, as Harvey carefully points out). This period also featured the rapid growth of the automobile industry, roads and expressways, urban sprawl, the proliferation of shopping malls, competitive and conspicuous consumerism, the rise of large transnational corporations, rapid technological innovations in many sectors, the destruction of entire city districts in the name of urban renewal, expansion of military production and weapons sales to regimes across the globe, and other familiar phenomena that continue into the present. All of this has been accompanied by a long series of reckless wars and military coups in various parts of the globe and an incredible (if uneven) toll of ecological devastation and loss of species and habitat, which in aggregate amounts to a sixth great planetary extinction spasm, the first to be engendered by human actions (Wilson 1992).

So what is really different about contemporary globalization? Is it not just more of the same colonial and imperialist exploitation and expansion? Perhaps, but the geographical scale is now more truly global than in the days of Lenin and Luxemburg. Contemporary globalization comprises a daunting set of interconnected processes that includes the information and telecommunications revolution, flexible "just-in-time" production systems, more extensive globalized trade networks, the capitalist revolution in agricultural production in both advanced industrial and many "Third World" nations (the "green revolution"), and, most important perhaps, the increased power and global organizational and market reach of transnational corporations (built up during the post–World War II Keynesian period). These factors have combined to spread the process of cultural imperialism (as capitalist monoculture) over most of the globe. This is not to argue that monoculturalism (global teenagers in global malls serviced by global sweatshops) has swept aside the great diversity of distinct cultures over the Earth. However, that threat is very real (Klein 2000). Just as biodiversity is threatened by globalization, so too is cultural diversity threatened (but not eliminated) by globalization (Scholte in Aulakh and Schecter 2000).

Harvey (2000) points to four major shifts that signify why globalization has taken on a "new allure" and importance after the Keynesian period. The first is financial deregulation, initiated in the United States in the early 1970s as a response to the breakdown of the Bretton Woods system of international trade and exchange established toward the end of World War II. Deregulation allowed the global system to be coordinated through the market and "made the financial conditions of capitalism far more volatile" (61). Furthermore, the rhetoric accompanying this shift promoted the term "globalization" as a virtue. Noam Chomsky (1999) and a growing number of other critics refer to this shift as the Washington "consensus," an array of market-oriented principles designed by the government of the United States. These include stringent structural adjustment programs, whose basic rules are liberalize trade and finance, let markets set prices, end inflation, and privatize.

The second major shift, the rate of technology transfer and imitation across and throughout different zones of the world economy, accelerated by leaps and bounds in the final decades of the twentieth century. It was facilitated by the increase of educated and scientifically trained elites "capable of adapting and adsorbing technological knowledge and know-how from anywhere and everywhere" (Harvey 2000, 61-62). While capitalism has historically always engendered succeeding waves of technology change, the current wave of profound technological change and product innovation is particularly concentrated in time while taking place (unevenly, of course) over greater geographical areas of the globe than ever before.

In the third major shift, the information revolution brought significant changes to the organization of production and consumption as well as to the definition of entirely new wants and needs. Dematerialized "cyberspace" in the form of the World Wide Web, originated by the military apparatus, was immediately seized upon by financial institutions and transnational capital to coordinate their activities instantaneously over space. The space and time of electronic media and communications imploded in a world where the monopolization of media power was already a problem for democracy, in spite of right-wing utopian claims that the information revolution is inherently emancipatory. Harvey (2000) goes on to warn that we should not ignore the strong totalistic tone of this technologically determinist rhetoric, "perhaps best captured in Margaret Thatcher's famous declaration that 'there is no alternative'" (62-63).

And, in the fourth major shift, the cost and time of moving commodities, production operations, and people tumbled, liberating many activities from former spatial constraints and permitting rapid adjustments in locations of production, consumption, and populations. Harvey (2000) emphasizes the importance of synergistic interactions among all four elements: "Financial deregulation could not have occurred, for example, without the information revolution, and technology transfer (which also relied heavily on the information revolution) would have been meaningless without a much greater ease of movement of commodities and people around the world" (63).

Over the past two decades, the shifts described above constitute a post-Keynesian shift in the process of globalization launched by the industrial revolution that could be viewed as an attempt to recapture the halcyon days of "laissez faire" liberalism of the late nineteenth century, organized and led by Great Britain (thus the current term "*neo*liberalism," also referred to by some as "neoconservatism"). It was during this earlier "free-trade" period that private business corporations first consolidated and then extended their great power through a variety of means, which included legalization of the corporation as a "person," limited liability for corporate shareholders, the ability of corporations (as persons) to own other corporations, and the "immortality" of the corporation (Grossman and Adams 1993; Kelly 1999; Korten 1995; Polanyi 1968; Yaron 2002). In the closing years of the twentieth century, the new period of "free trade" (the term preferred by its proponents over neoliberalism or capitalist globalization) was led jointly by Thatcherism in Great Britain and Reaganism in the United States.

There are several important effects or impacts of globalization that help to capture its meaning more fully. The first has been a weakening of the authority of nation-states vis-à-vis market forces. This is a pervasive theme in globalization literature (Schecter 1999, 71-73). It speaks to a decline in the power of the nation-state to regulate global corporations, markets, and finance capital. The information and electronic revolutions have facilitated the twenty-four-hour, instantaneous, and ceaseless flow of capital and information that even the mainstream US-based magazine *Business Week* once referred to as the "global casino" (Henderson 1991). The ability of the state (any state, even the United States) to regulate exchange and interest rates has consequently lessened a great deal. As well, accelerated technological change, increased product flexibility, trade, and financial liberalization have allowed the market to function with increasingly fewer social and political constraints (Zoninsein in Schecter 1999). This loss of power to control capital mobility has meant that state operations have become more "disciplined" by finance capital than ever before; global capital in the form of international banks and global corporations now demands structural adjustment and fiscal austerity. Consequently, "the state has been to some degree reduced to the role of finding ways to promote a favourable business climate" (Harvey 2000, 65). However, Chomsky, Harvey, and others critically analyzing globalization also see a continuing important role for the state under neoliberalism, not only in terms of promoting economic development, but also in terms of maintaining consensus and social control (Chomsky 1999; Harvey 2000, 180-81; Lentner in Aulakh and Schecter 2000; Schecter 1999, 61-101). This concern has, of course, been heightened since 9/11. Thus, we now see huge expenditures on military production, severe tax cuts and, consequently, massive increases in the federal debt from the self-described "war president" George W. Bush.

A second important effect of economic globalization over the past two decades has been a distinct tendency toward cultural convergence or global monoculture. Global markets, mass media (e.g., CNN), cyberspace, global brand names, and so on have given planetary currency to a wide range of symbols, ideas, habits, rules, words, products, and experiences that take on supraterritorial dimensions (Klein 2000; Scholte in Schecter 1999, 71). For Harvey (2000), however, it is far too simplistic to see globalism as purely a movement toward "homogeneity in global culture." We must consider that a range of global corporations now markets cultural difference, and there are intense cultural reactions in many places against the homogenizing influence of global markets (67). Nevertheless, this "diversity" marketing, as Klein (2000) has compellingly argued, appears more realistically as a "candy-coated multiculturalism," as a kinder, gentler packaging for homogenization – in effect, a monomulticulturalism, a "One World placelessness" created by an "ethnic-food-court approach" that, rather than "selling America to the world," delivers a kind of "market masala to everyone in the world" (117).

The third effect is that globalization has engendered the actual geographical dispersal and fragmentation of production systems combined with the increasing centralization of corporate power, the increasing geographical dispersal of a growing world labour force, and the increasing cultural heterogeneity of labour forces due to massive migrations in the latter half of the twentieth century. The combination of a greater global geographical reach of corporate power and an increased centralization of command and control functions clearly highlights the centrality of corporate power in the process of neoliberal globalization.

The migration of world labour has gone hand in hand with a rapidly accelerating migration to urban regions (from hinterlands both near and far). This migration is occurring at such a rate that it is better understood as hyperurbanization: that is, the current phase of urbanization is super rapid and largely unplanned, creating a totalizing effect on urban regions. With this development, the city and city region have become much more important as competitive entities in the global economy (Harvey 2000, 64). In the advanced capitalist countries, most people now live in cities. On a global basis, the world's urban population grew from 13 percent of total population in 1900 to 47 percent in 1999 (Jenks and Burgess 2000), with much of this urban growth occurring in the last half of the twentieth century. As well, there have been dramatic increases in the volume of global output and trade and in the number and size of cities as the global economy has shifted from the primary and rural to the secondary and tertiary urban sectors. Finally, the global economy has expanded threefold, and the human population has ballooned 30 percent to over six billion in the twenty-two years since 1980 alone (Rees 2002). Yet, in the neoliberal worldview of the late twentieth century, these cities and regions had to compete against each other in the increasingly liberalized markets of the process of globalization in order to continue (if not accelerate) the pace of growth. Moreover, attempts to internalize regional environmental costs (pollution, environmental degradation, etc.) and create sustainable and equitable regional development are seen as threats to regional "competitive advantages," leading capital to pursue its interests elsewhere (Burgess in Jenks and Burgess 2000) or to pursue legal challenges under NAFTA or the WTO. Thus, corporate globalization, reflected in policies of neoliberal "free trade"· (the Washington Consensus), is – in principle – against *any* local regional economic diversity and integration with goals of self-reliance.

Along with the growth of urban regions under neoliberal globalization, we have seen the rise of local, urban "growth machines" – coalitions of business, labour (often construction trades), and municipal governments – designed to attract capital investment based on some local comparative advantage. Neoliberal growth machine politics conceives of the city as an entrepreneurial entity imitating the outlook and financial business practices of the private sector, as a risk taker, and as an active competitor in the economic sphere. In this view, public-private partnerships between municipalities and urban developers are seen as essential to urban growth and revitalization. The private developers need the permits, licences, zoning changes, and so on, while the municipality needs the capital and organizational reach of big business. However, growth machine political economy has led municipalities into a zero-sum game of interurban and intra-urban competition to attract redevelopment capital via public-private "partnerships" that have been fiscally, socially, and environmentally damaging and narrowly focused on private gain in spite of proponents' claims to the contrary (Harvey 1989; Leitner and Garner 1993; Molotch 1993). This second wave of urban renewal since World War II has produced some miserable failures even when evaluated on the narrow economistic terms of their proponents (Flint and Detroit, Michigan), while others, widely hailed as great successes (Baltimore's Harbour Place or Milwaukee's Grand Avenue Project), exist in cities whose surrounding neighbourhoods continue to decline, demonstrating the failure of the "trickle-down" effect of globalization (Harvey 2000; Molotch 1993).

Ironically, these redevelopment projects, promoted on the basis of the comparative advantages of locality and place, end up mimicking each other and producing sameness in the name of the comparative advantage of the diversity of places. Their apparent success is therefore often short-lived or made redundant by alternative or parallel "innovations" reproduced elsewhere (Harvey 1989). Moreover, far from being "inevitable" outcomes of globalization, on closer inspection urban growth machines are revealed as the results of special interest, pro-growth actors – namely, the coalitions themselves (Molotch 1993). In sum, the result of urban growth machine development and heightened interurban competition "is a way into rather than out of capitalist crisis in the long run" (Harvey 1989, 55), which embodies the very manic logic about which Greider, Harvey, Korten, and a growing number of critical thinkers have been deeply concerned. Simply put, credit-financed shopping malls, sports stadia, and other spectacles of leisured consumerism are high-risk projects that can easily fall on hard times (Harvey 1989, 2000). Urban growth machines, like the global growth machine, represent a mostly ephemeral, fragile house of cards, as recent events have shown. We have only to think here of the spectacle of Giuliani, the mayor of New York City during the aftermath of 9/11, or President Bush pleading with Americans to return to shopping activities so that America can return to its normal business of commodity consumption.

There is already since 9/11 a nascent perception that people are beginning to spend more time in family and community activities rather than in the usual shopping mall excursions. If this proves to be a real and lasting shift, then the possibilities for a civil society–based cultural and social transformation away from the global manic logic of unregulated growth and consumerism become more imaginable, more desirable, more realizable,

Figure 1   Pentagon, by Don Carr. "Pentagon" is a metaphor for what Lewis Mumford called the US "power complex," the controlling nexus of the US military industrial complex. "Pentagon" also refers specifically to the Pentagon building in Washington, DC.

and more grounded in people's actual relationships with each other and in emerging alternative behaviours. This book was written in the hope that a change in direction is possible, that people will be able to bring about a revival of community and democratic associational life in civil society, leading to a change in the culture of consumption and to corresponding and necessary changes in the economic and political structures and institutions of civilization. That a diverse movement (composed of many different groups in shifting alliances concerned with a host of pressing issues) has already begun to emerge is reflected in a growing discourse on the rise of civil society (Douglas and Friedmann 1998; Sandercock 1998).

During the same decades of neoliberal globalization described above, there has also been a proliferation of social movements and citizens' organizations – cultural, economic, environmental, political, and social – in Eastern and Western Europe, South and Central America, Mexico, the United States, Canada, and elsewhere that have given rise to a widely proliferating literature based on the revival, reconstruction, reemergence, or rise of civil society (Cohen and Arato 1992; Douglas and Friedmann 1998; Edwards et al. 2001; Keane 1988; Korten 1998; Lipschutz 1996; Sandercock 1998; Schecter 1999; Walzer 1995). The bioregional movement is part of this spectrum of civil society initiatives that include social and environmental concerns as well as economic and political issues and problems. More recently, as many people are now aware, there is also an emergent global movement of peoples challenging corporate globalization. This movement has mounted large public demonstrations in Europe, the United States (Seattle), Canada (Quebec City), Italy (Genoa), Mexico, India, Central and South America, and elsewhere, most often at meetings of the WTO, the G-8, and other global elite institutions, protesting exploitation of workers, environmental destruction, and erosion of human rights, civil liberties, social justice, and democracy.

This movement, often characterized in the corporate-controlled media as an "antiglobalization" movement, is perhaps better viewed as a movement *for* socially just, democratic, and ecologically sustainable approaches to globalization. It is a movement *for* creating forms of global democracy. The global movement against corporate or neoliberal globalization increasingly sees itself as being of and for civil society, taking an inclusive approach to issues of social justice, democracy, and environment (Independent Media Center 2000). The term "civil society" is used explicitly by many in the movement, influenced, in part at least, by the use of the term by the Zapatista Liberation Movement (EZLN) in Chiapas, Mexico. The origins of the global movement are located in an international network called People's Global Action (PGA). PGA was formed out of a 1998 Zapatista *encuentro* ("gathering") in Barcelona, Spain. Its founding members include anarchist groups in Spain, Britain, and Germany, a Gandhian socialist peasant league in India, the Argentinian teachers' union, the Brazilian landless peasants' movement, indigenous groups such as the Maori of New Zealand, the Kuna of Ecuador, and the Zapatistas who inspired the *encuentro*. Most of the movement's techniques (consensus process, spokescouncils, even mass nonviolent civil disobedience itself) were first developed in the global south (Graeber 2002). The *encuentro* in Spain was modelled on the first *encuentro* organized in Chiapas, Mexico, by the Zapatistas in 1996.

Like the literature on globalization, the literature on civil society and the concepts and models used under the term is proliferating rapidly. There is even the concept of a "global" civil society spreading in the literature (Drysek 1997; Korten 1998; Lipschutz 1996; McGinnis 1999; Schecter 1999). For clarity in what follows, the concept of civil society needs to be defined and explained. My own theoretical perspective in this book is deeply informed by civil society theory, particularly by the work of Jean Cohen and Andrew Arato (1992). I will introduce this theory, which I have borrowed and then revised, in order to integrate a vital ecological dimension that it totally lacked.

Most often the definition of civil society and the social and political economic analyses that flow from it depend on the model used to picture the relationships between civil society and the state or between civil society and the market. Many analysts of civil society (whether liberal or Marxist), including those using global civil society concepts, use a two-sphere model that depicts relationships between civil society and the state. These models include the corporate sphere as a part of civil society (see, e.g., Lipschutz 1996; Schecter 1999; Walzer 1995; and Warkentin 2001). Such definitions of civil society thus include citizens' organizations or alliances, nongovernmental organizations (NGOs) whether formal or informal, trade unions, and private business corporations large and small. These models are seriously flawed. As Jean Cohen points out, the two-part (or two-sphere) model of civil society vis-à-vis the state, whereby civil society includes everything outside the state sector, can at best be a slogan, a mere starting point for mobilization against dictatorial statist regimes but not adequate for serious analysis of Western-style democracies. Planning theorist John Friedmann (1998) has also made an important contribution to civil society theory. For Friedmann, two-part models are useless in terms of making any real contribution to radical thought about social change (personal communication, 26 October 2001).

The major problem is that the two-part model ignores (or, at best, fails to focus on) the undemocratic relationships between powerful economic actors (banks, large corporations) and civil society. However, such relationships, based on economic power, can be "as great a danger to social solidarity, social justice, and autonomy as the power of the modern state" (Cohen in Walzer 1995, 36). Cohen adds that the autonomy of civil society is not the same as the autonomy of the market, since the former is based on normative principles "still oriented to the utopian ideals of modernity," including plurality, publicity, legality, equality, justice, voluntary association, and individual autonomy (37). This contrasts with the autonomy of the capitalist market driven principally, if not solely, by the profit motive. Historically, under capitalism, Cohen argues, economic society has been "more successfully insulated from the influence of civil society than political society" (38). In the current era of neoliberalism, this tendency is more pronounced than in the preceding Keynesian period. More than ever, the formal market sphere, now globally dominated by money capital and a rogue financial system, operates outside any human regulation, profiting from and contributing to the volatility of global money and speculative markets (Korten

1995). It follows that a three-part (or three-sphere) model is needed. Such a model requires a distinct economic sphere (as well as state and civil society spheres) to ensure a proper or adequate focus on the formal market sphere and its problematic relationship to civil society. There is another important reason to abandon two-part models of civil society. That is the concern among post-Marxists and interested others to create a democratic theory of radical social transformation that abandons the concept and strategy of "capturing state power."

In contrast, Cohen and Arato (1992) have made an important contribution to an emergent body of theory thematizing a broad democratic transformation firmly based in civil society. This radical democratic theory offers promising insights for all social movements – and anyone – seeking to address the crisis of modern civilization. Self-proclaimed as "post-Marxist" theorists, Cohen and Arato break with the Marxist theory of the dictatorship of the proletariat and with the conception of the working class as the primary agent of social revolution. Also abandoned is the old dream of abolishing the state. Instead, a dual strategy, based in civil society, is proposed to replace it. Crucially different, though, is that in this three-part model (described in great detail by Cohen and Arato in their important contribution to democratic theory), civil society is differentiated from both political and economic spheres. In this conception, the working class is only one of many agents of transformation along with a wide diversity of other actors in civil society. Civil society is thus a much more inclusive sphere in which to situate and on which to base citizen action for democratic social change. In differentiating civil society from both the political sphere (dominated by the state) and the economic sphere (dominated by financial capital and large corporations), the theory also focuses on the necessity of democratizing large private economic institutions while retaining a focus on democratizing the state as well. Two-part statist/civil society models ignore this crucial strategic consideration.

Thus, this three-sphere model supports a strategy that views civil society as the sphere, or terrain, of "emancipation," the sphere of the self-defence of society against both the economization of society on the one hand and the bureaucratization of it on the other (Cohen and Arato 1992). Its primary strategic purpose is to defend and strengthen democracy in civil society, reinvigorating grassroots democracy. Thus, "horizontal" actions target other actors within civil society, so that "civil society proper is the target and terrain of this politics of identity" (Cohen in Walzer 1995, 39). This basic strategy envisions horizontal communicative action targeting identities, norms, and institutions in civil society to form the democratic basis from which to initiate a second strategy in relation to the other two state and corporate spheres. This second dual strategy is aimed at democratizing both political and economic spheres through campaigns for reforms of laws and institutions of state and corporate sectors alike. Horizontal actions toward democratizing civil society are thus combined with "vertical" campaigns of bridging or developing influence for democratic legal, policy, and institutional reforms within the dominant state and corporate sectors. The combined horizontal and vertical strategies must support each other for lasting social change, as we shall see in Chapter 1.

It seems to me that, among the plethora of civil society theories, only two models, that of Cohen and Arato and the four-sphere model of Friedmann, engage the complex reality of modern, global capitalist society clearly and critically enough (with respect to both state and corporate institutions and power) to shed some light on possibilities and paths for radical but democratic alternatives. I have found the Cohen and Arato three-sphere model the most analytically useful with respect to the dual strategy theorization.

However, their civil society theory lacks both an ecological critique of globalism and a cultural critique of its underpinnings based on the narrowly conceived modernist construct of "economic man" (sic). As such, their model fails to integrate ecological thought and analysis. In the entire 600-page text of their major work, *Civil Society and Political Theory*, there is no definition of ecology, nor is there any discussion of an ecological dimension to civil society theory. In my view, no theory of social transformation can overlook the central importance in our time of ecology, given the immense, varied, and complex dimensions of global ecological crises, the profound cultural rift between dominant modern "Western" civilization and the natural world, and the importance of a wide diversity of literature on these questions (Berman 1981, 1989; Brown et al. 1996; Brown and Kane 1994; Evernden 1985; Merchant 1980; Naess 1990; Rowe 1990; World Commission on Environment and Development 1987; Worster 1985). So the primary theoretical goal of this book is to make a contribution to the integration of ecological, spiritual, and sustainability concerns with civil society theory, particularly with respect to the three-sphere model of Cohen and Arato. In my view, civil society theory must become fully inclusive of ecological, spiritual, and sustainability concerns in order to engage in any real way with both the concerns themselves and the movements in civil society that address those concerns. Theories of social change that do not engage with practices of social change remain merely formal academic constructs. By employing a civil society theoretical framework to explore the strengths and weaknesses of bioregionalism as a grounded alternative to neoliberal globalization, I intend to contribute to the development of an ecologically and spiritually informed civil society theory and to reveal some important lessons for developing an understanding of strategic democratic change in civil society aimed at democratizing both state and corporate sectors. In this way, strategies to expand democracy in both political and economic spheres are thus given urgent attention and opened to serious exploration and examination.

Bioregionalism is a philosophy with values and practices that attempt to meld issues of social and economic justice and sustainability with cultural, ecological, and spiritual concerns. Furthermore, bioregional efforts at democratic social and cultural change take place primarily in the sphere of civil society. What would an encounter between democratic civil society theory and bioregional philosophy and practice be able to tell us about the strengths and weaknesses of bioregionalism? Conversely, what insights might bioregional experience contribute to civil society theory, especially with respect to its lack of any ecological dimension? Moreover, the bioregional movement has developed a praxis of social change that challenges the modernist construct of "economic man" upon which neoliberal globalization rests. Civil society theory, like bioregionalism, questions neoclassical economistic constructs that deny/negate broader enlightenment conceptions of humans as social, communicative beings (Friedmann in Douglas and Friedmann 1998). It seems to me that employing democratic civil society theory as a means to explore bioregionalism as an emergent alternative to globalism promises to enrich both civil society theory and bioregional vision and practice. Moreover, this encounter might reveal important lessons for all social movements concerned with developing strategies to defend and enhance democracy in the face of the globalizing capitalist world order.

This book weaves together stories of the bioregional movement in Canada, the United States, and Mexico from its birth in the early 1970s to 1998. Through these stories, the vision, values, social change strategy, and community-building and networking tools/methods of the movement are revealed. Questions essential to movement building are explored. How does a movement rooted in social and cultural change and community building begin? How does it grow? What problems do local bioregional organizers and cultural change participants encounter in their efforts to move toward a more equitable, just, and sustainable society? What lessons can we draw from bioregional experiments in social, ecological, and economic sustainability? In presenting these stories, I pursue an extended inquiry into the possibilities for broader social and cultural change in one of the consumerist heartlands of global capitalism, North America.

The stories and examples presented here show that bioregionalists integrate cultural change into the centre of their paradigm of social transformation. Bioregionalists critique conspicuous consumption, and they work to implement changes in their lives and those of others, chiefly through horizontal efforts in civil society, building place-based communities and networks that respect ecological limits. Bioregionalists promote strategies aimed at reducing both aggregate and individual consumption. They attempt to live their daily lives in ways that greatly reduce their personal levels of consumption. Such efforts are seen by bioregionalist practitioners not as sacrifices that they must make for the environment or for social justice but as real, achievable improvements in the quality of their own lives. Reductions in consumption and the demanding life work of organizing for sustainable social change have been supported – in the experience of many bioregionalists – by certain emotional/spiritual benefits of bonding both with other humans and with the natural world in particular places. Using an analytical tool that I call "ecosocial capital," I have identified this vital bonding process as a synergistic energy involving spiritual feelings of joy and love.

The concept of ecosocial capital emerges from the current discourse on social capital, specifically a social capital critical of concepts of undersocialized, "economic man" as an atomized, hyperindividualistic consumer. Social capital theory, like civil society theory, emphasizes the importance of horizontal bonding relations of peers based on trust. Simply put, social capital refers to and includes norms of cooperation, reciprocity, and mutual aid; relations of trust; and organized social networks (Putnam 1993a, b). It is important to note here, since so many commentators have overlooked it, that social capital inheres in the structure of relationships of information and trust built between and among individuals (Coleman 1990). Thus, social capital cannot be measured quantitatively. Rather, it is about relationships. As such, it is already, implicitly at least, an ecological concept.

My use of the concept of social capital is different from that of either Coleman or Putnam. I have adapted social capital as a "sensitizing concept" to aid in the exploration and interpretation of emergent patterns of sociocultural relationships in the bioregional movement. Research using sensitizing concepts seeks grounded, interpretive explanations through naturalistic research that also seeks to improve the analytical tools themselves (Pyne Addelson 1991, 91). In this book, I attempt to show how bioregionalists have created social capital through their horizontal community-building strategies and how the profound emotional and spiritual rewards of social capital and ecosocial capital help to support this work.

While bioregionalists spend a great deal of their daily efforts in this horizontal work in civil society, they also put effort into pursuing vertical reforms. However, they have not sufficiently theorized their strategy vis-à-vis either the state or the corporate sectors with respect to strategic vertical reform and its relationship to horizontal community building. That is, they have not sufficiently theorized their strategy for vertical political and economic institutional transformation that would support lasting cultural and economic changes in civil society. In particular, they have not developed any common theory or strategy with respect to the entrenched power of banking capital and large corporations. Yet, as the economic system becomes increasingly globalized through the global reach of corporate and financial power, it is clear that, unless we learn how to effect democratic change within the corporate sector (as well as the state sector), movements for social change will not be successful in achieving deep and lasting reforms necessary for sustainability and justice. Reforms in the political sphere alone are not sufficient to democratize the corporate and finance capital sector, since, as already discussed, under the contemporary neoliberal order, global corporations and financial capital are outstripping the ability of states to regulate or even monitor their global activities.

After considerable thought about this problem over several years, I believed that a serious inquiry into bioregionalism could draw crucial cultural insights from its local community building and networking. This knowledge could then be used to inform civil society theory, strengthening it considerably by including cultural change as a fully integrated dimension of theory. In turn, this reconstructed, integrated theory (with its previous understanding of combined horizontal-vertical strategies) might inform social movements such as bioregionalism with some key insights into selected vertical strategies for political and economic institutional change in both state and corporate spheres. Such vertical strategies for democratic change would complement and support grassroots efforts at horizontal change in the sphere of civil society.

The search for cooperative and democratic solutions to the global crisis of civilization inevitably raises questions as to what is most fundamental about human nature and culture. These are questions about the ability of human beings to live cooperatively, about the relationship between humans and the rest of the natural world, and about the meaning of human life. Some, following classical conservative philosopher Thomas Hobbes, argue that humans have never lived cooperatively, that the original condition of humankind was a war of all against all.

Today there is good evidence, some of which I present in Chapter 2, to suggest that, during humanity's early days in the domestic mode of production (gathering, hunting, and gardening), many human groups did live cooperatively in extended families and communities and did so in the context of a worldview that conceived of humans as an integral part of the greater family of life on planet Earth. This is a worldview that places the human community squarely within the greater "community of beings" (the natural world). I make the case that modern society has some important lessons to learn from these societies, lessons about cooperative living among humans, about living with care and respect for all life, and about the conservative and careful use of natural resources. Informed by an anthropology with both sociocultural and ecological underpinnings, my review of the domestic mode of production – which serves as an introduction to my exploration of bioregionalism – challenges the narrow construct of the acquisitive and selfish human individual of neoclassical economics with a socialized concept of the human being.

My theoretical approach is located in the radical planning tradition that has been referred to as the tradition of social mobilization (Friedmann 1987, 75). Radical planning asks the general question how does social mobilization to effect radical transformation occur? Thus, my approach falls within both social science and the humanities since it includes anthropological and sociological dimensions as well as historical and philosophical inquiry. Traditionally, the social sciences and the humanities have confined themselves to human-centred questions and concerns, leaving the natural sciences to deal separately with questions of a nonhuman nature. Few social scientists holistically address questions concerning relationships between human and nonhuman nature. In contrast, my work is informed by an ecologically centred perspective. Social questions remain crucially important in my approach. However, since human cultures and economies are, in fact, located within natural systems, the study of human systems and cultures must be undertaken through a more holistic social ecology. A social ecological perspective challenges the separate and anthropocentric treatment of human social science and recognizes both the interdependence of human and natural systems and the primacy of humankind's "obligate dependence" (Rees 1990) upon the natural world. From within the research framework of an ecocentric scientific paradigm, the test of "good" science is not that it works in the sense of enabling humans to exploit the world around them more efficiently but that it works in the sense of assisting and enabling them to live in ways that preserve and foster the health, safety, and well-being of both the human and the nonhuman communities (Eckersley 1992, 116).

Chapter 1 examines both the neoclassical economic argument for globalism that supports constant increases in consumption/production and an opposing ecological analysis of the problem, including an exploration of the decline of community accompanying the drive for growth. This provides a context for a discussion of the theory of civil society and ecosocial capital.

In Chapter 2, I take up the question of human nature and the ability of humans to live cooperatively in community by looking at our roots in the domestic mode of production. I conclude with a discussion of contemporary civil society and the role of the informal economy.

Chapter 3 is an exploration of bioregional philosophical values that have emerged from the bioregional movement in Canada, Mexico, and the United States, values that deeply challenge the notion of "economic man."

In Chapter 4, I examine the bioregional movement's organizing strategy and tools for community building toward cultural and economic conversion to sustainable society. This is both a philosophical and an experiential exploration using many examples.

Chapter 5 presents five stories or narrative accounts of bioregionalists' efforts at reinhabitation in two large urban regions and three rural watersheds in the United States, Canada, and Mexico.

In Chapter 6, I present the story of the continental bioregional movement through narrative accounts of seven continental congresses.

Finally, the conclusion returns to theoretical considerations of civil society and bioregionalism, outlines my development of an ecocentric civil society theory, and attempts to draw some lessons for democratic social transformation in the face of corporate globalization, not only for the bioregional movement, but for social movements and society more generally.

1
Civil Society against Consumerism

Fatal Consumption

Today there is a growing fear that conspicuous consumerism, especially in North America, may be devolving into a culture of extinction. What is the basis of this urge to consume? What props it up? The problem of overconsumption in modern society is supported ideologically by the dominant cultural construct of "man" as an individualistic consumer, often referred to as *homo economicus*. *Homo economicus* relies on an ever-increasing dependence on material (manufactured) capital accumulation for personal security and self-esteem. The result of this negative dynamic is the overconsumption of resources in the advanced capitalist consumer societies, particularly in urban regions, that necessarily accompanies the accumulation of material capital. This phenomenon has been described as "fatal consumption" (Woollard and Ostry 2000). Both overconsumption and the economic concept of the human individual are promoted on a daily basis by a hegemonic capitalist paradigm through a multibillion-dollar advertising industry. Consequently, these two problems are intertwined. And, as we shall see, the rise of *homo economicus* has generally been accompanied by the decline of cohesive human community, especially in these urban regions.

Two different worldviews take almost diametrically opposed stances to the problem of fatal consumption. They are the economic or neoclassical worldview and the ecological worldview. For the proponents of the neoclassical economic worldview, there are few problems of overconsumption that economic growth and technological development under free-market conditions cannot solve. For example, Lester Thurow has dismissed resource availability as a problem for economic growth with an abstract theoretical argument that the interplay of demand and supply necessarily solves the problem: "The world can consume only what it can produce. When the rest of the world has consumption standards equal to those of the U.S., it will be producing at the same rate and provide as much of an increment to the world-wide supplies of goods and services as it does to the demand for goods and services" (Daly and Cobb 1989, 40). In this view, the only problem is the human technological ability to produce the required output. With this argument, any possible physical exhaustion of resources is simply ignored or dismissed. In a similar idealistic vein, George Gilder rejects biophysical limits to growth: "The United States must overcome the materialistic fallacy: the illusion that resources and capital are essentially things, which can run out, rather than products of the human will and imagination which in freedom are inexhaustible – because economies are governed by thoughts, they reflect not the laws of matter, but the laws of mind" (Daly and Cobb 1989, 109). In this view, the only limits to growth are in our heads! Economist Julian Simon totally agrees with this view. In discussing the inexhaustibility of natural resources, Simon has this to say: "You see, in the end, copper and oil come out of our minds. That's really where they are" (Daly and Cobb 1989, 109).

Like Simon, also using free-market ideological reasoning, economist Walter Block has argued that, "far from economic growth and population being a danger to the human race, the very opposite is true. Additional people can create more resources than they use up, thanks to technological improvements and a marketplace that allows specialization, division of labour, and world-wide economic coordination" (1990, 305). Moreover, Block adds his own "empirical" argument that, with respect to the human population, "the earth is virtually empty, as anyone can attest who has taken an airplane ride and bothered to look out the window" (304). These arguments are tellingly illustrative of some of the better-known proponents of the now dominant free-market economic worldview that simply denies biophysical limits to either economic or human population growth and increasingly refuses to even discuss theoretical arguments. This obvious dissociation from the real world has been condemned by no less an economic thinker than J.K. Galbraith: "Modern economics ... seems to be, mainly, about *itself*" (2000, 1). He continues: "The deeper problem is the nearly complete collapse of the prevailing economic theory – of the structure of thought that supports their policy ideas. It is a collapse so complete, so pervasive, that the profession can only deny it by refusing to discuss theoretical questions in the first place" (4).

Opposed to the free-market economic worldview is the ecological worldview of a smaller but growing number of thinkers (e.g., Daly and Cobb 1989; Goodland 1991; Rees 1995; Wackernagel and Rees 1996). In this view, the Western industrial growth model of capitalistic production and consumption has become unsustainable. For example, members of the UBC Task Force on Planning Healthy and Sustainable Communities estimated that industrial society has overstepped the limits of the planet's natural carrying capacity by up to 30 percent (Rees 1996b; Rees and Wackernagel 1994; Wackernagel and Rees 1996). Their figures are supported by independent research from several other countries. These studies tell us that the dominant Western philosophic/scientific paradigm embodied in our global industrial system cannot be made sustainable by mere minor reforms (IIED 1997; Rees 1995).

The reasons for this situation are becoming increasingly apparent to many. As William Rees argues, in its single-minded drive for GDP growth, "the modern market model eschews moral and ethical considerations; ignores distributive inequity; abolishes 'the common good'; and undermines intangible values such as loyalty to person and place, community, self-reliance, and local cultural mores." Similarly, with respect to the natural world, Rees adds, "market prices merely reflect current availability, not ecological scarcity, and the whole approach remains incompatible with ecosystems behaviour. Because of such 'non-trivial losses of information,' commoditizing nature is misleading and potentially dangerous" (Rees 2002, 255).

As Rees comments, it is now obvious that the neoliberal model is not adequately delivering, even on its own terms: that is, its long-standing promise to alleviate poverty (Friedman 1962). On the contrary, despite increasing GDP growth, Rees (2002) argues, chronic poverty prevails in many developing countries, and the income gap between high-income OECD countries and the south is growing. In 1970, the richest 10 percent of the world's citizens earned nineteen times as much as the poorest 10 percent. By 1997, the ratio had increased to 27:1. By that time, the wealthiest 1 percent of the world's people commanded the same income as the poorest 57 percent (United Nations Development Program 2001). This uneven geographical development of globalism is characterized by Rees as "eco-apartheid."

In the ecological view, economic growth of the dominant global industrialist system has a cumulative global ecological impact that has been called the "ecological footprint" of human society (Rees 1996a; Rees and Wackernagel 1994; Wackernagel and Rees 1996). The ecological footprint is important as a critical heuristic (or learning tool) in thinking about and measuring levels of consumption. The ecological footprint begins with the assumption that every category of energy and material consumption and waste discharge requires the productive or adsorptive capacity of a finite area of land or water. By adding the land requirements of all categories of consumption and waste discharge of a population living in a given area, the ecological footprint measures the land area required for that population to maintain its levels of consumption "wherever on Earth that land is located" (Wackernagel and Rees 1996, 51-52).

The aggregate or global ecological footprint is already excessive. That is, there is insufficient natural capital to sustain a growing industrial society more than a few decades with prevailing technology, given ozone depletion, climate change, desertification, deforestation, resource draw down, and destruction of and threats to foodlands (Brown and Kane 1994). In the ecological view, the sheer size of the human enterprise combined with both human population growth and throughput growth now threatens irreversible global ecological destruction. Moreover, ecofootprinting reflects the eco-apartheid of uneven global geographical development. Each resident of the United States, Canada, and many Western European and other high-income countries requires five to ten hectares (twelve to twenty-five acres) of productive land/water to support his or her consumer lifestyle. By contrast, the citizens of the world's poorest countries have average ecofootprints of less than one hectare (Wackernagel et al. 1999).

Perhaps the most alarming indicator of the profound sustainability crisis of consumer/industrial civilization is the accelerating rate of loss of biological diversity now occurring on the planet. Currently, according to the self-admitted conservative estimate of Harvard evolutionary biologist Edward O. Wilson (1992), we are losing 27,000 species every year. Moreover, Wilson warns that the current spasm of extinction that we are entering promises to be the greatest of all extinction spasms in the planet's existence. The primary cause of species extinction is loss of habitat due to human-induced appropriation of material and energy flows from nature that would otherwise sustain other species (Ehrlich and Ehrlich 1981; Wilson 1992).

Just as the proliferation of Western industrial civilization has destroyed habitat and endangered biological diversity, so too has it undermined the diversity, strength, and character of human community. The hegemony of productivist/consumerist civilization has never seemed so complete. The loss of community is arguably more advanced in those societies where consumerism is most developed, particularly in the advanced industrial consumer countries. In these countries, especially in certain urban centres, large ecological footprints testify to enormous consumption levels (Folke et al. 1997; Rees 1996a; Wackernagel and Rees 1996; Wackernagel et al. 1999). Wackernagel and Rees explain that the size of the ecological footprint is not fixed but dependent on money income, prevailing values, other sociological factors, and the state of technology. Most importantly, they warn that the ecological footprint of a given population is the land area exclusively needed by that population to maintain its consumption levels and that "flows and capacities used by one population are not available for use by others" (1996, 52). Since much of the material and energy flows used by high-consumption centres in the advanced capitalist countries is drawn from areas outside those centres, both in the hinterlands of the advanced consumerist countries and in many underdeveloped areas in the rest of the world, it is clear that the ecological footprint is also a measure of the inequalities of global economic imperialism. Moreover, high consumption in advanced centres, because it does deliver goods and services to those populations, can compensate them with commodity consumption for any loss of community relations. This dynamic highlights the crux of the problem posed for the transformation of civil society in the Western consuming nations.

It is precisely in these high-consumption centres where community is perhaps the least robust. Indeed, a wide range of thinkers has discussed the decline of human community in the West (Daly and Cobb 1989; Freund and Martin 1993; Friedmann 1987; Harvey 1989; hooks 1990; Polanyi 1957; Relph 1987). What about the high-consuming populations in the advanced industrial and high-tech centres of the hierarchy? I argue that a decline in community is evident in cities and urbanized regions of high-consumption societies. What do I mean by "community," and why do I and others claim that it is in decline?

The Decline of Community

The term "community" has been used to define social interaction from small-scale, close-knit groups of people living together in some common vision of collective living arrangements to various, more loosely defined, groups of people at the neighbourhood, district, regional, national, and even global levels. It has often been overused to the point of near meaninglessness. Something more precise is needed. When I use the term "community," I prefer that it has a geographical dimension. Yet others prefer not only to include communities of interest in the term but also to favour interest over geographical place. Some even appear to be hostile to geographically de-fined community in the name of contemporary urban, large-scale organiza-tion and cosmopolitanism of modern cities that they assume can provide suitable substitutes for the values of the human community that they de-stroy. Herman Daly and John Cobb have critiqued this globalist view (1989, 171). They argue against individualism and cosmopolitanism as solutions to problems of community life, and I side with them.

Daly and Cobb define community broadly as a normative term that meets four conditions: one, membership in the community contributes to self-identification; two, there is extensive participation by its members in the decisions by which its life is governed; three, the society as a whole takes some responsibility for its members; and, four, the responsibility includes respect for the diverse individuality of its members (1989, 172). I would also include in my definition of community the requirement that to be mem-bers of a community people must plan together over time for their long-term common betterment and need to have at least some personal acquaintance with other members (Boothroyd and Davis 1991). Like Boothroyd and Davis's definition of community, mine focuses on personal involvement and com-munity living as essentials. It eschews anonymity yet remains open to a broad pluralistic sense of community that avoids parochialism and homo-geneity. These latter are not inevitable aspects of local, geographically based community. The Boothroyd and Davis definition is open to both communities of place and communities of interest, but it rules out large interest groups such as labour unions, professional associations, business corporations, or churches. My definition of community also rules out whole cities but permits neighbourhoods, districts, and towns up to about 5,000 people. That is, there is a necessary size limit to the notion of community if anonymity is to be avoided.

In this context, Kirkpatrick Sale (1980) has reviewed a range of anthropological and historical evidence showing that humans evolved in small communities or bands that averaged about 300-500 members. Larger tribal groupings and early cities averaged about 5,000 individuals (179-91). Urban planner Hans Blumenfeld has suggested that the size of community in which people can know every other person by face, voice, and name is about 500 (Blumenfeld in Sale, 183). The figure of 5,000 for the larger groupings of early medieval cities, and neighbourhood districts within contemporary cities, is based on historical experience and a variety of planners' estimates of optimal spatial scale – small but still viable units through which individuals can traverse fairly easily by walking – yet is large enough to contain and support schools, playgrounds, various stores and services, public buildings, as well as private residences (185-86). Based on this evidence, Sale has argued that these two ranges of suggestive numbers, one about 500, the other about 5,000 to 10,000, represent optimum face-to-face community for the former and an extended association or wider alliance for the latter. Sale also argues that the larger number represents the optimum for an effective economic society in which basic specialization of production for goods and services as well as legislative, legal, political, and security tasks would be supported. He points out that several real-world independent states and self-administered dependencies work well at this size, including Anguilla, the Cayman Islands, the Falkland Islands, and Saint Helena (187-88).

My definition of community, then, combines both interest and geography. It is a flexible definition that includes small face-to-face communities as well as broader associations of people in somewhat larger economic units. I also want to include a sense of "polity" in my definition of community similar to John Friedmann's concept. A political community, Friedmann argues, defends itself against external powers that threaten to restrict or abolish its own powers. From the state, it demands both responsiveness to people's wishes and accountability for its actions. From the corporate economy, it demands service for the common ends of the community, and from civil society it demands conduct in conformity with the moral norms agreed to in assembly (1987, 338-39). Finally, in my definition of community, I want to include something that the male thinkers above have left out, something emotional that is essential to at least the small face-to-face scale of community. American cultural critic bell hooks has expressed the deep emotional experience of community that she felt growing up in a segregated community of black people in small-town Kentucky. This was a sense of belonging and togetherness, a sense of caring and support, a sense of power (though contained), and a sense of "sweet communion" that hooks understood was "rooted in love, relational love, the care we had towards one another" (1990, 35).

While my definition of community includes communities of interest, it places more emphasis on communities that combine both interest and geography. This is key because some might argue that the decline of geographical community has been compensated for by the rise of communities of interest, such as those formed through use of the Internet. While this may be true in some cases, it is crucial to keep in mind that the vast majority of humans do not have access to the Internet. It is also worth noting that an Internet community may know no loyalty to place (particularly if it "substitutes" for place-based community). Internet communities would therefore be preferred by the corporate sector since indifference to place exposes local resources to exploitation without resistance.

Why do I and others claim that community as broadly defined above has declined, especially in advanced urban centres of the so-called First World? There are many reasons. First, since the last half of the nineteenth century, there has been an enormous growth in size, economic power, and political influence of private business corporations. Economic anthropologist Karl Polanyi (1968) has made this phenomenon one of his major themes. Simply stated, it is this: the pursuit of material self-gain and economic power in the formal market economy has become an institutionally enforced incentive to participate in this type of economic life. Such economic domination has worked to erode social and community life. It has generally resulted in the decline of community power to make decisions regarding daily life, with decisions over every aspect of life being increasingly made in corporate boardrooms. This tendency is even more pronounced in the era of globalization (see Introduction).

The decline of community life has not been a strictly linear process. For example, in the first third of the twentieth century, many communities in Canada organized producer co-ops, consumer co-ops, and credit unions to foster community growth (Boothroyd and Davis 1991). Social capital inherent in the rich networks of active community life was actually increased in Canada after an earlier period of decline. However, during the economic boom of the 1950s and 1960s, many co-ops either withered or consolidated into large mainstream businesses administered with little community involvement in decision making. Also, the rise of welfare state ideology changed how people thought about the relationship between communities and the state. The growth of the welfare state saw governments willing and able to support people to stay in their communities even if the local economic base had collapsed. The community became a place with survival rights, but it had ceased to be an agent of planning (Boothroyd and Davis 1991).

This was the period of top-down master planning, the heyday of operations research and systems analysis, developed in great part out of military logistics for large-scale planning in World War II. In the bomb-ravaged cities of Europe after the war, redevelopment took the form of "clean sweep planning" (Relph 1987, 144). Such planning has no regard for physical or historical constraints. Edward Relph has pointed out that its main rationale was that there should be as few obstacles as possible to an entirely modern solution, assuming that there was little or nothing of anything old worth saving. Bombed-out cities in Europe provided perfect palates for clean-sweep planning. Between 1945 and 1960, in working-class districts of London, Amsterdam, and Paris, great open-block complexes of Bauhaus- and LeCorbusier-style apartment residences were built to replace row houses and tenements that had been destroyed in the war or subsequently declared unfit to live in. Most clean-sweep developments resulted in dreary groups of prefabricated concrete sections surrounded by open spaces too barren and windswept to be of much use for anything. The modernist, master-planning promise of community renewal failed to materialize. The real social effect was to undermine community life since local communities had no part in the planning: "The drab new surroundings frequently seem to have promoted not the egalitarian happy city of tomorrow but a whole range of personal and social problems including depression, vandalism, difficulties of supervising young children in ground-level playgrounds from upper floor apartments, and the joyless experience of sharing elevators with gangs of juvenile delinquents" (Relph 1987, 146-47).

In Canada, and especially in the United States, clean-sweep planning – without the bombed-out cities – was promoted as "urban renewal" and slum clearing, beginning in the early 1950s. Urban renewal was seen as a form of radical surgery to clean out unsafe, unsanitary, overcrowded dwellings that fostered social and economic problems. The philosophy of the entire process was captured by a US Supreme Court ruling rejecting an appeal against the expropriation of a store in Washington, DC: "Experts concluded that if the community were to be healthy, if it were not to revert again to a blighted-out slum area, as though possessed by a congenital disease, the area must be re-planned as a whole – it was important to redesign the whole area so as to eliminate the conditions that cause slums" (Relph 1987, 147). In this spirit, many poor or black communities were entirely bulldozed out of existence, to be replaced by "projects" of grey or dull brown apartment slabs in bleak, windswept landscapes.

Another aspect of urban renewal that has worked to undermine community in poor neighbourhoods is the thoroughly paternalistic approach taken to slums and slum dwellers. Jane Jacobs has argued convincingly that attempts to wipe away slums and their populations succeed, at best, in shifting them from one place to another. However, the more common result has been to destroy communities. For Jacobs, urban renewal "destroys neighbourhoods where constructive and improving communities exist and where the situation calls for encouragement rather than destruction" (1992, 270-71). Moving people out or encouraging the more successful slum dwellers to leave actually perpetuates the process of slum creation. Such "development" has destroyed many neighbourhoods in the United States that started unslumming by building on the forces of regeneration that existed within the slums themselves. One exception to the urban renewal process was Jacobs's own neighbourhood in New York City, which was saved from "disastrous amputation only because its citizens were able to fight city hall" (272). Unslumming, then, depends on the retention of a considerable part of a slum population and on whether the residents and businesspeople find it desirable and practical to carry out their plans right there. In other words, it depends on the retention of community vitality within the slum area itself, where the people, in Friedmann's sense, act together as a political community.

Another major reason for the decline of community since World War II was the rapid spread of automobiles and the proliferation of road and expressway systems beginning in the 1950s and still continuing today. The automobile is much more than just an artifact. In the twentieth century, it was a major means of expanding consumerism and throughput growth. Not only has the automobile played the major role in the organization of industrial expansion named and known as Fordism, but it also symbolizes the implementation of the ideology of consumption. Freund and Martin have pointed out that the automobile is the centrepiece of a vast system of auto-centred transit. They define such transit as a technological system with major impacts on public policy, land use, cultural patterns, social relations, community, natural resources, environmental quality, and options for the spacial mobility of individuals. In an auto-centred transport system, the car is the dominant, or only, means of conveyance used for everyday activities (1993, 1-2). People have become dependent on the automobile. Cars are the major means of transportation in most cities of North America. With respect to issues of community, there are several ways in which the auto and auto-centred transport systems have contributed to the decline of community in North American cities.

The road and expressway system has experienced enormous growth since 1945 in both the United States and Canada. Highway planning and engineering in the Keynesian era greatly expanded a landscape first begun in the 1930s, a relatively featureless landscape oriented exclusively to machines and machine speeds (Relph 1987, 158). This landscape has contributed to the paved-over destruction and fragmentation of wildlife habitat as well as to what Jacobs calls the erosion of cities. She argues that, while the erosion of cities has been an incremental process, the cumulative effect is enormous: "And each step, while not crucial in itself, is crucial in the sense that it not only adds its own bit to the total change, but actually accelerates the process. Erosion of cities by automobiles is thus an example of what is known as 'positive feedback,' an action produces a reaction which in turn intensifies the condition responsible for the first action, and so on, ad infinitum. It is something like the grip of a habit-forming addiction" (1992, 249-50).

Expressways, freeways, boulevards and streets, vast bridges, road widenings, endless parking lots, malls, used- and new-car lots, laneways, driveways, garages, and gas stations together comprise the extensive auto-dominated environments in cities that have contributed immensely to the erosion of cities. Ironically, all this has been promoted as urban renewal. In fact, many communities in many cities have been uprooted by this process.

Another effect of the automobile system has been to allow the planning of segregated cities. This refers to the creation of large, single-use districts in many cities since 1945 (Relph 1987, 138-65). This was also part of the clean-sweep planning approach to urban renewal. The mobility gained through the creation of segregated cities was paid for by the loss of urban communities. Expressways penetrate, weave through, and loop around almost every city in the developed world. They have made the enormous scale and segregation of cities possible by making all districts theoretically accessible from other districts by a quick auto trip. They have also divided up cities functionally, socially, and geographically, separating industrial districts from residential areas, poor ghettos from rich districts, and so on (Relph 1987, 162). Jacobs (1992) railed against this loss of diversity at the district level, arguing that such segregated land uses contributed to the loss of diversity essential to the vitality of urban communities.

Apart from expressways, road widenings, parking lot proliferation, and other manifestations of auto-dominated land use, the sheer number of automobiles came to dominate many streets and contributed to the erosion of urban community life. A 1970 study of a residential neighbourhood in San Francisco by Donald Appleyard illustrates the phenomenon. The Appleyard study showed the corrosive effects on community life of the growing zone of influence of cars. Through interviews and actual mapping of the residential use of street and yard space, Appleyard was able to show that, as traffic increased, what was defined as "home territory" by residents progressively shrank. This loss of home territory proceeded in stages from full use of the street carriage way, sidewalks, front yards, porches, and interior front rooms to the loss of each space, until even the front rooms of the homes were abandoned because of excessive traffic noise. The final stage was moving out of the neighbourhood altogether to become traffic refugees. As the residential use of streets and yards declined, so did the friendly neighbourly visits. Exchanges, acquaintances, and friendships evaporated. Eventually, long-term meaningful relationships fractured, and community life declined (Engwicht 1993, 48-54).

Geographer Edward Relph has commented on the sameness or monotony of the modern urban landscape. The elements that came together since 1945 to make the segregation, automobilization, and cosmopolitanism of cities were represented in planning through newly instituted official planning processes. These planning processes drew on a limited repertoire of ideas and procedures, mostly conceived before the war. They included single zoning of land uses, neighbourhood units, Bauhaus-style layouts for public housing, and assembly line standardization of town planning, or what Relph calls "planning by numbers" (1987, 140-41).

This top-down form of master planning was also called "rational" planning. It spread at first in the developed industrial countries, later more globally. Rational planning by experts removed or seriously eroded the ability of local communities to control their own destinies. Some now refer to the modern urban landscape, the rational planning process behind it, and the corporatization of cities as "global monoculture." Its success represents the advantage of space over place. What David Harvey remarked about the power of the international financial class of the nineteenth century remains true of those who control the forces of the modern global megamachine in this century: "Those who built a sense of community across space found themselves with a distinct advantage over those who mobilized the principle of community in place" (1989, 32). In the twentieth century, the automobile system was the major driving force for both the growth of consumerism and the decline of community life.

What are the sociocultural aspects of the drive for growth and consumption and the rise of aggressive individualism? The deep roots of this global phenomenon probably go back to the foundations of Western civilization (Mann 1986; Schmookler 1984). However, the more immediate economic and cultural roots of this phenomenon can be found in nineteenth-century economic liberalism and the institution of "laissez faire" or free trade initially launched by Great Britain. This was accomplished by the "great transformation" that took place as the economic sphere was freed of its social and political fetters via the market mechanism to the point where the economy was no longer embedded in civil society (Polanyi 1957). By this, I mean that the economy no longer directly served the needs of civil society but followed the "grow or die" ethic of nineteenth-century free-market liberalism. People have thus come to serve the economy as much as or more than the economy serves them. A disembedded or largely autonomous formal economic sphere also meant that exchange value became privileged over use value, national markets over local markets, and the formal market over the informal economy in civil society. All of these aspects further undermine local community.

The late-nineteenth-century creation of huge corporate trusts and the concentration and centralization of capital were facilitated by the legal transformation of corporate entities into "persons" with full individual rights but limited liability (Dodd 1934; Grossman and Adams 1993; Korten 1995). This expansion in size and reach of financial and corporate power, in combination with the creation of national markets and the creation of mass advertising, formed the basis for the growth-driven productivist/consumerist society of the mid-twentieth century (Ewen 1976). The expansion of the state in the Keynesian period, which rivalled the growth of huge corporations, eventually helped to ameliorate some of the worst working and living conditions created by nineteenth-century industrialism (at least in the advanced capitalist countries). However, the expansion of the state sector came at a cost: the creation of a hierarchical, state-citizen relationship of dependency in which the increasingly isolated individual citizen became more and more dependent on the growing state. These vertical state-citizen relations of dependency helped to undermine horizontal social relations in civil society (Cohen and Arato 1992, 39-40). In this century-long process, civil society became increasingly (if unevenly) separated from and dominated by both formal economic and political spheres.

On an even broader historical stage, the roots of this system have been traced to the Renaissance with the marriage of scientific materialism and mercantile and colonial capitalism (Berman 1981; Merchant 1980). This is still the dominant form of culture informing the capitalist industrial growth model today. Concealed behind the conspicuous consumption and possessive individualism fostered by the advertising industry is the dominance of finance capital and transnational corporate control over social and geographical space. Those who have built geopolitical and economic hegemony across space now dominate place-oriented communities in cities and urban regions. In turn, urban regions dominate their rural hinterlands. Marxist geographer David Harvey, in his historical analysis of the rise of this phenomenon in the last half of the nineteenth century, underlines the specific advantages of space over place: "The Parisian revolutions of 1848 and 1871 were put down by a bourgeoisie that could mobilize its forces across space. Control over the telegraph and flows of information proved crucial in disrupting the rapidly spreading strike of 1877 in the industrial centres of the United States. Those who built a sense of community across space found themselves with a distinct advantage over those who mobilized the community in place" (1989, 32).

Harvey's analysis refers to a logistical military advantage. At the level of culture, a somewhat parallel advantage pertained for space-oriented economies of growth over place-oriented economies of subsistence. Within the mass culture of urbanization in North America, social competition with respect to both lifestyle and command over space helped to create and mobilize consumer "sovereignty." This mobilization would ensure that consumption for consumption's sake matched capitalist industrialism's drive toward production for production's sake and accumulation for accumulation's sake (Ewen 1976). Urban regions in the upper levels of the global hierarchy have become the centres of consumerism, dominating vast regional and global hinterlands and drawing down their resources. The aggregated ecological footprints of such regions now span the globe (Folke et al. 1997; Rees 1996b, Rees and Wackernagel 1994; Wackernagel et al. 1999). Thus, the erosion of community through the control of space over place was compensated for and masked by the mass consumption of commodities in the advanced industrial/consumer nations.

The Great Transformation and the Rise of "Economic Man"

The accelerating depletion of vast rural hinterlands is a real problem facing all humanity, but it is generated primarily in the consumption centres of the global system. Locating concepts of sociocultural, political, and economic transformation in a North American urban regional context means focusing on the spatial core of the sustainability problem, at least for this continent. How can we build, or rebuild, healthy and sustainable communities in such centres of conspicuous consumption whose material reach is global?

To address the question of overconsumption, a purely economic analysis is not sufficient. The question begs a cultural understanding. The increase of international finance capital and rise of corporate power in the nineteenth century, their subsequent concentration and centralization in urban centres under the control of a small elite, and the great transformation in market relations led finally to the creation of the global megamachine in the twentieth century. This development was accompanied and made possible by another transformation, the shift in cultural consciousness about what it meant to be human. We need to understand how the great transformation to a capitalist market economy driven by excessive consumption in the centres was made possible by a change in the concept of the human being. That is, we need to consider the cultural core of "economic man."

As national and international markets grew, undermining the independence of local and regional markets and businesses, a new concept of the human individual as utility-maximizing economic man, or *homo economicus,* came forth to take the place of the culturally diverse, tradition-oriented, more communally and socially embedded human being. *Homo economicus,* the modern middle-class image of the acquisitive and selfish individual, disconnects that individual from traditional community at the level of self-understanding (Bowers 1993, 26). Instead of the community or even the family as the basic social unit, private accumulation by the atomized individual – cut off from community involvement – becomes the chief measure of success in a society based on unlimited consumption.

In a predominantly cultural analysis of the "great social transformation" from kinship and local community to the world of the capitalist market, Robert Bellah and his colleagues link the cultural changes surrounding this great social transformation to the emergence of the modern middle class in America (Bellah et al. 1985, 117-21). They point out that the term "middle class" emerged only in the last decades of the nineteenth century. This, of course, is the same period of the great economic transformation (to a laissez faire market society) analyzed by Polanyi (1957). The eighteenth-century concept of the "middle rank" of society as a moderating force for equilibrium between extremes of wealth and poverty gave way in the nineteenth century to a perception of a middle class composed of people on the rise – aggressive, mobile, calculating, and ambitious. This new class and the society that it more and more defined were seen as rising indefinitely to new levels of affluence and progress. In the United States at least, this concept of the middle class, the utilitarian/expressive individual primed for consumption, supplied the dominant cultural model for an all-encompassing process of escalation that would eventually attempt to include the entire globe.

For Bellah and his colleagues, this middle-class concept gives us "our central, and largely unchallenged, image of American society" (1985, 119). This late-nineteenth-century definition of the middle class as an aggregate of such individuals, as a group that "seeks to embody in its own continuous progress and advancement the very meaning of the American project," reveals a "peculiar resonance" between middle-class life and individualism in America (151). Indeed, this new self was the very image of the middle-class consumer that was heavily promoted by the emerging advertising industry in the late nineteenth century, the new "captains of consciousness" (Ewen 1976). Today this concept of the atomized individual consumer is central to the hegemonic culture of growth-driven consumer capitalism. It is promoted daily through the mass media by our contemporary "captains of consciousness."

In England, a very similar concept of "man" emerged as early as the seventeenth century. The Aristotelian idea of man (all of this thought is deeply patriarchal; see Bigwood 1993; and Plumwood 1993) as essentially purposeful, rational activity became even more narrowed over the centuries until it became a severely atrophied concept of rationality whose behavioural essence "was increasingly held to lie in unlimited individual appropriation, as a means of satisfying unlimited desire for utilities" (MacPherson 1973, 5). This new behaviour and the individualistic utilitarian concept that informed it increasingly became more deeply rooted in the expanding market society as part of the liberal tradition from John Locke onward. For C.B. MacPherson, the result was an uneasy compromise between two views of man's essence: man as consumer, and man as creator. Liberal thought evolved in an emerging market society and assumed, quite correctly, that society was a market society operating by contractual relations between free individuals who offered their powers in the market with a view to getting the greatest return that they could. However, these powers of the individual, whether "natural or acquired," were seen as merely instrumental to maximizing utilities; humanity's real essence was as an "infinite" consumer.

For ecological economists Daly and Cobb (1989), the view of humans as *homo economicus* is the most important of all the ideological abstractions of contemporary economic theory. They point out that the chief feature of *homo economicus* as a utility-maximizing individual is extreme individualism. Economic theory built on an anthropology of *homo economicus* has no doubt encouraged a much less inhibited quest for personal gain in the business world, yet Daly and Cobb dispute the reality of *homo economicus* as the natural state of human nature. If humans were normally or naturally insatiable, they point out, then aggressive want-stimulating advertising and planned obsolescence would not be necessary. However, *homo economicus* has encouraged the separation and abstraction of the extreme individualist from sociocultural concerns over justice, fairness, or the well-being of the community as a whole (85-89). The individualism of *homo economicus* encourages a view of society as merely an aggregate of such isolated, alienated individuals. Consequently, argue Daly and Cobb, the image of humans as *homo economicus* is a major obstacle to the development of a concept of the individual as a person in community (159). I consider the dominant, economistic image of the individual in our contemporary consumer society to be at the cultural heart of the problem of social transformation, an enormous barrier that must be addressed directly.

The roots of individualist thought are deep. They go back at least to the beginning of the modern era. The individual, for John Locke, existed alone in a state of nature, prior to any society, which itself comes into existence only through the voluntary contract of individuals trying to maximize their own self-interest, not through cooperative or kinship relations. For Bellah et al. (1985), the Lockean position, enormously influential in America, amounts to an "almost ontological individualism" (143). The ontological individual, they argue, is the conceptual basis for both the utility maximizer and the expressive individualist. Expressive individualism was part of the romantic rebellion against the concept of the human as a calculating utility maximizer. Bellah and his associates hold up Walt Whitman as an example of expressive individualism in its clearest form, as an individual concerned not with material acquisition but with the rich emotional, sensual, and intellectual development of the self.

There is also an important patriarchal dimension embedded in the American middle-class character. As Bellah and his colleagues (1985) explain, utilitarian and expressive individualism correspond with the split between public life in the economic/occupational sphere and private life in the family sphere. Many feminists have argued, and Bellah and his colleagues also point out, that in the nineteenth century middle-class American family women were seen to be invested with the characteristics of expressive individualism (the heart, the emotions), while men embodied those of the calculating utility maximizer (88-89). Under the patriarchal relations of the nineteenth century, this split privileged the utility-maximizing male individual, the utilitarian, over the expressive individual. This split between male and female, mind and body, reason and emotion, and the autonomous self and the separate other is essentially dualistic Cartesian thinking put into the service of the industrial and financial capitalist revolution of the nineteenth century. In this great cultural, social, and economic transformation, the middle-class consumer, economic man, became the model for the twentieth-century explosion in consumption for all classes in the advanced industrial world.

As Bowers (1993) has pointed out, the conundrum of the infinite utility-maximizing consumer presents a particular responsibility to those who are part of Western consumer society, a responsibility for the ideology of consumerism. This ideology, which arose in Europe and reached its maximum extension in the United States, equates personal identity and success with consumerism. The example of the atomized middle-class consumer as a model for the whole world in our era of global markets has now become the dominant form of culture, equating cultural identity and meaning with success in the marketplace and with the ever-expanding consumption of commodities.

In short, the material problem of overconsumption has both an economic and a sociocultural basis. The growth momentum of the global megamachine, combined with the pervasive sociocultural influence of *homo economicus*, demands more than merely minor reform. Rather, it suggests a profound need for another, very different, great transformation: a transition away from an acquisitive, materialistic, alienated culture and toward a sustainable society rooted in qualitative relationships among whole individuals integrated or embedded in healthy families and communities. The above twofold real-world problem – the decline of community and the rise of economic man – provides the context for the broad theoretical problem central to this book: how to think more profoundly and strategically about sociocultural as well as political-economic transformation in an era of globalization.

Civil Society Theory

Historically, there has been much theory making on political economic transformation but little work on integrating it with theory on cultural transformation. A diverse body of thought has been preoccupied with the problem of the revolutionary transformation of capitalism. Its roots are in the nineteenth century and the thought of utopianism, social anarchism, and, in particular, historical materialism (Marxism). Planning historian John Friedmann has located the thought of these "three great oppositional movements" within the planning tradition of social mobilization or radical planning (1987, 225). In particular, Marxist thought contributed much to political theory with respect to the role of the state and broad institutional transformation.

However, certain theory builders in Europe have recently emerged from the Marxist tradition with a very different framework both from more traditional Marxist thought and from neo-Marxist thought on political, economic, and social transformation. I believe that this new framework has an important contribution to make to theory in social transformation toward sustainable society even though it does not concern itself specifically with sustainability issues or challenge the dominant cultural ideology of anthropocentrism (human-centred thought).

Two major thinkers of this emerging theoretical framework are Jean Cohen and Andrew Arato. These two social theorists have played a central role in advancing civil society theory in *Civil Society and Political Theory* (1992), an extensive review of Marxist thought about the role of civil society and its relationship to the state. Arato worked at the Max Planck Institute, where he became familiar with Habermas's theory of communicative action. Cohen was sponsored by Habermas for a research fellowship at the same institute and taught political science at Columbia University. According to Cohen and Arato, it was the circulation of post-Marxist ideas that initiated the contemporary international dissemination of theoretical discourse about civil society (1992, 71).

As I noted in the Introduction, civil society theory breaks with the Marxist conception of the working class as the sole or primary agent of societal revolution (or social transformation) and consequently with the theory of the dictatorship of the proletariat. Also abandoned is the dream of abolishing the state, which, in Marx, is identified as the hegemonic element of a state–civil society relationship. In its place is the theorizing of a radical but democratic alternative in which the state is not overthrown but democratized on the basis of a diverse, inclusive, and democratic civil society.

For their part, Cohen and Arato (1992) argue for a three-part conceptual model that includes civil society, the state sector, and an economic sphere. They credit the Italian Marxist Gramsci for first developing this "highly original" three-part conceptual framework. They also observe, however, that his concept of civil society was presented in a confusing terminology, sometimes defined as the counterpart of the state, or as a part of the state along with and counterposed to political society, or as identical with the state

(144-45). This confusion in Gramsci is perhaps the reflection of a long and changing history of the term going back to classical and even medieval political thought. For Hobbes and Spinoza, "civil society" was inseparable from the state and its laws (Keane 1988, 38). For Marx, the state was the determining element and civil society the element determined by it (Marx and Engels 1975, 615). Thus, in Marx's conception, civil society was identified not with liberation but with bourgeois rule from above. Gramsci's definition was influenced by the work of both Hegel and Marx. Marx stressed the negative, atomistic, and dehumanizing features of civil society (Cohen and Arato 1992, 117). For Marx, civil society included all classes and their economic relations. Thus, the will of the state in modern history is determined by the changing needs of civil society, the supremacy of one or another class, and the development of the productive forces and relations of exchange (Marx and Engels 1975, 616).

On the other hand, Thomas Paine and Alexis de Tocqueville clearly opposed civil society to the state. For de Tocqueville (1969), civil society was a self-organizing, legally guaranteed sphere not directly dependent on the state (see Everton 1996). De Tocqueville, of course, based his conclusions on his observations of what he termed the rich associational life of free citizens in a strongly democratic America in the first half of the nineteenth century. The upshot of all this is that the concept of civil society has been marked by two very different theoretical approaches: the promise of liberation from below on the one hand and links to rule from above on the other (Cohen and Arato 1992, 118).

Gramsci, still within the Marxian tradition, tended to treat civil society in functional terms as the sphere responsible for the social integration of the whole and, therefore, for the reproduction of bourgeois hegemony or for the creation of socialist hegemony. For Gramsci, then, "civil society appeared as the central terrain to be occupied in the struggle for emancipation" (Cohen and Arato 1992, 144). However, Gramsci never critiqued the Soviet system, which, having captured state power by using the self-organized institutions of civil society, then effectively abolished civil society and its institutions. In contrast, Cohen and Arato break with this tradition by treating civil society as both an end in itself and the societal means and base for continuing and expanding the democratic revolution launched by the enlightenment toward the end of the eighteenth century.

It was for this reason that Cohen and Arato (1992) proposed their theoretical model that differentiates among three spheres: civil society, political society, and economic society. They argue that, from the point of view of what they call civic humanism, we cannot properly theorize modern social relations in the hope of transforming those relations if we do not differentiate among these three spheres or subsystems. Following Polanyi (1957), they point out that the industrial revolution in the nineteenth century produced an economic society, the formal market economy, that threatened to ultimately subsume and reduce autonomous social norms, relationships, and institutions of civil society (Cohen and Arato 1992, 122). Cohen and Arato advance their three-sphere model as a civil society–centred model. They point out that their model focuses on the empirical possibility of democratization in civil society while also underlining the normative necessity of democratization because civil society norms since the Enlightenment call precisely for democratization (411).

It is important to note, since many commentators using a two-sphere model of civil society and state (see Introduction) have ignored or misunderstood this point, that a theory of democracy is normative by necessity. Indeed, the critique of one set of norms (neoliberal, capitalist) implies the need for a new set. As philosopher Arne Naess has argued, science is also a field of communication; therefore, when one worldview is deeply opposed, it is entirely necessary for the emergent worldview to announce its new norms as directly and concretely as possible for these new deeply held values to be clearly understood (1990, 68-72). These normative acts thus become part of a dialectic of transformation. This does not mean that a democratic theory of civil society cannot also be used as a heuristic tool of analysis to explore the empirical possibility of democratization when analyzing social and/or cultural movements. As we shall soon see, Cohen and Arato have done exactly that.

Finally, they emphasize that their model lends itself to the defence and expansion of civil society against, first, the deleterious effects of a greatly expanded, dominant, corporate economic sphere and, second, the overextension of the administrative apparatus of the interventionist state into the social realm (1992, 24). For Cohen and Arato, the political inference of their model, and the reason they are specifically *post*-Marxist, is that civil society–based social transformation theory abandons the Marxist theory of the dictatorship of the proletariat and the use of social mobilization for the purpose of overthrowing the state. In this view, the theoretical concern for social transformation (as opposed to mere social reform) remains, but the emphasis shifts to theorizing about democratic forms of transformation.

In Cohen and Arato's model, the civil society sphere is composed of both public and private elements: the intimate sphere or the family, the sphere of associations (especially voluntary associations), social movements, and institutions of culture and public communication. It also includes a domain of individual self-development and moral choice as well as a legal domain of laws and rights needed to "demarcate" all the other components from the state and the economy (1992, 346). For Cohen and Arato, the concept of civil society indicates a terrain that is endangered by the logic of both administrative and economic mechanisms but is also the primary locus for the potential expansion of democracy under liberal democratic regimes (vii).

In the latter sense, civil society is the sphere of emancipation, of freedom. Clearly, we see here that the civil society concept in Cohen and Arato remains a contested terrain, susceptible to colonization from without via the logic of the self-regulating market, the bureaucratic apparatus of the welfare state, or a combination of them.

Again a note is necessary to address the apparent confusion of so many commentators on civil society who have characterized the civil society concept as a fuzzy, idealized notion of the "good society," and/or as somehow homogeneous (Edwards et al. 2001, 1-8; Friedmann in Douglas and Friedmann 1998), or as Eurocentric (Warkentin 2001). Any careful reading of Cohen and Arato should make it clear that civil society is to be understood as a contested terrain. The very development of the concept out of Gramscian thought should also make that clear. Friedmann is also clear on this point when he warns that civil society must not be read as a homogeneous sphere, since deep divisions run through it, "creating an internal dynamic that is based on social class, gender, religion, ethnicity, so-called race, access to household resources and other social markers" (in Douglas and Friedmann 1998, 23). Nor is the concept Eurocentric. The roots of its current revival lie as much in Latin America as in Europe, as Friedmann (21) and many others have pointed out. Indeed, one of the best examples of the use of civil society theory (and practice!) is by the Zapatista Liberation Movement in Mexico in the defence of the Zapatistas themselves by a mobilized Mexican civil society and to create a political space for reforms (Marcos 2001; Ross 2000).

The political sphere in the Cohen and Arato model, in addition to the dominant state sector and parliament, also includes political associations and parties. It is by definition a public sphere. For Cohen and Arato, political society in the form of representative democracy shares with the modern civil society sphere two key institutions that mediate between them: the public sphere and voluntary associations. Politically relevant public discussion through public media, political clubs, associations, and parties is on a continuum with parliamentary discussion and debate. The civil and political spheres thus share a large portion of the public sphere. It follows that in representative democracies political society "both presupposes and must be open to the influence of civil society" (1992, 412-13). However, Cohen and Arato (and Polanyi 1957) refer to the fact that, since the creation and expansion of the market economy, the state sector likewise has experienced enormous and complementary growth in tandem with the market sector, leading to the rise of the welfare state. Cohen and Arato then note, as have many from the left and the right, that the success of the welfare state has created a great crisis of solidarity. The welfare state disorganizes social networks and replaces mutualist forms of association, self-help, and horizontal cooperation with vertical, functional, reified, state-citizen relations in which the citizen is reduced to the role of a client. This process, they explain, "fully matches the effects of the capitalist market economy" whose growth has also replaced horizontal relations with vertical relations (40).

The economic sphere in Cohen and Arato's model principally represents the formal market-dominated sector, but the economic sphere also includes, for example, collective bargaining and representation of workers on company boards. Cohen and Arato point out the low degree of public participation in the essentially private economic sphere and speculate that mediation in this sphere might involve a plurality of forms of property (e.g., consumer and producer cooperatives) in which civil society could both gain footholds in economic society (1992, 713 n. 340) and seek innovative forms of limiting capitalist economic hegemony as well as political hegemony by the state (471).

Cohen and Arato (after Habermas) repeatedly stress that we should not lose sight of "the utopian promise" of the liberal and democratic norms of modern society inherited from the Enlightenment. They argue that we should not reduce these to mere legitimation devices for capitalist industrialism, as has so much of Marxist and neo-Marxist analysis. Regardless of this important caution, Cohen and Arato do adopt Habermas's theory of the colonization of civil society, analyzing both the monetarization and the bureaucratization of social relations that have created a set of social benefits and securities at the cost of creating a new range of dependencies and destroying or severely atrophying existing horizontal solidarities. All this has served to undermine people's capacities for self-help and cooperative forms of horizontal communication for resolving problems at the base of society – in civic communities. Cohen and Arato cite, as one example, the "therapeutization" of everyday life fostered by social service agencies that contradicts the very goal of therapy – the autonomy and empowerment of the patient – creating a cycle of dependency between the individual citizen turned client and the therapeutic apparatus (1992, 445-51).

While Cohen and Arato make a major contribution to breaking with the Marxist theory of the dictatorship of the proletariat and of the working class as the sole or chief agent of societal transformation, they have little to say about the ecological problematic of modern society. For example, they do not address the problem of overconsumption. Consequently, perhaps, they do not include any substantial discussion integrating a cultural analysis into their theory that challenges the anthropocentric dimensions of the dominant modern Western worldview on consumer society and its construct of *homo economicus*. However, their three-sphere framework, since it focuses on civil society, does integrate a cultural domain for theoretical analysis – the normatively democratic "terrain of cultural modernity" (1992, 7, 25).

At the same time, their framework may contribute to theoretical clarification with respect to the political sphere in the thought of those contemporary movements that do put much more emphasis on ecologically centred cultural transformation and consequently do challenge both anthropo-centrism and *homo economicus* more profoundly. Specifically, for social move-ments in modern civil society, Cohen and Arato propose a concept of "self-limiting revolution" or "self-limiting radicalism" as an alternative to limited reform on the one hand and totalizing revolution on the other (26, 32, 72). In this view, social movements concerned with societal transforma-tion should pursue a dual strategy of democratization from their base in civil society. With respect to civil society, the strategy would be a horizontal one, targeting cultural models, norms, and institutions of civil society fo-cusing on processes of communicative action that would constitute the "re-flexive [focusing on process] continuation of the democratic revolution" (26, 523). This "defensive" strategy would seek to defend and enhance civil society by preserving and developing its communicative infrastructure through efforts to redefine identities, reinterpret norms, and develop egali-tarian, democratic associational forms. With respect to the political sphere, the "offensive" strategy would seek to develop spaces within political soci-ety that could be democratized through a politics of bridging and building influence for institutional reform (531-32). The envisioned goal of this prong of the dual strategy is "the reflexive continuation of the welfare state" rather than its abolishment (26). This part of the strategy would seek to "accom-plish the work of social policy by more decentralized and autonomous civil-society-based programs" (26). In Cohen and Arato's concept of self-limiting revolution, then, both the political and the economic spheres remain par-tially differentiated from the civil society sphere rather than being collapsed into civil society by a totalizing revolution that attempted to abolish the state and the formal market economy. The term that they use for this is "de-differentiation."

To illustrate their dual strategy, Cohen and Arato discuss the example of the feminist movement of the 1970s and 1980s in the United States. On the one hand, the feminist movement pursued a strategy of contesting norms and structures of male dominance in civil society through a focus on iden-tity, self-help, consciousness raising, and proselytizing through the under-ground press, their own alternative publications, and the universities. This was a horizontal strategy of spreading feminist consciousness and achiev-ing institutional changes in social relations based on traditional, inegalitar-ian gender norms in civil society. On the other hand, the feminist movement also pursued a strategy of focusing on political and economic inclusion and attempting to exercise influence vertically throughout the legal and po-litical system to fight discrimination and attain equal rights (1992, 551). Cohen and Arato point to the extensive political and legal successes of this dual strategy achieved by the feminist movement. They conclude their case study by suggesting that "as most analysts stress ... these political and legal successes have as their prerequisite and precondition success in the cultural sense – in the prior spread of feminist consciousness" but also that, "without a politics of influence aimed at political society, success in the first respect would be unlikely and limited" (552-53).

Given all of the above, the general theoretical problem that I am addressing can be focused on the need for more understanding of how to go beyond Cohen and Arato by integrating ecological thinking into their theory. In turn, there is the need to understand how a reconstructed Cohen and Arato framework can contribute to the strategic thought of current movements in civil society, such as bioregionalism, that make ecologically centred cultural transformation an integral part of their praxis.

Social and Cultural Capital

Social and cultural capital are two concepts that have the potential to contribute to theoretical insight and reflection on a civil society–based strategy for social transformation, especially with respect to cultural and ecological issues related to overconsumption. The concept of social capital has been used to challenge cultural claims of free-market neoclassical economists built in great part, as we have seen, on an anthropology of *homo economicus*. Social capital, developed (but not invented) by social theorist James Coleman (1990) and refined and applied by social scientist Robert Putnam (1993a, 1993b), refers to features of social organization, particularly networks, norms, and relations of trust that facilitate cooperation for mutual benefit.

However, the social capital concept has also been adopted by a wide range of academics and by the World Bank for a variety of purposes very different from the particular use that I make of it in this book. As a result, the concept has been severely critiqued for its origins in both rational choice and social exchange theory, its association with neoclassical economics, its resulting eclecticism, as well as its wide but uncritical acceptance and use as an analytical, empirical, and policy panacea (Fine 2001). In his examination of the origins of the social capital concept, *Social Capital versus Social Theory*, Ben Fine argues that the indiscriminate application of social capital has meant that social capital has begun to replace serious political economic analysis with intellectual remains rooted in a framework of methodological individualism and its associated formal methods and is therefore "incoherently attached to the social and informal" (2001, 95-96). While I agree with much of the criticism of Fine about the indiscriminate use of social capital, only once does he even allude to (but otherwise ignores) the powerful attack on *homo economicus* found in the work of both Coleman and Putnam in their discourse defining and explaining social capital (77). In my case, it was precisely for this quality of the concept – its association with the social and with the public good – that I realized it could be useful in spite of its origins and association with neoclassical economics. On the contrary, I discovered that the concept was compatible with a framework that was, in fact, critical of capitalism and globalism.

Since its inception, the social capital concept has been associated with local community relationships. In the 1970s, the term "social capital" was used by economist Glen Loury to refer to the resource endowment of "nontransferable advantages of birth" conveyed by family and local community relations, peer influences, and friendship networks that are useful for the child in later-life productivity and social development (1977, 1987). This particular origin has had much influence in the subsequent development of the concept in Coleman and later Putnam. In this usage, social capital is generated through family and community relationships. It is a community good that can benefit the individual.

Coleman developed the concept more fully than Loury, elaborating and enhancing the social relations content of the term. Coleman challenged the "broadly perpetrated fiction in modern society" of the independent individual fostered in part by the conception of *homo economicus* in classical and neoclassical economic theory (1990, 300-2). As we have already seen, in the abstract concept of *homo economicus,* society consists of a set of independent individuals acting to achieve independently arrived at goals guided by the "invisible hand" of a perfectly competitive marketplace. This "under-socialized" concept of humans as atomized economic maximizers in self-regulating markets supports a narrow view of social relations as merely (at best) a "frictional drag that impedes competitive markets" (Granovetter 1985, 484). In contrast, for Mark Granovetter (who influenced Coleman on this point), the atomized and anonymous "man" of neoclassical economics is virtually nonexistent in real economic life, where economic transactions of all kinds are rife with actual social connections. This is to say that attempts at purposive action by economic actors are always embedded in ongoing systems of social relations. Granovetter explains that the embeddedness argument stresses the role of personal relations and structures or networks of such relations in generating trust and discouraging malfeasance. Put another way, market relations do not totally order or overdetermine all relations. There is a life world beyond the market upon which the market is dependent for its existence. In spite of the structural influence of the capitalist market, there is at least some independent agency in social relations.

Taking his cue from Granovetter, Coleman has emphasized that social capital inheres in the structure of relations between persons and among persons, being lodged neither in individuals nor in the implements of production. Coleman conceives of social capital as social-structural resources that can become a capital asset for the individual. That is, social capital acts as a social-structural resource for individuals that can be used to realize their interests. It is therefore an important resource for individuals and "can greatly affect their ability to act and their perceived quality of life" (1990, 305, 317). However, this is not to confuse social capital with human capital. Human capital is defined by Coleman (and many others) as those skills and capabilities that are acquired by individuals to enable them to act in new ways. Human capital is embodied in these skills and knowledge in the individual. Social capital is contained in the relations among persons, but it can be an important resource to enhance and support the development of human capital.

The emphasis of Granovetter and Coleman on networks of relations in defining social capital has been taken up by Robert Putnam (1993a, 1993b). Putnam stresses dense and horizontal networks. He argues that dense horizontal social and political networks can foster strong norms of generalized reciprocity. Reciprocity refers to a continuing relationship of exchange that is at any time unrequited but that involves mutual expectations that a benefit granted now should be repaid in the future. However, in generalized reciprocity, expectations of repayment are lax and not measured by an economist's weigh scales and narrow time-limited calculations (see Chapter 2 for further discussion on general reciprocity). Putnam is interested in generalized reciprocity as a norm that engenders trust. In this view, social trust is an important component of social capital that arises from two related sources: norms of reciprocity and networks of civic engagement (1993a, 171-76). For Putnam, reciprocity practised over time builds trust, and "trust lubricates social life" (1993b, 37). It is crucial to note that Putnam's analysis is based on the horizontal nature of these dense relationships. It is through horizontal reciprocal relationships that the trust essential to the creation of social capital is most effectively realized.

Now, Putnam argues that the norm of generalized reciprocity serves to reconcile self-interest and solidarity and is therefore highly productive because communities with this norm can more effectively restrain opportunism and resolve problems of collective association. Dense networks of social interaction also facilitate communication and coordination that amplify information about the trustworthiness of individuals. In addition, dense social ties facilitate gossip and other ways of cultivating reputation, information on which trustworthiness is built. Finally, networks of civic engagement embody past successes at collaboration that can serve as a cultural template or norm for future collaboration. Putnam stresses the self-reinforcing and cumulative aspect of social capital: "Successful collaboration in one endeavor builds connections and trust – social assets that facilitate future collaboration in other, unrelated tasks" (1993b, 37).

Social capital also has a public good aspect that "distinguishes it from the private, divisible, alienable goods treated by neo-classical economic theory" (Coleman 1990, 315). Coleman explains that, because it is an attribute of social structures in which an individual is embedded, social capital is not the private property of any of the actors who benefit from it. Rather, social capital as a concept that refers to relationships between individuals has, by definition, a public good aspect. However, it is this relational quality of the concept of social capital that lends a certain "intangible character" to it (Coleman 1990, 319). Social capital is not a material substance like physical capital, nor is it easily measurable like financial capital or even human capital. On the other hand, the concept of social capital lends itself to qualitative social ecological analysis in the sense that it is about relationships rather than things. While this is perhaps the reason for its intangible and even ambiguous character, it is also the most salient aspect of the concept from the perspective of social transformation. Therefore, it is this relational character of social capital that I make use of when examining the bioregional movement. Unlike many social scientists (Edwards et al. 2001; Harvard Center for Population and Development Studies 1996), I am not concerned with measuring social capital. Even Coleman placed much more emphasis on its use in qualitative analysis of social systems (1990, 305-6).

Yet, from an ecologically centred perspective, problems remained with the social capital concept. Putnam's study of social capital in making democracy work in Italy, however shaky his data (Fine 2001, 85-89), takes no account of the growth problematic. The most successful regions in terms of effective citizen participation in regional programs were those in the more industrialized north, where industrial throughput growth (and thus consumption) is strongest. Moreover, the concept of social capital in both Coleman and Putnam is thoroughly anthropocentric: it challenges *homo economicus* as an atomistic entity but not the culture of consumption that utility-maximizing *homo economicus* embodies. If humans cooperate more effectively in their development, but continue with exponential industrial growth and consumption, then the problem remains – at best – only partially solved. While social capital points to the need to theorize cultural transformation, it fails to specifically address the ways in which humans relate to the natural environment; it fails, that is, to address the relationship of human capital to natural capital or, less prosaically, to nature. However, another concept has emerged to address this gap.

Fikret Berkes and Carl Folke (1994) have advanced a definition of cultural capital that is designed to capture a range of sociocultural variables similar to those that define social capital but that also specifically seeks to integrate the missing ethical or moral variable that relates to natural capital. They define cultural capital as the interface between natural capital and human-made capital. Human-made capital refers to the produced means of production generated through economic activity. It is also referred to as "manufactured capital." However, it is important to caution that Berkes and Folke's use of the term "culture" includes a recognition of many distinct societies (cultural diversity) and of many different definitions of culture among anthropologists. Their definition also recognizes that the concept of "nature" is itself culture-specific. They argue that a cultural diversity of ways to deal with the natural environment is a significant part of cultural capital, quoting Madhav Gadgil to point out that cultural diversity may be as important to conserve as biological diversity. Cultural diversity, in this view, may be an adaptive strength in the pursuit of sustainability. Philosophy, values, ethics, and religion of a culture are central to Berkes and Folke's definition of cultural capital.

Berkes and Folke emphasize that manufactured capital is never value-neutral but is a product of and embodies evolving cultural values, norms, and worldviews. For example, with respect to the modern system of production, they analyze how cultural capital and manufactured capital reinforce each other in a positive feedback loop that diminishes natural capital:

> Technologies (tools, skills, and know-how) which mask the society's dependence on natural capital encourage people to think that they are above nature. The more extensive this change, the more of similar type of technologies will be developed and the more impacts on natural capital there will be. Positive feedbacks between cultural capital and human-made capital are established which enhance this trend. There will be resource depletion and environmental degradation to feed an industrial society that requires ever increasing amounts of raw materials, and that generates ever increasing amounts of waste. Therefore, cultural capital plays an important role in how we use natural capital to "create" human-made capital. Thus, human-made capital is never value neutral, but a product of evolving cultural values and norms. (1994, 132)

In particular, coming from an industrial society that has masked our dependence on natural capital, we need, in Berkes and Folke's view, to "restore a semblance of the 'community of beings' world view of ancient pantheistic traditions" (1994, 144). Restoring this ancient ethic as an important part of our cultural capital, they submit, would be a creative use of this form of cultural capital to help meet the contemporary challenge of reintegrating people with nature.

I have borrowed the "community of beings" form of cultural capital to provide a new context for analyzing social capital development or formation. Social capital that is informed by the "community of beings" ethic is a new, adapted form of social capital that I call ecologically centred, or ecocentric, social capital. By this, I mean an ecosocial capital concerned with both interhuman and interspecies relationships. Ecosocial capital, then, is concerned with the formation of both interhuman and interspecies bonds.

From Theory to Action

Coleman has pointed out that losses of social capital in modern society raise the important question of social capital formation: that is, how can social capital be brought into existence (1990, 362, 663)? What does it take to generate social capital? Indeed, given my focus on ecosocial capital, the question becomes: How does social capital that is informed by a "community of beings" ethic come into existence in civil society?

Theoretical concerns about the creation of norms of cooperation and reciprocity, trust, and networks of civic engagement – when put into a framework of democratic theory building – are properly located within the radical-planning tradition. This tradition relies on action from below, from the space of civil society, where the people, as planning theorist John Friedmann argues, can break into politics to reassert their voice as the legitimate arbiter of their collective fate. Moreover, Friedmann explains, the concerns of radical planning are quite properly a part of planning in the public domain. Planning is not exclusively a function of the state. Indeed, as Friedmann has argued, "planning in the public domain could originate anywhere, including civil society" (1987, 298). More specifically, as Friedmann has also pointed out, "in social transformation, theory and practice become everyone's concern: responsibilities for both are multiple and overlapping" (393). In the 1990s, Friedmann also came to focus on civil society as a pivotal dimension of transformational change (1990, 1998). In the radical-planning tradition, then, theory and practice are not viewed dualistically; ideally, there is a dialectical convergence of the two in what is known as "praxis" (the integration of theory and practice), whereby practice informs theory, which in turn informs practice.

In the last half of the twentieth century, particularly since the 1960s, certain radical traditions have arisen within society, raising questions about cultural (as well as economic and political) transformation to an ecological worldview and a sustainable society. Such movements include feminist, gay and lesbian, indigenous, environmental/ecological, ethnic/racial, age, and ability concerns. Originally analyzed as "new social movements" (Tourraine 1979), many are emerging as international or global, partially through effective use of the Internet (Castells and Hall 1997, 69-83; Klein 2000; Ronfeldt et al. 1998, 7-22). Oppositional movements such as social ecology, deep ecology, ecofeminism, and bioregionalism have also been viewed as part of the radical alternative in planning thought (Beavis 1991, 75-82; Douglas and Friedmann 1998; Friedmann 1990; Sandercock 1998). These movements typically place a much deeper emphasis on cultural change as a foundation for sociopolitical and economic transformation than Marxism generally has. That is, Marxism has tended to view culture as a dependent variable (for a very informative review of this entire body of thought from an ecocentric perspective, see Eckersley 1992).

In contrast to Marxism, bioregionalism has emphasized cultural transformation in both its thought and its practice. However, bioregionalism as a movement in civil society is not solely cultural. Rather, the bioregional movement has developed a broad strategy for initiating struggles for economic, political, and structural transformation from below, a fact that links it to the older concerns of transformative theory and the traditions of radical planning. Bioregionalism is one movement (perhaps the only one) that has managed to combine many of the features and concerns of social ecology, deep ecology, and ecofeminism as well as a number of other radical movements. These diverse origins and expressions are combined in a social and cultural movement that in many ways incorporates much of the cultural diversity and sensibilities of the "new" social movements of the 1960s (Carr 1990). For these reasons, the bioregional movement presents an important paradigm to explore from the perspective of integrating cultural analysis within transformative theory. It is particularly relevant in the context of a culturally diverse contemporary globalizing society that nevertheless remains ideologically dominated by anthropocentric *homo economicus*, at least in the leading consumer/industrial countries.

Bioregionalism is based on a strategy of building local communities of place in civil society that are networked at broader geographical scales from the local watershed and larger regional watersheds to the continental scale. Bioregional activist and writer Peter Berg has defined the term "communities of place" as self-organized communities with the intention of overcoming modern individual alienation by learning to cooperate and work together toward restoring and maintaining natural systems, finding sustainable and self-reliant ways to meet human needs, and developing support for individuals engaged in this work (Andruss et al. 1990, 137-44). This strategy of bioregionalism situates each community within the natural "place" that it inhabits. In turn, these local communities of place are envisioned to become networked at broader scales as a greater community of communities. Bioregionalists believe that this strategy can assist individual human beings to make major changes in their cultural and economic lifestyles toward healthy relationships with each other and with the natural environment (Forsey 1993, 1-9).

However, while bioregionalists spend much energy and time in horizontal efforts aimed at redefining and reclaiming identities, norms, and institutions in civil society and some effort in vertical campaigns for political reform, they have not sufficiently theorized their strategy with respect to either the state or the corporate sector. Particularly, the bioregional movement has not developed either a theory or a strategy to contend with the entrenched power of international finance capital or the large corporations. Thus, an inquiry into bioregionalism that reveals cultural insights from its attempts at holistic vision and practice might have some valuable lessons for civil society theory with respect to the latter's lack of ecological understanding and cultural critique of economic individualism. In turn, a revised civil society theory (with its understanding of combined horizontal-vertical strategies) might have some valuable insights into strategies to democratize state and corporate sectors.

2
Ecocentric Social Capital: The Ecology of Kinship

Modes of Production

The existence and use of social capital can be most clearly explored, defined, and understood by first looking at societies where small communities were the predominant or sole form of social organization, communities in which there was no state and the economy was not seen as separate from society. In such small communities with high stocks of social capital, what we moderns call "the economy" was so deeply embedded in social relations that it was not even perceived as a phenomenon. It was simply part of the life of those societies characterized by a different mode of production. Fine, but what is a mode of production?

A conventional definition of a mode of production refers to an entire system of production of goods and services in a society that encapsulates both the forces or means of production and the social relations of production. Mode of production has been a central concept for Marxism, but non-Marxist sociologists now also use the concept widely. The forces of production are sometimes referred to as factors of production. Conventional definitions of mode of production traditionally include four factors of production: land, labour, entrepreneurial skills, and capital, with capital sometimes subdivided into finance capital and physical capital. Also, a conventional, neoclassical mode of production analytic framework regards these factors merely as inputs into the production process.

In my definition, inspired and informed by ecological economic thinking on forms of capital and by Marxist political economy, the human production system or mode of "production" is viewed as a mode of production *and* consumption: that is, production and consumption are seen to be directly related aspects of an integrated human economic system. The way in which we consume is closely tied to the way in which we produce, and the way that we produce strongly influences the way that we consume. It is a dialectical relationship: as production grows, so does consumption; as consumption grows, so must production. For example, when the industrial mode of production became so productively successful in the nineteenth century, it became necessary to create masses of consumers and national markets to supplant the great variety of small local and regional markets. As discussed in Chapter 1, this was done through the creation of advertising and mass media. In turn, the rise in consumption subsequently stimulated further increases in production and so on in a huge, positive feedback loop that is now leading us into the global marketplace.

My definition of a mode of production and consumption includes six factors of production: natural capital (not only land but also all of nature's goods and services), human capital (skills and knowledge of labour and management), social capital, cultural capital, physical or human-made capital, and finance capital. Thus, I have collapsed labour and entrepreneurial skills and knowledge into one category (human capital), and I have added two other factors of production: social capital and cultural capital.

As noted, all human modes of production are actually modes of production and consumption. We therefore cannot consider the various factors as merely inputs into production; we must also consider their role in consumption. For example, natural capital is a factor in production, but natural capital can only be a factor of production by being consumed. Social capital can replace some, or even a great deal, of natural capital as a factor of production and therefore can reduce natural capital throughput while enhancing and supporting human capital. Human-made capital will also have a different relationship to both human capital and natural capital if ecocentred social capital grows to replace a sufficient amount of natural capital throughput to achieve sustainability.

In part, the purpose of this chapter is to develop an understanding of economic activity that is truly embedded in dense systems of horizontal, many-sided social relations that are themselves embedded in the greater ecological community. In this analytical probing exercise, I also attempt to deepen the notion of ecocentred social capital so that it becomes a useful tool for exploring the role of social capital in contemporary society.

Consider first the question of embeddedness: that is, the fact that our modern industrial market society is the *only* society in history in which the economic sphere has not been embedded within social relationships and instead has come rather to dominate the sphere of civil society (as the work of Cohen and Arato and Polanyi has shown). In other words, our modern society, far from being the "universal" model that its ideology has led us to believe it is, is in fact atypical.

If we want to shed light on the relationship between economic society and civil society in any potentially sustainable future way of life, then we need to advance beyond the perceptual boundaries of our atypical market society. Contemporary thought is too narrowly restricted by the very economic norms of the industrial model that we seek to change. Since our

modern society is atypical, we need to understand how more typical societies function. We need to examine our human roots in societies where civil
society – not economics – was the dominant sphere of social relations. Such
a comparison might aid us in casting a clearer light on our own contemporary situation, in particular on the possibilities of transforming the capitalist industrial/consumerist mode of production into a sustainable mode of
production.

The Domestic Mode of Production

With roots deep in the Paleolithic period, the domestic mode of production
(DMP) used by gathering/hunting and horticultural societies was by far the
longest-running production-consumption system that humans have ever
experienced, comprising more than 99 percent of our time on Earth. This
fact alone speaks volumes for the sustainability of this system. Many different cultures are included within the DMP, but thanks to the fairly comprehensive overview provided by the economic anthropology of Marshall
Sahlins (1974) we have a definition and an analytical framework that help
to capture certain common features of the spectrum as found in a broad
range of societies still practising the DMP in the nineteenth and twentieth
centuries. Furthermore, Sahlins's broad examination provides a basis for
comparison with our own industrial mode of production.

In contrast to the industrial mode of production (IMP), the DMP may be
defined initially as a form of social organization for material production
and consumption in which the required level of resource throughput is
determined largely by the nature of its social relationships and its "connectivity" to nonhuman nature. This is an entirely different form of economy
from our own, in which, as discussed, a positive feedback type of relationship between production and consumption drives throughput growth. It's
actually very difficult to speak of "an economy" as such in reference to the
DMP. Sahlins has pointed out the following important caveat when discussing Paleolithic or Neolithic societies: "Structurally speaking 'the economy'
does not exist in the DMP. More precisely, 'economy' is something that
generalized social/kinship groups and relations, notably kinship groups and
relations, *do*" (1974, 76, emphasis in original). It is not a distinct, separate,
specialized organization. In other words, economy is a function of society,
for it is society, in the form of family or band production groups producing
for their own subsistence, that directs what is to be produced (and therefore
what is to be consumed). Furthermore, Sahlins adds, "the household is to
the tribal economy as the manor to the medieval economy or the corporation to modern capitalism: each is the dominant production-institution of
its time" (1974, 76). In the DMP, the household is charged with production,
with the deployment and use of labour power, and with the determination
of economic objectives. Of course, "household" here conveys a range of

different family forms, mostly some form of extended family. Cooperation in production can (and occasionally did) extend beyond the household, but such cooperation does not compromise the autonomy or economic purpose of the household, the domestic management of labour power, or the prevalence of domestic objectives across broader social activities of work. Given the centrality of the domestic management of production, Sahlins named this system the *domestic* mode of production.

Karl Polanyi has also compared gatherer/hunter societies with modern economies. He has observed that in the household economy the individual's motives spring from situations set or governed by facts of a noneconomic order, whether of family, politics, or religion. He remarks that the term "economic life" in this context would have no obvious meaning: "In contrast to kinship, magic or etiquette with their powerful keywords, the economy as such remained nameless" (Dalton 1968, 85). Again the economy is seen as thoroughly embedded in civil society to the point that the very concept of an economy did not exist.

If the household is the management unit of production (of the deployment and use of labour), then the household is also where what moderns would call economic objectives are determined. The principal relations of production are therefore the inner relations of the family or domestic group. All of these production decisions are domestic decisions for the purpose of domestic consumption, satisfaction, health, and happiness. As Sahlins explains, "the built-in etiquette of kinship statuses, the dominance and subordination of domestic life, the reciprocity and cooperation, here make the 'economic' a modality of the intimate" (1974, 77). Production, then, is attuned to the family's customary requirements. For Sahlins, this means that production is for the benefit of the producers, who are also the consumers. In the DMP, he finds an economy that is ordered primarily by kinship relations.

The "Zen" Road to Affluence

What are the main features of the DMP with respect to the potential of social capital to replace natural capital? In our materialistic consumer society, we tend to consider affluence in terms of the possession of things, the endless accumulation of material products. Indeed, this propensity to accumulate forms the core of the definition of economic man. In contrast to modern affluent consumer civilization, Sahlins counterposes what he calls the "original affluent societies" (Paleolithic gatherer-hunters and Neolithic agriculturists) of the DMP. Perhaps the most striking feature of such societies is what he calls their "structure of underproduction" (1974, 41).

This structure of the DMP refers to the observed reality across a number of ethnographies from around the world reviewed by Sahlins where production was not only low in comparison with more materialistic societies but also low relative to the existing possibilities and abilities of those societies themselves. Underproduction in this sense was not necessarily inconsistent with a kind of affluence. That is, all the material wants of the people could easily be satisfied even with "the economy" running below its production capacity, given their modest (by our modern exaggerated standards) ideas of satisfaction. In Sahlins's terms, these underproductive economies do not use all their available labour power, or fully engage all their technological means, and therefore also leave many of their natural resources untapped.

We moderns have consistently seen these subsistence economies as materially impoverished, surviving only in a state of brutal hardship. This view is changing, but to regard such societies as "affluent" still shocks our consumerist sensibilities. However, as Sahlins points out, poverty is, at least in part, a social status and in this sense is an invention of civilization. For Sahlins, poverty is neither a small amount of goods, nor just a relation between means and ends, but above all a relation between people. In this sense, poverty has actually grown with civilization. Our contemporary, overproductive, global economic era in the last half of the twentieth century was also a time of mass starvation, more than any other in the history of humanity. While Paleolithic and Neolithic communities had what we would call a "materially low" standard of living, the lower material wants of peoples within a domestic mode of production were usually met; they did not suffer from mass starvation. For Sahlins, referring to the low material wants of these societies, there is a "Zen" (Zen is noted for its simple austerity) road to affluence: "Adopting the Zen strategy, a people can enjoy an unparalleled material plenty – with a low standard of living" (1974, 2). It was simply a structure of production for livelihood.

Sahlins points out that production for livelihood is essentially production for use value. Production for livelihood, then, is by definition production for a "specific useful character responding to the producers' customary requirements" (1974, 84). Production within the producing/consuming domestic group (the household) merely meets the materially low, "Zen" demands. Sahlins further observes that, even when there is exchange between households, clans, or broader groups, both the exchange transaction and the production for it are oriented toward livelihood, not profit. Thus, in the DMP, production is under no compulsion to advance to the physical capacity that it would if oriented for exchange value on a market. On the contrary, Sahlins argues that production for use value is discontinuous and irregular and sparing of labour power. Viewed from within our modern, overproductive, consumer culture, production for use value is seen by Sahlins as a system of production for livelihood with limited economic goals defined qualitatively (*not* quantitatively) in terms of a way of living. Production, then, "is under no compulsion to proceed to the physical or gainful capacity, but inclined to break off for the time being when livelihood is assured for the time being" (84). Production is intermittent. In this ancient (and in some places still extant) system, what we moderns call "economics" is only a part-time activity or an activity of only part of the society (86). Furthermore, work in the DMP has an entirely different character from work in our modern market economy. In the DMP, there is what Sahlins calls an intrinsic discontinuity in the very way that work is organized: "Work is accordingly unintensive: intermittent and susceptible to all manner of interruption by cultural alternatives and impediments ranging from heavy ritual to light rainfall" (86).

As well, Sahlins notes, much work was seasonal and often required considerable effort over a concentrated period of time. Nevertheless, the typical "working week," if averaged out, was found to be fifteen to twenty hours in many of these societies (1974, 14-32). The evidence discussed by Sahlins draws on a number of empirical, quantitative studies of more or less contemporary gatherer-hunter societies, including Richard Lee's work on the !Kung Bushmen, James Woodburn's on the Hadza in Africa, and several more from Australia (20-32). Based on this evidence, Sahlins argues that "a good case can be made that hunters and gatherers work less than we do; and, rather than a continuous travail, the food quest is intermittent, leisure [is] abundant, and there is a greater amount of sleep in the daytime per capita per year than in any other condition of society" (14).

The misnamed 1966 Man the Hunter conference in Chicago, based on new field research at the time, was a watershed in thinking about gatherer-hunter or, more properly perhaps, foraging societies. First, the notion of "man the hunter" as the major breadwinner of early societies was overturned. As Richard Leakey commented almost thirty years after the event, the conference was important "not least for the recognition that the gathering of plant foods provided the major supply of calories for most gatherer-hunter societies" (1994, 63). This understanding helped to overturn the male bias in anthropology that had ignored or downplayed the role of women as gatherers. In his paper at the Chicago conference on the Kalahari !Kung Bushmen, Richard Lee showed that vegetable foods comprised 60-80 percent by weight of their total diet and that, although men's work and women's work were roughly equal in terms of time spent, women provided as much as two to three times as much food by weight as the men. Lee commented that, through his own and others' work at the conference and previous to it, "we have learned that in many societies, plant and marine resources are far more important than are game animals in the diet" (Lee and Devore 1979, 30).

Since Sahlins published his work, a variety of other cultural and ecological anthropological literature confirms – from a range of analytical approaches – the seemingly light impact of the underuse of natural resources in Native North American societies (Brody 1981; Cronon 1983; Feit 1973;

Tanner 1985; Turner 1983). For example, the work of ecological historian William Cronon confirms Sahlins's work from the perspective of a different framework, using a different methodology. Cronon (1983) examines in great detail the life of First Nations peoples in early colonial New England. With extensive multidisciplinary documentation and rigour, he lays out the evidence for the abundance of wildlife in the forests and along the shores inhabited by the tribal nations of Micmac, Abenaki, Mohegan, Delaware, Penobscot, Powhatan, and so on at the time of the Europeans' arrival. His reconstruction of ecological history is based on an interdisciplinary methodology that includes early travellers' descriptions (tempered by a critical approach to the European ethnocentric Christian mind-set of those centuries), ecological succession theory and the concept of ecosystems, an investigation of relict stands of old-growth forests in Connecticut, tree ring and pollen analysis, extensive research into the pattern of colonial legal activity, archeological evidence, and a review of modern ecological literature on the condition of contemporary eastern forests. His treatment of the relationship between culture and environment explores and explains the ways in which people created and re-created their livelihoods, analyzed through changes in both their social and their ecological relationships. Cronon focuses on relations at the local level, "where they become most visible," with the small region as his unit of analysis (6-14). Thus, Cronon describes the great diversity and abundance of forests and seashore habitats encountered by the early colonists, including the great abundance of mammal, bird, fish, and forest life, as well as the great variety and patchwork of forest plant associations across the regional landscape (22-32). His historical witnesses all agreed upon the "incredible abundance of New England plant and animal life" (22).

In this broad context, Cronon describes in detail the Native peoples' daily, seasonal, and annual patterns of adaptation to the cyclical and changing ecological dynamic. He describes how the Natives lived in seasons of abundance and of occasional winter scarcity, for both existed, as his detailed account clearly shows. Two broad regional variations are described: the hunting and gathering societies of northern New England above the latitude for maize growing, and the mixed economy of those groups in southern New England that grew maize and supplemented it with hunting, gathering, and fishing. Cronon describes how the Indians, both agricultural and nonagricultural, adapted their lives to the cycles of the seasons and to both abundance and scarcity. The principal social and economic grouping of New England Indians was the village of a few hundred people. However, the villages were not fixed geographical entities. Their size and location changed on a seasonal basis, breaking up and reassembling as social and ecological needs required. Mobility was an important key to light impact on the landscape.

Early European visitors such as Thomas Morton characterized New England Indians as being "rich in Land, and poor in all the Comforts of Life" (in Cronon 1983, 79). Cronon points out that, like Morton and other European observers of Indian life, the philosopher John Locke failed to notice that Indians did not recognize themselves as poor and that the endless accumulation of capital that he saw as a natural consequence of the human love for wealth made little sense to Indians. Cronon himself makes the link to Sahlins's "Zen road to affluence": "'Wants,' Sahlins says, may be 'easily satisfied' by producing much or desiring little" (80).

Cronon has also documented the Indians' relaxed attitude toward personal possessions, using various early accounts of what anthropologists now call usufruct rights. For example, the Micmac of Nova Scotia were described by one contemporary as "so generous and liberal towards one another that they seem not to have any attachment to the very little they possess, for they deprive themselves thereof very willingly and in very good spirit the very moment when they know that their friends have need of it" (in Cronon 1983, 61-62). Cronon comments that Europeans often interpreted such actions as the supposed generosity of the "noble savage" and suggests that a better interpretation would place such behaviour in the context of their seasonal round of life in which accumulation of possessions made little sense. Moreover, Cronon adds that in New England Indian society a system of reciprocity existed similar to the potlatch ceremonies of the Pacific Northwest, in which wealthy individuals gave away much of what they owned to establish reciprocal relations of obligation with potential allies (46).

In difficult seasonal circumstances, some households did not always meet their own modest "Zen" consumption requirements. If this was so, how can Sahlins defend the system as affluent? The answer lies in the system of generalized reciprocity that pertained at the level of the domestic group (whether foraging bands or villages), especially with respect to the sharing of food. In the DMP, food sharing between haves and have nots was an important key to the success of generalized reciprocity (Sahlins 1974, 210-19). A simple definition of generalized reciprocity refers to a system of total sharing within the family, band, or village, associated especially (but not only) with food sharing. It does not necessarily mean that food is divided equally among the people, but it does mean that no one goes hungry if food is available. If food shortages exist in the territory, then food will be shared with visitors or those seeking help (Leacock and Lee 1987, 8).

However, the concept of general reciprocity is also used by Sahlins to convey the sense that a form of exchange takes place. Several forms of reciprocity represent a continuum of forms of exchange. For Sahlins, the most generalized reciprocity is the solidarity extreme in which the material side of the exchange transaction is repressed or subsumed by the social side. In this form of reciprocity, the expectation of return exchange for "gifts" is indefinite, not stipulated by time, quantity, or quality. This form takes place within close kinship relations. Failure by the recipient to reciprocate even over a long period of time does not cause the giver to stop giving. This is crucial because this extended giving (called "general reciprocity") suggests that merely instrumentalist or economistic explanations for such behaviour are insufficient.

From this generalized reciprocity extreme, the continuum moves out to less "pure" forms of kinship dues and chiefly dues where there is a more definite expectation of commensurate return within a finite period of time. This continuum proceeds on to "balanced reciprocity" or direct exchange. Balanced reciprocity can take the form of either "gift exchange" or out-and-out trade in which the material side of the transaction is at least as critical as the social side. At this extreme, transactions are conducted with those beyond immediate kinship relations. Sahlins characterizes the distance between these poles of reciprocity as a "social distance" (1974, 196). Reciprocity, then, whatever form it took on the continuum, was the cultural norm that governed redistribution in the DMP, normally ensuring nutritional success for all families.

In the DMP, we see civil society writ large. In it, the economy of production for livelihood exists only as a function and attribute of kinship relations; it is deeply embedded in those relations. As we have seen, what we would call "economic" activity is a part-time affair whether from the point of view of the individual or the domestic group. Extended kinship relations – civil society itself – are where economic direction is set, decisions are made, and most of the essential production and consumption are carried out. Kinship relations set the pattern for and embody the relations of production. The relations of production are therefore contained within civil society and are not part of a separate economic or political sphere.

In the DMP, the quality and extension of kinship relations are not limited to those who are strictly kin. Even within the most extensive clan organizations, people still behave toward each other as if they are kin. More than this, though, as anthropologist Stanley Diamond has argued, all meaningful social, economic, and ideological relations have a kin or transfigured kin character. Diamond refers to this character as a "personalism" extending from the family outward to society and ultimately to all of nature (1974, 144-45). However, I have found the best explanations of such a personalism to be those of certain First Nations writers. It is captured in the popular phrase "all my relations." For example, Native American author Dennis Martinez (1993) points out that the relationship between the people and the Earth, expressed in the well-known ceremonial phrase "all my relations," is really an indigenous concept of general reciprocity. Reciprocity, in this sense, is a powerful but simple and straightforward concept that means helping our relatives so that they will help us, in this case *all* our relations:

the plants, the animals, the birds, ecological relationships, everything on our Earth. This personalism of relationships is understood as a "caretaking responsibility" associated with a subsistence livelihood. Note also that this indigenous understanding of general reciprocity takes us beyond a merely human-centric notion of social capital.

If relations of production are embedded in kinship relations, then what are the essential features of such relations? Much has been written about this topic already, so I have merely arranged a composite list of these features from a number of sources that I think we need to consider in order to better analyze social (and cultural) capital in the DMP. I should point out for the sake of clarity that the following list, which includes an important First Nations contribution (Clarkson, Morisette, and Regallet 1992; Diamond 1974; Leacock and Lee 1987; Mander 1991), is an attempt to reflect only some broad parameters of what the literature says about similar features of many, if not most, of the societies practising the DMP.

1   Ownership of the means of production – the land or natural capital – is collective, at the level of the band.
2   There is general access to technology – virtually everyone has skills for making essential tools.
3   There is reciprocal access – beyond the band level – to the means of production through marriage ties, visiting, and coproduction.
4   There is little or no emphasis on accumulation.
5   Generalized reciprocity occurs within the family, band, and clan.
6   Dense social networks exist in small communities.
7   There is intensive and extensive nurturing of children.
8   There is cultural integration – sacred and secular are united – and all life is sacred.

Clearly, levels of social capital were extremely high in the DMP. Moreover, at the scale of the family, band, or clan, social capital was ubiquitous in both production and consumption. Norms of reciprocity, cooperation, pooling, sharing, and mutual aid were the social institutions comprising these dense networks of intense, horizontal interaction. Direct and many-sided personal and social relationships gave rise to high levels of information about one another and enabled the formation of deep bonds of trust based on this information. Of course, this should not be read as if DMP societies did not experience "bad actors" in their populations or that there was no social conflict. What I mean is that, in comparison with our modern, alienated, atomistic society, societies that practised general reciprocity as a basic norm of life in small groups reflected relatively high levels of social capital expressed in strong kinship relations. Such societies engaged intensively in the sharing of oral histories through storytelling and public

ceremonies and rituals, bonding people to each other and to their ancestors. The fabric of social life was evidently rich indeed. We have also seen
that human capital, the knowledge and skills associated with technology in
the DMP, was perhaps as ubiquitous and developed as social capital. What
we today would call civic engagement was almost universal in the DMP, a
daily fact of life for the individual in society, the civic individual.

From the point of view of replacing natural capital with social capital,
high throughput of natural capital was neither necessary nor desirable in
such societies. This is very encouraging and hugely significant, for it suggests that high levels of social capital can provide a meaningful and powerful substitute for heavy consumption of natural capital in our society, if we
can learn to build and enhance dense, horizontal, mutual relations and
institutions of our own – if, that is, we are prepared to learn some essential
lessons in civics from foraging peoples.

Sahlins's work has been critiqued by anthropologists who argue that the
studies he drew on were based on small numbers of individuals (Bird-David
1992). More than that, the work of Sahlins, Lee, and others has been ac-
cused of inventing (or socially constructing) the very categories "hunter-
gatherer" and "forager" in order "to illuminate and legitimize a crucial area
in Euroamerica's symbolic reconstruction of its own ontology" (Wilmsen
and Denbow 1990, 494). However, new studies using a culturalist method
of economic analysis that examines the metaphors and language used by
gatherer-hunters themselves to gain more insight into their behaviour have
confirmed Sahlins's initial insights into gatherer-hunter "affluence" and general reciprocity (Bird-David 1992). Essentially, this debate reflects an ideological split between anthropologists who view the gatherer-hunter way of
life as different from that of economic man and those who argue that
gatherer-hunters behave the same as do members of modern market economies (Gowdy 1998). Analysis of gatherer-hunter/forager metaphors shows
that these societies do indeed have relaxed attitudes about what we would
call economic security. Sharing is a primary metaphor and is used to encompass the sense of a "life-long engagement of sharing," and "in the course
of their life activity they normally engage with it as if they were in a sharing
relationship" (Bird-David 1992, 31). This includes a sense of sharing with
the natural world, which is viewed animistically as a world that shares with
them, exactly the opposite of the neoclassical economic paradigm, which
views the natural world as a world of "scarce resources" separate from the
human realm. In short, gatherer-hunters adopt the sharing path to affluence in a "cosmic economy of sharing" (Bird-David 1992, 30).

In responding to accusations of imposing his Western social construc-
tions on gatherer-hunter peoples, Lee also returned to the people whom he
studied, the !Kung: "What is the !Kung view of their own history? The !Kung
see themselves as a people, increasingly circumscribed and threatened, but

a people nonetheless with a strong sense of themselves. When told that they were really tributary appendages, long integrated into the economies of their more powerful neighbors, they were surprised and not a little offended" (1992, 40).

This is a reference to the fact that gatherer-hunter peoples are today everywhere endangered (as is the natural world) precisely because of the ongoing expansion of the global megamachine. Lee points out that "it is striking how the largely male, White, and Western poststructuralists are proclaiming the death of the subject, precisely at the moment when alternative voices – women, people of colour, Third World and Aboriginal peoples – are struggling to constitute themselves as subjects of history, as the makers of their own history" (1992, 36). In a more recent reader on gatherer-hunter economics that includes new research, John Gowdy (1998) concludes that the positive view of gatherer-hunters as the original affluent societies has held up well in the decades since Sahlins's *Stone Age Economics* was published.

The next section looks more closely at cultural capital to examine indigenous views of what I call "ecological kinship." First let me briefly compare the domestic mode of production (or the cosmic economy of sharing) with the modern mode of production, capitalism. In the modern system, the economic sphere is not only *not* embedded in civil society but also *dominates* civil society and consequently kinship relations. In modern capitalist society, the private corporation is the dominant production institution of our time. This means that production is geared not to use value or the needs of kinship or civil society but to exchange value and the self-regulating market mechanism. Particularly over the past 150 years or so (the period of the great transformation), the market mechanism has worked to create what can be seen, in contrast to Sahlins's structure of production for livelihood, as a structure of overproduction geared to commodity consumption.

What has emerged from my analysis of the DMP is the simple fact that in a structure of production for livelihood a large amount of time is available for the creation, development, and nurturing of social capital. In the "Zen" road to affluence, material production of basic necessities is not allowed to interfere with or fragment the profoundly rich social, cultural, and spiritual lives of the people. Rather, material production is itself part of – embedded in – kinship relations. Indeed, as we have seen, kinship relations govern material production. In any truly affluent society, the affluent will have plenty of time to enjoy their affluence. Affluence can be viewed, in this more basic sense, as the disposable time of individuals and groups to enrich their social, cultural, and spiritual lives.

Social capital increases through use (see Chapter 1); therefore, those with social capital tend to accumulate more through even greater use. In societies where affluence is measured in the richness of social relations (rather than the amassing of material wealth or the frenetic consumption of commodities), everyone's time is freed up to produce high-quality, diverse, and many-sided social relations. Social capital in extended and intense use does require a lot of time, but it produces even more social capital while also enriching human capital. In societies with relatively high levels of social capital practising the DMP, the required time to build up these levels through intense use appears as a crucial additional factor for the further flourishing of social capital.

In societies where productive – or economic – activity is embedded in social relations, social capital is also built up through organized work sharing. This is unlike the economic sphere of modern industrialism, where mass-production work is alienating for so many, is characterized by vertical relations of dependency, and robs labour of valuable time to build a rich social and cultural life. In the DMP, in contrast, productivity is not associated with quantitative success in material production. Rather, it is associated with modest or subsistence production of material life. Furthermore, the productivity of social capital in the DMP is associated with its own reproduction and growth. The general result, then, of the productivity of social capital in the DMP is the production of rich, many-sided, dense, horizontal networks of social relations while conservatively using both natural capital and human labour. This is the "secret" to the productivity of social capital in the DMP. I would also suggest that it is the secret to the impressive longevity, to the proven long-term sustainability, of the DMP. One does not give up such a rich, socially affluent, way of life easily. It took a long time for agriculture to spread across Europe. From its origins in the Near East around 8000 BC, agriculture advanced across Europe "at a snail's pace" to reach Greece around 6000 BC and Britain and Scandinavia some 2,500 years later (Diamond 1992, 183).

The Community of Beings and Ecological Kinship

As we saw in Chapter 1, the concept of cultural capital was designed to capture a range of sociocultural variables mostly similar to those defined by the term "social capital" (Berkes and Folke 1994). In my exploration of the DMP, we have seen, first, that kinship relations were extended from the family to the band and clan levels. In other words, kinship relations were extended out into civil society to the point where kinship relations were coterminous with civil society. That is, all social capital in this situation took on a kinship or transfigured kinship character. Second, we have seen that kinship relations were not considered to be limited to the human community.

The extension of transfigured kinship relations to all of nature noted above is also captured by Berkes and Folke's "community of beings" ethic discussed in Chapter 1. In this remarkable and ancient ethic is the crucial link between social capital and cultural capital. Obviously, as we have seen, Earth-based societies, whether from the Stone Age or our age, do not make the hard and fast distinctions that our modern industrial culture makes between human and nonhuman life, between the social world and the natural world. This simple fact has enormous bearing on the conservative use of natural capital in the DMP. Such cultural capital considerations are entirely absent from Sahlins's otherwise outstanding analysis of Stone Age economics. More generally, it is difficult to find any discussion of the community of beings ethic in the anthropological literature, other than as anecdotal accounts of "superstitious" beliefs. Therefore, to understand how cultural capital reflected in the community of beings ethic informs behaviour vis-à-vis the relationship between social capital and natural capital, I have consulted literature from a variety of First Nations.

The Haudenosaunee or Iroquois Six Nations Confederacy is known for the fact that its Great Law provided both inspiration and ideas embodied in the US Constitution. In 1977, the confederacy presented a series of position papers to the United Nations in Geneva on the global crisis facing humanity. This address to the Western World was later published by Akwesasne Notes as *A Basic Call to Consciousness* (Six Nations Confederacy 1986). It identifies Western civilization – a whole way of life – as the very process of abuse of both humanity and nature at the root of our global crisis. The basic call advanced by the Iroquois Confederacy is that humans need to reclaim consciousness of the Earth as "a very sacred place" (1986, 49) and that the role of humans, according to their own ancient traditions or "original instructions," is to be "the spiritual guardians of this place" (49). For the Iroquois, human relations are thoroughly integrated with and dependent on all life. The following quotation captures this relationship beautifully in poetic prose:

> In the beginning, we were told that the human beings who walk about on the Earth have been provided with all the things necessary for life. We were instructed to carry a love for one another, and to show a great respect for all the beings of this Earth. We are shown that our life exists with the tree life, that our well-being depends on the well-being of the Vegetable Life, that we are close relatives of the four-legged beings ... We give a greeting and thanksgiving to the many supporters of our own lives – the corn, beans, squash, the winds, the sun. When people cease to respect and express gratitude for these many things, then all life will be destroyed, and human life on this planet will come to an end. (49)

This philosophy of kinship with and sacredness of all life forms was not peculiar to the Six Nations. Similar sentiments can be found over and over again among the First Nations. In a report written by a team of Native people published by the International Institute for Sustainable Development in Winnipeg, First Nations authors Linda Clarkson, Vern Morisette, and Gabriel

Regallet describe why, in Native traditions, respect for people and respect for the Earth are linked for people to survive and care for at least the next seven generations:

> When we begin to separate ourselves from that which sustains us, we immediately open up the possibility of losing understanding of our responsibility and our kinship to the earth. When we view the world simply through the eyes of human beings we create further distance between ourselves and our world. When the perceived needs of one spirit being [are] held above all others, equality disappears ... From this basic understanding, our ancestors assumed their role as the spiritual guardians of the earth. One of the most significant illustrations of this is the central belief that the whole of creation is a sacred place ... At the first level of understanding we can see the relationship between humans and their basic biological needs as they relate to the earth. The second level creates the relationship that ties the biological need to the spiritual. This is a dialectic relationship. More than ingesting the fruits of our labour through one orifice and discharging them through another, it is a fundamental alliance with the earth. (1992, 5)

In this worldview, sacred and secular, spiritual and material, human and nonhuman are tightly woven together. Here we clearly see the crucial link between general reciprocity and the community of beings ethic. Reciprocity, expressed in the phrase "all my relations," is extended beyond the merely human as a kinship ethic that includes the whole Earth. The practice of this ethic informs the use of both social capital and human capital as well as the very respectful way that natural capital was used in the DMP. It is evident that the ancient community of beings ethic was responsible for the high quality of care practised in the use of other organisms and resources. It was a matter not only of using fewer resources but also of using them with care and spiritual attention.

What has been learned about social capital and natural capital from the foregoing analysis of the DMP? First, there is a definite, strong, negative correlation between social capital and consumption: that is, high levels of social capital are associated with low throughput of natural capital. This inverse relationship contributes an enrichment of the social capital concept, one that is directly relevant to replacing natural capital with social capital. Moreover, a reflective consideration of cultural capital, in particular the community of beings ethic, has itself enriched and transformed the social capital concept by expanding the concept of kinship relations beyond human social relations to all other species and to the biosphere. Broadening the norm of general reciprocity to include all of life is not simply a symbolic act but is also directly related to the conservative and spiritually respectful use of natural capital in the DMP.

Second, this exploration has revealed a more nuanced understanding of the concept of ecosocial capital than that discussed in Chapter 1. Ecosocial capital both informs and subsumes social capital. High levels of social capital in DMP societies are associated with the ecosocial character of the community of beings ethic. The deeply spiritual meaning attached to this Earth-centred ethic provides a potentially strong motivation for the careful, respectful, and sparing use of natural resources, viewed not as mere commodities but as kin. The ecological kinship norm found in the community of beings ethic is thus identified as a spiritual resource for humans. If affluence is to be associated with the richness and diversity of one's social or, rather, ecosocial relations, then the possession of commodities appears to be a very poor substitute.

Civil Society and the "Love" Economy

What can we learn from the analysis of the DMP in terms of the three-sphere analysis of our modern industrial mode of production? How much of what was the norm to the peoples practising the DMP could apply to modern society, a society in which the formerly all-embracing kinship/civil society sphere has become atrophied and dominated by the economic and political spheres? A brief examination of the sphere of civil society in our contemporary industrial era will help to clarify the potential for democratization of our modern, civil society sphere.

The contemporary industrial/consumer mode of production provides an almost total contrast to the DMP. In our society, natural capital is squandered, and civil society has been marginalized by the political and economic spheres. The hub of the domestic mode of production, the household, has been trivialized or ignored altogether as a factor in production. As many feminist analysts have pointed out, women's work in the home does not even count as productive labour. Marilyn Waring (1988) has given us a detailed analysis of the consistent omission of women's domestic labour in both the United Nations System of National Accounts and in many different systems of national accounting. In all these systems, the household is simply not counted as part of the economy. Women are invisible as producers in their capacities as housewives. Their knowledge and skills do not qualify as human capital. Of course, this also applies to men who do domestic work in the home, but, as Waring and others have shown, the vast majority of the work done in the home is still done by women, even after twenty years of feminist organizing and education. However, what is relevant here is the question of the size of the household and community economy.

There are several different names for the household and community economy in modern society: the hidden economy, the informal economy, the dual economy, the grey (or black) economy, the barefoot economy, and the cooperative or love economy. Hazel Henderson, who uses the term "love economy," makes a useful distinction between economic activities such as illegal drug and other criminal activities (transnational corporate barter deals, tax dodging, and cash moonlighting) of the formal economy on the one hand and all the "traditional, loving, unpaid work in the subsistence, household and community sectors described earlier by Sahlins, Polanyi, et al." on the other hand (1991, 152). The former list she categorizes as the undocumented "underbelly" of the GNP formal sector. The latter list, of course, is what concerns us since it comprises activity in the sphere of civil society. Henderson refers to sociological studies (economists generally ignore the informal economy) in France, Sweden, Canada, and the United Kingdom, showing that about 50 percent of all productive work is unpaid (120). These figures suggest a huge potential for a civil society–based informal economy based on horizontal forms of social capital.

Another aspect of the love or caring economy is the volunteer sector, which itself is huge. Barbara Brandt in *Whole Life Economics: Revaluing Daily Life* cites another study showing that 51 percent of all US residents over the age of seventeen do volunteer work (1995, 20). While there remain difficulties with measuring the informal economy, it is clear that this sector is enormous. Brandt has made a very useful list of the various components of the informal economy that helps to characterize its size, importance, and potential for transformational analysis and action in the civil society sphere. She presents six major sources of informal human economic activity that have emerged to make this formerly invisible economy visible: (1) unpaid domestic activities for home and family, commonly known as women's work; (2) women's biological activities of pregnancy, childbirth, and breastfeeding; (3) household production and neighbourly exchanges of goods and services; (4) volunteer activities for community and public good; (5) innovative new economic models and institutions, such as worker ownership, consumer cooperatives, land trusts, community money systems, et cetera; and (6) economic forms from non-Western and nonindustrial cultures. As Brandt points out, many of these informal activities are becoming more broadly recognized as spaces in the struggle for democratization, partly because of the efforts of women, partly because of changing values, and partly because of the growing failure of the formal sector to meet people's needs (108-10). The size of all these activities taken together is impressive. Moreover, it is clear that these are all activities that take place in civil society. For Henderson, Brandt, and a number of feminist analysts, the "home-grown economy" functions as a support base for the formal economic sector. Equally, or perhaps more importantly, Henderson's "love economy" can provide a minimal social safety net from the GNP-dominated "world trade roller coaster" (1991, 119).

What I find hopeful in this analysis is that, in spite of the real marginalization of the hidden economy (its domination by state and corporate sectors), it remains a huge terrain with potential for a strengthened democratization through the building of ecosocial capital. While the economic and political spheres have come to dominate civil society over the past century and a half, civil society and its concomitant economic life as represented in the informal economy have not disappeared. Civil society, then, remains the most promising sphere for the theoretical and practical effort to begin building democratic relations in our time.

Wild

I thought I could become wild once
Me, a city girl born and bred
Gone to the country following a dream
Made life real.

Splitting wood and carrying water
Prepared me for living outside
For raising my food, our food
For building our shelters

We were wilder then
Chickens in the toolshed
Goats on the porch
Sleeping outside as many seasons as possible
Hanging out around fires
Living for the out-of-doors

I felt at home outside
Strength was in my arms, my hands
My sense of self too long trapped
In the aridity of my skull
Began to descend toward my toes
Taking up a new, more succulent,
More earthy home in my gut

I woke up to being animal
Delighted in my tireless feet
Moving over forest trails
To mountain ridges
Across dancing streams and creeks

Felt joy in the sureness of body
Finding its way over
Ice-crusted paths, through mud and snow
We carried our life with us on our backs

We tasted mammalness, now and then
Saw how humans could be different living in nature –
    wild and yet
Self-domesticated
Caring for ourselves
Satisfying our animal needs for food and shelter
Rearing our young in our ways

– Alice Kidd, December 1990

3
Bioregional Vision and Values

Bioregionalism is both a philosophy of life and a social movement in civil society. The movement is based on cultural and social praxis in which bioregionalists attempt to integrate an economic and political praxis. In simple terms, the bioregional movement is inspired by and organized around the concept of healthy and sustainable local communities, complemented by broader efforts at social change through regional and interregional networking in both rural and urban environments. For example, bioregionalists were among the first to initiate and attempt to implement community projects, proposals, and visions toward ecological or green cities in the early 1980s (Berg 1983, 1986; Berman et al. 1981; Todd and Todd 1984; Todd and Tukel 1981). The term "green city" first appeared in bioregional popular literature in 1983. Bioregional green or "ecocity" projects and proposals have been directly traced to the earlier visionary work of Lewis Mumford and the Regional Planning Association of America (Aberley 1985).

The long-term goal of the bioregional movement is to establish bioregionally self-reliant economies of "place" networked geographically across "space" via communications and limited trade links. Self-reliance, in this sense, means producing most or all of your basic necessities while engaging in trade only for specialty items. This vision is directly at odds with the neoliberal agenda of a single global market dominated by finance capital and transnational corporations. In the ideal globalized order, urban and regional economies produce commodities for the global marketplace according to their relative comparative advantages while importing a plethora of other commodities from around the world, each produced according to the comparative advantages of its regional or national economy. The two worldviews could not be much further apart.

In its first two decades, beginning in the early 1970s, the bioregional movement slowly but steadily grew. In 1984, the first Planet Drum Directory listed about fifty groups that identified with bioregionalism (Goldhaft 1989). By 1995, Doug Aberley's content analysis of *Raise the Stakes* (the major continental networking journal of the movement) showed about 100 such groups and another 278 classed as allies of bioregionalism (personal communication, 29 April 1996).

Bioregional educator Frank Traina (Traina and Darley-Hill 1995, 9) has pointed to two major problems with measuring the impact of the bioregional movement: first, many people and groups are doing things advocated by bioregionalists without necessarily being aware of the formal bioregional concept (projects in stream restoration and "daylighting," urban design and sustainability, sustainable livable regions, etc.); second, few people are bioregionalists only, often identifying themselves as also greens, environmentalists, ecofeminists, social ecologists, deep ecologists, conservationists, restorationists, ecologically concerned Christians or Jews, green Buddhists, neo-Pagans, or Earth-oriented spiritualists, et cetera. There are also First Nations peoples who practise bioregional ways of life. Furthermore, bioregionalists do not pay dues to any organization, nor do local bioregional groups report to any larger organization. All of this makes counting bioregional heads difficult.

The numbers may be greater than Aberley's content analysis of *Raise the Stakes* shows. In any event, there is no question that bioregional ideas are spreading throughout the environmental movement and even more generally (though to a somewhat lesser extent) in society at least in the United States, Canada, and Mexico, in both government and corporate environments. There are over 60 bioregional publications in English and Spanish (most of these are regional or local magazines or journals), plus another 140 publications that include material on bioregionalism (Aberley, personal communication, 29 April 1996).

A number of published bioregional thinkers are now well known in the environmental movement and beyond: Thomas Berry, Wendel Berry, Earnest Callenbach, Dolores LaChapelle, Joanna Macy, Stephanie Mills, Bill Mollison, Judith Plant, Kirkpatrick Sale, Gary Snyder, Starhawk, and John and Nancy Todd. Others who are well known, empathetic to bioregionalism, and/or published in the bioregional press include Jane Jacobs, Helena Norberg-Hodge, Jerry Mander, Reed Noss, Richard Register, Jeremy Rifkin, Vandana Shiva, Charlene Spretnak, and David Suzuki. Still other sympathizers publish in local and regional magazines, journals, and newspapers of the bioregional movement, in all representing a rich diversity of thought. The movement includes activist poets and ecophilosophers, scientists and back-to-the-landers, urban and (bio)regional designers and planners, urban geographers, educators, ecocity neighbourhood activists, and creek restorationists.

Some bioregionalists do not regard bioregionalism as a social movement, particularly at the continental level. Traina suggests that by certain definitions it may make more sense to speak about a bioregional community (Traina and Darley-Hill 1995, 9). In my view, bioregionalism is a social movement, but it is also a community of communities. Community or social movement, the key question here is how do bioregionalists go about building their communities and networks?

In the bioregional movement, there is great respect for cultural, social, and religious diversity. Bioregionalism is greatly enriched by the diversity of people, ideas, and social movements out of which the movement arose. Relevant social movements include the green movement, the ecofeminist movement, the permacultural movement, social ecology, deep ecology, the Mexican ecology movement, various indigenous peoples, the Christian "creation spirituality" movement, certain new left groups, the neo-Pagan or Wiccan movement, Zen Buddhism, the Earth First! movement, and the Rainbow Tribe or Rainbow Gathering movement.

Consider some typical activities carried out by bioregionalists. They undertake ecological restoration projects such as creek and stream daylighting and restoration, permaculture design, community gardens, urban forestry, bioregional mapping, bioregional education, and renewable energy projects (including solar, wind, and microhydro projects and home or business retrofitting). Bioregionalists campaign for and support proximity or mixed-use, integrated density design, planning and zoning reforms, socially and ecologically sustainable regional planning, urban ecovillage projects, alternative transit planning, and recycling and reuse projects. Bioregionalists help to organize and promote ecocity "green" calendars and volunteer directories, community currency and barter-exchange networks, community land trusts, a variety of all-species projects (see Chapter 4), and various publishing groups. These activities are social capital and human capital intensive rather than finance capital intensive, often depending on large amounts of volunteer time, cooperation, and initiative.

Bioregional thought appears in essays, poetry, local and regional journals, books, and the self-published proceedings of the North American Bioregional Congress (see Chapter 6). This expanding literature reveals a philosophy rooted in the activities of building local community and networking regionally and interregionally in diverse social movements across North America (or, as bioregionalists refer to the continent, "Turtle Island," after a common and fairly widespread indigenous expression). The overwhelming majority of bioregionalists' efforts at social change take place within the sphere of civil society. This is a movement wherein philosophy lends itself to direct action, to implementation in the here and now. Most bioregional thinkers are attempting to live in place or reinhabit their cities and bioregions within a wide variety of projects, communities, and settings. Peter Berg, one of the key founders of the movement, constantly challenges himself and others with the motto "what's the *do* of it"?

Much bioregional literature attempts to integrate thinking and feeling, poetry and philosophy, vision and ideas, often with step-by-step practical suggestions about what to do next. Indeed, at the epistemological heart of the bioregional paradigm is the coming together of ecofeminism and bioregionalism, rooted in a praxis of what ecofeminist/bioregionalist Judith Plant has called "thinking feelingly" (Andruss et al. 1990, 79-82). Bioregional literature weaves thought and feeling together to engender emotional as well as intellectual inspiration. The philosophy and poetry, the vision of transformation, as well as stories of the now numerous attempts to implement the vision in various contexts in Canada, Mexico, and the United States all hold something of this character.

Bioregional values represent a revolution in our way of thinking about human society and the natural world. There are five core concepts at the heart of bioregional thought upon which we can say that the bioregional paradigm (in the larger sense of culture and worldview) rests: place, reinhabitation, bioregion, home, and community.

Place

A fundamental premise of bioregional thinking is that all humans live in places and that we have a responsibility to those places for the essential life support that they supply. Developing a philosophy and practice around place is the foundation of bioregionalism. Berg has perhaps expressed most directly this understanding of responsibility to place:

> Wherever you live the place where you live is alive and you are part of the life of that place. No matter how short a time you've been there, or whether or not you're going to be leaving it and going to another place, it will always be that situation throughout your life. The place that you end up being in is alive and you are part of that life. Now, what is your obligation and your sense of responsibility for the sustenance and support that these places give you and how do you go about acting on it? (in Cayley 1986)

As well as responsibility to place, we see here a strongly held ecophilosophical view that humans are part of a living planet, the so-called Gaian worldview. However, in bioregional understanding, the spirituality of the living planet is experienced directly, not abstractly, through direct relationship with one's immediate place. The essence of this specific, grounded phenomenological experience of place is perhaps most powerfully expressed in the poetic prose of "Living Here," an early bioregional document of the Frisco Bay Mussel Group, the first self-consciously "bioregional" group:

> The uniqueness of each place comes in part from ecology and climate, but even more from the biota, the animals and plants that live there, shaping the landscape, its character, and one another as they evolve together. Each species which forms a strand of a living community has its own history and

has entered the regional fabric at some point in geologic time, bringing the mysterious information of its own previous being.

This subtle and deeply resonant wisdom of place deserves respect and reverence, for those who thoughtlessly destroy information so long in the gathering are guilty of a crime against consciousness ... We should protect it and as much as possible restore it, for these living roots which penetrate far into the past not only maintain the biological integrity of our home region, but nourish our spirit and sense of place as well. (Berg 1978, 128)   .

Human responsibility to place is owed in return for the life support and spiritual nourishment that resonance with place furnishes. A great deal of bioregional spiritual sensibility is grounded in this resonance with place; it involves an empowering form of ecological reciprocity. It is directly out of this emotive responsibility to place that the idea of reinhabitation flows.

Reinhabitation

Reinhabitation is a key concept for a grounded social and cultural praxis that suggests answers to Berg's question of how we should act on our responsibility to place once we have accepted and begun to respect the biosphere's vital life-support functions. Peter Berg and Raymond Dasmann, an ecologist working at the time with the International Union for the Conservation of Nature, created the following definition early in the development of the movement. It is perhaps the single most quoted phrase of bioregional literature:

Reinhabitation involves learning to live-in-place in an area that has been disrupted and injured through past exploitation. It involves becoming native to a place through becoming aware of the particular ecological relationships that operate within and around it. It means understanding activities and evolving social behaviour that will enrich the life of that place, restore its life-supporting systems and establish an ecologically and socially sustainable pattern of existence within it. Simply stated it involves becoming fully alive in and with a place. It involves applying for membership in a biotic community and ceasing to be its exploiter. (in Berg 1978, 217-18)

From this definition, we can see that bioregional praxis relates simultaneously to ecological restoration and an evolving social/cultural commitment to living in place, a praxis of becoming "native to a place." Bioregional planner, mapper, and teacher Doug Aberley has described bioregionalism as "a teaching which helps people to both describe the bioregion where they live, and then to live within its natural capability to support life on a sustainable basis" (1985, 145). This praxis of "becoming fully alive in and with a place" clearly implies involvement of the whole person. A transformation of the self is implied in this cultural/social praxis, a revolution grounded in an awareness of particular ecological relationships of place developed through one's attempts to reinhabit that place.

While the awakening of ecological awareness (of self and other) through the experience of place can occur almost any place at any time with any person, the growth of that awareness over time into ecological wisdom and both personal and sociocultural behaviour change is a profoundly engaging process. Learning to reinhabit a place as a responsible member of the larger ecological community takes time and personal commitment. One must break out of old habits and move beyond modernism and its critics to actual behavioural change. A sustainable pattern of life cannot merely be proclaimed or made into "policy" by politicians or planners. Ceasing to be exploiters of biotic communities cannot be achieved simply by recycling, becoming a vegetarian, wearing cotton clothes, riding a bicycle to work, or living a subsistence lifestyle in the country, though all these behavioural changes might be part of a bioregional praxis. Moreover, bioregional living is not only about individual behavioural change, as valuable a starting point as that is. Social and cultural transformation is vital and implies a profound shift in political, economic, and ecological relationships. Reinhabitation must become a lifelong process for both individuals and communities. Indeed, many bioregionalists acknowledge that, for true social transformation, bioregional reinhabation must become a long-term, intergenerational process.

Another critical point about praxis is Berg and Dasmann's stress on reinhabitation taking place in "an area that has been disrupted and injured through past exploitation." In fact, there are few pristine "wildernesses" left, few areas that have not been injured by the megamachine of industrial growth society. This emphasis on ecological restoration is particularly crucial for its potential application to disturbed urban regions. Despite its rural roots in the back-to-the-land movement, bioregionalism at its core implies a reinhabitory approach to urban regions, where, after all, most people in advanced industrial countries actually live.

Bioregion

In the past few years, the bioregion concept has had fairly widespread use in certain government and even corporate circles and on the Internet, often in a merely biogeographical sense. Yet its definition in the bioregional movement is much richer and includes a vital cultural dimension. In "Growing a Life-Place Politics," Berg defines bioregions as "unique life-places with their own soils and land forms, watersheds and climates, native plants and animals, and many other distinct natural characteristics" (1986, 5). This definition supports a concept of bioregions as unique regions, literally *life* regions, each with its own makeup, all interconnected in the web of life that comprises the ecosphere. Bioregionalism supports a holistic understanding that values the parts as well as the whole. It is an understanding that respects bioregional difference while acknowledging larger life-support processes that each bioregion contributes to the ecosphere and, in return, is supported by the same ecospheric processes. This understanding, fundamental to bioregionalism, links the local to the regional and ultimately to the planetary. It is comprehensive, broad, and inclusionary rather than parochial, narrow, and exclusionary.

As a first approximation of a specific identification of a bioregion, Berg and Dasmann argue that it can be determined by the use of climatology, physiography, animal and plant geography, natural history, and other descriptive natural sciences (in Berg 1978, 217-20). Berg and Dasmann explain that in a gross sense nobody would confuse the Mojave Desert with the fertile valley of California. Between major bioregions, the differences are sufficiently marked "that people do not usually attempt to practice the Sonoran desert way of life in the Oregonian coastal area" (218). However, they also recognize that there are many more subtle biogeographic intergradations between bioregions. Seemingly simple at first glance, the concept of bioregion actually encompasses many complexities.

Jim Dodge, an early bioregionalist and writer, provided a list of the physical and biological criteria often advanced for defining bioregions: biotic shift, watersheds, land forms or topography, and elevation (Andruss et al. 1990, 5-12). Biotic shift is the percentage of change in plant/animal species composition from one place to another. The percentage of change is not always agreed upon and can vary from 15 to 25 percent. The biotic shift concept also suggests soft and permeable boundaries between bioregions. Soft boundary interpretations appear to be favoured by most bioregionalists. For Dodge, watershed, usually taken to mean drainage area, can often be a defining criterion for determining a bioregion's shape and extent. However, he also added that rivers, especially large and long rivers, can pass through areas with different soil, climate, vegetation, elevation, and latitude, areas that look and feel quite different from one another.

Dodge also discussed two other criteria for defining a bioregion: cultural/ phenomenological, which implies "you are where you think you are," and "spirit places" or "psyche-turning power-presences" (Andruss et al. 1990, 7). With this latter criterion, the concept of bioregion moves beyond mere descriptive geography or natural science ecology increasingly employed in government and corporate spheres. Dodge's thinking accords with other early bioregional thought that the cultural dimension of the bioregion concept is integral to its very definition.

Berg and Dasmann actually began their groundbreaking definition of a bioregion with the assertion that "the term refers both to geographical terrain and a terrain of consciousness – to a place and the ideas that have developed about how to live in that place" (Berg 1978, 218). This inclusion of culture in nature distinguishes the bioregion concept from many natural science ecological concepts of "ecoregions," which typically exclude human culture from the natural world, generally considering cultural issues separately from issues of natural science ecology. In contrast, the concept of a bioregion is a fluid, dynamic, and fairly open one that places human community within natural communities and recognizes vital links between human terrains of consciousness and geographical terrains. The very process of defining a bioregion, far from being merely a natural science ecology exercise, is grounded in attempts to locate culture in nature through the praxis of living in place.

There is yet another dimension of bioregions. The concept of bioregion transcends a strictly local definition of place. As Berg and Dasmann have put it, reinhabitation involves developing a bioregional identity. This wider bioregion-scale identity means that the terrain of consciousness extends beyond the local ecosystem scale. The question of what geographical scale we should attempt to reinhabit thus becomes a fluid one dependent on the diversity of scales both physical and sociocultural found in different bioregions and in the consciousness of reinhabitants.

For bioregionalists, the question of appropriate geographical scale is thus an open one, linked to the question of the appropriate scale of human community. A reinhabitory strategy beyond the scale of local place includes thinking about broad (bio)regional approaches to self-reliant economic and institutional changes. For example, Berg, in a 1983 article challenging classic environmentalism to go beyond "more than just saving what's left," conceives of four different inhabitory zones within urban bioregions: the city, the suburbs, rural areas, and wilderness areas. Each zone would have a distinct focus for reinhabitation, which I explore in Chapter 4. The key point here is that reinhabitation is conceived of early in the chronology of bioregional literature both to have an immediate local inhabitory community locus and to include a broader transitional strategy toward societal change beyond the local scale. For Berg, to focus reinhabitation at the scale of the bioregion calls for "a full pronouncement of values and a thorough implementation of social, economic, technological, and cultural practices that affirm the natural basis of the human species in life-sustaining processes of the planetary biosphere" (1983, 1).

Home

Bioregionalism is thus, in great part, a profoundly cultural approach to social transformation. A good illustration of this is the movement's redefinition and revaluation of the notions of home and community. The revaluing of home is informed by connections between ecofeminism and bioregionalism. Judith Plant, a pioneer in drawing these links, writes about the notion of home as follows: "Home! Remembering and reclaiming the ways of our species where people and place are delicately interwoven in a web of life – human community finding its particular place within the living and dying that marks the interdependence of life in an integrated ecosystem. This is the pattern of existence that bioregionalism explores. For this term is about being and acting and is more than just a set of ideas. It is the practice of coming to terms with our ecological home" (Andruss et al. 1990, ix-xi).

In bioregional thought, home is very much a place-grounded concept, but it is also valued in a broader, ecologically centred way. The actual or direct experience of home in a particular place and in particular ecosystems is linked to a sense of kinship with all life. In short, it is a "remembering and reclaiming" of the ancient community of beings ethic.

In the face of modern alienation, atrophy of community, and hierarchical patriarchal relationships, bioregionalist ecofeminists see the redefinition of home as crucial. Plant writes of the need for a redefinition and revaluing of the concept of home from both a feminist and a bioregional point of view. This revaluation of home by both ecofeminism and bioregionalism is a core concept for each. It has done much to draw bioregionalism and ecofeminism together.

As many have pointed out, the word *ecology* comes from the Greek *oikos,* meaning "home." Learning to be at home on Earth through reinhabitation, through coming to experience ecological relations "in place," implies a much broader concept of home than even an extended family concept. As we have seen, our industrial growth civilization has so expanded the domain of the market that the domestic sphere has seriously atrophied. Feminists have been concerned with revaluing both the personal and the political spheres, both the domestic and the public spheres, particularly in the sphere of civil society. In revaluing home, we need to expand the personal to the political as well as bring the political into the personal. Ecofeminist-bioregionalist thought has advanced the concept that home, understood as the domestic sphere, needs to be revalued and reclaimed by men as well as women. For Plant, the reality, both historical and present, is that these life activities have been undervalued and a source of oppression for women. The concept of reinhabitation is enriched by its relationship to a redefined concept of home. It means, for men and women alike, revaluing home in both an ecological and a socio-politico-cultural sense. On the one hand, bioregionalists redefine home to include the local watershed, the other species of the watershed, the local landforms, et cetera. However, the bioregional sense of home also means expanding the intimate sphere of care and responsibility, of family and kinship, usually associated with home outward to include one's larger bioregion. Home implies both ecological and civic, as well as domestic, responsibility.

Socioculturally, home means reuniting the personal and the political spheres, the domestic and the public spheres, by transforming both. Transforming the patriarchal sense of home, ecologically and culturally, does more than simply redefine the roles of men and women in the home. It also enlarges the importance of domestic life to include public aspects and dimensions of the civil society sphere once again. Culturally, the civil society/ public sphere (where concern for and experience of community values have atrophied and where the values of care and nurturing have been undermined by the power of the formal economy and the welfare state) is being revalued and reclaimed in bioregional thought. Bioregional reclaiming of civil society means bringing the kinship values of the domestic sphere, restricted under the patriarchy to the sphere of women, out into the larger civil society domain. The expansion of kinship values into civil society has been a major philosophical contribution to bioregional thought by ecofeminists in the movement.

Conversely, in bioregional thought, political power needs to be decentralized a great deal and much more fully democratized. Numerous bioregional thinkers have emphasized that bioregionalism is very much about the decentralization of power, about more self-governing forms of social organization. Plant additionally argues that "the further we move in this direction, the closer we get to what has traditionally been thought of as 'woman's sphere' – that is home and its close surroundings. Ideally, the bioregional view values home above all else, because it is here where new values and behaviours are actually created" (Andruss et al. 1990, 81). In a social capital reading, the importance placed on an enhanced, expanded domestic sphere, home – with its inclusion of the local web of life – is identified as a nurturing incubator of ecocentric social capital. A bioregional view of broader kinship, like the ancient community of beings ethic, subsumes social capital under ecosocial capital. In other words, a broader community of beings kinship ethic embeds caring and bonding among human kin within a larger ethical realm. Again, this is an inclusionary, expansive philosophy that links the local to the planetary.

The central importance of a transformed concept of home is reflected in the fact that the North American Bioregional Congress (NABC), the original continental networking organization of the movement, adopted a mission statement called "Welcome Home!" at its initial congress in 1984. "Welcome Home!" makes a connection full of feeling between local human community and ecological community health. It is an excellent example of thinking feelingly:

A growing number of people are recognizing that in order to secure the clean air, water, and food that we need to healthfully survive, we have to become guardians of the places where we live. People sense the loss in not knowing our neighbours and natural surroundings, and are discovering that the best way to take care of ourselves, and to get to know our neighbours, is to protect and restore our region.

Bioregionalism recognizes, nurtures, sustains and celebrates our local connections with:

Land

Plants and Animals

Springs, Rivers, Lakes, Groundwater & Oceans,

Air

Families, Friends, Neighbors

Community

Native Traditions

Indigenous Systems of Production & Trade

It is taking time to learn the possibilities of place. It is a mindfulness of local environment, history, and community aspiration that leads to a sustainable future. It relies on safe and renewable sources of food and energy. It ensures employment by supplying a rich diversity of services within the community, by recycling our resources, and by exchanging prudent surpluses with other regions. Bioregionalism is working to satisfy basic needs locally, such as education, health care and self-government.

The bioregional perspective recreates a widely-shared sense of regional identity founded upon a renewed critical awareness of and respect for the integrity of our ecological communities. (Andruss et al. 1990, 170)

An Earth-centred or ecological social capital reading of "Welcome Home!" highlights the combined ethic of community ecological health and restoration. "Welcome Home!" invites people to take care of the ecological health (including, of course, the human ecology) of the places where they live and work. In this core statement about home, the values of care and kinship normally associated with the nuclear family are extended to the entire local ecological community and even to their wider water connections with the oceans. In this way, the kinship ethic of social capital is given a much broader ecological dimension. So the broadest planetary ethic is very much celebrated and nurtured yet remains grounded locally in the immediacy of recognizing needs at home.

In revaluing home, a bioregional, ecofeminist view also revalues traditional men's and women's roles. As Plant argues, the patriarchal concept of home will not be transformed without the enlightened perspective offered by feminism: "We know that it is non-adaptive to repeat the social organization which left women and children alone, at home, and men out in the world doing the 'important' work. The real work is at home. It is not simply a question of fairness or equality, it is because, as a species we have to actually work things out – just as it is in the so-called natural world – with all our relations" (Andruss et al. 1990, 21-23). Such ecofeminist values challenge the neoclassical view of *homo economicus* promoted almost daily in the mainstream press, where, for example, the definition of adaptation is narrowly conceived as accumulating capital and maximizing consumption.

Bioregional Community and Ecological Kinship

Community is another deeply held core value for bioregionalists, one that is closely associated with home. For bioregionalists, community has a much different meaning from the many diverse definitions of community that remain purely human-centred. In part, bioregional thought on community has been inspired by their explorations of the meaning of community for Earth-based cultures that themselves display great diversity in culture and community organization.

Helen Forsey, an ecofeminist bioregionalist who has lived many years in a rural intentional community, has outlined common uses of the community concept by bioregionalists. Forsey begins her overview by pointing out that in our contemporary society the word *community* has been so overused that its meanings have become so diffuse as to be almost useless. Yet she also argues for its continued use because "the images it evokes, the deep longings and memories it can stir, represent something that human beings have created and recreated since time immemorial, out of profound need for connection among ourselves and with Mother Earth" (1993, 1).

Forsey outlines four uses of the word by bioregionalists. The first is "intentional community," in which people have deliberately chosen to live and work together with clear common agreements and ties to a particular place. The second refers to existing neighbourhoods or villages where people already living in close proximity to each other are looking at the reasons why they are there and building on their basis of unity. The third refers to temporary communities formed in the context of political resistance, such as blockades, marches, or peace camps. The fourth refers to geographically dispersed but still close-knit networks of common concern and mutual support. In my experience and understanding, bioregionalists are involved in all four types. However, when I use the phrase "communities of place," I mean intentional communities as defined by Forsey, whether rural or urban. I also use the term in Forsey's second sense to refer to local neighbourhoods and in her fourth sense to refer to networks as communities of interest and mutual support.

Despite some of the differences among bioregionalists over the concept of community, there is strong agreement that community is key to building a bioregional movement. At the first continental congress of the movement in 1984, NABC I, the Community Empowerment Committee linked human community to ecological community and to the work of reinhabitation: "Human communities are integral parts of the larger bioregional and planetary life communities. The empowerment of human communities is inseparable from the larger task of reinhabitation – learning to live joyfully and sustainably in place" (Henderson et al. 1984, 16). At NABC III, many participants spoke about local community as a fundamental building block of bioregionalism. The congress as a whole passed a resolution "to support the community movement as an essential way to carry out the ideals of the bioregional movement" and an affirmation that the continental congresses were held "in the spirit of community" (Zuckerman 1989, 73).

Let's consider some examples of how community in Earth-based societies is understood in the bioregional movement. These viewpoints present a very different conception of humans from the utility-maximizing individual of neoclassical economics. In my experience, many bioregionalists subscribe to a view of the human individual in prehistoric society as a genuine social being. This social being evolved in a cultural context of intensive small-group cooperation, whether in foraging bands or Neolithic villages. An important part of this concept is the idea that the local community was the primary unit of human habitation rather than the individual (Henderson et al. 1984, 16). Bioregionalists have drawn on anthropological sources to support their view, including the works of Leakey, Lee, Sahlins, and others who all emphasize the importance of close cooperation in the early cultural and social evolution of humans. In addition, the work of Kirkpatrick Sale (discussed in Chapter 2), pulling together studies on the small scale of early human cooperative social organization, has informed bioregional thought on human community with respect to the important question of the ability of the human individual to know and engage in many-sided relations with a certain but finite number of others. This human scale criterion for community may be critical for the successful building of trust and mutual aid, two key dimensions of social capital. Examining and learning from the long story of human origins in gatherer-hunter societies and how humans have adapted for thousands of generations have been at the core of much bioregional thought about community. Various bioregional writers and thinkers have contributed to this examination (Andruss and Wright 1984; Berg 1978, 1; Berry 1988, 180-93; Snyder 1977, 1980, 23-30).

All human cultures have roots – however distant they may be – in Earth-based traditions. The time when humans lived with an understanding and a way of life that respected other species and the life process extends over thousands of generations. With respect to sheer long-term sustainability, that ancient Earth-based way of life dwarfs our own modern period. The modern industrial system has so far lasted for only about twenty generations. Even the beginnings of large-scale agricultural production occurred only some 500 generations, or 10,000 years, ago. In contrast, band life in the Paleolithic era lasted for thousands of generations. A critical question emerges from this reflection. Why and how were early human societies successful for such a long time? Bioregionalists suggest that the answer lies in adaptation through cooperation.

My own introduction to this aspect of bioregional understanding has been largely informed by long discussions with several bioregionalists in British Columbia. Among them, Van Andruss and Eleanor Wright have written of the organized set of customs that integrated human life with nonhuman life (1984). For Andruss and Wright, the way of life of gatherer-hunters was integrated not only in the sense of being integrated with their ecological community but also in the sense of being a whole culture: that is, one in which humans organized their lives in the larger ecological community through cooperation, through close social and cultural bonding in small groups or bands with each other. They argue that such whole cultures spanned the generations: that is, there was strong cultural continuity from one generation to the next. For Andruss and Wright, small human bands were self-governing adaptive units of social and cultural primates. This argument clearly locates human activities and ways of life within a long animal heritage.

Why were these societies able to succeed for so many generations? Kelly Booth, another BC bioregionalist, observes that there is more to human adaptation than can be learned in the lifetime of one individual. Learned patterns, Booth argues, were "registered in the customs of the group" (Andruss et al. 1990, 73). Thus, adaptation seen as a group affair or process challenges the individualistic capitalist view of adaptation. The revolution in anthropology discussed in the previous chapter advanced a similar understanding of gatherer-hunter cultures. In the bioregional view, whole cultures lived out their myths (or origin stories) together. The term "whole cultures" refers to generations of societies linked by their origin stories. Through the collective telling, retelling, and reenacting of their mythologies, the people produced and fostered continuous, adaptive cultures whose very meaning formation was taken from and depended on the local biota and ecology. Bioregionalists attempt to emulate such practices in contemporary settings. In the next chapter, we will see in detail how such practices can assist in building communities of social beings.

What do bioregionalists mean by "social being"? Dolores LaChapelle, a bioregionalist from the Rocky Mountains of Colorado, writing about "our roots in the old ways," discusses anthropologist Dorothy Lee's experience of what it meant to be a "social being" living in a society that practised general reciprocity (1988, 84-85). After experiencing and absorbing through participant observation something of the way of life of the Tikopia, an isolated Polynesian island people, Lee realized one day through the simple experience of embroidering a blanket for her daughter that, even though she did not like the task, she was thoroughly enjoying the experience. On reflection, she saw that she wasn't just sewing to please her daughter; rather, her action was taking place within a relationship that contained social value. Lee discovered what it meant to be a genuine social being, not merely Dorothy Lee, an individual. For her, somehow, a boundary had disappeared. This discovery gave her the key to understanding certain social motivating forces in the lives of the Tikopia whom she was studying. The usual anthropological terms such as "obligation" and "duty," attempting to describe Tikopian social being and the Tikopian practice of general reciprocity, failed to capture what was really a process that, experienced phenomenologically, "brimmed with joy." Lee realized that, for an individual in this society, external incentives such as obligation were not needed to motivate the individual to be a social being. After her direct experience, Lee began to understand that the previously defined limits of her self had begun to change and that the Tikopian concept of self was different from the Western concept of self. Her profound experience helped her to understand that in Tikopian society the individual was embedded in a system of social relationships in which affection was not merely an expression of the ego but also "a sharing, a social act." Similarly, work among the Tikopia was always socially shared. Lee points out in her summary that, with this social definition of self, work can take place among the Tikopia without the incentive of reward or the fear of punishment because work as social participation is meaningful. Moreover, the "social" understanding of being that Lee encountered was embedded in a concept of "universal inter relatedness," because for Tikopians "man was not the focus from which relations flowed." Here again we see social capital subsumed by ecosocial capital and with it the enhanced motivating power of this deeper direct participation in kinship.

To explain further the ecocentric kinship perspective and the powerful social motivation for the individual embedded in a system of generalized reciprocity, LaChapelle also draws on the experience of Jaime de Angulo, who lived with the Pit River Indians of northern California in the early part of the twentieth century. De Angulo reported that, for the Pit River people, the generations were part of a continuous flowing process: "The total society generates and the children belong to that society ... Everybody really exists in a continuous world of generations, of being the children of the world they are living in, so you're a very bad child if you do not venerate Father Tree, or any other aspect of your parent world" (LaChapelle 1988, 86).

In this society, the world of generations is both human and nonhuman. Sharing in this kinship world, as LaChapelle points out, grows out of relationships embedded in the generations. Indeed, the generations are so tightly interconnected in this view that everyone participates in "being the children of the world they are living in." In a sense, then, social capital among humans is also a bonding across generational time. Yet the "social" space in this world of extended kinship stretches beyond the merely human. Children and adults alike venerate "Father Tree" and other aspects of their "parent world."

The motivating power of such synergy for the individual living in these cultures is well illustrated by the personal experience of Dorothy Lee. Living among the Tikopia, Lee directly experienced social being wherein the self is understood as part of a universal interrelatedness in which relations do not start from the ego, nor are they "defined in terms of the emotions of the ego, but rather as ... a sharing, as a social act" (LaChapelle 1988, 84-85). I cite Lee's example partly as an illustration of how social capital acts to inform and nourish human capital, especially when we understand human capital to include not only skills and knowledge but also wisdom. This woman from modern, individualistic society was able to personally experience a strong motivating synergistic force, so strong that the direct, joyful experience of it helped her to redefine the boundaries of her self. Such synergy is an expression of what I understand to be the motivating power of social capital. It is the emotional joy in social capital that both Putnam and Coleman omitted from their concepts. The joyful personal experience of social capital, its synergistic motivating power, I identify as an essential nourishing and motivating force for community building.

Communities were adaptive, LaChapelle argues, because they were truly ecological: that is, human communities were an integral part of their local ecological communities. In short, they were true communities of place: "Community is sharing a particular physical place, an environment, not only with other people but with the other beings of the place, and fully realizing that the needs of all the beings of that place affect how you live your life" (1978, 120). In LaChapelle's community of beings definition, we see the ancient kinship ethic woven into the present era, implying that we moderns may yet reclaim an Aboriginal sense of ecological community. Indeed, such an ecological understanding and valuing of community is broadly shared among bioregionalists.

These five concepts – place, reinhabitation, bioregion, home, and community – are closely linked. Together, although focused on the local, they form a philosophical ground for a truly broad understanding of need for a planet-wide transformation that challenges globalism based on economic man. Other typologies that capture the essentials of bioregional thought could be constructed. However, few if any bioregionalists would disagree that these five would be included in any typology of core bioregional ideas and that – taken together – they are specific to bioregionalism. There are also a number of other important key bioregional values, essential for a fuller understanding of the bioregional value system.

Other Basic Bioregional Values

One excellent way to review other major bioregional values is to reflect on the set of bioregional education values approved by full consensus at NABC I and III and reaffirmed at NABC IV. The following twelve principles generally reflect other key bioregional values.

1 Bioregional education emphasizes the interdependence and kinship of humans with all that exists, based upon our understanding of local ecosystems and their relationships with the planetary ecosystem.

2 Bioregional education values self-respect and respect for one another as essential components of respect for other life forms and all ecological processes.

3 Bioregional education recognizes no separation of learning from life. We are all teachers and students. The process of bioregional learning is one of active participation and sharing within the human community and the natural environment.

4 Bioregional education honours the products of intellect while remaining grounded in a joyful and empowering awareness of spirit.

5 Bioregional education affirms the importance of handing down traditional local knowledge and wisdom.

6 Bioregional education is guided by the vision of long-term sustainability of the Earth community, and it promotes the transformation from anthropocentric values to geocentric and biocentric values.

7 Bioregional education is assisted by publicizing existing and developing new clearinghouses for networking information on ecological data, theory, social ecology, local knowledge, and methods of innovative learning.

8 Bioregional education proceeds from the premise that Earth is a community of entities, a living organism of which we are part.

9 Bioregional education shows us how our daily actions and those of our society affect the health of the Earth community.

10 Bioregional education validates and nurtures bonding between the individual and the planet through sensory, emotional, spiritual, and intellectual channels.

11 Bioregional education integrates social and ecological justice issues. The domination of people and the domination of nature have a common root.

12 Finally, bioregional education facilitates discussion, planning, and action for a sustainable, humane economy and society. (Henderson et al. 1984; Hart et al. 1987; Zuckerman 1989; Dolcini et al. 1991)

The first of the twelve education values is based on, as declared above, "our understanding of local ecosystems and their relationships with the planetary ecosystem." The expression of these relationships is phrased precisely in terms of an Earth-based understanding of ecological kinship. Considered through an ecocentric (or Earth-centred) social capital analysis, the bioregional value statement linking interdependence with kinship can be understood as a restatement of the ancient community of beings ethic. While it is clearly inspired by and grounded in a certain modern ecological under-standing that values integration of social and natural ecologies, it also joins with many ancient human traditions, Earth-based traditions, whose cul-tural foundation rested on nonanthropocentric or Earth-centred value sys-tems. As we saw in Chapter 2, a certain profound quality of social capital informed by a kinship form of cultural capital distinguishes many hunting and gathering societies by their high levels of social capital. Bioregionalists often see themselves as merely joining in the millennia-old mainstream of human cultures that have always valued kinship this way. As David Haenke commented in the proceedings of the first continental congress in 1984, "bioregionalism is rediscovery and reinterpretation (to creatively deal with the ecologically-diminished reality in which we presently live) of the old ways by those who see that we cannot continue in the present profane ways" (Henderson et al. 1984, 3). But what do bioregionalists mean by "the old ways"?

At the heart of this long continuity of belief is the ancient connection with the land. Bioregional poet, essayist, and reinhabitant Gary Snyder, in a series of essays entitled *The Old Ways*, has observed that those "inhabitory" peoples practising the old ways will speak about a piece of land being sacred or all the land being sacred – "an attitude that draws on the mystery of life and death; of taking life to live; of giving life back – not only to your own children, but to the life of the whole land" (1977, 59-60). In this particular essay, based on a public talk given in 1976, Snyder is speaking about reinhabitation as a rejoining of the old ways, turning again to the land and to place, but this time infused with a contemporary ecological critique of some essential problems of modernism:

> The wisdom and skill of those who studied the universe first hand, by di-rect knowledge and experience, for millennia, both inside and outside them-selves, is what we might call the Old Ways. Those who envision a possible future planet on which we continue that study, and where we live by the Green and the Sun, have no choice but to bring whatever science, imagi-nation, strength, and political finesse they have to the support of the inhabitory people – natives and peasants of the world. Entering such paths, we begin to learn a little of the Old Ways, which are outside of history, and forever new. (1977, 66)

Of course, by "outside of history" Snyder does not mean some abstract, ahistorical truth; rather, he is referring to the remarkable continuity of a sacred inhabitory ethic across great stretches of time and among many different indigenous cultures. In an interview some years later, Snyder asserts that the real "norm," the real "grain of things" in the larger picture for humans across the millennia, is living close to the Earth, more simply, more responsibly (1980, 112).

Native people who have participated in bioregional movement gatherings have often spoken about our human connectedness and interdependence with the Earth. At the first continental congress of the bioregional movement, the Native Peoples Committee in its statement of philosophy asserted the profound spirituality of the kinship ethic: "Spirituality is the foundation for our way of life. We affirm that our spiritual roots are the source of the strength, endurance and wisdom necessary for our struggle to transform our culture. Indigenous Indian spiritual traditions and those of other Indigenous People of the world provide essential support for a way of life which respects connectedness with all creation. Humans are a species dependent upon, not more important than the universe, the plants and the animals" (Henderson et al. 1984, 25).

Interdependence with all life, the sacredness of all life, and kinship with all life together form one intertwined thematic continuity linking contemporary bioregionalism with indigenous cultures of the past and the present. This profoundly spiritual kinship understanding is the ancient community of beings ethic that clearly has not died out. Rather, it is still alive and is now growing once again in the bioregional movement and in many indigenous communities and nations reclaiming their traditional wisdoms, territories, and practices.

For bioregionalists, interdependence is both a local and a planetary ecological reality. In the first resolution on bioregional education, interdependence includes – as part of the kinship ethic – the understanding that local ecological relationships are interdependent with the Earth's ecosphere. This statement clearly contextualizes place-oriented human interdependence, at the local ecosystem and bioregion scales, within a broad ecological recognition of planetary interdependence and kinship systems. Such a thoroughly interdependent value claim supports the broadest interpretation of bioregional spiritual philosophy, a philosophy that embeds human values within a planetary kinship system. Far from being a parochial philosophy, a bioregional understanding of kinship opens itself to the ancient human cultural mainstream.

The second bioregional education value integrates and embeds human self-respect and respect for other humans with respect for all life forms and processes. This value makes more explicit what was already implied in the first education value. Philosophically, recognizing kinship with *all* life forms and processes also implies and values human respect for one another as humans. Furthermore, something else is added in this resolution: self-respect.

It is included and embedded in the larger respect for human and nonhuman others, but it is also affirmed as a value itself. Here the strengths of Earth-centred kinship values with respect to both human and nonhuman life forms, and both self and other, are conjoined as essential components of a more ethically profound understanding of respect. Such respect for self and other is essential to building Earth-centred social capital in an ethnically mixed postmodern society. The bioregional movement is only one among a number of social movements struggling for the healing of intercultural social relations.

Resolution three places emphasis on learning directly from life processes – beyond the classroom – through active participation and sharing in human and natural communities. In such a direct learning-from-life approach, ecocentric social capital can be generated through the shared learning process itself. This dynamic is explored more thoroughly later.

Resolution five affirms the crucial importance of traditional local knowledge and wisdom. As we have already seen in our discussion of place, bioregional reinhabitory praxis grounds itself in local knowledge of both biophysical and cultural history. Without absorbing these local values in one's lifelong learning process, the bioregional project cannot really begin. Bioregional and Mohawk-Cree educator Sharilyn Calliou, discussing implications of bioregional education for the classroom teacher, has stressed the importance of developing locally based materials, and, through this local grounding process, the principles of bioregional thought deemed necessary for species and planetary survival can be imparted. While bioregional praxis does stress skills development, bioregionalism "is not merely [about] imparting skills, but about developing conscious philosophical understandings guiding life" (Traina and Darley-Hill 1995, 67-75). The question, then, for Calliou, is how to teach the intangibles of bioregional thought necessary for species and planetary survival. This can be best achieved by teachers who practise the principles of living in place. For Calliou, local ecological caretaking must become a primary reason for schooling.

Resolutions six and eight explicitly recognize that bioregional education values involve a transformation from current anthropocentric values to geocentric and biocentric values guided by the vision of long-term sustainability of the Earth community. Bioregional education is based on the premise of the Earth as a community of entities that forms a living organism, which includes the human community. Thus, this broad vision of a diverse planetary community is viewed as complementary to – and as important as – the bioregional emphasis on local place and community.

Resolution ten states that bioregional education values and nurtures bonding between the individual and the planet through intellectual, sensory, emotional, and spiritual channels. Note that none of these is privileged over the others. This value affirms a holistic, phenomenological approach to education that recognizes that learning is most profound and lasting when bonding via all these various "channels" takes place through an experiential learning process. When successful, such experiential bonding is the living expression, or manifestation, of interdependence and kinship. The community of beings ethic is experienced phenomenologically through such bonding.

Resolution eleven affirms the need to recognize that the domination of nature and the domination of people spring from the same source and that we need to integrate social and ecological justice issues. Bioregionalists understand that the destruction of natural ecologies is being accomplished by the same system and the same systemic processes that are destroying social ecologies. Bioregional thought explicitly values social as well as environmental justice.

Finally, resolution twelve affirms that bioregional education involves and facilitates planning and action toward a sustainable society. Again, praxis is stressed over mere intellectual content, holistic praxis linking teaching and learning with planning and action. This resolution explicitly links bioregional education values to a generalist concern for social change in society as a whole, a concern that has become atrophied in our society under the influence of individualism and consumerism. As we saw in the Introduction, the middle-class, utilitarian, individualist ethic – the dominant cultural mode of the late nineteenth century – has spread almost everywhere with the growth of middle-class consumer values and behaviours. A key problem for civilization is how to build social capital, particularly Earth-centred social capital, when it has been so pervasively undermined in the past 150 years. Bioregionalists propose that education in the broadest sense, including both formal and informal learning in and out of schools, must be carried out and modelled by individuals who work to become re-embedded social beings at several levels: home, local community, neighbourhood, watershed, and bioregion. The work must then be complemented by networking continentally and even globally as well as by celebrating and spreading bioregional values across these broader geographical scales.

With respect to the formal education system itself, Calliou has made the point that a bioregional education that accents the interdependence and kinship of humans with all that exists cannot be merely another add-on program but must have an interdisciplinary, "across-the-curriculum resonance" (Traina and Darley-Hill 1995, 71). She argues that the concern of bioregional education to engage in discussion, planning, and action toward sustainable society be accompanied by teacher education empowering teachers to reflect on their own life situations, to speak out, and to act: "Bioregionalism could provide teachers with a way to focus dialogue about becoming empowered to live in an ecologically responsible life-way and empowering learners to also do so. The school alone cannot provoke social change. Healthy schools can only exist in healthy societies and bio-regionalism discusses ways to think about change needed to heal our local and global collectives" (70).

With respect to the problem of the autonomous utility-maximizing individual, bioregional education values point to a conception of the human individual in society, a socially concerned and embedded individual who exercises the rights and responsibilities of a full citizen of the biosphere in individual and collective ways, locally and globally.

Bioregional education is more than a classroom adventure. It is about spreading general bioregional values far and wide like pollen on the wind to be received by those ready for them. The first journal devoted to bioregional education, *Pollen*, was published by Frank Traina, a bioregional educator and writer who has been focusing his efforts on bioregional education for many years. At the earlier continental congresses, Traina worked with others in the education committee to help formulate the above education values. Other bioregionalists, including Peter Berg, speak of bioregional "seed" groups and "seeding" other movements (Carr 1990, 168). Also, Berg has spoken about education as the "insinuation" of bioregional values and ideas into other contexts: "We didn't want to own bioregionalism. We knew we couldn't. If it was to be successful, people would start thinking of it as a useful tool to start fitting their interests with, and we would make it our job to keep the information about bioregions coming – in a way that you could say, it was insinuated" (Berg 1996b).

Berg's comment underscores an important point. Dogmatism in social movements in the radical planning tradition, particularly sectarian politics around ideologically "correct" interpretations, plays a very destructive role with respect to fostering the key ingredient of trust in social capital formation. In bioregionalism, on the contrary, education is not about owning bioregional ideas but about giving the bioregional vision and bioregional values away to take root and grow in their own ways, just as each seed is unique and takes root in soil that is particular to that place. Moreover, bioregional education is about much more than new pedagogical techniques. As Calliou has pointed out, bioregional education is a paradigm shift reteaching humans to learn how to live within the carrying capacity of a natural, local eco-system: "Teaching about one's eco-social home has possibilities for restoring an ethical foundation to a very secularized Eurocentric worldview" (Traina and Darley-Hill 1995, 74).

Bioregional education has much to do with reclaiming and regenerating a form of cultural capital informed by the community of beings ethic. The vision of education worked out at the continental gatherings was created by practitioners, teachers, educators, and reinhabitants. For Traina, a fundamental obstacle to implementing this ancient ethic is the lack of respectful values and feelings about nature. Drawing specifically on education resolution ten above, he argues that bioregional education addresses a fundamental problem of modernity when it validates and nurtures bonding, defined as the building of a personal relationship with nature, including feelings of connectedness and emotions as well as respectful values and feelings about nature. Traina believes that this personal, emotional component of bioregional education is crucial to the success of the cultural paradigm shift that bioregionalists seek: "Having been raised in a culture which treats natural things as resources, we have to unlearn this attitude and learn another, and we have to help ourselves and others learn a different way of relating to nature ... The method of bioregional education is to bring back romance into our relationship with nature. In this respect it can be viewed as a reaction against the cold scientific treatment of nature which sets nature apart from the human" (Traina and Darley-Hill 1995, 94-95). In short, profound personal bonding to the other (in this case the "romance" of human and nonhuman) is essential for regenerating a community-of-beings–informed cultural capital as a reclaimed societal ethic.

Ecopsychologist Elan Shapiro has also discussed bioregionalism's values and what they can tell us about ourselves as modern alienated individuals. Shapiro argues that prevailing economic and psychological pressures move us to think of ourselves as individual units, as supposedly autonomous individuals. Thus, what we're specifically missing are actual feelings of connectedness. In modern society, most of us have become alienated, disconnected from where we live. Bioregionalism, Shapiro argues, is saying that we cannot have a sense of self that's separate from a sense of place and that we need to join self and place again to have the richness and the connectedness that both individual humans and human communities need:

> For example, if you think of a person as part of a web of life, a web of
> intimate, reciprocal relationships, then everything is feeding our lives. We're
> feeling fed by what's around us and we're feeding back into what's around
> us ... What bioregionalism means – which people might not get from terms
> like "Gaia consciousness," or "deep ecology" or "planetary healing" is that
> in order to survive on this planet, in order to be whole, we need to realize
> how important it is that we're a part of the immediate place where we live.
> We need to know this place in detail, we need to love it in the detail. (1993,
> 17-19)

The profound place-specific and grounded emotional bonding described by Shapiro and Traina and advanced by bioregional education values integrates and "feeds" ethical concerns for healthy social and natural ecologies. Romance and love – that is, feelings of connectedness with the natural world – are identified as essential, nourishing, experiential components of the community of beings ethic. This loving emotional bonding to both other humans and the "community of all beings" in the places that we live I can now identify as necessary for the building of Earth-centred social capital. Such bonding generates Earth-centred social capital, which in turn nourishes individual human capital.

As we saw in Chapter 2, social capital is about relationships, but the extended relationships described in the definition of Earth-centred social capital have their reflections, their meaning content, manifested within the hearts and minds of individuals. The emotional meaning for individuals that such bonding imparts has the potential to supply the spiritual fuel and motivation necessary for *homo economicus* to transform away from individualism and consumerism and toward socially embedded individuals in ecologically embedded societies. In other words, high levels of social capital, far from representing deep sacrifices in the abandonment of consumerist heaven, promise rich earthly rewards of nurturing emotional interconnection for the embedded ecosocial individual.

Although not exclusive to bioregionalism, diversity is another value central to bioregional understanding. This value includes both biological/ecological diversity and sociocultural diversity. One of the early bioregional publications, *Reinhabiting a Separate Country*, is in great part a celebration of ecological and cultural diversity in northern California. It contains many different stories and oral histories of people and places in the city, the river and delta, and the mountains and a recognition that adaptive and diverse human cultures offer humans as a species the richest possibilities for wholeness and survival (Berg 1978). The "Welcome Home!" mission statement discussed above is, in part, a celebration of diversity (both ecological and cultural). At NABC IV in 1990, a "Declaration of Bioregional Autonomy" recognized the "biological, geological, climatic and cultural uniqueness and diversity of each bioregion the world over" (Dolcini et al. 1991, 26). In the first publication of the New Catalyst/New Society Bioregional Series *Turtle Talk*, the editors gave tribute to diverse approaches to the "regeneration of culture" within the bioregional movement: "In the final analysis it is the diversity of approaches represented in 'Turtle Talk' that is most appealing. Here, at last, there is recognition by key thinkers and activists in the movement that they hold just one straw of truth, and that the way to prevent that truth from being broken is for the straws to be combined in a strong whole" (Plant and Plant 1990, 10).

Diversity is understood in the bioregional movement as a strength. However, it is important to caution that "diversity" should not be read to mean unlimited ideological diversity. The goal is to reach a unity within the diversity. For example, feminists often recognize diversity as a way to value differences within a larger unity, using the metaphor of the patchwork quilt to express this concept. Bioregionalist women honoured this concept at NABC I by organizing the sewing of a patchwork quilt representing the back of a turtle to celebrate bioregional diversity across Turtle Island. Bioregionalists have attempted to implement their belief in diversity in their own lives as reinhabitants and in their encounters with each other during events such as the various regional and continental congresses and gatherings. Chapter 6 explores this praxis through a look at the history and experience of the continental congresses.

In modern Eurocentric society, wilderness as a concept has been infused with contradictory meanings. Keith Thomas (1987, 254-69) traces the changing history of the term from the seventeenth century to the nineteenth century in Europe. In the seventeenth century, "wilderness" meant an inhospitable barrenness, a terrible wasteland, unproductive, unattractive, and frightening to civilized people. By the beginning of the nineteenth century, "wilderness" had been converted, in part by the growth of better roads and tourism, into a highly valued aesthetic and even a religious experience. For the Romantics of the nineteenth century, nature improved by human touch was nature destroyed, so real wilderness was conceived to be pristine or absent of human influence. In the United States, as William Cronon has observed, a similar conversion occurred later in the nineteenth century with such thinkers as Thoreau (1996, 69-90). The idea of wilderness as pure and unsullied by human presence still has great influence in the environmental movement today. The Sierra Club's naturalist founder John Muir fought to make the pristine Yosemite Valley a national park. This battle was central to the founding of the Sierra Club. From the early photographs of Carlton Watkins to Ansel Adams, Yosemite became America's most photographed park, a model of untouched, sublime wilderness. This romanticism ignored the real history of Yosemite in which the US Army emptied the valley of its original inhabitants, the Miwok people, in 1851. This was almost twenty years before Muir arrived there – without any knowledge of the previous human presence – to discover the "untouched" wilderness, which moved him to flee civilization. Now we know that it was the Miwok people's use of controlled burns that contributed to the biological diversity and parklike beauty that inspired Muir and so many others (Solnit 1992). Cronon critiques this conception of wilderness, arguing for a concept of wilderness that includes human homemaking (1996, 69-90), similar to a bioregional understanding of wilderness.

Bioregionalists recognize both otherness and kinship in wilderness. Pulitzer Prize-winning poet and essayist Gary Snyder, his family, and a group of neighbours are bioregional reinhabitants in the foothills of the Sierras in northern California. Snyder writes of otherness and kinship in wilderness. In *The Practice of the Wild* (1990), he points out that the term "wild" has been defined in our dictionaries in largely negative terms: undomesticated, unruly, uncivilized, uncultivated, uninhabited, dissolute, unrestrained, licentious, loose, wanton, spontaneous, et cetera. Snyder proposes that we turn this around 180 degrees and look at wilderness for what it is rather than what it is not. He suggests that we view wild animals as free agents living within natural systems. Similarly, plants can be viewed as self-propagating, self-maintaining, flourishing in accord with innate qualities. Land can be seen as a place where the original and potential vegetation and fauna are intact and in full interaction and the landforms are entirely the result of nonhuman forces.

Conversely, Snyder also argues for a sense of kinship in wilderness: "It has always been a part of basic human experience to live in a culture of wilderness. There has been no wilderness without some kind of human presence for several thousand years. Nature is not a place to visit, it is *home* – and within that home territory there are more familiar and less familiar places" (1990, 7). While Snyder is perhaps most known as a poet, his expression of values is actually grounded in a long practice of reinhabitation in a particular place.

With these bioregional concepts of wilderness, an image of nature very different from that of the dominant Western one begins to emerge. This image is new only in comparison to the dominant cultural mode of Western civilization. Bioregional concepts of wilderness are part of the rebirth of the ancient community of beings ethic in which wilderness and home were synonymous with human be-ing in the world. In fact, Kirkpatrick Sale has traced the etymology of the word *human* to its oldest roots. The ancient Indo-European word for earth, *dhghem*, is the root of the Latin *humanus*, the Old German *guman*, and the Old English *guman*, all of which meant "human" (1985, 7). To be a wild human is to be part of Earth, to be an Earthling.

For Peter Berg, wilderness should be the greatest shared value for an ecologically sustainable society, because wilderness embodies systems, designs, and purposes that are "eco-energetic" (efficient in terms of using energy and resources). Berg further argues that the idea of wilderness has the power to help people become liberated from what he calls "late-industrial" forms of control. Wilderness as a value can inspire people, including people in the city, "the new urban person who belongs in the ecological era," to become more conscious of resources, of what they consume, and then to get involved in "neighbourhood culture" to create urban wild habitat, urban stream restoration, community gardens, solar retrofitting, secondary materials recycling industries, and so on (Plant and Plant 1990, 22-30). Moreover, wilderness is "the enduring source of a bioregion's spirit and regenerative power," to be maintained both for its own sake and as a "reservoir for reaffirming natural systems through reinhabitation" (Berg 1983, 1-2). In Berg's sense, wilderness plays a key role in reinhabitation on an urban bioregional scale as an anchor for the four "inhabitory zones" within every bioregion: wilderness zones, rural areas, suburbs, and the inner city, as we saw in the above discussion on bioregions. Wilderness is a liberatory spiritual value for bioregional reinhabitation in all four zones.

Spirituality is another important value for bioregionalists. A discussion of fundamental values for any culture (even a culture in a process of emergence such as bioregional culture) must include the subject of spirituality or religion. Strictly speaking, as Frank Traina has remarked, bioregionalism itself is not a religion, yet the spiritual values of the movement could be described as representing the religious institution of the movement (Traina and Darley-Hill 1995, 6). Bioregionalists are generally tolerant and supportive of inclusiveness with respect to spirituality. At the continental gatherings of the movement, for example, there has been a healthy acceptance of a wide diversity of spiritual practices. This acceptance raises the question of whether there is any common theme in bioregional spirituality. Traina has observed a certain commonality in bioregional spirituality: "Because bioregionalism takes such a strong moral stand with respect to the well-being of nature and the Earth, and since it demands commitment and offers people meaning, it takes on – even unwittingly – a spiritual tone. People from many different religions and philosophies consider themselves bioregionalists. The movement has a pervasive sense of the sacred" (6).

This "sense of the sacred" common among bioregionalists centres on a belief in the sacredness of all life, including all the interdependent creatures and ecological systems of the Earth. It is associated with bioregionalists' sense of the Earth as a "community of entities" (education values eight to ten above). Clearly, bioregional spirituality is linked to a community of beings ethic. Yet, as Traina has also pointed out, some bioregionalists have argued that the topic of spirituality should be kept entirely separate from the bioregional movement. There is considerable controversy within the movement over this topic (see Chapter 6).

The final key bioregional value identified is celebration. Bioregional reinhabitant Marnie Muller describes the process of getting to know our bioregional "homeplace" as bringing forth a deep sense of celebration and appreciation. For Muller and many other bioregionalists, bioregional celebration grows out of a sense of community and communion with the life of the region. Muller further argues that celebration and appreciation are at the heart of bioregional education, and getting to know our bioregional homeplace through reinhabitation brings forth this deeper sense of celebration and appreciation:

> It is a way of exploring our ecological as well as our cultural heritage. Celebration can take the form of an All Species day or it may take a more quiet form, like a walk in the woods. Bioregional celebration grows out of a sense of community as well as communion with all the life of the region. It is the

sense that we are all dwelling in this shared homeplace. We are always in an intimate relation to our bioregional homeplace. Its life systems of air, water, soil, and carbon pass in and through us each day. Knowing home is an integral aspect of knowing ourselves. (Traina and Darley-Hill 1995, 91)

Celebration offers a way to experience the joy of communing with the life of the bioregion. Often bioregionalists experience the connection as an interaction. Muller illustrates this interactive sense of communion in a brief story: "A talented dulcimer player who is a friend of mine once confided, 'I don't really play music, it plays me.' Perhaps, getting to know one's bioregion is like that; perhaps it 'plays' us as much as we 'play' it. May we sing the bioregion as it sings us" (Traina and Darley-Hill 1995, 91).

Celebration is identified as a key part of the bonding process between humans and the community of beings essential to ecocentred social capital formation. The bonding process engendered, affirmed, and fostered by celebration offers a positive, proactive alternative to the alienation and anomie of modern civilization. It underscores the centrality and vital importance of cultural transformation advanced by bioregionalists with respect to the relationship between humans and the rest of nature.

Traina, in his discussion of celebration as a bioregional value, refers to the often depressing message of the environmental movement in its efforts to motivate people to "save the earth," citing Theodore Roszak to highlight the problem: "Are dread and desperation the only motivations we have to play upon? What are we connecting with in people that is generous, joyous, freely given, and perhaps heroic?" To Roszak's complaint, Traina offers "the values and practices of bioregionalism" that "emphasize a positive loving relationship with the natural world and seek to joyfully celebrate the natural world" (Traina and Darley-Hill 1995, 9). Again love and joy are identified as aspects and key motivating dimensions of a community of beings experience.

Brian Swimme (nuclear physicist) and Tom Berry (bioregional thinker and writer) have even gone so far as to argue that the principal role of the human in the universe is celebration: "If we were to choose a single expression for the universe it might be 'celebration,' celebration of existence and life and consciousness ... We remain genetically coded toward a mutually enhancing presence to the life community that surrounds us ... Our own special role is to celebrate this entire community to reflect on and to celebrate itself and its deepest mystery in a special mode of conscious self-awareness" (Traina and Darley-Hill 1995, 9).

While not all bioregionalists would agree fully with this affirmation of genetically encoded mutualism, most would agree that celebration is essential to building community. Celebration in the bioregional movement is a useful community-building tool as well as a value to be held. Celebration, growing out of and contributing to a sense of bioregional community and communion with all life, is identified as crucial for the intense bonding essential to the regeneration of Earth-centred social capital.

Bioregional values aspire to a strong version of Earth-centred social capital, similar in two fundamental ways to Earth-based societies of the domestic mode of production. First, bioregional values incorporate a sense of the community of beings ethic, the form of cultural capital identified as essential to an Earth-centred understanding of kinship in gatherer-hunter/ horticultural societies. This is not to say that bioregionalism would have us move back to a gatherer-hunter or horticultural mode of production. I have never read or heard anyone in the bioregional movement make such an impossible claim. What it does mean is that the sense of ecological kinship captured by the ancient community of beings ethic is a form of cultural capital that informs bioregional community-building values in contemporary society. This ethic profoundly challenges the core values of *homo economicus* and global neoliberalism.

Second, in the vision and values of the bioregional movement, kinship with the Earth and its biological diversity includes a strong kinship with others of our own kind as well, similar to the strong sense of kinship that we saw in societies practising the domestic mode of production. Thus, in both cases, we see that social capital is subsumed by ecosocial capital, but this also suggests that the formation of ecosocial capital may be a more powerful motivator than social capital as conceived by Coleman or Putnam. That is, the recognition of kinship with other species, far from undermining interhuman kinship, appears to strengthen it.

We have also seen that, with respect to the social capital concept of Coleman and Putnam, a personal experience of intense joy in genuinely social acts can reward the individual immensely and is therefore another potentially strong motivator. The motivating quality of this synergistic, joyful energy is thus identified as an aspect of social capital ignored or overlooked by Coleman and Putnam. There is an obvious potential in this direct experience of synergy in social capital formation that merits further investigation.

In the literature on social capital, a range of quantitative studies has generally ignored qualitative, cultural aspects of the concept (Harvard Center for Population and Development Studies 1996). Spirituality, joy, and love, for example, are totally omitted in such studies. Yet such cultural capital content appears to be essential to an understanding of how either social capital or ecocentric social capital is generated and maintained when bioregionalists go about building communities of place.

Finally, it is clear that the philosophical, or ecophilosophical, values of the bioregional movement present a profoundly challenging, comprehensive, ethical, and cultural alternative to the pathologically narrow set of social constructs about the human being centred on *homo economicus*. The

monocultural construct of modern man that provides the cultural and ethical underpinning for the global neoliberal economic order is revealed, in
comparison, to be dangerously narrow, crassly materialistic, and entirely
dismissive of the richly variegated biological and cultural diversity of planet
Earth.

The Salmon Circle*

Chorus

And the salmon circle from the sea to the sea, up the rivers of life

endlessly, and they always return to the place they began, for a million
years they

swam and swam and swam

Figure 2 "Salmon Circle," drawing by Alison Lang

Verse (1, 2, 4)

Round the rocks in the pool, in the river below, they are

turning and turning Oh so slow, and they've been there forever in that

sacred dance, round and round they go, it's a water romance And the
(to chorus)

Verse 3

Red backs, moving in the stream; Hump backs dancing in a dream;

Nose to tail, they circle round and round, Go back to the spawning
ground (to chorus)

Verse 2

To the long slow rhythm of a four-year cycle,
to the pounding beat of the oceans that are like a
drum that sounds clear across the globe,
and it's calling its children,
it's calling its children home.

Verse 4

By the taste of the waters they return to the
source
lay down their eggs feel the life force
resting safe in the gravel pass the winter through,
these great fish are dying
but in the spring life renews.

*This song is intended to be performed with a salmon circle costumed
dance.

– Fraser Lang and Alison Lang

4
Bioregional Strategy and Tools for Community Building

Bioregional Organizing: From Local to Continental Scales

Because of bioregionalism's great emphasis on living in place and home, some analysts have misunderstood the movement as a parochial philosophy. We have already seen that this is not the case. Bioregionalists locate and ground their efforts at social transformation in particular places, but they do so within a planetary ecological consciousness and value system. Moreover, bioregional values and ethics inform a broad regional (or rather bioregional) and even broader continental networking strategy. Local communities of home and place are linked across vast spacial distances through direct face-to-face meetings and gatherings and via mail and e-mail. As well, bioregional values and practice link local community building to broader sociocultural transformation, as we shall see.

Considered in light of a geographically informed civil society theory, bioregional strategies appear most evidently as locally rooted ways to ground the work of networking politically and culturally across space in the creation and nourishment of local communities of place and bioregion. As the bioregional strategy of political and economic conversion unfolds, its primary emphasis on horizontal organizing, networking, and community building in the sphere of civil society is revealed. In this strategy, there is no hint of "capturing state power." Rather, bioregional politics relies on cultural transformation and an economics that begins to address the building of institutions in civil society that meet basic human needs while attempting to restore natural systems.

Peter Berg has always been at the forefront of bioregional political thought. In 1976, he wrote a political essay that had widespread influence among early bioregionalists. *Amble toward Continent Congress* called for local groups to initiate a broader political process of networking and alliance building at a continental scale. This essay preceded the first continental congress by eight years. Ten years later, in 1986, in another influential article, "Growing a Life-Place Politics," Berg advocated locating bioregional political activity in a culturally based politics of place. The same year, the second continental congress of the movement took place. The movement was attracting new adherents. It was a good time to advance a vision of local organizing networked at broader scales.

Berg, as a good political pamphleteer, has the ability to both capture the essence of what people are doing and thinking and then nudge them a little further with an enhancement of the developing vision. In "Growing a Life-Place Politics," Berg argued that bioregional politics starts with individuals who identify with real places and find ways to interact with the life web around them. He advanced three "reinhabitory" principles to guide this work: restoring natural systems, satisfying basic human needs, and developing support for individuals engaged in reinhabitation. In this essay, Berg attempted to answer the question of how to develop support for individuals. He took a social ecological approach to the question. For Berg, bioregional political work depends on working together cooperatively with "closeby watershed neighbours" to form "seed groups," the basic units of "bioregional political interaction" (in Andruss et al. 1990, 139). From there, several seed groups of neighbours working on a wide variety of different projects can join together to form a broader community organization at the local watershed scale. Berg argued that the local watershed level of organization should become a "watershed council," a new institution acting as a forum for addressing watershed issues based on the three reinhabitory principles. At this level, reinhabitants can more effectively engage and contend with established local government agencies and organizations to deal with immediate problems while pressing for "eventual self-determination in the watershed." Finally, the local seed groups and watershed councils would eventually join together to form an even broader network, a federation or congress, at the level of the entire bioregion. In Berg's view, the most basic level of politics for these groups should be oriented to transforming the local culture of the people involved from an industrial, commodity-consuming culture to a culture of reinhabitation or living in place. However, this local horizontal strategy in and for place rooted in civil society must inevitably lead to broader political questions. For example, when I asked him what a bioregional politics would look like, Berg responded, "from my point of view, the politics will follow the culture; the culture of reinhabitation in a bioregion will lead the politics, and the politics will be 'how do you carry that out?' At what point do we need the power of control over our own lives here and to what extent?" (Berg 1989).

For Berg, political work is necessarily embedded in cultural work, in the work of incubating a "culture of reinhabitation." In his political essays and pamphlets, Berg consistently links political action to the problem of cultural transformation. To become sustainable, cultural change at the level of individuals and local seed groups is seen to require support by broader levels of social, economic, and political organization. Berg has played a key role in helping to articulate this understanding in the bioregional movement.

All these geographical and social levels of organization (seed groups, councils, and congresses) are meant to be applied in both rural and urban settings. As Berg has succinctly and ironically commented in discussing urban contexts for a life-place politics, "Cities don't hover on space platforms. They are all within bioregions and can be surprisingly dependent on fairly close sources for food and water, at least ... Green City proposals aren't based on simply cleaning up the environment but rather on securing reciprocity between the urban way of life and the natural life-web that supports it" (in Andruss et al. 1990, 141). In the bioregional movement, it is generally understood that cities are a key part of a broader bioregional perspective and strategy of societal change. Bioregionalism is not simply a back-to-the-land movement. In fact, bioregional green city proposals call for achieving reciprocity between urban regions and their life-supporting ecosystems. This is a bioregional recognition of the profound implication of human dependence on natural systems as a prerequisite for a transformatory cultural approach that frames political organizing. In moving toward reciprocity with the natural life web, the cultural change that this requires informs the political work. This envisioned strategy, rooted socially in civil society and geographically in place and bioregion, ultimately implies the political need to seek changes in government and state institutional structures of power that would support the cultural changes taking place in civil society. Berg's question – "How do you carry that out?" – remains for the moment only partially answered.

The next level or scale of organization is the continental congresses. In his life-place politics, Berg suggests that continental congresses can become "an important new political forum" that can engage people in organizing exchanges of expertise, work parties, and cultural events to support member groups and help focus attention on crisis situations in particular life places as well as fostering the work of "thinking like a continent" (in Andruss et al. 1990, 142). Here Berg directly confronts the apparent contradiction in bioregionalism of thinking on a much broader geographical scale ("like a continent") while also committing much effort to local organizing. Berg openly recognizes that, from a local bioregional perspective, it is difficult enough to understand one's own watershed and bioregion. However, he also argues that this broader continental level of bioregional movement organization is necessary to "confront the problem of arbitrary (and multiple) government power over bioregions" (in Andruss et al. 1990, 142). Many bioregionalists agree with him and have demonstrated it by putting in the enormous time and effort (compared to the small resources of the movement) needed to organize a series of biannual continental gatherings in which broader political and networking issues have been accorded important places.

However, not all bioregionalists support the continental level of organization, while others are sometimes simply too busy working at reinhabitation
at both local and bioregional scales to attend, as personal conversations
with bioregionalists attest. In any case, many bioregionalists have attempted
to implement this extremely demanding multilevel strategy for over two
decades, demonstrating an extraordinarily broad social and geographical
consciousness and creating lifelong bonds of cultural and political solidarity across space. So far, a picture is emerging of a horizontal bioregional
strategy, located in the civil society sphere in immediate space (and place)
and time, that foresees the need to transform institutions of political power.
Questions remain about how that might be accomplished – that is, which
interactions should take place in the intersecting spheres of civil and political society to facilitate the transition to a more democratic form of governance involving both spheres in forms of decision making and
implementation. There is also, of course, the economic sphere.

Bioregional Economic Conversion
Bioregional economics, like bioregional culture and bioregional politics,
begins with place, community, and neighbourhood but extends across place
and space to include watershed and bioregion. For Berg, bioregional economic formations must meet basic human needs and support the work of
reinhabitation to be sustainable. Principles of bioregional economics contrast sharply with neoclassical or conventional economics. The cold, calculating language of *homo economicus* is absent in bioregional economic
thought. In sharp contrast, bioregional economics has been inspired, in
great part, by the "small-is-beautiful" Buddhist economics of E.F. Schumacher
(note the parallel with the "Zen" road to affluence of Buddhist economics
in the domestic mode of production analyzed by Sahlins). The following
vision statement about a bioregional economy, passed by consensus at the
third continental congress, exemplifies the caring, compassionate, "Buddhist" character of bioregional economic thought:

> A bioregional economy manifests itself through qualities of gift, trust, and
> compassion. Bioregional economics is a tool for implementing a social
> agenda informed by relationships, interdependence, and diversity; and is
> sensitive to the scale of the Earth's systems. Bioregional economics distrib-
> utes the gifts of the Earth to sustain the health and richness of the bio-
> sphere in which we live and through which human needs are fulfilled.
> Decision-making is based on principles of local, democratic self-control and,
> secondarily, through mutually friendly, cooperative and compassionate re-
> lationships between and among individuals, groups, communities,
> bioregions, federations, and all species. A bioregional economics is expres-
> sive of a universe of beings evolving and working harmoniously toward the

fulfillment of our individual destinies and our common future. A bioregional economy reflects the oneness of all life. (Zuckerman 1989, 67)

In this vision statement of economies that manifest through "gift, trust and compassion" and reflect "the oneness of all life," we can identify three key aspects of ecocentric social capital: trust, norms of general reciprocity, and kinship with the community of beings. Bioregional economics is by definition about trust, interdependence, mutual aid, and cooperative and compassionate relations among humans and between humans and all species. In these envisioned economies, a bioregional economics is embedded in a cultural/philosophical matrix. Such a total contrast in thought and feeling between this bioregional vision and the entrenched capitalist economics of *homo economicus* raises challenging questions about the difficulties of implementing a vision so different from capitalist economics. Bioregionalists recognize the challenge and have begun to address the need for a long-term strategy that embeds its economics in a philosophical and sociocultural matrix. As we saw in Chapter 1, Karl Polanyi viewed such embedding of economics as essential to avoid the catastrophic collapse of civilization, while Jean Cohen and Andrew Arato would prefer to see a partial embedding rather than the complete dedifferentiation of the spheres.

Bioregionalists see the core of a bioregional economy as a "web" or network of strong, local economies. Bioregional economic thinker Susan Meeker-Lowry, in *Economics as if the Earth Really Mattered*, explains that a strong local economy means a broadly diversified economy that favours the use of local skills, knowledge, ingenuity, and local resources (1988, 231). This envisioned web of local economies (to be examined in more detail shortly) parallels and supports a bioregional political strategy of seed groups, watershed councils, and bioregional and continental congresses.

Furthermore, the concept of an economics of human communities, both local and (bio)regional, is expanded to encompass the larger community of beings. For example, bioregional essayist Tom Berry writes eloquently in *The Dream of the Earth* (1988) that both social and natural ecology concepts intertwine in an economics of the larger Earth community. In this vision of bioregional economics, "the natural world is the larger sacred community to which we belong." Here we encounter the broad vision of an economy of kinship with all beings, the ancient community of beings ethic. One crucial ecophilosophical implication of this integrated human and natural ecological understanding is that cultural transformation as well as social and political change are seen as vitally necessary for human economic systems to fit truly sustainably into natural ecological systems.

The primary goal of bioregional economics is ecological sustainability, not economic growth. One term for a bioregional economics is "reinhabitory economics." Peter Berg and Raymond Dasmann envisioned that the object of a reinhabitory economics is to maintain natural life system continuities while enjoying them and using them to live (in Berg 1978). Given this goal, these bioregional thinkers boldly suggest that reinhabitory economics may be more aptly defined not as an economics at all but as an "ecologics."

A framework for bioregional economies would aim for self-reliance at the level of the bioregion (rather than self-sufficiency, which implies a closed system). The difference between the two concepts, self-sufficiency and self-reliance, cannot be overemphasized. There has been great misunderstanding on this point by some who have criticized the notion of self-reliance by confusing it with self-sufficiency and parochialism. Self-reliance does not imply an absence of trade and exchange between bioregional economies. If implemented, a developed, self-reliant bioregional economy would include careful, extensive recycling, diversification, production for food and basic fibres first, minimization of throughput energy and materials, maximization of nonpolluting processes, high-quality and durable goods production, organic agriculture, and permaculture. It would also include horizontal communication and transportation networks, community-based currencies and exchange systems for local economies, and community control of investment, production, and sales.

The enormous gap between the existing global capitalist market system and the still-to-be-realized vision of bioregional economies underlines the perceived need for a prolonged process of bioregional economic conversion to support and complement the cultural work of reinhabitation. At the continental gatherings, bioregionalists have worked hard in brainstorming sessions to conceptualize at least a sketch of a conceivable long-term process for bioregional economic conversion. That strategy, worked out over the third and fourth continental congresses, comprises four general components. It has been called a "four-prong conversion strategy." Its primary emphasis is on building community at the base in the informal economic sector of civil society; it begins with a horizontal appeal to local civil society to begin acquiring ecological, biogeographical, and biophysical knowledge of place and region.

The first prong was named "Know where we are today" (Dolcini et al. 1991, 39-40). It begins at the local community/neighbourhood level, working with the community to identify major issues, community values, and resources, helping to mobilize the community to come to know its own situation in detail. This knowledge requires investigating and/or cataloguing the natural environment, wildlife and domestic animals, migration routes and patterns, and the human population; determining the percentage of the basic needs currently being met by the community; and identifying what kinds of production services need to be initiated by the community. This process has been called an "ecological/production audit." It also investigates the kinds of production taking place, how harmful the processes are socially and ecologically to the bioregion, and so on. It includes bioregional mapping and inventories (statistical and by interviews) to define the bioregion; resource audits – natural, human, energy, and technology; social relations; sacred/unique sites; history; consumption/waste audits; and "power audits" (what are the social/political networks?).

The second prong of the conversion strategy is to oppose and undercut the dominant system in those areas where it is not in alignment with bioregional principles, through community education, boycotts, corporate divestiture campaigns, political organizing, and ecological/bioregional education.

The third prong is to redirect the energies and power of the old industrial/consumerist system into emerging sustainable systems through developing support for revolving loan funds, community-based credit unions, community-based banks, various kinds of co-ops (worker, child care, agricultural, marketing, consumer, and housing), community-supported agriculture, remanufacturing (recycling for local production), integrating appropriate technologies, implementing workplace democracy, and land use policies that promote sustainability.

Finally, the fourth prong is to establish new sustainable systems in alignment with bioregional principles: markets for cottage industries, land trusts, community currency, barter/exchange networks, cohousing, intentional communities, regional/municipal investment to support community-controlled production, priority to the local economy, optimum self-sustainability (including limited nonexploitive exports, maximum self-sufficiency in food production, maximum diversity, energy, and water self-sufficiency), community ownership/control of resources, and participatory democracy (Dolcini et al. 1991, 39-40).

This entire strategy – an attempt to develop a comprehensive approach – was put forth by the economics committee at NABC IV. It was recognized by the entire congress through consensus as a sketch, or simple outline, of a process for bioregional economic conversion. The congress recommended the strategy as a model for bioregional activists to adopt (and adapt where necessary) and encouraged its implementation wherever possible as an important dimension of bioregional organizing. As can be seen, this four-pronged process of economic conversion focuses primarily on building up the integrated strength of local institutions within the informal economy sectors, in the sphere of civil society. Clearly, this is primarily a horizontal strategy targeting norms of cooperation and collaboration and "participatory" democracy in both political and economic spheres. Yet there is also here more than a hint of vertical strategies in both spheres, for example the corporate divestiture campaigns and the call for changes in land use policy and political organizing.

The bioregional economic strategy is a transitional strategy complementary to the bioregional political strategy. Both are based in civil society;

both are founded in local community–scale activity. Both envision broader networks of exchange across geographical and social space. Like the bioregional organizing strategy of growing a life-place politics through seed groups, councils, et cetera, bioregional economics is a transitional strategy in that it provides concrete places to begin in the civil society sphere at the local community level and, at least, an initial outline for a long-range strategy of economic transformation involving democratization in civil society and the beginning of a strategy for more democratic governance in the political sphere and more socially accountable corporations in the formal economic sphere.

Bioregionalists have given considerable thought to the time frame expected for realization of the bioregional political economic vision. Bioregional reinhabitation as described, complemented, and supported by the development of bioregional reinhabitory economics is understood in the bioregional movement as a process of transformation that will by necessity take several generations to accomplish. For example, bioregional and ecocity thinker Richard Register describes a 140-year process (in several stages) for the long-term implementation of "Ecocity Berkeley" (1987, 57-130). Other bioregionalists whom I have discussed this matter with also understand that bioregional political economic strategy requires a long-term, intergenerational process of cultural transformation to become sustainable. Bioregionalists recognize that such a profound transition in worldview and in human institutions cannot be achieved overnight or even in one generation.

The above transitional strategy can be viewed as a framework to be compared with the Cohen and Arato framework for sociopolitical transformation. Both rely for their implementation on actions from "below": that is, transformative democratization of the whole of society must be based on and grounded in dense horizontal networks of people's organizations in civil society. On this point, both frameworks are based on apparently similar radical notions of political and economic transformation based on social mobilization in the civil society sphere. Without these changes at the base, both frameworks indicate that no lasting democratization can happen, that no political or policy changes from above can be insured for sustainability against the whims of opportunistic politics or corporate neoliberal globalization schemes. However, as noted in Chapter 1, the Cohen and Arato framework, while theoretically appealing in many respects, offers no account of how cultural change in civil society might begin.

Bioregionalists, in contrast, do have many direct experiences of initiating cultural, political, and economic change. They work hard to form local communities of home and place, seed groups and watershed councils, and congresses in civil society at a variety of geographical scales. The primary work is based on horizontal initiatives to establish norms of cooperation, to create as well as target cultural identities of place in social, ecological, and spiritual terms, to build and nourish trust, and to build networks of information and knowledge communication and exchange and solidarity. Bioregionalists employ a range of tools for implementing and realizing their long-term, multiscale community strategy of place and space. They can be assessed as tools for creating and nourishing social and ecosocial capital.

How do potentially motivating dimensions of social and ecosocial capital – synergistic joy and love and other spiritual dimensions – get expressed in bioregionalists' self-understanding of these tools and how they work? What is the role of trust? From this exploration, what more can be learned about the character of social and ecosocial capital, especially with respect to the potential motivating power for their formation? Are the bioregional values of interhuman and interspecies kinship experienced as motivating emotions through the use of these tools? Does their use generate and/or strengthen the experience of kinship for bioregionalists? All of these questions focus on the horizontal character of the bioregional movement's strategy in the civil society sphere.

Tools and Methods for Building Seed Groups, Watershed Councils, Congresses, and Communities of Place

There are various methods and processes used by bioregionalists to aid in building seed groups, councils, congresses, communities, and networks. I consider these processes/methods as tools for developing norms of social solidarity, cooperation, and mutual aid – tools, that is, for building community. How can the use of these tools help to overcome modern barriers of anomie and alienation blocking the formation of social capital or ecosocial capital? To try to answer this question, I have categorized my list of tools into two sets: first, those that are generic to creating and fostering seed groups, councils, networks, et cetera; second, those that are specific forms of activity in themselves, such as permaculture, ecological restoration projects, and bioregional education projects. I discuss the generic tools first. This list includes consensus-building processes (including conflict resolution techniques, reevaluation counselling, etc.); movement-building activities such as undoing "isms" workshops (race, gender, class, age, etc.); the use of sharing circles; the bioregional use of story; interspecies communication (or all-species work); the use of ritual, theatre, dance, music, poetry, mime, costume, and art; and bioregional mapping.

Consensus Decision Making

In group decision making, bioregionalists normally use the consensus process. Many bioregionalists have learned consensus from Caroline Estes, a Quaker and rural reinhabitant in Oregon, who has over 35 years of experience practising and teaching consensus decision making. Estes facilitated the first five continental gatherings of the bioregional movement, greatly influencing the movement in consensus praxis. Consensus processes were developed by Quakers in the nineteenth century and later by the human potential movement in the 1960s and 1970s. It is widely known that the consensus process was also used by many indigenous cultures well before the Quakers. Knowledge of consensus decision making has become fairly widespread, particularly in social movements. In spite of this, the consensus process is often misunderstood or only poorly understood and applied as a form of "group think" dominated by a few articulate or overly assertive participants. In the bioregional movement (and in many social movements), this is not accepted as good consensus process.

In the bioregional movement, consensus decision making means that all members must agree, or at least none seriously disagree, on any group objective. This puts great responsibilities on each member to listen very carefully, remain open-minded, and reflect deeply, knowing that she or he must accept the consequences of the decision, since each individual is considered indispensable to both process and decision. Estes explains that consensus is based on the belief that each person has some part of the truth, but that no one has all of it, and on a profound respect for all persons involved in the decision that is being considered (Andruss et al. 1990, 165-69).

True consensus process needs four ingredients: "A group of people willing to work together, a problem or issue that requires a decision by the group, trust that there is a solution, and perseverance to find the truth" (Andruss et al. 1990, 166). Its great strength is that there is never any decision that does not have complete or at least strongly held agreement. With such commitment to the process, there are no disgruntled minorities or weak, divided groups. Consequently, good consensus process can be a powerful tool for building social capital, because it focuses as much on developing horizontal bonds of trust, mutual understanding, and respect for the process and those involved in it as it does on decision outcomes.

Consensus process begins with a clear statement of the problem, in language as simple as possible. Estes emphasizes that the problem not be stated in such a way that an answer is built in. On the contrary, there should be an openness to looking at all sides of the issue. Good consensus process also needs a skilled facilitator. For Estes, the facilitator role cannot be too strongly emphasized: "Traits that help the facilitator are patience, intuition, articulateness, ability to think on her/his feet and a sense of humor. It is important that the facilitator never show signs of impatience. The facilitator is the servant of the group, not its leader" (in Andruss et al. 1990, 166).

Good consensus process calls for active participation by all participants. Each participant, not just the facilitator, must take some responsibility for the quality of the entire process. Estes stresses that the consensus process is a "direct application of the idea that all persons are equal" (in Andruss et al. 1990, 165-66). She argues that, if we do trust one another and do believe that we all have parts of the truth, then at any time one person may know more or have access to more information, while at another time others may know more or have better understanding. Even when we have all the facts before us, Estes warns, "it may be the spirit that is lacking and comes from another who sees the whole better than any of the persons that have some of the parts. All these contributions are important. Decisions which all have helped shape and in which all can feel united make the carrying out of the necessary action go forward with more efficiency, power and smoothness" (in Andruss et al. 1990, 166).

This definition of consensus helps to reveal the importance of trust as an essential ingredient of social capital formation, trust built on cooperative practice, mutual respect, and perseverance in searching for truthful solutions. Good consensus process appears as a primary tool for generating social capital.

Given the above definition and understanding of consensus process in the bioregional movement, what is the experience of it? Can it really help to build trust? Estes describes the empowering experience of the consensus process at the first North American Bioregional Congress:

> Over 200 persons arrived from all over the continent, and some from abroad, and worked together for five days, making all decisions by consensus. Some of those present had used the process before ... but many had not used it, and there was a high degree of harmony and unity. On the final day of the congress, there were a very large number of resolutions, position papers and policies put forward from committees that had been working all week long. All decisions that were made that day were made by consensus – and the level of love and trust amongst participants was tangible. Much to the surprise of nearly everyone, we came away with a sense of unity and forward motion that was near miraculous, but believable. (1984, 19)

Thus, for bioregionalists, good consensus processes are, at bottom, about working together to build common bonds in order to move forward together whether it be in a seed group, at a congress, or in an intentional community. That is, consensus is much more than just a decision-making technique. The above example illustrates the effectiveness of good consensus process in creating the trust, the sense of cooperation, and the group solidarity needed to clarify important issues and to work together toward defining common goals. Good consensus process contributes to fostering a deeper, common understanding of the issues involved and assists greatly in building agreement and unity. Consensus process has been an essential tool for social capital formation in the bioregional movement. Furthermore, it is clear that love, as well as trust, can be generated by good consensus process. Here is another clue to enhancing the Coleman/Putnam definition of social capital. Love (again) appears as an important bonding dimension of social capital.

The above discussion may have left the impression that consensus process is easy to implement. This is a mistaken reading. Consensus often requires hard work among participants. Understanding and achieving good consensus-building process requires patience by all participants. Estes recommends that, when a decision cannot be reached, it is often best to put it off until a future meeting so that participants can have time for deeper reflection. This practice is sometimes called "laying aside," after Quaker custom. For the practical person, this may seem unnecessary or impractical, but it means that individuals' opinions and feelings are highly respected and that social relations are not damaged in the rush to move forward by making quick decisions.

In the bioregional movement, one person who seriously believes that the group is about to make a wrong decision may move to block consensus. In such circumstances, Estes observes, good consensus process requires "that the meeting see the person who is holding up the meeting as doing so out of that person's highest understanding and beliefs" and that the "individual(s) who are holding the group from making a decision must also have examined themselves well to know that they are not doing so out of self-interest, bias, vengeance or any other emotion or idea except the very strong feeling and belief that the decision is wrong – and that they would be doing the group a great disservice by allowing it to go forward" (in Andruss et al. 1990, 169). In her own intentional community experience over many years, Estes has seen consensus blocked on only a few occasions, and each time the person blocking was correct in the sense that the group would have made a mistake by moving forward too quickly and without due consideration.

In group processes, conflicts sometimes arise for which no quick and easy solutions appear. Two or more individuals may be in conflict. To deal with such problems, bioregionalists have adopted conflict resolution and group facilitation techniques (some originally developed by the Quakers) also used by peace groups, civil rights organizations, women's consciousness-raising groups, groups in the environmental movement, and so on. Such techniques started to appear as a formal process in the late 1960s and had become widespread by the late 1980s (Kaner 1996, ix). They are based on a willingness by involved participants to reach a mutually acceptable resolution. One example will suffice to illustrate this approach.

A typical conflict resolution method is "no-lose" (or win-win). In this method, all parties to the dispute participate with a facilitator in a seven-step process: (1) define the problem in terms of both people's needs, with each person identifying the conflict in his or her own terms; (2) restate the problem in such a way as to include both persons' needs; (3) brainstorm alternative solutions on a sheet for all to see without discussion until each person sees on the list solutions with which she or he is willing to work; (4) individually evaluate the alternative solutions, eliminating any that are unacceptable for any reason; (5) decide on the best solution acceptable to everyone involved in the conflict and make a mutual commitment to try it; (6) implement the solution and set aside time to evaluate the progress; (7) evaluate how it is working, and, if anyone believes that it is unfair or won't work, repeat the process from step one (Coover et al. 1977, 90).

The win-win process relies, in part at least, on a technique called "active listening" (Coover et al. 1977). This technique attempts to clarify the conflict by having the individuals involved explore their feelings on the issue(s) with a friend or someone who is considered "safe." Active listening is a way of helping a person to solve his or her problems by listening attentively for the feelings behind the person's statements and reflecting them back to the person without making any judgments about the person, belittling the problem, or trying to suggest solutions. The "active listener" simply tries to reflect the person's own feelings back for clarification. This technique is designed to resolve conflicts in which real needs are being frustrated by miscommunication. However, it is not meant to resolve conflicts based on differences of belief or deeply held values.

Conflict resolution methods are often used in conjunction with consensus. As noted, the use of these processes is common in a wide number of movements in civil society. Their use in the bioregional movement also increased in the late 1980s and in the 1990s. These methods can help to build up levels of information and trust between participants by revealing real blocks in communication and more accurate information on genuinely held beliefs and values. Such methods are potentially invaluable for social capital formation. Reevaluation counselling is another more elaborate method used by bioregionalists and others when two individuals are having severe problems working or living cooperatively.

Reevaluation Counselling
Reevaluation counselling is a form of co-counselling by peers, without professional intervention. It was founded as a practice in the 1950s by Harvey Jackins in Seattle. Subsequently, it was advanced as a theory in the early 1960s out of years of experiences with solving people's emotional problems and neuroses (Jackins 1975). It grew quickly as a movement of peer counselling communities and networks outside the practice of professional counselling (Rowan 1988).

To the extent that reevaluation counselling has a precursor, it can be found in the person-centred counselling developed by Carl Rodgers. The essence of his approach is based on the assumption or principle of the basic goodness of the person and his or her capability to find the answers to his or her problems given the time, space, encouragement, and loving support to do so (Rowan 1988). Similarly, reevaluation counselling theory assumes that everyone is born with enormous intellectual potential, natural zest for life, creativity, and lovingness but that these qualities often become blocked and/or obscured in people as a result of accumulated distressful or hurtful experiences that begin in (but are not limited to) childhood (Jackins 1975).

Glen Makepeace, a veteran bioregionalist who is trained in and practises reevaluation counselling, observes that in the theory of reevaluation counselling everyone in modern society is keeping painful experiences out of her or his awareness:

> In other words, they're using part of their life energy to keep these blocked feelings away ... A child that begins to tantrum is invariably stopped from doing it, or they're allowed a little bit of a tantrum, they're not allowed to continue, and the natural process of healing is blocked ... It is less acceptable for men to cry than it is for women. What happens because of the nature of the distress pattern when we get into a situation that is sufficiently similar to the original place in which the pattern was installed on us, the pattern will be restimulated, and this is an explanation of neurotic behaviour, the repetition compulsion. (1997)

Counsellors trained in reevaluation counselling learn to recognize these distress patterns locked up in our bodies. When adequate emotional discharge (unloading hurts and other feelings by crying, laughing, raging, etc.) of these hurts can take place, the person is freed from the rigid pattern of behaviour and feelings left by the hurt. The bodily release of blocked distress patterns is viewed in reevaluation counselling theory as a natural healing process. In recovering and using the natural discharge process, two people take turns counselling and being counselled. The person acting as the counsellor actively listens, helps to draw the other out, and permits, encourages, and assists emotional discharge. The person being counselled talks, discharges, and reevaluates. Then the roles are reversed. In the peer counselling process, it is recognized that the "client" has to do the work and is in charge of her or his own therapy throughout the entire process. The person acting as counsellor does not comment on, evaluate, or share experiences with the client. Rather, the role of the counsellor is to encourage the client to talk about and come to terms with the problem by actively listening to the client, by really being there for the client in loving attention and awareness of the inherent nature of the person being counselled: "The term used in peer counseling is 'delightful attention.' It's what the Rodgerians call 'unconditional love' for the person. And even just that alone will frequently help the person to discharge quite a bit, because when do you ever get such attention?" (Makepeace 1997).

In reevaluation counselling, the peer relationship is crucial. The ongoing counselling of the counsellor is important. The theory and practice of reevaluation counselling are learned by everyone in the reevaluation counselling community so that no part of the process is mystifying for participants. Reevaluation counselling spreads mostly by one-to-one communication of the theory. Practice is communicated by an "each-one-teach-one" basis (Jackins 1975, 17). According to its founder, group and community activities and networks grew out of paired co-counselling relationships. Reevaluation counselling communities have developed various kinds of group activities, from group counselling sessions, to public workshops on peer counselling, to peer counselling discussion groups. Women's and men's groups and race and ethnic groups based on relationship to oppression were also developed (Jackins 1975).

The use of reevaluation counselling to liberate blocked energy for the purposes of community building and societal transformation became of great interest to a growing number of bioregionalists in the 1990s. Makepeace describes his experience in the bioregional movement. He first encountered peer counselling in 1990 and immediately recognized its value for a social movement. Makepeace refers to the success that he felt when he enthusiastically offered a workshop in coevaluation counselling at the 1990 Maine continental bioregional congress with Joyce Marshall, who had been doing peer counselling for some years with her husband, Gene, and a friend of theirs, Jean-Marie Manning, also a bioregionalist. Makepeace also worked successfully with a few people at the Maine event, helping them to deal with the problems that they were having even though he himself was new to the process.

Makepeace views peer counselling as very useful for several purposes related to building bioregional community. First, it's a good way to get yourself in good emotional shape so that "you're basically coming into a situation with a good perspective on other people, and with your own abilities available to you [you're] not caught up in whatever distresses you might be having" (1997). Second, Makepeace, a trained group facilitator, found that reevaluation counselling was a useful tool for facilitators. For example, if someone is having problems during an event and disrupting it, he or she can be taken aside for a peer counselling session. Or a facilitator experienced in peer counselling could recognize behaviour driven by some blocked emotions and set up reevaluation counselling. Often that's all it has taken in Makepeace's experience.

Makepeace identified a third use of reevaluation counselling from his experience living in his own bioregional community in the Bridge River: "In many of the problems that have come up over the years, we've dealt with them by doing co-counselling. Marital problems or relationship problems are common ones, where a person is having a difficulty and it's hard for them to be in something like a community with somebody they're not getting along with. And co-counselling is very useful in that kind of a situation" (1997).

Clearly, in the modern era, in which anomie, alienation, and denial are epidemic, reevaluation counselling appears as a necessary tool for several reasons related to the generation of social capital. It fosters relationships of openness and honesty, most essential for building trust. Trust then aids a participant to unblock and discharge pent-up feelings and installed patterns of oppression. Reevaluation counselling consciously uses love as an aid in trust building and emotional discharge. This movement of feelings between co-counsellors stimulates bonds of trust and love. Again love is identified as another important factor in the bonding process. Furthermore, the feelings are established on the basis of a peer relationship, or, in other words, the bonds are horizontal.

Bioregional Movement Sharing Circles

The use of the circular form by bioregionalists is, in part, based on ancient peoples' understanding of the power of the circle. While such an understanding is not common in our modern culture, the circle is a form used extensively by humans since the first fire circles, the first "hearths," at the dawn of humankind, when early humans gathered around fires. Ancient stone circles are evidence of the use of the circle in prehistoric times. Stonehenge is only one of over 900 ancient stone circles found in the British Isles, used to study the cycles of the sun, the moon, and certain stars but also used for various, if not well understood, ceremonial purposes (Krupp 1983; Wood 1980). Available evidence indicates that Stonehenge and many other stone circles were likely temples or ritual sites of some sort. After examining a good deal of this evidence, E.C. Krupp concludes "with reasonable certainty" that the circle's formal architectural arrangements and alignments, its imposed "symbolic and visual order," along with buried human bone fragments, indicate both astronomical and ceremonial purposes, the marking and enclosing of "sacred space" (1983, 214-30).

Krupp also refers to about fifty stone circles, most found on the eastern slopes of the Rockies or on the open plains below in both the United States and Canada. One in Saskatchewan is shaped like a turtle. The turtle is a common First Nations symbol for "Turtle Island" (North America). Today we know these circles as medicine wheels. One is the Bighorn Medicine Wheel, high up on an exposed shoulder of Medicine Mountain in Wyoming, only slightly smaller than the large stone circle at Stonehenge. Information on the stone circle in Wyoming is found in *The Rocky Mountain Bundle*, one of the early Planet Drum Foundation publications.

The medicine wheel, common to many North American indigenous peoples, is a symbolic and sacred circle. Brooke Medicine Eagle is a Métis teacher and healer who gained experience in the white academic world before returning to her Native roots. Medicine Eagle writes simply and powerfully of the power of the circle symbol/medicine wheel:

> The form of the circle, in which all are equally important and responsible, is a natural way to practice oneness. Coming together, again and again, to physically maintain the perfect roundness of the circling spiritual dance is a vital learning, even when there are ripples in the circle, such as individuals wishing to withdraw or wanting to run the show differently or feeling personal discomfort with others in the group. Their ability to maintain the basic harmony of the circle, even with these challenges before them, affirms their awareness of building community together ... The circle becomes the container of all things, all happenings, concerns, celebrations, mourning, anger, all joy, so that no one and nothing is ever left out. It is within the circle, then, that the healing is created. It is within the circle that we create the wholeness and the holiness. (1991, 419)

There were many different medicine societies, but common to most was the concept of the medicine wheel as both a circle and a path that people moved through as their life cycles unfolded. The medicine wheel, then, is a symbol for each person's life cycle. But it is also understood as a series of teachings or lessons for living life according to traditional ways.

Not only is the medicine wheel understood as a symbol for life and a teaching of how to live life in harmony and balance, but it can also be used to mark out a specific ceremonial space, to mark the "wheel" of the seasons, and to help practitioners live in "a sacred manner." Jamie Sams is a medicine teacher and a member of the Wolf Clan teaching lodge of the Seneca Nation. She is of both Iroquois and Choctaw descent, trained in Seneca, Mayan, Aztec, and Choctaw medicine. After consulting the grandmothers and the elders who had been her teachers, Sams came to understand that it was time to share the sacred teachings of the medicine wheel with non-Natives.

Sams writes about the use of stone circles for ceremonial space that mark special or sacred places and lessons of birth, of growth, of death and rebirth: "The Stone Circle of the Medicine Wheel is a symbol of Sacred Ceremonial Space that has been honored by our people for centuries as a place to come and experience the beauty of the cycles of physical life. These cycles of planting, gestation, birth, death, and rebirth are the life lessons of the Sacred Hoop ... When we as Children of Earth lose our sense of where we fit into the Medicine Wheel of life, we lose sight of the unified circle and how to live in a sacred manner" (Sams and Carson 1988, 85-87).

Bioregionalists have been strongly influenced by such traditional philosophies and practices. Dolores LaChapelle is a bioregional reinhabitant in the San Juan Mountains of the Colorado Rockies, the founder and director of the Way of the Mountain Learning Center, and a member of the Academy of Independent Scholars. She has been studying, practising, and teaching the use of the sacred circle for solstice and equinox celebrations for many years. She points out that, while stone medicine wheels were used by only some indigenous peoples, many traditional people throughout the world literally "lived within their medicine wheel": that is, they practised sacred ritual "walks" or journeys around sacred places or features of their land, thus turning the whole of their territory into a sacred circle or medicine wheel. LaChapelle gives several examples of peoples who did this and argues that forms of stone circles have been used by humans since the Paleolithic period, some 20,000 years ago (1988, 188-90).

For bioregionalists in contemporary society, the circle is also a symbol and a tool for individual and community empowerment. From the early days of the movement, bioregionalists have been aware of the symbolism and power of the circle. Planet Drum is the name of the original educational, publishing, and networking organization founded in 1973 by Peter Berg, Judy Goldhaft, and others. The very name Planet Drum is suggestive of many associations; the planet is circular, and so is the drum. I asked Berg where the name came from:

> Shamans play a hoop drum and written on it are symbols of natural events, cycles, other species, whatever. And the shamans sing a song from that drum as a kind of ouija-board reindeer collar bone moves around among these symbols. Well, that's what we thought of the first things we published which were loose, separate articles in an envelope that you opened up, they fell on the floor, you rearranged them. We thought the articles were the symbols on the drum and the person reading them was the shaman; but, since then of course, we've had all kinds of other associations with it: like "daily bugle," so "planet drum," a drum for the planet. (1989)

At bioregional events, gatherings, and congresses, the circle form is used on a daily basis for many different kinds of group activity. From working together in local seed groups and committees to watershed councils and bioregional and continental gatherings and congresses, bioregionalists learned to meet and work together in circles for various purposes: healing, decision making, ceremony and ritual, and community building. In fact, the practice of meeting in circles is associated with most bioregional activities. For example, there are drumming circles, plenary circles, men's and women's circles, elders' circles, youth circles, sunrise and sunset ceremonial circles, healing circles, opening and closing circles, and many others.

Bioregionalists, in adopting the circle form as a healing and experiential teaching tool (a kind of medicine wheel), are not "reinventing the wheel" but respectfully reclaiming ancient traditions of Earth-based peoples from Turtle Island, Old Europe, and elsewhere. Used in respectful and noncommercial ways, the medicine wheel circle is a tool for the direct experience of community, but not just human community. Bioregionalists are using circle power as one way to experience the healing power of the community of beings ethic. The understanding of its teaching and healing power described above is often experienced by bioregionalists in healing circles and community ceremonial circles as a potent spiritual motivation for building inclusive bioregional communities. Examples of such direct experiences in the bioregional movement are narrated in the following chapters.

Story

Story is another bioregional tool for reclaiming and rebuilding communities of place. Story is perhaps as old as humanity, as old as the first fire circles around which humans gathered to tell, share, and enact their stories. We usually refer to these ancient stories as myths. Many (if not all) peoples have a foundational myth or origin story. Indeed, eminent scholar of myth Mircea Eliade provides a definition of myth that emphasizes common cultural origins. In Eliade's view, the following definition captures what is most comprehensive in myth with respect to gatherer-hunter (Eliade uses the term "archaic") societies: "Myth narrates a sacred history: it relates an event that took place in primordial Time, the fabled time of the 'beginnings.' In other words, myth tells how, through the deeds of Supernatural beings, a reality came into existence, be it the whole of reality, the Cosmos, or only a fragment of reality – an island, a species of plant, a particular kind of human behaviour, an institution. Myth, then, is always an account of a 'creation'; it relates how something was produced, began to *be*" (1968, 5-6).

It is Eliade's definition of myth that I use here – myth as sacred origin stories from the "primordial Time, the fabled time of the 'beginnings.'" One key point that Eliade makes about myth is that, in prehistoric societies, people were obliged to remember and periodically reenact their origin stories in public ceremonies and rituals. Oral cultures passed down their traditions through such regular reenactments. Ceremonial reenactment of myths, in which everyone participated, was often done at important times of the yearly seasonal cycle. The telling of these stories could last for days. A few years ago, at an environmental conference hosted by the Huron First Nation at Cape Croker on the Bruce Peninsula (Ontario), participants were told the story of the Great Peacemaker, founder of the Iroquois Confederacy. I witnessed the storyteller, Native elder Tom Porter, take two hours to tell the story in considerable detail. Then he announced that this was a very shortened version. In the old days, the complete story took ten days to tell. It was accompanied by visiting, feasting, drumming, and singing. It was a reenactment of an ancient bonding, the coming together of five different peoples for the original act of creation, inspired and led by the Great Peacemaker, that birthed the Iroquois Confederacy.

Bioregionalists have explored links that Earth-based cultures made between story and place. The gods, goddesses, mythic figures, and powers in the old stories of animistic societies were often familiar animals, plants, or other beings of place, and they were usually local deities. Dolores LaChapelle has argued that, even in the case of the Greeks, most of the original Greek gods were animals and that the Romans, before they adopted the Greek gods, believed not in gods but in *numina* or powers associated with particular places (1988, 120). Many other examples of myth linked to place in place-oriented cultures are provided by LaChapelle. One is a story told by Dennis Tedlock about travelling with the Zunis in New Mexico: "You're going by in a car, going by a mesa with pink and yellow stripes of sandstone and about 300 feet up the side of it there's a cave up there. You're going along with a Zuni and the Zuni says 'That's the cave, you remember that story about Aatoshle ogress. That's the cave where she lived when that little girl wandered into her cave to spend the night. Right There'" (in LaChapelle 1988, 188).

Even today, LaChapelle argues, humans can adapt to the pattern of their place through stories that grow from place. Following what she calls our "root-traces," the patterns of relationship both within us – as evolved over millennia – and in nature outside us, we can discover our own story of place. Even more, LaChapelle argues, the story of a society is about the way that a people can adapt to or "fit" into place: "Humans, too, can begin to fit just as beautifully into the pattern of their place, but not through conscious willing; instead it's more like playing. 'Story' grows out of this type of play. As the festival grows through time, the story develops. The story of a society is the way that a people fits into its place. The place gives us the *li*, the pattern, and the story is how we fit into that pattern" (1988, 91).

Tom Berry, another bioregional philosopher who has deeply investigated human cultural forms as story, writes about the central importance of story for viable and sustainable human cultures: "It's all a question of story. We are in trouble just now because we do not have a good story. We are in between stories. The old story, the account of how the world came to be and how we fit into it, is no longer effective. Yet we have not learned the new story" (1988, 123). What is the new story in Berry's view?

Berry finds the beginning of a new story in his search for a synthesis of the modern scientific story and what he calls a "numinous" view of the universe. For Berry (who comes from the Christian scholastic tradition), the Christian overemphasis on the story of redemption is unbalanced, thus diminishing the importance of the creation aspect of the Christian story.

Moreover, the scientific story (what Berry calls the "life sequence" discovered by Darwin) has largely replaced the redemption-oriented Christian story. However, Berry argues that the secular story of the Western scientific worldview does not see either the numinous quality or the deeper psychic powers associated with its own story. In *The Dream of the Earth*, Berry proposes a new "universe story," one that involves a change in our "cultural coding" that melds our scientific understanding with a numinous view of the universe and the "earth community" (1988, 123-37, 194-215).

Berry gives this new universe story a bioregional focus through his understanding that this planet "presents itself" as a complex of highly differentiated regions (bioregions) caught up in the comprehensive unity of the planet itself (1988). Each region has its own special story. Berry provides as an example, in narrative essay form, a specific story of the Hudson River valley, where he lived for many years. He tells a story of the valley from the time of the formation of its mountains to the glaciation that covered it with a thousand feet of ice; then come the retreat of the ice and the current geographical configuration of the valley. For Berry, the story of the Hudson valley is also the story of the Indian peoples, the original dwellers in the region, who interacted with the land successfully over millennia. Berry then brings the story to the present with the coming of the white man and the changes wrought by farming and industry. I cite the beginning of this story at length because it illustrates a characteristic bioregional sensibility about the intense emotional bonding power of story to evoke feelings of ecological community and kinship. I find it most evocative when read slowly, aloud:

> Tell me the story of the river and the valley and the streams and woodlands and wetlands, of the shellfish and finfish. Tell me a story. A story of where we are and how we got here and the characters and roles we play. Tell me a story, a story that will be my story as well as the story of everyone and everything about me, the story that brings us together in a valley community, a story that brings together the human community with every living being in the valley, a story that brings us together under the arc of the great blue sky in the day and the starry heavens at night, a story that will drench us with rain and dry us in the wind, a story told by humans to one another that will also be the story that the wood thrush sings in the thicket, the story the river recites in its downward journey, the story the Storm King Mountain images forth in the fullness of its grandeur. (1988, 171-72)

Many bioregionalists take this spirit of story found in Berry's engaging, narrative, poetic prose and, using older oral ways of storytelling, weave stories of place together in communal settings with children, friends, and extended family. Story is used in circles at gatherings of every geographical level – local, bioregional, and continental. Here in these circles, among stories of place and culture shared by the participants, the story of the emerging bioregional movement/community is told for newcomers to orient themselves and for veterans to remember and celebrate.

One key purpose of bioregional storytelling is bonding people together in reclaiming their places. Bioregional stories emerge from and are informed by the places where people live. Told in the old oral ways, in a circle or around a fire circle, at important times of the yearly cycle such as solstice or equinox, or during the full moon, stories can stimulate powerful bonding among participants. Such stories bond people to place and to each other to produce a social cohesion grounded in place. Story, as used by bioregionalists, is thus identified as another cultural tool for building ecosocial capital through a shared, integrated bonding of people with people and people with place. Story is an inclusive form of sharing, a sharing among peers and equals, face to face in circles sharing personal stories, building up information about each other, sharing feelings as well as thoughts, building trust levels, bonding horizontally.

The bioregional use of story, like the ancients' use of story, can facilitate the creation and use of ecological social capital. Through the telling and sharing of stories, meaning becomes relational. All participants in the story circle share to some profound extent the individual stories, increasing social bonds of information, trust, and mutuality. Furthermore, through sharing their stories of place *in* a place, the participants begin to weave these stories together as part of a broader common story of place and region. Ecological social capital is thereby created, grounded in particular places.

David Abram, bioregional all-species activist and academic philosopher, who has done an extensive phenomenological study of differences between oral and literate cultures, writes about the direct experience of oral storytelling. I cite the following passage at length because it so clearly explains how storytelling helps humans to connect "in the flesh" with phenomena and how phenomena are experienced as kin.

> Stories, like rhymed poems or songs, readily incorporate themselves into our felt experience; the shifts of action echo and resonate our own encounters – in hearing or telling the story we vicariously *live* it, and the travails of its characters embed themselves into our own flesh ... If the story carries knowledge about a particular plant or natural element, then that entity will often be cast, like all of the other characters, in a fully animate form, capable of personlike adventures and experiences, susceptible to the kinds of setbacks or difficulties that we know in our own lives. In this manner the character or personality of a medicinal plant will be easily remembered, its poisonous attributes will be readily avoided, and the precise steps in its preparation will be evident from the sequence of events in the very legend

that one chants while preparing it. One has only to cite the appropriate story from the Distant Time, about a particular plant, animal, or element in order to recall the accumulated cultural knowledge regarding that entity and its relation to the human community ... By invoking a dimension or a time when all entities were in human form, or when humans were in the shape of other animals and plants, these stories affirm human kinship with the multiple forms of the surrounding terrain. They thus indicate the respectful, mutual relations that must be maintained with natural phenomena, the reciprocity that must be practiced in relation to other animals, plants, and the land itself, in order to ensure one's own health and to preserve the well-being of the human community. (1997, 120-21)

Abram's careful explanation of how oral story sharing can create lived experience of the community of beings for participants illustrates the spiritual communal bonding potential of story as a cultural tool for affirming "human kinship with the multiple forms of the surrounding terrain." This insight into the process of ecosocial capital formation links myth as origin story to that "Distant Time" when "all entities were in human form, or when humans were in the shape of other animals and plants." "Distant Time" is what Eliade (as noted above) refers to as "primordial Time," the time when the event first took place, the prodigious sacred time of myth.

Ritual and Ceremony

Ritual is used by many cultures, including modern industrial society. Rituals that bioregionalists perform are often inspired and informed by forms of ritual practised by Earth-based cultures. Ritual is an enormous subject within which I focus on a specific concern: how does ritual assist in helping people to bond with each other and with nonhuman nature? That is, how does ritual assist bioregionalists to experience ecological kinship? How do bioregionalists understand and use ritual for bonding and community building?

Traditionally, ritual occurs in a number of different forms, including initiation rituals or rites of passage, potlatch or give-away rituals, world renewal rituals, healing rituals, rituals to honour animals and other nonhuman species and place dimensions of nature, rituals to celebrate community and mutuality, and ritual journeys around the region or territory of inhabitation of a given cultural group. All of these are practices with ancient roots. Although much diminished in European cultures since the Inquisition and the suppression of Pagan practice, ritual use is being reclaimed and thus continues in our time. While certain uses of ritual have been controversial within the bioregional movement (see Chapter 6), ritual is nevertheless widely practised among bioregionalists.

Some bioregionalists have studied, practised, and taught the use of ritual. A smaller number have also written publicly about ritual. Among the most well known are Starhawk and Dolores LaChapelle. For bioregionalists, ritual is used to connect humans to each other as well as to nonhuman nature. LaChapelle, who has led and taught Earth ceremonies and rituals for over twenty years, advances a threefold typology of ritual: (1) biological ritualization in animals and its further development in humans; (2) general human ritualizations such as habitual, repetitive, stereotyped, compulsive, or obligatory acts or methods of formalizing, routinizing, conventualizing [sic], et cetera; and (3) "sacred ritual" – that which enables humans to connect to or evoke "the sacred" (1988, 151). It is this last category that interests LaChapelle. By "the sacred," she means the direct personal experience, the intense sensation and definite awareness of being an integral part of, being alive with, the whole of life, all of it, all relations simultaneously.

This sense of holistic awareness is also described as an experience of entering or reentering the "process of becoming." The experience of being connected to all of life has been described in similar terms by a number of other ecocentric thinkers and is understood as an "embodied" awareness, not merely a mental connection. This view of the sacred means that what is sacred "is not outside the world, but manifests in nature, in human beings, in the community and culture we create" (Starhawk 1987, 21). John and Nancy Todd (of the former New Alchemy Institute) name this immanent, embodied connection "a sacred ecology," and they identify it with the ancient animistic worldview of many traditional cultures (1984, 80-81).

For LaChapelle, life's goal is to "live in a sacred manner" by including and setting up "ritual structures in our lives where we can feel nature moving deep within us, in response to the patterns of all of nature without" (1988, 128). One central purpose of contemporary "Earth rituals" (a synonym for sacred rituals) for people in modern Western culture, then, is to restore – through lived, embodied experience – the lost connection between humans and nature.

LaChapelle wanted to help other people "begin to feel a real connection with the non-human beings of their own place" (1988, 203). She understood that many people from the dominant culture of "Industrial Growth Society" (her name for the industrial consumerist mode of production) had a difficult time connecting with nature. She created a ritual just for this purpose, the "Breaking Through Ritual," which she first performed in 1979, adapting it from a Hakkow ceremony of the Plains Indians. Each year the participants follow the same route with LaChapelle and her cofacilitator, Rick Medrick. They journey together through the mountains for several days. During this time, participants ritually greet "other beings" that they encounter: trees, rivers, mountains, and rocks. Chanting, drumming, and dancing are performed throughout the ceremonies. The idea is that the ritual structure, adapted from the land itself, enables bonding with all the beings of place. LaChapelle tells the story of her own experience of it:

I began to recognize just exactly what the land form does to people in each place. The resulting human/earth bonding astounded us. The more skilled Rick and I become at recognizing what the land wants from us the easier it becomes; because it's not us; it's the mountains and the river who do the bonding. We spend two days in a secluded valley, giving our people the necessary skills and beginning rituals; then two days white water rafting on the Arkansas River; followed by four days in the alpine Crestone Peaks area. I teach Tai Chi every day and we do rituals whenever the mountains or rocks or trees tell us to. (1988, 204)

LaChapelle reports that many participants in the "Breaking Through Ritual" journey testify to life-changing experiences for themselves – after which they can no longer "take Industrial Growth Society seriously," in the sense at least that they have broken through the boundaries of its narrowly rationalistic worldview and connected profoundly with nonhuman nature. LaChapelle argues that such a ritual journey provides a "fundamental pattern" for restoring the connection between humans and nature: "When you give a group of people the chance to live as hunter-gatherers always lived, daily moving together through the place, where the trees and rocks and waterfalls are 'sacred' – worshipping the beauty and chanting the songs these natural beings give you – then you 'remember' deep inside that 'this is how it always was.' And then you are home!" (1988, 204).

How does ritual work to achieve this deep embodied bonding? As someone who has experienced similar "sacred" feelings on numerous occasions, I know that it is extremely difficult to convey effectively a sense of what happens during an Earth ritual to produce the bonding effect to someone who has never experienced it. Margot Adler, who did a comprehensive study on neo-Paganism and contemporary Earth religions in the United States, reports that a certain professor giving an arts class on ritual stated that "the only way you can learn anything important about ritual[s] is by doing them" (1986, 163).

The idea that ritual can actually work to bring about experiential knowledge of a "sacred ecology" is not considered rational, not in Western positivist and postpositivist thought at least. Nevertheless, there is a neurobiology of ritual, a Western neurophysiological explanation of how ritual works, that LaChapelle has reviewed extensively. She begins her discussion by pointing out that Carl Jung opened up the study of the deeper layers of human consciousness to include the human unconscious and the collective unconscious. Jung described the psyche as reaching down from the "daylight of the mentally ... lucid consciousness into the nervous system that for ages has been known as the 'sympathetic'" (in LaChapelle 1988, 154). LaChapelle also gives an account of two decades of empirical research on the physiological processes of the nervous system that occurred since Jung's initial work.

In presenting her overview of this research, LaChapelle observes that previous biological research on repetitive stimuli on the brain to facilitate a state of ritual-induced awareness was not sufficient to explain all its effects because the body organs are interconnected by the nervous system as well as the brain. Thus, synoptic research on the entire nervous system was needed for a deeper understanding of the effects of ritual action.

Modernists tend to think that all of consciousness can be found in the neocortex (LaChapelle 1978, 72). LaChapelle offers ritual as an essential cultural tool for the mind to reconnect with nature through reconnecting more holistically with our own nervous systems and our own bodies. LaChapelle (drawing on work by systems philosopher Gregory Bateson) argues that, while the mind as a whole is an integrated network of circuits, the conscious mind registers only the bits and pieces of the ongoing circuits that go through all three levels. In this view, the neocortex is dependent on the older parts of the brain.

Ritual, carried out over several hours or more, LaChapelle goes on to argue, can act as a catalyst for going below the conscious "rational" part of the mind in the neocortex to access information from both halves of the older brains rooted in our neurophysiological systems – that is, in our bodies. In Earth rituals, several different techniques are used simultaneously: drumming, chanting, dancing, and other repetitive actions. It is this multi-technique approach that provides "the necessary redundancy so that the message goes through all levels and to all participants" (LaChapelle 1988, 155). This connecting action at all levels of the brain, including the autonomic nervous system (ANS), is the "tuning" of the nervous system. In this way, we reach into our own nervous system to access information long suppressed by our "rational" neocortex.

As additional evidence, LaChapelle cites the finding of researchers Gelhorn and Kiely on the bonding effects of tuning: strong rhythm or repetition "of itself produces positive limbic discharge resulting in decreased distancing and increasing social cohesion" (1988, 155). Yet neurobiological explanations of how ritual works to bond individual participants to their own, older, neurophysiological roots ignore the meaning of ritual for participants. We need to inquire into the experience of those who, like LaChapelle, learn about ritual by doing it.

Chanting

In her introduction to chanting in ritual, LaChapelle comments that, when a group experience a ritual event together, more things happen than any one person can comprehend, much of it registered subliminally. Chanting together rhythmically can focus some of these happenings for participants. Chanting, LaChapelle explains, is the mechanism that facilitates communication between our conscious brains and the older brains within us: "When the group begins to chant together, much of the unconscious material can surface and become conscious and embedded in the chant ... In chanting one can be totally oneself and yet totally with all the others ... If everyone is totally being oneself there results a mutual sense of worth that builds up in everyone concerned, which leads to the unexpected gift of joy that can happen in chanting ... the overflowing abundance of joy which continually happens in chanting" (1988, 277-78).

LaChapelle emphasizes that chanting, when performed for some time, "begins to dissolve the 'boundaries' we've artificially set up around our single individual person in this Euro-centric culture. The longer you chant the more the boundaries of the self extend." But, LaChapelle warns, this is not some airy, spacy, abstract, "spiritual" concept. This opening of the self occurs "only because you are grounded in that particular place where you are circling around, circling around, chanting and chanting" (1988, 280).

.I think that it's important in this context to reflect a moment on the much maligned concept of the "ecological self." For LaChapelle, the separate self of "Euro-centric culture" is an artificial creation; even more, it's a delusion. The "ecological" or "extended" self that she is speaking of is not about the dissolution of the psyche or the bland and vacuous unity of some abstract, disembodied, "universal" self. Rather, the ecological self, for LaChapelle, is about relationship that is firmly grounded in place by the bonding experience of chanting and circling together in sacred ritual. The ecological self in this sense is about relationship between self and other, both human and nonhuman other. Through chanting, the chanters connect with their own deeper selves, with each other, and with the other nonhuman beings of place. In this understanding, "the sacred" is about relationship, not substance. LaChapelle contrasts this extended, relational self with the atrophied, ego-centred self of Eurocentric culture. In the same passage that deals with the "Euro-centric self" (a synonym for *homo economicus*?), LaChapelle specifically points out that chanting in the context of an Earth ritual is a powerful means "to begin to move out of the narrow, meaningless life as mere 'economic man'" (1988, 276-77).

Here we encounter another, rather subtle, bonding phenomenon produced by ritual practice, in this case through chanting. The concept of economic man, the major cultural underpinning of neoliberal globalization, as discussed in Chapter 1, is both narrow and abstract, yet it is a pretentiously universalized concept. In contrast, the concept of the human self discussed by LaChapelle is a relational one, dependent on the specificities of place, both human and nonhuman. There is a movement of the self from Eurocentric economic man to a relational bonding with one's own body and with the other beings of place. In this process, we see the link between social and ecosocial capital formation. This connection with our deeper selves and our relational selves, this "mutual sense of worth," can release an "abundance" of joyful energy that has enormous empowering potential for the psyche. Thus, another aspect of social and ecosocial capital is revealed: the great potential for releasing psychic energy from the connection of self and other, experienced as a joyful, spiritual empowering. Furthermore, this spiritually empowering energy of ecosocial capital can also be seen as an empowering resource for individuals. Such empowering experiences, explored further in Chapters 5 and 6 in a variety of settings, hold huge potential for replacing the urge to consume, to unself-consciously continue to live as a utility-maximizing, egocentric, alienated individual, a privileged consumer in the neoliberal global marketplace.

Drumming

The drum is perhaps the most commonly used item in rituals (LaChapelle 1988, 271; Redmond 1997). Generally in ritual, the drum serves to mark and to change the rhythm. LaChapelle points out that drumming has the overall effect of connecting many different parts of the brain as well as preventing the rational, "merely human" aspect of the brain from taking over. For LaChapelle, an important aspect of drumming is the fact that we live in a syncopated world from our earliest existence. In the womb, the fetus floats in amniotic fluid that carries sound far better than air, and the baby's heartbeat is twice as fast as the mother's, so the two heartbeats, superimposed on one another, produce a syncopated rhythm that is the baby's entire world for many months (1988, 284). Drumbeats can "speak" to these patterns deep in the psyche/body.

In ritual, the lead drum sets the rhythm and acts to synchronize all the drummers and the dancers. The effect can be very powerful, and when it continues for hours energy builds up, the rhythms surge up and down the spine, muscles become relaxed, and the entire body and nervous system are stimulated holistically by the pounding rhythms. In "ritual dance," LaChapelle observes, "the drum is important to us because we are freed to move once again with the syncopated heartbeat of the world" (1988, 284). The drumming embodies the dancers and the drummers in the rhythms. Rhythms bind the ritual participants together in embodied resonant movement with "the syncopated heartbeat." Ecosocial capital, then, can also have a sensuous, musical dimension. The ability of one rhythm to draw another into harmonic resonance is called "entrainment." The harmonic resonance of drumming has been traditionally used by shamans and oracular priestesses to move ritual participants toward a state of ecstatic union with the "divine rhythms of the earth" (Redmond 1997, 174).

Dancing

Ritual dancing can take many forms, but often the circle or spiral sets the pattern. The dancing acts to enhance the effects of chanting and drumming.

When done over many hours, muscles and joints of the body are loosened, the dancers' bodies moving with the syncopated rhythms of the drums. In this "long dance," as LaChapelle calls it, "all aspects of the mind: conscious and unconscious, as well as the sympathetic and parasympathetic nervous systems are 'tuned' together within the individual so that bonding occurs both throughout the group and with nature in that place" (1988, 288). Dancing is movement. In Earth ritual, the movement is syncopated, repetitive, insistent, sensual, embodied. Interconnection is experienced viscerally as well as emotionally.

In LaChapelle's multimethod approach to Earth ritual, all elements of sacred ritual act together to produce the altered state of awareness called "tuning." The form of the circle (with or without a stone medicine wheel or henge), the creation of sacred space, the telling of story and its enactment in ritual, the chanting, drumming, and dancing (sometimes accompanied by the shaking of rattles) – all combine to "break through," to peel back the layers of Eurocentric delusion, and through the tuning effect to connect with other participants and with the nonhuman beings of that place. In this bioregional understanding of ritual, the practice of ritual works to embody a people within the circle of their land community. The theoretical model is an embodied model.

Note that, while this examination sets out to explain the bonding action of ritual between humans and nature, the explanations also encompass interhuman bonding. Bioregionalists who practise Earth rituals emphasize the importance of both. For example, LaChapelle states that the purpose of Earth ritual, as she describes and practises it, includes "putting all parts of the human together deep inside the individual, ... putting humans together in society and ... facilitating human interactions with nature" (1988, 149).

Starhawk has led rituals at two continental bioregional gatherings (and at many other events, including antinuclear demonstrations, feminist gatherings, and more recently demonstrations against globalism in Ottawa, Quebec City, Seattle, Genoa, and elsewhere). Starhawk uses the power of ritual to bring people together, to ground people to be more effective in grassroots political actions in modern society. She writes from her own experience about ritual as social bonding, telling the story of the mass arrest of 600 women for nonviolently blockading the Livermore Weapons Lab in California, where nuclear weapons are designed. The women were held in a gymnasium that had been the site of experiments with radioactive substances for twenty years. They struggled with the guards, who attacked one of the women. Violence seemed to be inevitable. One woman started to chant. Starhawk describes vividly what happened next:

> The chant is wordless, a low hum that swells and grows with open vowels as
> if we had become the collective voice of some ancient beast that growls and

sings, the voice of something that knows nothing of guns, walls, night-sticks, mace, or barbed-wire fencing, yet gives protection, a voice outside surveillance or calculation but not outside knowledge, a voice that is recognized by our bodies if not our minds and is known also to the guards whose human bodies, like ours, have been animal for a million years before control was invented. The guards back away. "Sit down," a woman whispers. We become a tableau, sitting and clasping the woman as if we are healing her with our voices and our magic. The confrontation has become a laying on of hands. The guards stand tall, isolated pillars. They look bewildered. Something they are unprepared for, unprepared even to name, has arisen in our moment of common action. They do not know what to do. And so, after a moment, they withdraw. The chant dies away. It is over. For a moment, mystery has bested authority. (1987, 5)

Starhawk then reflects on the meaning of this experience: "In that moment in the jail, the power of domination and control met something outside its comprehension, a power rooted in another source" (1987, 5). The "source" is the bonding effect evoked by the chant as a sacred connection with life. For Starhawk, this intense bonding experience is a form of empowerment or "power-from-within," which also connects the individual with his or her deeper self and with other humans. But there is another aspect of power involved here too. Starhawk names it "power-with." She explains how power-with worked to unite the women protesters: "We joined in the chanting begun by one woman in the jail because we respected her inspiration. Her idea felt right to us. She had no authority to command, but acted as a channel to focus and direct the will of the group" (1987, 10). Thus, power-with is a horizontal, shared power, the power of differences working in unity, in interlocking rhythms. Horizontal power is feared by the global captains of consciousness. As RAND documents produced for the US military show, there is great concern in certain circles of the military-industrial complex about growing consciousness of and direct citizen action against neoliberal globalization (Ronfeldt et al. 1998). However, from an ecological civil society theory perspective, tools that can help to raise horizontal grounding, bonding, and participatory social power to nourish civic collaborative action are highly valued.

Another way to look at ritual is as a means of communication. For La-Chapelle, the root meaning of communication, *communicare*, means to "make common to many, to share, to participate." This interactive meaning of communication goes beyond giving a message from one individual to another and concerns an evocation of a shared or mutual experience of *communitas*. The knowledge coming from this direct experience LaChapelle calls "understanding." Understanding must be evoked or called forth (1988, 298). Furthermore, this form of knowledge must be called forth with the help of the body. "Calling forth" implies, in one sense, that the knowledge obtained from the experience of *communitas* is already there buried under immense amounts of modern conditioning. What knowledge is called forth? Knowledge of a sacred ecology, of *communitas*. In other words, the knowledge evoked is that of the community of beings. So, to reflect on the meaning of ritual for a moment, it now seems to be clear that the practice of Earth ritual evokes – through the bonding experience generated by the action of ritual – a personal knowledge of ecocentric social capital. Moreover, the knowledge is acquired through an embodied process; the knowledge is an embodied knowledge. It is the result of a movement, a "breaking through" from Western culture's encrusted mind/body and human/nature dualisms to the joyful experience of spiritually awakening to and connecting with the community of all beings.

Bioregionalists employ ritual in many different ways and situations, some of them very public. Indeed, bioregionalists have been creative in their innovative efforts at including newcomers in their rituals and at performing more accessible and more public forms of ritual than those discussed by LaChapelle. For example, bioregional activist Amy Hannon, philosopher, drummer, teacher, and organizer of community ritual events such as the Coastal Carolina All Species Project, has observed that an incremental approach to Earth rituals may begin by something so simple as coming together on a regular basis at prescribed times corresponding with natural rhythms such as solstice, equinox, new or full moon, sunrise and sunset, planting and harvesting times, et cetera. For Hannon, it is of key importance to plan the ceremony in conjunction with Earth's rhythms: "The physical changes that occur everywhere in the planet during these moments register in everything that lives, including the cells of our own bodies. By ritually acknowledging the power of these moments, we begin to deepen our awareness and to remember our connections" (Traina and Darley-Hill 1995, 143-44). Hannon points out that she has found it practical, when involving the broader community, to limit the ceremonies of simple solstice or equinox celebrations to about an hour, perhaps followed by a potluck supper and social. Whatever the actual arrangements, she recommends keeping the core ritual event within bounds determined by the energy of the community. One form of public Earth festival often used by bioregionalists is All Species Days.

All Species Days and Projects

All Species Days are collaborative community celebrations involving the use of street theatre, parades, costume, masks, mime, puppetry, poetry, music, dance, and public ceremony. They are held annually to celebrate the story of the places where they are performed. The first such event was held in 1978 in San Francisco, where the parade proceeded to City Hall and the mayor proclaimed the first All Species Day. They have been celebrated in at least thirty-five communities in the United States and Canada (Kraft et al. 1993; Traina and Darley-Hill 1995).

The All Species Project was developed by bioregional activist and educator Chris Wells to celebrate and promote All Species Days. Wells was instrumental, along with teacher John Mcleod, in organizing the first annual All Species Day in Santa Fe in 1980. Often described and promoted by its creators as a process of "community pageantry," All Species Day activities began as a way to discover and celebrate human connection to all species and to the Earth and to represent the needs of plants, animals, and the Earth to the human community.

In 1987, Wells and Mcleod planted "seeds" of the all-species idea in Kansas City, and then the Heartland All Species Project grew into a separate organization. Wells travelled far and wide planting seeds, which have also grown into All Species Days, in many other cities. He has also shared his vision, music, mask making, and stilt skills with teachers and others at the North American Bioregional Congresses I, II, and III. Soon, as Hannon observed, "different versions of All Species Day were being celebrated all over the continent" (Traina and Darley-Hill 1995, 129).

Wells describes the purpose of All Species Projects in terms of the bioregional value of interdependence: "All Species Projects are strides towards making us actively aware of our interdependence with animals, plants, and elements. Our search is for the creatively contagious collaborative projects which engage a community in exploring its ecological connection. Once we feel this connection, we can face the facts and figures with an understanding and a new capacity to act in relation to the world on which we depend" (Traina and Darley-Hill 1995, 126). Here again we see a strong emphasis on the active participation of the community in creating the event and the empowerment (or the power-with of Starhawk) that enables collaborative action.

In fact, All Species Days do not happen without extensive preparation and community involvement and collaboration. The idea behind the All Species Project is to create an arts and education program working with schools, community centres, educators, artists, and others over a full year to plan the all-species festival. While the avowed purpose of the All Species Project is to understand and celebrate human interdependence with all species and the Earth, the reliance on and encouragement of community collaboration in the events also make all-species processes a useful tool for bonding participants to each other. Bonds of trust and solidarity are built through sharing in both the work and the celebration. In addition, organizational networks are formed. As Wells expresses it, "We also create out of this a community troupe, a familial network of skilled educators, artists, and concerned citizens who are recruited into teams of varying size depending on the nature and requirements of each project" (Traina and Darley-Hill 1995, 126).

In Santa Fe, for example, Wells's report of the day's events of 20 May 1988 illustrates the public educational success that communities can achieve by fairly large-scale organizational networking among many small, diverse, autonomous groups, each creating its particular project. The day begins with multicultural opening ceremonies. First the San Juan Tewa Buffalo Dancers perform an opening ceremonial dance. Then the DeColores Singers honour the landscape of New Mexico in Spanish song, which the crowd joins in, singing the eighteenth-century hymn "For the Beauty of the Earth." The parade starts up, led by rhythm sections with the "ecological" floats moving slowly among several thousand children, teens, parents, and contingents of "creatures." The "creatures" are masked and costumed local species: roadrunners, rattlesnakes, pinion trees, coyotes, river otters, red-tailed hawks, western flickers, mosquitoes, and antelope. The parade of about 4,000 people arrives at a large park for the annual giant puppetry pageant theatre, "Aldo and the Wolf," dedicated to wildlife biologist and ecocentric thinker Aldo Leopold. A quartet plays Pachelbel from their wheelchairs. A group of teenagers from a local drug abuse program come in as stilt-dancing performers in a crane dance. The wolf study group from a local school club, JADE (Juveniles Against the Destruction of the Earth), make their choreographed stalking moves in masks made from recycled materials, as full-size buffalo puppets appear out of a cloud of smoke. The pageant theatre has begun. Later, during sideshow time, three elementary schools present their plays on wilderness topics under the previously agreed-on theme "Why Wild?" Mimes and musicians, puppeteers, dance groups, and speakers each perform repeated shows on ecological themes. Live bison, wolves, and raptors in the care of local ranchers and animal doctors arrive. Wells concludes his report on the day's events with the following reflections: "Images of nature in its glory and balance, scenes of family and community overcome oppressive forces of ignorance and destruction. The world for a moment seems turned rightside up again. People are seen in the course of the day crying and laughing, thinking out loud with strangers, and in a few paved hearts seeds of appreciation are starting to germinate" (Traina and Darley-Hill 1995, 127).

Months of preparation and collaboration by teachers and students, church groups, clubs, scouts, artists, mimes, and musicians have helped to produce – as one of the outcomes – the social cohesion so important to the building of community. Here is social capital grounded in a spiritual connection with the various species of the place – in other words, ecosocial capital. The public educational work under an Earth-centred all-species theme has contributed in an incremental manner to the birth of a broader cultural shift, manifested in a budding emotional identification with other species and a bonding with the landscape and the stories of Santa Fe and New Mexico. The long cooperation to produce the event, the music, dancing, and drumming, the all-species puppetry, mime, and street theatre, has helped to bond participants socially and ecosocially. All-species work represents an important attempt to help humans connect with other species and to recognize and feel that connection. This is the creation of rooted culture, of human beings who flower into multiple interconnected identities, ecosocial beings so very different from *homo economicus*.

Undoing "Isms" Workshops and Talking Circles/Alliance Building

From its inception, the bioregional movement has been concerned with issues of racism, sexism, classism, and other forms of oppression – that is, issues of social justice. These issues have often been discussed in terms of building alliances among the bioregional movement and other social and cultural movements of oppressed peoples. This history, including controversies and problems, will be examined in Chapter 6. The immediate task now is to explore the tools that bioregionalists have used to address these issues and problems.

Margot Adair has contributed to the bioregional movement (and, more generally, to other movements and groups throughout the United States) by developing tools to approach issues of race, gender, and class and building alliances across "cultural difference." Adair developed what she calls "tools for change," including undoing "isms" workshops, talking circles, and other means to address thorny issues of social justice. Adair and Howell (1988) write about these issues and about the pressing need to deal with them in social movements. At the fourth continental gathering in 1990, she and Roberto Mendoza led an all-day workshop on undoing "isms" (see Chapter 6).

Before looking at the tools themselves, I think that it's necessary to examine some major reasons why such tools are seen by Adair (and generally the bioregional movement) as vital for bioregionalism to develop stronger community relationships. Her work has been influenced by her life in San Francisco, where she has been part of efforts to bring together insights of Marxism, spirituality, personal relationships, and institutional change. Adair is one of a number of individuals who entered the bioregional movement out of previous experience in the National Organization for an American Revolution. Referring to the poisoning of the land, air, water, and people, as well as pervasive social ills in the United States, Adair and her coauthor, Sharon Howell, argue that to survive Americans need to rebuild communities that are life-affirming. For Adair and Howell (1997), diversity is the essence of community. Without working across class, race, gender, and other differences that have divided people through unequal access to power and privilege, people will not be able to weave the community ties that are essential to building alliances toward a socially just, as well as an ecologically sustainable, society.

Adair and Howell also argue that the prevailing modern middle-class model of the individual in the United States, particularly for those of European descent, has worked to strip away their cultural heritage. The authors, themselves of European descent, focus on the racist character of the middle-class Euro-American individual in the United States. They argue that conformity to the model of the competitive individual has created a culture in which individuals hide their inadequacies and idiosyncrasies for fear that they will be used against them. In such a culture, trust among people is very difficult to build, yet, as we have seen, trust is essential to building horizontal bonds and networks in civil society. Moreover, Adair and Howell argue, there is a distinctly racist character to the model of the competitive individual. "White" has been the great melting pot for people of European descent, especially in the United States: "People from distinct and separate cultures have all been poured into the pot, rising to the top of society through the process of having their heritage boiled away. All that is left is to identify how far up one has risen. People are judged by what they own; their character and wisdom are deemed irrelevant. Loyalty to social movements, to principles, people, place, and past have evaporated. Opportunism is rewarded while generosity is seen as sentimental. 'White' is solely an identity of privilege. This is the 'wonderbreading of America'" (1997, 11).

In such a situation, Adair and Howell argue, race is a political category (1988). The creation of "white" meant giving privileges to some while denying them to others with the justification of biological and social inferiority. The term "white" was established as a legal concept after Bacon's Rebellion in 1678 to separate the indentured servants of European and African heritage who had united against the colonial elite. The colonial elite, Adair and Howell conclude, created "white" as an identity of superiority for people of European descent when compared with other "races." However, the hierarchical order of success for such an identity denied the true diversity of European cultural heritage, family ties, loyalty to place, and rootedness in community. All of this is renounced for consumerism, a rootless identity of self with what one owns. Here we encounter a more nuanced definition of economic man, one that includes race and ethnicity but only by obliterating all difference, including the differences of European origin! As we have seen, the monoculture now puts different faces in its logo ads (Klein 2000), but only *homo economicus,* the artful consumer, remains inside the faces.

Middle-class culture, Adair and Howell argue, is a constricted culture. Conformity to the model demands that people be in control of themselves, the situation, and the facts. People want to be sure that they are not blamed when things go wrong. Any problems are interpreted as a threat to one's public image. This dynamic is especially strong when people think about interacting with those whom they perceive to be different. When faced with those whom they consider less advantaged, people often respond with blame or guilt. Dominant cultural concepts of individual achievements and failures encourage the belief that people must be poor because of their own limitations. The tendency under these conditions is to avoid questions of privilege and power. The emphasis on individual freedom hides the fact that the options available to some are only made possible at the expense of others and the Earth. This is what Adair and Howell call "the power taboo" (1988).

For Adair and Howell, the process of building relationships across our differences begins with our willingness to look at power. The structures of power are maintained, they argue, not only through the functioning of institutions and instruments of force but also through the patterns of thought and behaviour "that we all learn as we grow and live in a society dependent on divisions, especially of race, class, gender and age" (1988, 2). Because middle-class culture has been so dominant, all of us raised in modern society are affected by these ingrained patterns of behaviour, including those in social movements that oppose the dominant culture. This is why, conclude Adair and Howell, those in social movements must place great importance on and spend much effort in breaking the old patterns, unlearning sexism, racism, and other "isms" and weaving new ties by building alliances among different social movements.

While Adair and Howell do not actually use the term "*homo economicus*," their analysis of middle-class culture, based on essentially the same social construct, economic man, contributes to it an understanding of the racist dimensions of the competitive and acquisitive middle-class, individualistic, utility maximizer. This analysis, developed out of their work in the National Organization for an American Revolution, calls for extensive work among oppositional social and cultural movements to recognize and address issues of power and privilege as essential to rebuilding communities that are life-affirming and alliances that are built both on respect for our differences and on new horizontal ties of mutual support. By openly grappling with the many questions that arise from living with difference, Adair and Howell argue that people can gain strength and, in the process, change. The horizontal links in building civil society–based alternatives to *homo economicus* are crucial in building social and ecosocial capital among oppositional social and cultural movements. More than that, horizontal linkages appear to be indispensable for the creation of a rainbow of movements in solidarity with all. The horizontal character of social capital relations draws attention to the importance of issues of power and privilege and identifies any vertical character that they may have as a problem for further inquiry and eventual action. How do social movements build trust in a context of vertical relationships created by power and privilege?

The tools for change that Adair and Howell work with have the goal of rebuilding trust. Trust, they argue, must be at the base of our relationships. Life-affirming communities and organizations can be sustained only when we trust and support one another. Such trust can be possible, they say, only when we are mutually accountable. Yet trust, they assert, has been "one of the greatest casualties of the movements of the 1960s" (1997, 13). There is therefore, they affirm, an urgent need to work to change old patterns of behaviour. A history of well-entrenched stereotypes of race, gender, and class is not easy to overcome. Adair and Howell offer a variety of tools for both individual and group work.

One tool for change advanced by Adair and Howell for different groups trying to work together is to "open the context" of issues that have been buried or obscured, by recognizing and naming the ignored realities: "When these undercurrents are named – from interpretations of history, to ways of doing everyday things, to access to resources – what has previously been left unsaid becomes part of the reality with which everyone grapples. The narrow norms which suppress the complexity of varied lives are broken" (1997, 16). Or, from a civil society view, the encrusted shell of modern economic man breaks open, creating the possibility of establishing relations of mutual respect based on shared knowledge of real, rooted, diverse traditions. On this new web of horizontal relations among peers, trust can be supported and thus grow.

In the experience of Adair and Howell, this process works because, when the content of what has been silent or hidden is named, people begin to share thoughts that they previously censored. Moreover, in their experience, this process works better when "naming" the ignored realities is done by someone with privilege, because it helps to avoid the dynamics of guilt and blame.

Breaking the power taboo by naming different oppressions helps to create a new dynamic. The "power of naming" breaks the taboo. Experiences no longer invisible become part of what everyone grapples with; they are no longer just "his problem" or "her problem." A vertical barrier has been crossed. Moreover, explain Adair and Howell, when experiences kept hidden are named and revealed, people are no longer forced to deny themselves. They no longer have to choose between self and other: "The boundaries of the situation expand, our humanity is enriched, and the basic assumptions of the power structure have to be reexamined. Naming power begins our process of reclaiming it" (1988, 8-9). Naming power begins a process of creating webs of horizontal relations in civil society. The wider and stronger these webs grow, the more effective they become in supporting diversity and democracy against the monoculture.

Another tool employed by Adair and Howell is talking circles. They make a particular use of talking circles to address alliance building. Such circles are defined by Adair and Howell as a method for transforming the diverse dynamics of competition, domination, and submission in which some do all the talking while others fade into the background. Their purpose is to facilitate the creation of an atmosphere in which all participants feel safe enough to be honest and to share their experiences even though doing so may be painful. Adair and Howell (1997) note that they were inspired to use this form by a ceremonial practice of some Native American peoples and by women's consciousness-raising groups. How do such talking circles work?

Before beginning the talking circle, everyone must agree to strict confidentiality in order to help provide the sense of safety that people need. Participants are encouraged to speak from the heart and the spirit. In the circle, the person talking has the attention of the whole group, sharing whatever may move her or him. Everyone else gives the speaker her or his full attention, listening without judging, without deciding what it all means, just listening with his or her own heart and spirit. There is no discussion of people's remarks, and each participant strives to speak directly out of his or her own experience rather than respond to or analyze what someone else has said. After everyone in the circle has had a turn, a theme that has emerged may be discussed if participants want to focus on it. Adair and Howell emphasize that this discussion must be undertaken with sensitivity since "people have spoken with their hearts and no one likes their heart trampled on" (1997, 27).

Adair and Howell also emphasize the importance of working to know each other as full human beings, building relationships with more than just ideas. Making the time and space to share our stories and to really listen to one another can begin the process of building new, more holistic relationships. Adair and Howell additionally stress the importance of enhancing this process and strengthening the connectedness that it generates by sharing in song, dance, silence, meditation, prayer, and various activities rooted in the participants' different histories: "When our work includes sharing our hearts, bodies, and spirits – we heal our fragmentation and experience our wholeness. It is good to mark the beginning and end of our meetings with these kinds of activities – even something as simple as a few moments of breathing together, listening to a poem, or lighting a candle. When we do, we cultivate a generosity of spirit toward each other and all life. An atmosphere of openness and appreciation for our shared humanity is created, in contrast to situations in which pettiness thrives" (1997, 28). Here we see that alliance-building efforts, while especially focused on interhuman bonding work, are carried out in a context of "generosity of spirit toward ... all life." Sharing stories, songs, poems, or simply silence encourages the sharing of broader, relational selves open to the community of beings ethic.

Adair and Howell provide several "focusing questions" that they have found useful in creating an open context for this deeper sharing. How did the people who raised you make a living? How did they feel about it, and how did it affect you? Name one thing from your heritage that gives you strength and one that limits you. Tell stories that you remember about your grandparents. What do you never want to hear again from people different from yourself? What do you want from an ally? When do you feel a sense of community?

Another tool to use in conjunction with talking circles is "constructive feedback." For Adair and Howell, constructive criticism or feedback is necessary to enable us to transform destructive attitudes and behaviours. Building trust requires honesty, courage, and caring in unlearning old patterns. However, they caution, constructive critical feedback should always be given in the context of common goals, not to point a finger at the "bad guy," which is merely blaming behaviour. They provide a list of simple dos and don'ts for individuals wanting to engage in constructive feedback: be concrete; avoid value judgments and name-calling. The purpose is change, not blame. Use "I" statements, not "you" statements. Don't assume that you're right without collective investigation. Look at all sides; nothing is all bad.

Be self-critical; since you are in relationship with one another, be conscious of what you may be doing to contribute to the problem. Ask how you can support change. A final caution given by Adair and Howell is that constructive feedback should "always be directed at the attitude and the act, while supporting the person receiving it" (1997, 26).

For Adair and Howell, given the hold of the dominant culture on us, it is crucial that alliance-building work be informed by a politics based on principles of social and ecological justice. We can do this work by evaluating our decisions on the basis of whose interests are being served, who benefits, what is gained, and what is lost. Because our dominant monoculture obscures social relationships, Adair and Howell advance a framework for the critical examination of outcomes. They suggest a list of questions that must be asked to address the impacts of our decisions on both people and the Earth (1997, 17-18). Examples include:

What resources are used – whose labour and what raw materials make the situation possible? Are the exchanges fair – does everyone equally benefit?

What is the impact on the Earth? Who has the power (ownership, decision making, information, influence)?

Who establishes policy? Who is accountable to it? What decisions have been made? Who benefits? Who loses? Who are allies?

What is the vision of what would be better? Does everyone share the same vision? If not, can the differences coexist?

Bioregional Mapping

Maps and mapping have been central to the development and activities of the bioregional movement since its inception. Mapping has fulfilled several different key purposes for bioregionalists. First, mapping has contributed to the very development of the concept of bioregions. The first bioregional maps were created by Raymond Dasmann and Miklos Udvardy in 1973 for a United Nations study of biotic provinces (Aberley 1993). Peter Berg and Raymond Dasmann were inspired by the maps to work together to develop and popularize the concept of bioregions. Bioregional poet and mapper Gary Snyder was also central in the genesis of the bioregion concept, linking First Nations cultural life patterns with biogeographical patterns (1980).

Second, bioregional mapping is used for public education and inspiration. Bioregional maps were used in the mid-1970s by the Planet Drum Foundation to illustrate a reinhabitory vision for California. They were also used to illustrate the Planet Drum journal *Raise the Stakes*. Cascadian bioregional poet, teacher, and mapper David McCloskey has used a mapping process to "call forth" a vision of Cascadia and as a learning tool for "finding home" (Aberley 1993, 18). Freeman House and the Mattole Restoration Council use mapping to inform themselves of the history of the destruction of salmon habitat in the Mattole Valley in California. They also use maps as a watershed restoration educational tool for the residents of the valley and as a political tool to interact with and educate relevant government institutions. In 1985, the first systematic method of describing the characteristics of a bioregion via a mapping process was created by Doug Aberley.

The first bioregional mapping process applied to the concept of urban reinhabitation was outlined by bioregional thinkers John Todd, cofounder of the widely known New Alchemy Institute, and George Tukel, a bioregional planner, in *Reinhabiting Cities and Towns: Designing for Sustainability* (1981). They called the process "place patterning." By overlaying patterns of human settlement on patterns of natural succession, Todd and Tukel envisioned the possibility of planning urban settlements to adapt to and fit into changing patterns of ecological succession and disturbance in order to contribute to the maintenance of ecological stability of the bioregion. A key part of this mapping process was to develop a "solar income budget" for the bioregion to assess the potential for living within the solar energy supplied by the bioregion. This form of mapping represented an early attempt by bioregionalists to conceptualize living within the carrying capacity of a bioregion.

In their approach to place patterning, Todd and Tukel look specifically at ecological succession as a powerful conceptual tool for visioning the design and reshaping of urban human communities within the matrices of their bioregions. For these writers, seeing the city in the bioregion as a whole is the first step in the evolution of bioregionally based design practices. They see place patterning as an exercise in town and neighbourhood planning that can be applied at the neighbourhood scale and/or the much broader scale of the entire urban region.

The first step in place patterning (apart from physically exploring the bioregion, itself an essential prerequisite) is to overlay the "artificial terrain onto the natural one using maps to see where tensions or compatibility exist" (Todd and Tukel 1981, 20). This is done through compiling a series of overlay maps delineating all of the natural water flows; water-related functions such as harbours, docks, and marine terminals; railway lines; major road traffic arteries; airports; electrical power stations or major transmission and distribution substations; waste treatment facilities; areas zoned for residential, commercial, industrial, and governmental purposes; and agricultural activities.

Then a "biological map" is prepared, indicating water flows, landforms, soil characteristics, wildlife habitats, and native vegetation. All urban "green zones" are also plotted, including parks, open spaces, treed avenues, wooded ravines, wetlands, et cetera. Finally, by overlaying these maps, an overview of urban patterns and biogeographical patterns can be compared, with points of tension and compatibility being specifically located. This overview can also be seen over time by comparing the present mosaic with past ones through maps of the natural and social geography, old drawings, histories, photos, and stories of place from older residents. This exercise can also lead to identifying special places of local spiritual significance. Indeed, the vision of a "sacred ecology" noted above is the framework that informs the work of the Todds (1984), including the most "pragmatic" work of recycling and growing food.

With an overview of both patterns of natural succession and patterns of human settlement within the bioregion, one can begin to see, Todd and Tukel argue, how settlement patterns could be planned, or rather replanned, to adapt to and allow for the changing patterns of ecological succession and disturbance to maintain the ecological sustainability of the bioregion. A key point they make is that the overlay method allows the conceptual connection of the biological components, which they argue "should be almost continuous" (1981, 23). Prophetically, this concern for biological connectivity foreshadows the rise of the new science of conservation biology in the mid-1980s.

Doug Aberley is perhaps the most systematic, detailed, and comprehensive of all bioregional mappers. He has been developing his own mapping method for close to two decades. In 1993, Aberley published a collection of bioregional mapping stories, thought, and practice from the movement, including a detailed primer on how to map a bioregion entitled *Boundaries of Home: Mapping for Local Empowerment*. Interest in mapping workshops has grown steadily at the continental congresses. Aberley played an important role in stimulating this interest, leading mapping workshops at these gatherings. Mapping is now seen by many bioregionalists as an essential tool for bioregional reinhabitation in city or country.

Aberley describes several purposes of bioregional mapping: displaying graphically the destruction of land and culture caused by big business and centralized government; showing a vision for a sustainable future more clearly than thousands of words; depicting strategies of resistance to aid in blocking unwise development and helping to focus anger against such development; and charting patterns of complexity weaving together urban restoration of streams, open spaces, and ecologically integrated human settlements. Ultimately, Aberley argues, bioregional mapping is about processes and relationships rather than disembodied facts. What matters for him in bioregional mapping is not how good your cartography is but developing your ability to fill the world "with personal and communal descriptions of time and space." That is, his approach focuses on rediscovering one's relationships of place and bioregion by "tracing the aspirations that define self, family, and community" in both historical and actual contexts (1993, 5-6).

The chief purpose of bioregional mapping, for Aberley, is to build community, not to become an expert cartographer (Aberley et al. 1995). In fact, he recommends the use of existing topographic, local government, or other maps of one's home bioregion as ready aids for mapmaking (1993). His inspired vision for what he has called an "evolving atlas" of home merits a full citation:

> Imagine this. In the town hall of your community a large atlas that describes "home" in a great variety of ways is prominently displayed. It has several hundred pages that depict layers of biophysical and cultural knowledge: climate, soils, flora and fauna, historic places, wind patterns, how much food was harvested by place and year, plus a summary of a host of related community experience. It is a well-worn tome, referred to continuously by local citizens. In the margins are penciled notes, adding new information to that which is already shown. Every year or so, your community updates the atlas, growing another layer to the collective understanding of the potentials and limits of place. On the evening that each new edition of the atlas is unveiled, Elders are invited to "speak" each map, adding stories to further animate the wisdom that the flat pages tell. These are songs, dances, and ribald stories, all relating to the occupation of a well-loved territory. It is entertainment and celebration on one level; on another, it is an absolutely critical validation of larger community potential and purpose. This is the role mapping plays in the bioregional vision.

While the above examples describe the potential and purposes of bioregional mapping, some examples of actual uses of bioregional maps will provide a real-life context. Again, bioregional tools often work in combination. Story, song, dance, and celebration – in conjunction with mapping – have been used together in a variety of ways in diverse settings.

Chicago bioregionalist Beatrice Briggs describes the organizing break-through brought about by the creation of a map for her urban "wild onion" bioregion. In 1989, the Wild Onion Alliance was born at a conference entitled Re-Inhabiting Chicago. For the first four years after forming, alliance members developed a slowly evolving description of their bioregion, but without a map they could not define the watershed context for where they lived. Finally, they developed a base map that served several purposes. It provided a base for a series of overlay thematic maps to show the surficial geology, the glacial moraines, the forest cover, wetlands, primary Indian settlements before the arrival of the Europeans, and the history of population growth and development since 1832. Moreover, by showing the entire watershed context of the Upper Illinois Valley, Briggs notes, the mapping process allowed people to identify how the Wild Onion Bioregion fit into that context and taught their group "some important lessons about the place we call home" (Aberley 1993, 21).

Toronto writer and bioregionalist Whitney Smith writes about the need for residents of that megalopolis to visualize their bioregion. Map images, Smith explains, can really help to "focus the urban sprawling mind" so that we can begin to get a contextualized vision of where we live. For Smith, each place requires pivot points or "coordinates" that define it in the minds of its citizens – the images, myths, songs, and stories that make up a "living culture ... that anchors commonality" (Aberley 1993). A bioregional mapping process of an urban region can help to reveal those coordinates. A bioregional map – in Smith's view – should help to "seed" the bioregional idea by producing a picture that evokes images of and identity with "home." Smith reports that, before his group was able to produce a map of the Oak Ridges Bioregion, an "enlightened federal commission" (the Crombie Commission on the Future of the Toronto Waterfront) produced a map of the Greater Toronto Bioregion, a map with the same boundaries as the Oak Ridges Bioregion. This region is bounded by the Oak Ridges Moraine on the north, the Niagara Escarpment on the west, the Trent River system on the east, and Lake Ontario on the south. This map included greenlands, Aboriginal sites, wildlife features, et cetera. Smith reported that the map was published in a local magazine and produced a "significant effect" on public awareness: "People began to understand that they didn't just live in a city. They realized that a bioregion was a place where many things were considered" (Aberley 1993, 22-23).

Several bioregional mapping projects have been started in British Columbia. The Southern Gulf Islands Bioregional Project produced a manual on bioregional mapping, *Giving the Land a Voice*, out of a workshop with Doug Aberley, Malcolm and Briony Penn, Kathy Reimer, and Michael Dunn (Aberley et al. 1995). They also sponsored an art exhibition, Mapping Cherished Island Places. Twenty artists submitted pieces, some of which were reproduced in the manual. Another mapping project is the Haida Nation's on Haida Gwaii off the coast of British Columbia. For the past few years, Aberley has been working for the Tsleil-Waututh Nation within the Salmonopolis Bioregion (the lower Fraser basin, British Columbia), mapping sacred and traditional use sites to support the nation's land rights in the joint federal-provincial-First Nations treaty settlement process.

Aberley speaks of implicit and explicit uses of bioregional mapping. Explicit bioregional mapping is when mappers explicitly use the term "bioregional" to apply to their maps. Aberley reports that, in addition to North America, there is explicit bioregional mapping now being done in many places in Britain. Explicit bioregional mapping is also being done in the Po River valley in Italy, in South Slovenia, by the Karen people in North Western Thailand, and by tribal people in Burma. For Aberley, the Tsleil-Waututh Nation's mapping is "the purest example of a First Nation melding its aspirations with this bioregional tool" (1999). The Tsleil-Waututh are using bioregional maps to tell the story of the past, present, and future of their traditional territory. They start with hand-drawn maps, and over time those maps become very sophisticated digital images. The whole process of making these bioregional maps takes place within their community.

In implicit bioregional mapping, the term "bioregional" is not used. For Aberley, the greatest implicit use of bioregional mapping is by tribal people doing land use and occupancy studies. Examples reported by Aberley include the Nisga'a, the Gitxsan, and the Inuit First Nations. Gitxsan mappers have borrowed Herb Hammond's community forest use and planning model (1991), adapting it to traditional Gitxsan sociocultural organization and resource values in a new, holistic Gitxsan model rooted in Gitxsan traditional ecological knowledge and worldview, whose "central understanding" is about the "need to respect and acknowledge the spirit within all things and people" (Pinkerton 1998). In this model, traditional kin groupings called Wilps (Houses) are considered to own and be responsible for resources in their local geographical territories.

There is a third category of mapping reported by Aberley that borrows from bioregional mapping, sometimes explicitly using the term "bioregion." It is done by some government agencies. However, Aberley critiques these "mainstream" uses, which appropriate a biogeographical definition of bioregion without adhering to any of the cultural values of bioregionalism: "It is just natural resource management with no socio-cultural dimension" (1999). He cites two examples (1999): first, the California Resources Agency's 1991 Memorandum of Understanding, a protocol for a number of federal and state agencies for resource management of the bioregions of California; second, the Canadian Royal Commission on the Future of the Toronto Waterfront final report *Regeneration* (1992), which published maps of the Greater Toronto Bioregion (see Figure 3).

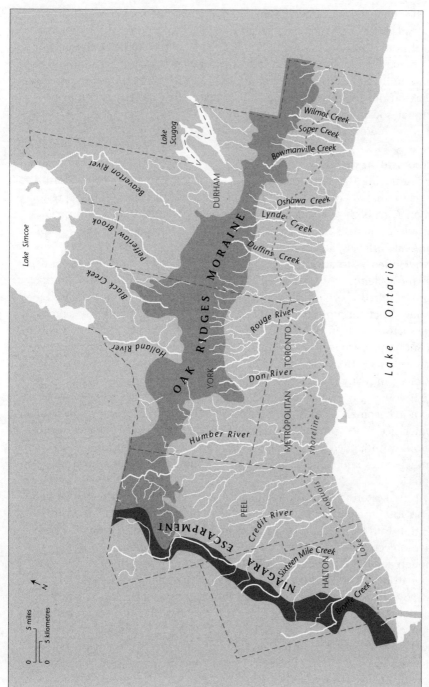

Figure 3 Map of the Greater Toronto Bioregion, modified from Royal Commission on the Future of the Toronto Waterfront, 1992.

The above visions of bioregional mapping promise to become an important social learning tool for a broad diversity of purposes: the popularization of the bioregional vision of home, kinship, and reciprocity; the shifting of popular consciousness from individualistic commodity consumption to community cooperation at living in place; and the visualization in popular consciousness of the long-term, intergenerational, bioregional strategy of cultural, social, and economic transformation (see Chapter 5 for an account of urban bioregional mapping).

Ecological Restoration

The Restoring the Earth conference held at the University of California, Berkeley, in 1988 marked the surfacing of a movement for ecological restoration with both scientific and popular components. Over 1,000 people, including scientists, consultants, students, environmentalists, youth groups, corporate officials, and "ordinary citizens" participated (Berger 1990). Topics included restoration of agricultural, forest, desert, and mined lands, aquatic systems, and strategic planning and land acquisition for restoration. Hundreds, perhaps thousands, of grassroots citizen groups engaged in a wide variety of projects to restore waterways. By 1989, there were almost 300 such projects in California alone. An Adopt-a-Stream model launched in Snohomish County, Washington, became a model for citizens in other states (Pollock 1989).

Today, in many cities across North America, thousands of citizen groups are involved in restoration activities and projects. Ecological restoration has also become a scientific discipline. Shortly after the Restoring the Earth conference, a new professional association, the Society for Ecological Restoration, was founded (Berger 1990). Many government agencies in both the United States and Canada now engage in numerous kinds of restoration work.

At the Restoring the Earth conference, ecological restoration was defined as an interdisciplinary approach to the benign or altruistic human intervention into biological processes toward restorative ends. However, others have objected to this definition on the basis that humans do not know enough about ecosystems or ecological processes or disturbance regimes to "fix nature." Chris Maser, a research scientist in natural history and ecology with over twenty years of experience, observes that "there is no such thing as reforestation ... We can't fix nature ... We can only put back pieces and allow nature to heal herself" (Andruss et al. 1990, 121). For Maser, management-oriented restoration is a mechanical concept dependent on knowledge that we don't have. Ecological sustainability, in contrast, is primarily an issue of managing ourselves (Maser 1992).

Restoration ecology, the process of restoring the land to health, is also "the process through which we become attuned with Nature, and through

Nature, with ourselves." Restoration ecology, therefore, is both the means and the end, for, "as we learn how to restore the land, we heal the ecosystem, and as we heal the ecosystem, we heal ourselves" (Maser 1988, 186). William Jordan III, the editor of *Restoration and Management Notes* and a founding member of the Society for Ecological Restoration, holds a similar view that places priority on the process of restoration and its ability to transform the human beings who inhabit and shape the landscape (Nilsen 1991). American writer Barry Lopez links ecological restoration's science dimension with both physical labour and spiritual renewal: "It is no accident that restoration work, with its themes of scientific research and spiritual renewal, suits a Western temperament so well. It offers the promise, moreover, of returning to us what we so persistently admire in indigenous cultures – a full physical, spiritual, and intellectual involvement with the Earth, and an emphasis on the primacy of human relationships over the accumulation of personal wealth" (in Nilsen 1991, 4-5).

Such views of restoration ecology are similar to a bioregional view of ecological restoration in which "restoration is, ultimately, a process of cultural change" (Daigle and Havinga 1996, 8). For bioregionalists, restoration work involves an embodied spiritual and intellectual engagement with the community of beings. This means that restoration work, in the bioregional movement, is not merely about natural science ecology but also about restoring our communities and our selves.

Freeman House, one of the original bioregional reinhabitants in the mid-1970s, has twenty-five years of practice in ecological restoration on a local watershed scale as an essential part of his practice of reinhabitation in his own watershed, the Mattole River Valley, on California's north coast. In 1995, at a conference of the Society for Ecological Restoration in Seattle, House proposed a merger between bioregional reinhabitation and ecological restoration. He called it a proposal of marriage: "The aspirations of reinhabitation and environmental restoration are entirely complementary and promise a synergistic adventure the particulars of which we can only begin to imagine." House argued that restoration projects that arise out of communities with reinhabitory goals provide the stimuli for reciprocal relationships that endure. The lessons learned from restoration projects – successes and failures – can provide "inhabitory peoples with the skills they need to pursue their cultural integration with local natural processes." Without the marriage, House added, any lessons learned often lie in government basements and with small numbers of restoration professionals. If the goal is cultural transformation, as it is for House, the most important work of ecological restoration lies always "in the vernacular life of local cultures." Such grassroots behaviour, House affirmed, is the only mechanism through which we might hope to attain self-regulation among groups of citizens who have extended their identities to include the surrounding life systems. The need for constant monitoring of ecological systems commonly stressed by professional restorationists can only be fulfilled by local residents: "Where else," House asked, "can we hope to find the systematic and enduring quality of attentiveness which this sort of observation requires, but through the informed eyes of residents of particular places who have learned that their daily lives are lived in the vastly dynamic and infinitely slow progressions of natural succession?" House also reminded the assembly that citizens' restoration groups are playing a role as important practitioners of the emerging sciences of restoration ecology and conservation biology as well as contributing to defining the goals of these new disciplines.

House, as a citizen practitioner and thinker, has become recognized in certain mainstream circles, often getting invitations to speak in academic and government venues. Speaking at the President's Council for Sustainable Development at Lake Tahoe in 1994, he argued that the initiative for restoration must come from citizens' grassroots work in their local watersheds. First, on the principle that, since human economic behaviour is the primary element in the destruction of biodiversity, "any picture of the future of ecological systems necessarily includes a scenario for how humans will act within any given landscape." Moreover, House argued, local allegiances and the unique character of local watershed ecological processes help to explain the fact that innovative leadership is already coming from grassroots groups since they are really the only people who can do the job on the ground. For House, "no amount of statistical analysis can replace daily observation and years of experience as a source of the detail necessary for site-specific sensitivity." In this view, ecological restoration is a process tool for primary use in civil society. Restoration work is community-building work, culture-changing work. For House, the community-building effect of ecological restoration projects is grounded in shared direct experience: "Shared visceral experience in projects like these can cut through the oversimplified ideological positions which had divided neighbors previously."

At the Fifth Shasta Bioregional Gathering in California, Restoring Our Watersheds, Our Communities, and Ourselves, in 1997, House expanded on the theme of community building through "hands-on" watershed restoration. He located the power of ecological restoration in what he called the particulars of place:

The beauty of "hands-on" watershed restoration is that it allows the place itself to become our teacher. As we engage in the particulars of our places, we begin to relearn how to live in a context that has always been there but in modern times become all but invisible. For myself, and I suspect it's true for a lot of you, I learned the importance of watersheds not from bureaucracies of scientists, but directly from salmon. Because watersheds were the

life-places of salmon, because salmon were important to us, watersheds became important as a unit of perception. (1997a)

House views the dominant US culture, where there has been a lack of
encouragement to learn either the skills or the benefits of community and
mutual aid, as the great barrier to cooperation and community building. He
locates this failing in the modern priority placed on skills of commerce and
trade. House refers to the growth of the culture of *homo economicus* reflected
in the changing meaning of the term "consumer," which only eighty years
ago had negative connotations of selfishness and wantonness (1996). For
House, it is "The Economy" and its "built-in strategy to create a global monoculture of consumers" that is a direct challenge to the survival and regeneration of local culture.

House locates his response within the process of reinhabitation, based on
his own long experience and that of his watershed community. For House,
restoration can act as a tool for building bioregional community:

Any serious move toward reinhabitation demands that we be inclusive,
which means each of us talking to people we don't necessarily like or who
don't like us. Those of us who are workers in the woods, fishers, school
teachers, shopkeepers, or ranchers need to be talking to each other. It is one
of the primary values of community-based watershed work that it provides
the occasion for this kind of communication to happen. As we work side by
side with people different than ourselves, we find a common teacher in the
place itself, in the particulars of our home landscape. And we discover that
this new context is much more conducive to the building of functional
community than the political processes that had previously separated us.
(1997a)

House concluded his talk at the Shasta Bioregional Gathering by affirming that its theme of "restoring our watersheds, our communities, and ourselves" is the spirit of restoration that we need to maintain as our ultimate
goal and to embody that spirit in our selves. House's view of restoration has
had much influence within the bioregional movement. In Chapter 5, I explore in more detail the effort of House and his coworkers in the Mattole
Valley to build reinhabitory community through ecological restoration.

Permaculture Design

Permaculture is a design philosophy and a "sister" movement of bioregionalism. Permaculture, an amalgam of "permanent" and "agriculture,"
is a word coined by Bill Mollison to refer to the development of what he
calls an interdisciplinary Earth science that he and David Holmgren created

in the early 1970s. Mollison defines permaculture as "the conscious design and maintenance of agriculturally productive ecosystems which have the diversity, stability, and resilience of natural ecosystems" (1990, ix). His definition includes the "harmonious integration of landscape and people providing their food, energy, shelter, and other material and non-material needs in a sustainable way" (ix). For Mollison, without permanent agriculture, there is no possibility of a stable social order. As a design system, permaculture is a "system of assembling conceptual, material, and strategic components in a pattern which functions to benefit life in all its forms" (ix). Permaculture, then, is a holistic design approach to sustainable human land use that is informed by an Earth-centred ecological philosophy.

For its originator and its growing numbers of practitioners, permaculture is as much about values and ethics as it is about design. Permaculture was founded upon "a philosophy of working with rather than against nature; of protracted and thoughtful observation rather than protracted and thoughtless action; of looking at systems and people in all their functions, rather than asking only one yield of them; and of allowing systems to demonstrate their own evolutions" (Mollison 1990, 3). The ethical basis of permaculture is care of the Earth (provision for all life systems to continue and multiply), care of people (provision for people to access those resources necessary to their existence), and setting limits to population and consumption (by governing our own needs, we can set resources aside to further the above principles).

Mollison believes that an ethic of caring for people complements and forms an integral part of an overall Earth care ethic. For him, associations of self-supporting species such as mycorrhizal fungi on tree roots (and other mutualisms in natural ecosystems) make healthy communities that humans can learn from to foster "an interdependence which values the individual's contributions rather than forms of opposition or competition." In this way, he explains, "we may evolve the mature ethic that sees all humankind as family, and all life as allied associations" (1990, 3). The fundamental ethic of interdependence and kinship espoused by bioregionalists is also central to permaculture. Indeed, some permaculturalists have begun to refer to permaculture gardens as "co-evolutionary kinship gardens" (Brentamar 1997). This means that with permaculture there is as great an effort to "grow" community as there is to grow food.

There is also a profound connection between the ethics of permaculture and a bioregional ecological restoration ethic. While permaculture focuses on already settled areas and agricultural lands, Mollison clearly affirms the interest of permaculture in conserving and maintaining natural systems for other species by taking a broader, landscape approach, one that uses land sparingly through a tight integration of food production and settlement: "One certain result of using our skills to integrate food supply and settlement ... will be to free most of the area of the globe for the rehabilitation of natural systems. These need never be looked upon as 'of use to people,' except in the very broad sense of global health" (1990, 6-7).

Permaculture implicitly fits well with the broader bioregional strategy of urban land use restoration and transformation described at the outset of this chapter. Mollison explicitly recognizes that, in order to supply our needs from existing settlements without the continued drawdown of immense quantities of natural capital resources from hinterlands far and near, we will have to govern our greed. For those in high-consumption societies, a cultural transformation away from the consumerism of *homo economicus* is integral to the vision and practice of permaculture.

Mollison's set of ethics on natural systems takes implacable and uncompromising opposition to further disturbance of any remaining natural forests (where most species are still in balance). This ethic includes vigorous rehabilitation of degraded and damaged natural systems to stable states. It demands the establishment of plant systems for our own use on the least amount of land we can use for our existence and the establishment of plant and animal refuges for rare or threatened species. Therefore, permaculture design focuses primarily on using the least amount of land that we can use for our own existence.

Permaculture design was developed initially on Mollison's own extensive theoretical and experiential knowledge of ecosystems. However, twenty years of developing as a "hands-on" civil society movement in both Australia and North America have added substantially to the diverse dimension of knowledge gained through permaculture praxis in place.

In one sense, permaculture is a practical design tool kit for bioregional reinhabitation on an individual site, in a small watershed, or on a neighbourhood scale. On the question of geographical scale, Mollison has pointed out that permaculture is an attempt to return to systems of small gardens in order to produce food for humans. Large-scale, chemical-based agriculture, he argues, actually produces far less human food than we are led to believe, and it does so in an ecologically destructive manner. In some countries, such as Russia, Mollison claims, gardens already produce 90 percent of the food. Permaculture design was originally conceived by Mollison as a response to the mess created by industrial agriculture, which he believes is "the most destructive activity on the face of the earth" (Permaculture Association of Western Australia 1996, 7).

At the fifth continental bioregional gathering, participants described permaculture as a "shed of tools" to assist communities to reinhabit their bioregions. Indeed, the elements of permaculture design encompass a total approach. Mollison outlines four major components: site components such as plants, soil, landscape, water, and climate; social components, including people, culture, and legal/financial structures; energy components,

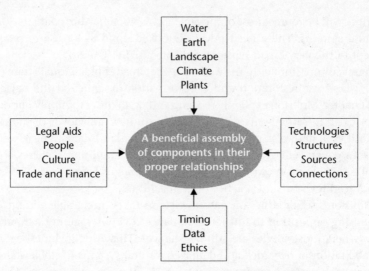

Figure 4 Elements of a total design; adapted from Mollison 1990.

including sources, linkages, technologies, and structures; and "abstract" components such as time, ethics, and information (see Figure 4).

At the heart of permaculture design strategy is what Mollison has called "entropy strategy." Entropy is dissipated energy. As we know from the second law of thermodynamics, the total entropy of the universe is increasing. Or, put another way, the universe is slowly running down. However, life systems constantly organize "against" entropy. Life creates complex storages from diffuse energy and materials, accumulating, decomposing, building, and transforming them for further use. As open systems, life systems make use of energy in many ways before it dissipates, building neg-entropy or essergy. Mollison's entropy strategy in his permaculture design process emulates life systems' strategies for dealing with entropy.

For example, instead of just leaving manure on a field to compost, we can first ferment it, distil out the alcohol, and then route the waste through a biogas digester in which anaerobic organisms convert it to methane (useful for a cooking or heating gas or as vehicle fuel). Next, the liquid effluent can be sent to fields for fertilizer and the solid sludge fed to worms, which convert it to rich horticultural soil. Finally, the worms themselves can be used to feed fish or poultry. This is just one of many examples supplied by Mollison.

Permaculture design principles can be used at several scales from the home garden to entire cities. Currently, cities are open systems that contribute to increased entropy by dissipating energy and material brought in from elsewhere. A permaculture design strategy for a city would emulate open living systems' strategies for building essergy by catching and storing energy in multiple ways before it dissipates to an unusable entropic level.

Nutrient cycling provides another lesson. For Mollison, a "cycle" is an interruption or eddy in the straight-line progression toward entropy. In a tropical forest, for example, almost all material nutrients are in cycle in life forms. Mollison regards cycles as niches in time, analogous to ecological niches in space: "If niches are opportunities in space, cycles are opportunities in time (a time-slot) and both together give harbour to many events and species" (1990, 23). So, in permaculture, unlike agriculture, the concept of yield is limited not to one crop but to the system as a whole. For Mollison, every cyclic event increases the opportunity for yield. In this sense, to increase cycling is to increase yield: "Cycles in nature are diversion routes away from entropic ends – life itself cycles nutrients – giving opportunities for yield, and thus opportunities for species to occupy time niches" (1990, 23).

The permacultural movement and the bioregional movement have developed as parallel streams over a similar time period. However, from the first continental bioregional congress in North America, permaculture has also been a part of the bioregional movement. Since then, the interest in permaculture and the integration of the two movements have continued.

Permaculture, then, like ecological restoration, is another tool for building communities of place. Bioregionalists view permaculture as a method or set of tools to connect a human kinship ethic with an ecological kinship ethic in "co-evolutionary kinship gardens." Social capital and ecosocial capital formation are linked in permacultural approaches to land use design. Like ecological restoration, embodied "learn by doing" permaculture methods, used in the practice of reinhabitation, are seen as an effective way to acquire knowledge of the integration of social and ecological kinship. Moreover, with permaculture design, growing food becomes another method of growing a community of beings while reducing human energy and material throughput. Using permaculture design, then, ecosocial capital grows, while human use of natural capital decreases. This is exactly the opposite of resource use in the neoliberal global economy, which is always seeking to expand the use of natural capital (limited only by the imagination of economic man), while globalized market relations of exchange intervene in the relationship between rooted cultures and their diversified local food production, effectively decreasing ecosocial capital (see also Chapter 6).

Bioregional Education and Community

We have seen in Chapter 3 that the process of bioregional education is understood by bioregional educators (and bioregionalists generally) as one of direct, experiential learning through active participation and sharing within the human community as an integral part of the Earth community. In one important sense, then, education, from a bioregional perspective, is viewed as a process of sharing.

All bioregional education is founded on learning directly about and from local ecologies: the climates, geologies, landforms, watersheds, soils, native plants and animals, as well as local cultures, histories, and current affairs. This is the core, embodied learning in place. Bioregional education is also founded on a broad Earth-centred ethic and a vision of long-term sustainability of the Earth community. Bioregional education is thus rooted both in place and in planetary ethical concerns. One curriculum outcome of this broader ethic, as bioregional educator Sharilyn Calliou has expressed it, is that bioregional education should create and promote "curriculum theory and materials grounded in a responsible land ethic which motivates social and political transformations" (Traina and Darley-Hill 1995, 67). Such a sweeping ethic demands enormous commitment. What, then, are the methods of bioregional education to address this ambitious curriculum outcome?

There are two major forms that bioregional education promotes: one is the use (or development) of schools and learning centres as community institutions, embedded in their local communities through outreach programs into their local neighbourhoods; the other is educational projects that take place outside the formal school system altogether.

One goal of bioregional education with respect to human community, Calliou argues, is to address the "deep human yearning we have to live in community in socially and ecologically healthy ways" (Traina and Darley-Hill 1995, 69). In bioregional education, learning about both our human community and our ecological community is a process of learning by doing. The focus for this grounded process is everyday life and place. For bioregionalists, there is no separation of learning from life. Whether carried on within formal school institutions or outside them, the method of bioregional education with respect to community building is to learn about community – together – through the experience of living and working in a community. Schools and learning are thus seen by bioregional educators as integral parts of the experience of building community.

In bioregional education, another essential method is to encourage the student to experience personally the energy of the interconnected web of life that is the Earth community and to experience a direct sense of kinship with it. Bioregional educator Frank Traina has written that in bioregional education "a personal relationship with nature is of primary importance especially as it includes a sense of caring" (Traina and Darley-Hill 1995, 93). For Traina, the fundamental problem of education with respect to the natural world is the lack of respectful feelings and values about nature. One central goal of bioregional education, Traina argues, is "to bring back romance into our relationship with nature" (Traina and Darley-Hill 1995, 95). This is an open recognition of the strength of romanticism, the reintegration of bodily senses, emotions, and intellect; but, Traina insists, this experience must occur with real plants and animals in real time in real places.

One excellent example of bioregional education outside the formal school system is found at Sunrock Farm outside Cincinnati. There Frank Traina has established a program of bioregional education for schoolchildren that deals with connecting with the natural world through a direct experience of farm life in combination with artistic and wilderness experiences. The totality of the experiences in the program is designed to encourage the child's knowledge and feeling of being connected to, being interdependent with, and having affinity for the natural world. At Sunrock Farm, the method is to allow the child to personally experience this flow of materials and energy. Traina calls this method "the art of enfolding" (Traina and Darley-Hill 1995, 92). This means that "nature" is both without us and within us. Traina explains that when we enfold the things of nature within us we expand our egos and grow outward. The art of enfolding, then, is knowing how to introduce the child to the wonders of nature. The concept of enfolding is another way to express what I have been calling bonding with the natural world, the sense of ecological kinship.

The "Guide for Teaching at Sunrock" explains clearly how bonding works:

> At Sunrock Farm children personally meet a few of their Earth-family members, and they do things with them. The farm is rich in sensory and emotional contact. They milk a goat, bottle feed kids, touch the pigs, feed goats and cattle, gather eggs, handle chicks, plant seeds, eat and smell plants, and so on. This is done safely and with joy. While it may look like we are merely entertaining the children, we are actually introducing them to other members of the Earth community. For most of our visitors this may be the first time they have ever met a real pig, cow, chicken, goose, sheep, goat, turkey, and our friends the (living) vegetables. And unlike in a visit to the Zoo, they can get to know the animals in a more personal way ... A farm tour helps to develop what Thomas Berry calls "inter-species bonding." (Traina and Darley-Hill 1995, 99-100)

Interspecies bonding is essentially direct, embodied, emotional experience of the community of beings. The Sunrock Farm program has also had considerable influence on the teachers. Traina (1994) reports that, once a teacher brings her students to the farm, she will keep coming back with more students for many years.

These contextualized examples of bioregional community- and alliance-building tools show that intent and use of the tools place cultural change at the geographical scale of home and small watershed community at the centre of a broader (in both social and geographical terms) bioregional strategy of transformation. Bioregionalists' self-understanding of their strategy for building community reflects a deep commitment to integrating cultural transformation into the centre of their efforts at broader social change in civil society. Clearly, if there are lessons for the Cohen and Arato theory of societal transformation, they are to be found in this culturally oriented bioregional praxis. Certainly, the horizontal character of the webs of relations that bioregional activists are building is clearly indicated. So far, we have seen that this is a movement acting primarily within the sphere of civil society, targeting other peers on issues of cultural, geographical, and ecological identity, encompassing democratic values of equality, cooperation, and collaboration, and seeking to engender respect for difference and reciprocity in building relations across difference.

Several points stand out. First, the community of beings ethic is a central spiritual resource for bioregionalists. Such ecological kinship is experienced viscerally and emotionally as well as intellectually, and that is the point about these tools. It is one thing to examine the community of beings as a bioregional ethic, but the tools are designed to stimulate and facilitate a holistic lived experience of the community of beings. Their use is intended for just this purpose, whether it be consensus process, ecological restoration, permaculture design, Earth ritual and ceremony, and so on. Even undoing "isms" workshops and alliance-building methods (with more strictly "social" goals) include something of this aspect of ecosocial capital. The abundance of joy and well-being from their lived experiences of the community of beings is a great resource for these individuals. Such intense experience is a potentially great source or wellspring of motivation for ecosocial capital formation that merits further exploration. In this light, the "breakthrough" potential from economic man to the ecosocial being of the community of beings holds promise for helping individuals to rethink their lives based on the growth of commodity consumption in the global neoliberal marketplace.

Second, consensus process, reevaluation counselling, and undoing "isms" workshops (tools that focus on interhuman problems), as used and understood by bioregionalists, reveal the centrality of trust as a factor in social capital formation and link it with the horizontal character of social capital bonds. This is important because it supports the argument of Robert Putnam on the horizontal nature of social capital, an argument that has been criticized by a World Bank study that argues in defence of vertical bonds for social capital (Grootaert 1998). Indeed, it appears that vertical relationships characterized by hierarchy and dependency prevent or undermine experiences of trust and mutual cooperation that work to build social capital. Moreover, in bioregionalists' use of consensus, trust is sometimes associated with feelings of love. In bioregional discourse on consensus, both trust and love are repeatedly identified as potentially powerful horizontal bonding agents in social capital formation. Trust, especially when accompanied by feelings of love, is thus identified as a potentially powerful motivation for the horizontal formation of social and ecosocial capital.

Third, as the example of the "breaking through" ritual illustrates, the lived experience of ecological kinship can transcend the narrowly conceived "Eurocentric self," in the process connecting not only with other phenomena but also with the relational "ecological self." As noted, this experience releases an abundance of energy, joyful energy, that I identified as an important source of empowerment for the individual psyche (just as James Coleman's social capital acts as a resource for individuals). Here is great potential for replacing the experience of materialistic commodity consumption with the profoundly spiritual (and embodied) experience of the community of beings.

Fourth, ecosocial capital includes and integrates social capital when permaculture, ecological restoration, story, Earth ritual, or bioregional education are practised in groups, as the contextualized examples in this chapter have indicated. This too requires further exploration and analysis.

Fifth, to this point in the story, the vertical dimension of the bioregional strategy is mentioned but clearly not developed beyond the initial outline of a long-term transitional vision. Bioregional praxis in several communities and at the continental gatherings and congresses must be examined in the next two chapters to glean a fuller understanding of bioregionalists' communication and bridge-building work in the political and economic spheres.

And sixth, there is the question of the tools themselves. Do the tools work? Do they help to form social and ecosocial capital? From the examples discussed in this chapter, it is clear that, for the bioregional actors involved, these tools do work to facilitate certain lived experiences of synergistic spiritual resources – joy, trust, and love – as motivating energies. Moreover, the examples are compelling in that they illustrate emergent, but deeply held, beliefs on the part of the bioregional actors. However, as we have seen, bioregionalism is a diverse movement with many different lived experiences. To better establish the case across the movement, the following two chapters report on more examples in a variety of contexts.

Cure for the Common Car

The cure for the common car is
buildings as mountains
legs flowering

edible keyhole gardens
rounding the corners
calming intersections

skyscraping skyfilters of rain
seen from above
all green

feeding waterfall dispersals
through vaults down under
lights going downward to free
O solar light or moon come full

sky above bunchgrass
respirating roots
to very berried canopies

so life-scaleable
from the beginning
1904 at 72nd Street
letting the sun sink in

where city
meets
its country self.

– Coco Gordon

5
Narrative Accounts of Reinhabitation in Rural and Urban Settings

Introduction

Both the long-term strategy and the tools used for community building associated with the bioregional movement are pursued in this chapter through an exploration of bioregional praxis in three rural and two urban settings until 1999. As we saw in Chapter 4, there is already compelling evidence that the bioregional strategy is located in the sphere of civil society and that it is primarily a "horizontal" strategy. However, bioregional local praxis "in place" is also beginning to develop corresponding vertical strategies in at least the political sphere as well. The bioregional political economic strategy adopted at the congresses takes on varied expressions in particular places.

Each of these settings is, of course, unique. Each has its own local set of natural and cultural contexts and particular history. The ways and means that bioregionalists have adopted and adapted to their special circumstances are also unique. As noted, the tools discussed in Chapter 4 can be employed in many ways, in different circumstances, and in different combinations with each other. Moreover, not all of the tools will necessarily be employed by each group or each community of bioregional reinhabitants.

Human experience takes place both in time and in geographical space. The phenomena that I am exploring here are best revealed as stories in time and place. The narrative accounts in the next two chapters are grounded in geography, in both a phenomenology of place and an existential or experiential sociology. These accounts into bioregionalists' experiences and their meanings for practitioners are also bioregional narratives and as such are inclusive of various and multiple voices (Cheney 1989), not merely that of the narrator. The stories make use of "thick descriptions" to throw light on the experiences and their meanings and to keep theorizing close to the empirical ground. My goal here is also to lead the reader vicariously into the experiences being investigated, into the details, nuances, and multiple dimensions of the phenomena.

Rural Community Building

Many bioregional experiences of community building are those of people who have left the cities to join the back-to-the-land movement of the late 1960s and 1970s. Most often these ex-urban people carried with them broader planetary concerns that have not been forgotten in their return to the land. Indeed, bioregionalists have spent considerable time and effort locating their reinhabitory experiences in broader social and geographical contexts, organizing for broader sociocultural transformation.

Actually implementing bioregional communities is not easy. In the preface to one of several story collections of rural reinhabitation, Judith Plant remarks that stories of bioregional community building are not "polyanna" tales promising utopia but substantive information on a variety of lived experiments in building local community, including the struggle against personal alienation and emotional damage from a patriarchal system of "power-over" (Forsey 1993). Building community and a networked movement of communities in modern, industrial societies – particularly in North America – where alienation, fragmentation, and depletion of healthy community life has been taking place for generations is readily acknowledged by bioregionalists as a very difficult process. From their direct experience, bioregional reinhabitants recognize that reciprocity and kinship, horizontal relations of information, trust, solidarity, mutual aid, and mutual empowerment do not come easily to peoples who have never known them or have experienced them only in weak, fragmented, and occasional ways. Helen Forsey, who lives in a small intentional rural community, recognizes the formidable challenges to community building. She locates their cause not in some ahistorically universalized "human nature" but in distorted attitudes and alienated behaviour cultivated by an "unnatural and oppressive" society (1993, 6-7).

In spite of the difficulties, a diverse store of experience with building small, face-to-face, bioregional communities has been gained over the past twenty-five years. The following three rural stories illustrate the use of consensus process, circles, story, bioregional mapping, ecological restoration, bioregional education, and/or ritual and ceremony. In addition, all three narratives illustrate the central role of cultural transformation in bioregional praxis, approaches that reach out not only to the strictly local community but also beyond it to the broader society at the (bio)regional and even continental scales.

The Mattole Restoration Council

The Mattole River Valley in northern California is an incredibly beautiful place. The watershed, in the Klamath-Siskiyou bioregion, covers an area of more than 300 square miles. The river, sixty-four miles long, flows roughly parallel to the coast never more than twenty miles from it, until it bends and empties into the Pacific near Cape Mendocino. In the late-August afternoon, as you approach the valley from the north along one of three highways into it, the fog that inundates most of northern California lifts to reveal rolling hills of coastal prairie land. The high dramatic rocks of Cape Mendocino block the fog, leaving the lower few miles of the Mattole bathed in golden California sunshine. It is just south of this point that the river meets the sea. The cape rocks; the golden undulating hills; the wide, long, gently sweeping beach; and the pounding white surf surging and spilling across the black sands present a powerful and stark beauty. The watershed itself receives 80 to 200 inches of rainfall per annum, while Arcata not far to the north receives only 30. The King Range of mountains rises higher than the surrounding hills of the Coast Range. They thus form the first landfall for storms from the Pacific.

Euro-Americans did not settle in the watershed until 1857. Within five years, most of the Mattole and Sinkyone peoples who inhabited the Mattole watershed had been killed or removed from the watershed to the Round Valley and Hoopa Reservations a hundred miles away to the north and southeast. This local holocaust was an "acting out" of the Euro-American doctrine of Manifest Destiny, "so rapidly and violently as to effect a nearly total break in the cultural continuity of the human presence" (House 1999, 175). The Euro-American pioneers initially drawn by the Gold Rush worked hard to convert the landscape into sheep and cattle ranches when the gold fever subsided, but the Mattole was on the remote north coast, and their numbers were few. Perhaps because of its relative remoteness even well into the twentieth century, the Mattole watershed did not attract large numbers of settlers until a large influx of countercultural, back-to-the-landers started about 1968. They quickly tripled the population to around 2,000 people.

David Simpson, formerly of the San Francisco Mime Troupe, was among those who went to the Mattole to homestead. He arrived just in time for the last of the rich salmon runs. Soon afterward, the fish runs rapidly dwindled to the point where the salmon population of the Mattole was endangered due to erosion caused by logging, overgrazing, and too many poorly built roads. When I visited Simpson and his partner, Jane Lapiner, he told me the story of the valley erosion that led to siltation of the Mattole, changing the ecology of the watershed.

In 1948, improved technology from World War II tanks adapted to forestry resulted in an unrestrained rush for Mattole timber, which formerly had been too remote and too difficult to log commercially. It was not until 1948 as well that electricity came to the Mattole. Then, in a forty-year period, 91 percent of the old-growth coniferous forest was removed. A lot of the original logging was done by "wildcatters" from Oregon, but some valley people also participated. The heavy winter rains, steep terrain, and logging led to heavy erosion and flooding. In 1955, a flood washed away the

Mattole's riparian forest. Again in 1964 and 1965, floods and continued logging caused more soil erosion. The silting of the river filled up the pools and spawning areas. Simpson and I discussed the role that civilization played in wasting soils, in particular the work of Edward Hyams on the role of several civilizations in the Mediterranean in wasting soil and thereby undermining their basis of existence. Simpson remarked that, in the Mattole Valley, the process was much quicker: "They rewrote the history of civilization in forty years" (1989).

It was not until 1975 that the logging industry was required to replant. Early efforts to restore a silver salmon run in Mill Creek were begun in 1978 by Simpson and a few others. They began to see salmon as an indicator species for a healthy watershed. In 1979, a friend of Simpson's, Freeman House, moved into the valley to homestead. House had worked with the Planet Drum group and had known Peter Berg as far back as the 1967 "summer of love" in San Francisco. Now Simpson and House are next-door neighbours in the Mattole Valley. I spoke at length with House in 1989 about his experience.

In the late 1960s, House came to understand that – in Western culture – a whole range of experiences had "been removed from us" – basic life experiences such as childbirth, death, and food. This realization led him to "attempt to experience real food." House acquired a fishing boat in order to provide primary production for the "free food" systems that the diggers had set up in San Francisco. For many years, he fished, working in Puget Sound in the Pacific Northwest and in Alaska.

In 1973, House read Michael Perlman's energetics analysis of US agriculture and then applied Perlman's methods to analyze his own fishing operation. He was able to determine that in chasing salmon around the ocean he was using more energy measured in calories than was coming out of the catch. Ironically, House observed, the salmon return from the ocean to congregate in their home rivers' mouths just at the time of their cycle when they are at the height of their strength and are most nutritious for eating. As a fisherman, House was easily able to relate these ecological considerations with an understanding that, in the market system, the fishermen were under the control of the canners, who financed their boats and were therefore able to dictate prices to them. Huge commercial hatcheries had taken control of the industry with "little or no provision" made for the wild salmon populations or their spawning grounds and habitats. House was frustrated by this situation. As he saw it, "efforts to assist the wild salmon population by improving natural spawning grounds are resisted by interests connected with construction contracts for new and enormously expensive hatcheries." All these considerations, in addition to his work with Planet Drum, eventually motivated House to change his life plans. He gave up fishing and moved to the Mattole Valley to engage in salmon enhancement and habitat restoration.

In 1979, soon after House moved to the Mattole, Simpson, House, and a small group of others began an effort, on a small scale, to propagate salmon. They eventually formed the Mattole Salmon Group. After a year and a half of negotiations with the Department of Fish and Game, they received a permit to trap small numbers of Mattole salmon. The technology that they used was extremely simple hatchbox systems – "backyard incubators" – always located near someone's home so they could be checked daily. The incubators run on gravity-fed creek water, involving no electricity. The young salmon fry are released into the wild after they've been given a chance to grow to the point where they are able to survive.

It was not long before the small group realized that, to save the salmon run, they first had to restore the entire watershed. House reflects on the group's early experience: "As soon as you get into salmonid enhancement, you recognize in a real concrete way the indicator species nature of the beast. And you realize that you can't restore natural systems by putting fish back into water. All you're doing is building yourself into a permanent interfering sort of relationship with natural systems" (Plant and Plant 1990, 107-8).

For the salmon trappers, restoring the watershed also meant recognizing the need for a structure to hold themselves accountable to the whole community. For House, this is an example of how salmon inform, and thereby help to organize, human activity.

For Simpson too, salmon restoration "prepared the way" for watershed restoration. Simpson explained to me that within the human community in the Mattole Valley it worked because everybody loved the salmon: ranchers, loggers, and homesteaders. And, as more women got involved with the "business" of salmon enhancement, Simpson recalled that the process became more celebrative, and "suddenly you were dealing in culture, in how to live" (1989).

The small group of salmon enhancers grew, and in 1983 they and a number of local watershed groups formed the Mattole Restoration Council (MRC). At the outset, the goals of the council were to improve the inhabitants' knowledge of the watershed, to identify the most important restoration projects, and to build a community of self-conscious restorationists.

The MRC is composed of several member groups, including the Mattole Salmon Group, the Mattole Valley Community Center, Petrolia High School, the Sanctuary Forest, the Soil Bankers, several creek watershed associations, and a range of individual members. The MRC engages in salmon enhancement and monitoring, reforestation, inventory mapping, stream bank restoration, road removal and restoration, monitoring all timber harvest plans, interfacing with government agencies and bureaus, as well as organizing cultural, educational, and social activities in the valley.

Here we see an example of one type of organization for community used by bioregionalists, the neighbourhood or village level where people already living in close proximity to each other begin to question the ecological basis of their own existence and then seek to build a basis of unity for social and cultural change. In this case, the "neighbourhood" (or district) scale is the local watershed of the Mattole River. A number of local "seed groups," the Mattole Salmon Group, the Soil Bankers, and the Sanctuary Forest group, joined with other local organizations to form a watershed-wide council with an initial basis of unity. The small seed group of salmon enhancers had networked with others to further the interests of the watershed as a whole. From the outset, one key goal of the MRC was to "build a community of restorationists" (House 1989). Their effort was not to be merely a functionalist approach to repairing a watershed but to be a social experiment in cultural change. By one important measure (the growing network itself), social capital was being created.

The MRC's first project was an inventory of salmonid habitat throughout the entire watershed. With the help of a local fisheries biologist, twenty valley people walked 260 miles of the Mattole and its tributaries to map salmon habitat. They were able to locate impediments to salmon migration upstream, to determine the extent and condition of spawning habitat, and to begin addressing these problems. Antisiltation efforts were launched by building log weirs and gravel beds, planting eroded shorelines and landslides, stabilizing stream banks with small rocks and mortar, et cetera. The MRC also began to take annual surveys of stream cross-sections at numerous points on the Mattole and inventoried the main sources of sedimentation. The council saw the watershed as a geographical unit that all residents could easily identify with and take responsibility for. Council members sought and received funding from both government and private sources. Soon they were able to afford to pay some of their workers. They envisioned that restoration work could become a significant part of the local economy, especially in light of Humbolt County's then 25 percent unemployment rate.

Bioregional education has been used in the Mattole to complement the work of restoration. Petrolia High School was founded in 1984 as an alternative school run by the valley people themselves. For ten years, it was the only high school in the watershed. David Simpson served on the board. The students studied Earth and life sciences. Hands-on restoration work was a central part of their program. The staff were both teachers and activists. They led children on backpacking trips exploring the watershed. They also started a theatre group that toured other regional high schools, helping to educate the students there about ecological restoration issues. In addition, they founded a dance group, the Feet First Dancers, which engaged in cultural, educational performances. For Simpson, "the restoration of culture must go hand in hand with the restoration of natural systems" (1989).

Today, the original Petrolia High no longer operates. However, the new high school run by the state has adopted many of the innovative programs launched by Petrolia High. The elementary school in the valley, a state-run school, has also involved children in the salmon enhancement program.

Bioregional mapping is another tool used in the Mattole in conjunction with restoration and education. In 1988, the MRC undertook an extensive mapping project of the entire watershed to determine the exact locations of remnant old-growth stands. Using a combination of aerial photographs and the efforts of some 200 volunteers, it completed the project and produced a map that it then compared with a US Forest Service map, based on 1947 aerial photographs. The MRC published both maps side by side. The maps revealed in graphic form the huge loss in old-growth forest between 1947 and 1988 (see Figures 5 and 6).

The maps were a key part of a broad public education project in the Mattole Valley aimed at watershed restoration. The two juxtaposed maps were sent to all 2,000 residents of the watershed. After the maps were published, many more valley people became involved in restoration work and in the battle for the preservation of the remaining old-growth stands. Hundreds of local people got into the work of restoration. Residents came to know their own watershed more intimately through a "learn by doing" approach to ecological restoration.

The project also provided local people with a political tool to face decision makers and a collective sense of empowerment. House comments on this dynamic: "Politically, the watershed information gives you real ammunition to deal with political entities: federal, state, and county. Often it's simply a matter of embarrassment – that you know more than they do. Sometimes it's more a technical matter of having reorganized the information into a format that makes managerial sense. And none of the official entities have yet bothered to do that. An awful lot of this information is emerging through the grass-roots" (Plant and Plant 1990, 108-9).

The campaign achieved an important victory, a manifestation of local empowerment. Illegal logging in the "Sanctuary Forest" (900 acres of unlogged coast redwood and Douglas-fir at the headwaters of the Mattole) was halted by a blockade of 150 local residents, including some from the MRC. The maps also enabled the MRC to provide clear evidence, for loggers especially, why there was not much work left in the woods (recall that no one was required to replant until 1975).

The MRC updated its old-growth map in 1997 from records of timber harvest plans since 1988. The map depicts which tracts of old growth have

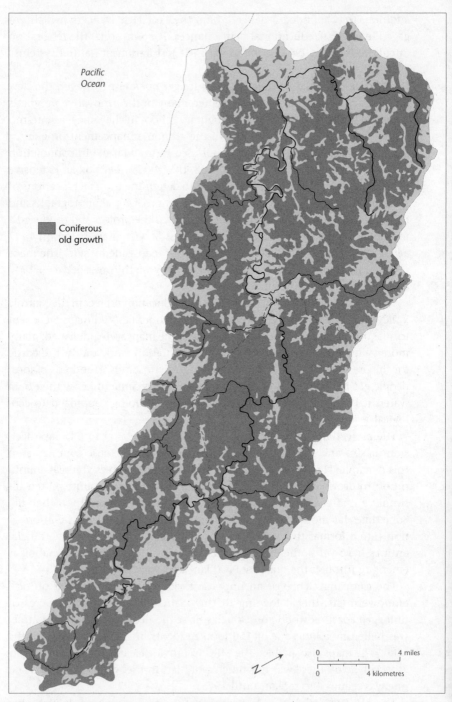

Pacific
Ocean

Coniferous
old growth

0   4 miles

0   4 kilometres

Figure 5 Distribution of old-growth coniferous forests in the Mattole River
Watershed, 1947; map by Eric Leinberger.

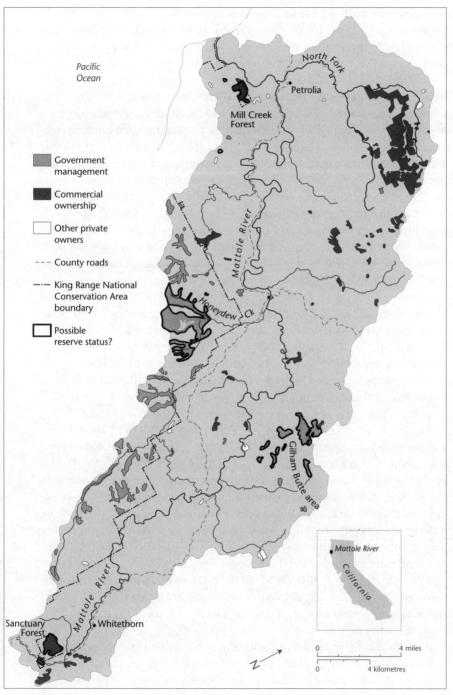

Figure 6 Distribution of old-growth coniferous forests in the Mattole River Watershed, 1988; map by Eric Leinberger.

been cut since 1988, which have been protected, and which are the subject of pending plans. One considerable success in this respect is the protection of old-growth forests since the first mapping project in 1988. The new mapping process helped the MRC to show that, of the 9 percent of old-growth habitat identified in 1988, none of which was in protected status, two-thirds were now fully protected as an ecological reserve (House 1997b). The 1997 mapping project also helps to clarify current MRC strategic restoration goals, which focus on identifying areas for priority protection based on their condition as high-quality habitat or refugia; the presence or absence of salmon and steelhead; water quality; and special features that residents and landowners believe to be high-priority areas for protection (Zuckerman 1997). In all, 3,700 acres of temperate rainforest habitat in the Mattole headwaters now have protected status. This amount includes seven salmon and steelhead tributary streams and all the old-growth forest in the headwaters (House 1998). The "Sanctuary Forest" in the headwaters is home to the mountain lion and the black bear and is a refugia for the endangered tailed frog, the northern goshawk, the torrent salamander, and coho salmon.

Sanctuary Forest, a nonprofit member group of the MRC, has steered the process of protecting the headwaters. Sanctuary Forest acts as a land trust, negotiating land purchases, sales, and trades; helping to establish conservation easements; and acquiring core area old growth, wildlife corridors, and riparian (or stream-side) habitat. Its members also engage in trail building to allow human participation in the reserve without compromising habitat. They run educational and recreational hiking programs, led by guides trained by Sanctuary Forest in forest ecology, Mattole history, and tour guiding.

The Soil Bankers (a.k.a. the Mattole Forest and Rangeland Cooperative), another member association of the MRC, planted 300,000 seedlings on contracts with the US Bureau of Land Management since 1986 on the 60,000-acre King Range National Conservation Area that comprises 10 percent of the Mattole Valley. They also planted thousands more with the MRC Reforestation Program and engaged in erosion control projects in the Mattole watersheds. Overall, the MRC has been a valuable resource for the valley people, supplying information on gully repair, revegetation, road problems, and road building and general advice on erosion problems. Several tributary groups of residents also formed in the creek watersheds to handle problems specific to their creeks. With hundreds now participating in the restoration work and new creek groups starting up, social capital has been building in the Mattole.

The MRC envisions a practice whereby small forest enterprises produce softwood and hardwood products while improving timber stands through ecologically based forestry. This practice is integrated with the preservation of all remaining old-growth stands and the provision of good water and fish and wildlife habitat. Many residents in the valley have come to see the crucial connection between preserving old growth and restoring salmon runs. House observes that restoration activity in the Mattole taught participants the necessity of what he calls "preventative restoration" (1997b).

While much of the work of the MRC has been carried out by volunteers, the paid work of the council has also grown over the years. By 1995, the annual budget of the council was close to $350,000. Well over 90 percent of income was generated by contracts, while less than 6 percent came from grants and donations (Dulas 1996). This suggests good potential for economic as well as ecological sustainability with the economic activity embedded in ecological and cultural restoration work.

The work of the Mattole Salmon Group and the Mattole Watershed Council has had a definite effect on the valley's culture. House (1989) recalled that, in the Mattole watershed, a certain cultural shift had already begun by the end of the 1980s. By then, many people in the valley had become familiar with the new language of restoration and had come to expect to hear it spoken. It was becoming part of their language. Public education projects contributed to the shift in values: public education work with the valley's schools through ongoing theatre performances, the Adopt-a-Watershed program involving students in the work of salmon enhancement, and a video about restoration work in the Mattole. As well, the Mattole Salmon Group began setting up hatchboxes in several local classrooms for hands-on experience with salmon eggs and fingerlings.

The Mattole Valley Community Center, founded in 1976, is another part of the MRC. It holds many community events, such as fund-raising cabarets and activities for preschoolers, and is available to valley residents for low rental rates. Popular theatre has also developed in the valley. In addition to being reinhabitants, David Simpson and his partner, Jane Lapiner, are experienced theatre people. They have collaborated with others in Mattole Valley stage productions and a travelling theatre company that occasionally tours the West Coast. The company has produced theatre pieces such as *Queen Salmon* and *The Wolf at the Door*, a musical comedy written by Simpson about the reintroduction of wolves into the wilds and poor, disenfranchised people in the "wild" urban landscape.

The Mattole Salmon Group understood from the beginning that making a difference in a watershed as heavily impacted as the Mattole was going to be a project of decades if not generations. Thus, the members persisted with their efforts even when stocks of chinook and coho continued to decline for ten years after initiating their hatchbox program. Since the low ebb in 1990, however, stocks have started a slow comeback. The program of the Salmon Group and the entire MRC has since become a model for the Pacific Northwest for how to undertake restoration and management of resources of an entire watershed and how local residents themselves can run a multidisciplinary, complex, and effective restoration program.

House sees restoration as a key means of communication and bonding through the common experience of sharing the work in the watershed. Working together in creek restoration groups provides "common experiential information" (Plant and Plant 1990, 110). The watershed itself provides some of this common information. Working together, people get to know each other better. Shared information is a key ingredient in building levels of trust. Common experiential information about each other and about the watershed – acquired while working together – enhances this effect. Information and trust levels build up; norms of cooperation and civic solidarity are developed. If this continues over time as it has in the Mattole, then new norms can become established. A cultural shift is under way. Individuals can feel more empowered politically by an emerging cooperative culture.

In speaking about the relationship of cultural transformation to political transformation, House (1989) pointed out to me that centralized political structures today represent at least the past 400 to 500 years of industrialism and its constructs, constructs that have come to live in us as individuals. That is, we have become disempowered to the extent that those internalized constructs control our thoughts and behaviours. Bioregionalism, House affirmed, gave him the tools to replace those structures, to chip away at his own conditioning.

Discussing broad cultural and political change led to a consideration of cross-cultural political work and alliance building. House sees alliance building as first and foremost the necessity to do cross-cultural work at home in the Mattole watershed. From his perspective, communicating with local ranchers, loggers, and farmers *is* a cross-cultural endeavour. For this reason, although House himself is one of the earliest adherents of bioregionalism, he hasn't placed much emphasis on using the word *bioregionalism* within Mattole Valley society: "People can understand restoration work pretty readily – but, if you have to stop and explain bioregionalism, it can get in the way" (1989).

In 1991, the theme of cross-cultural alliance building (between the countercultural restorationists and the ranching community) in the Mattole took a more concrete form with the birth of the Mattole Watershed Alliance (MWA). The MWA brought together a valley-wide spectrum of the watershed's residents, including ranchers, timber interests, restorationists, large and small landowners, and the Bureau of Land Management, a major land manager in the watershed. The MWA's broad interests coalesced around support for a variety of land uses, including healthy agriculture; livestock, forest, and fishery production; and the maintenance of open spaces, wildlife populations, and recreational opportunities. Members agreed on a broad, loosely defined program of improving the overall natural health of the Mattole watershed, including salmon habitat, timber regrowth, clean air and water, and soil erosion.

The advent of this cross-cultural alliance, House recalled, brought the realization to MRC stalwarts how purely countercultural (or isolationist) their efforts had been up to that point. House explained this belated realization by pointing to the fact that, in the Mattole, the counterculture made up a large majority of the total population. The founding meetings of the MWA agenda committee were difficult, with much "social venting" (House 1997b) by ranchers, timber producers, and others with whom the MRC had not communicated well. These groups frankly let the restorationists know what they thought of the MRC countercultural agenda and exclusivity. This venting process also gave House and the other restorationists the opportunity to convince others on the agenda committee that their MRC agenda was much more benign than some suspected. They argued that ecological restoration in the context of the entire watershed had taught the restoration groups in the Mattole the necessity of sensitive land management as "preventative restoration." After that, they were able to agree that land management issues were at least as important as "technical restoration." Finally, the different interests came together on the basis that working together to cooperatively plan land use was the *only* defence that they had against being overrun by centralized regulation.

The alliance met monthly and was run by consensus process. At first, consensus process was so variously understood that the members had to bring in consensus trainers from the outside. Yet enough people from all sectors of the economic and social spectra were willing to attend consensus workshops that, over a period of a year or two, consensus began to function. This meant that enough trust, information, and cooperative behaviour norms had built up within the alliance that people could begin to work together effectively. Social capital was being formed beyond the counterculture in the Mattole. Increased levels of action became possible.

The MWA was then able to implement some unprecedented actions. A recommendation to entirely close salmon sports fishing on the Mattole for a period of five years was made to the California Board of Forestry. Because the alliance was both broadly based and united around the issue, the recommendation prevailed, and a moratorium was implemented. For the first time, the board made special rules for an individual watershed in California (House 1997b).

Commercial fishing was the next issue to be addressed by the MWA. A committee of the alliance negotiated with local commercial fishers (the Humbolt Fish Marketing Association) to lay off fishing during the critical month of October, when the salmon congregated at the mouth of the Mattole. For House, this was a striking example of what could be accomplished by even a limited "sense of place," with alliance concerns being organized entirely around salmon. In House's view, it was the salmon that brought the old and new guards together in the Mattole.

At the same time, the MRC assisted the watershed alliance by supplying maps, mailing lists, and other information. Then, when the State of California cut funding for the Mattole Salmon Group (MSG) hatchbox program, the alliance successfully intervened to help restore the funding (Stemler 1991). Here we see the effective use of a combined horizontal strategy of alliance building in the sphere of civil society with a vertical strategy in the political sphere, opening lines of communication between both state agencies and the government of California. Horizontal strength through the watershed alliance was strong enough to be effective in restoring resources from the state to the local MSG hatchbox program.

With respect to the biological/ecological effectiveness of the hatchbox program, the results are encouraging but will require a longer trial for a full evaluation. In 1980, MSG fish counts indicated that 1,000 king (or chinook) salmon had returned to the Mattole. However, the 1980s saw a seven-year drought in the valley. Fish runs declined to a low of 200 in 1990. From 1991 to the winter of 1997-98, small yearly increases brought the count back up to 1,000 (House 1998).

The MWA functioned for a few years, but, when the group tried to address much more contentious timber management issues, the bonds were not strong enough to hold the alliance together in any real way. Two years were spent attempting to define "old-growth forest." The alliance was unable to reach a consensus even on a definition. It did not share a large enough common information base, and the members did not trust each other enough. Today the alliance no longer functions.

The failure of the MWA over timber management shows the limits of consensus process. Consensus decision making requires a certain level of shared meaning and intent as well as trust (see also Chapter 4). In the MWA, consensus worked well as long as the deeply divisive issue of timber management was not on the table. Consensus does not work when people's true positions are opposed to each other.

However, the work of the MRC continues. The work of both the Mattole Salmon Group and the MRC has expanded considerably in the past twenty years. From a handful of dedicated restorationists in the late 1970s to an active core of twenty or more, with hundreds taking part in the work at various times, watershed consciousness has grown to the point where the language of restoration is becoming a new norm in the valley. Here, in the work and lives of a significant number of active participants, is an example of watershed restoration wherein building a community of self-conscious restorationists is as important as restoring habitat. As observed by House and Simpson, cultural change toward stronger community bonds is under way in the Mattole. Moreover, for House, this shift in culture is informed by the place, the salmon, and the watershed.

A normative cultural shift has taken place. Among a significant percentage of the valley's residents, strong levels of common information and trust through shared work and experience in ecological restoration, combined with emergent norms of cooperation and civic solidarity, provide evidence of the successful formation of social and ecosocial capital in the Mattole.

A variety of tools have been used to assist this process of cultural change in civil society. The actual shared work of watershed restoration has been an important contributor to ecosocial capital formation in the Mattole. Another key tool has been bioregional mapping. Maps have been crucial in the effort to inspire an understanding of the Mattole watershed as a whole. Maps have also been crucial in the work of public bioregional education, in shifting consciousness about salmon and other watershed issues in the Mattole. Bioregional education (in the form of public theatre in the valley, local fund-raising cabarets, watershed tours, and the Mattole Restoration Newsletter) has been another important tool for shifting consciousness. Sometimes these tools have been used in combination, such as the use of maps as a form of bioregional education about the watershed as a whole or the use of consensus process in alliance-building work.

A definite shift in perception has been effected in Mattole civil society more generally. Much of the population of the valley is at least discussing restoration in the context of the entire watershed. House reports that by 1990 there was a more or less universal understanding of "the watershed concept" on the part of the people who lived in the watershed as well as at the regulatory agency level (1997b).

At this broad civil society level within the Mattole, though, severe disagreements remain with respect to timber and land use. However, even here some limited victories were achieved. Perhaps the most important was the attempt by MRC activists to break out of their countercultural isolation by working in the broader MWA. Even though this particular alliance was not successful enough to weather the storm of timber management issues, it was an important local attempt at building horizontal bridges in civil society, and it showed that horizontal linkages in the civil society sphere could be more effective when combined with vertical forms of communication and influence in the political sphere.

At the broadest level of Mattole civil society, House – reflecting on the changes in his valley since he arrived there – finds hope in the generation who have grown up over the past two decades helping to carry the fertilized native salmon eggs, incubate the young salmon, and release the fries as a part of their elementary school program. We are taken by this reflection back to the salmon themselves. House, at the end of his beautiful tribute to the salmon, *Totem Salmon: Life Lessons from Another Species*, muses on the comeback of the salmon as an emotional, personal issue for tens of thousands of people in salmon-bearing watersheds of North America: "Salmon is regaining its status as the totem creature of the North Pacific. Salmon, who spend most of their time in the vast oceans, return to instruct and feed us. They focus our attention on some of the smaller increments of the natural world – the streams that run through our rural homes or beneath our urban structures – at the same time as they instruct us regarding the indivisible relationship of one locale to another and the life lessons to be learned from the other species" (1999, 198-99).

Huehuecoyotl

Huehuecoyotl, a community of Mexican bioregionalists, is located in a part of Mexico rich in both biodiversity and indigenous and peasant cultural traditions. This is a story of people who came together to form an intentional community on a piece of land outside the village of Amatlan. Amatlan is one of seven outlying villages of the municipality of Tepoztlan, a town of about 28,000 people, located an hour and a half by car south of Mexico City. Tepoztlan and its surrounding area are in the State of Morelos, one of twenty-nine states of the United States of Mexico (see Figure 7). Mexican bioregionalists call the surrounding bioregion Cuauhnahuac, which means "close to the forest" in Nahuatl, one of the local indigenous languages (Kuri 1996).

Cuauhnahuac, for the most part, is a broad river valley of the Amacuzac River, which flows between the Ajusco Mountains and the Sierra Madre Del Sur, the mountainous spine of the Mexican isthmus. Two types of forest are found in the bioregion: upland temperate coniferous forest and lowland tropical brush of the valley. Ecologically, the region is the critical meeting place of the biological zones of North and South America (Weinberg 1996). It is a region of rich biodiversity, with 90 mammal, 350 bird, 79 reptile, and 30 amphibian species. The bioregion of Cuauhnahuac, roughly coterminus with the Amacuzac River watershed, is also coterminus with the State of Morelos, a correspondence that some Mexican bioregionalists think makes it significantly easier for its inhabitants to accept the concept of bioregionalism wherein human boundaries and natural watershed boundaries coincide (Kuri 1996).

Cuauhnahuac, "close to the forest," refers to the fact that, in former times, much of the land was forested. Even today some forests remain in the Yautepec watershed, the local tributary of the Amacuzac River. Upland pine-oak woods still survive below the craggy, steep, sandstone foothills of the Ajuscos, which divide this bioregion from Mexico City and the Federal District to the immediate north. Water is a problem here. It is in short supply due, in part, to centuries of deforestation for the sugar plantations of the

Figure 7 Map of area surrounding the municipality of Tepoztlan, in the
Cuauhnahuac bioregion, State of Morelos, Mexico; adapted from Lewis 1960.

post-Spanish Conquest oligarchy, which dominated Mexico before the revolution in 1910. It is also due to the contemporary deforestation carried on by the new oligarchy in Mexico City, which wants luxury homes, corporate complexes, and golf courses outside the urbanized and heavily polluted Federal District.

The village of Amatlan is regarded by local people and more broadly in Mexico as the birthplace of Quetzalcoatl, the feathered serpent god who "established" the Toltec empire. The region is rich in local traditions. In Amatlan and Tepoztlan today, homeopathic medicine and traditional indigenous religion are practised alongside Western therapies. Above the town of Tepoztlan, atop one of the sandstone peaks, a pyramid temple to Tepozteco, god of the wind, overlooks the bluish hills of the valley. At times, the polluted air from Mexico City spills over the Ajuscos into the valley, obscuring the hills.

In addition to being the heartland of Quetzalcoatl, the State of Morelos was a heartland for the Mexican revolution of 1910. Here Emiliano Zapata organized a peasant rebellion and army. The city of Cuernavaca, only twenty-one kilometres from Tepoztlan, was Zapata's centre of operations. In this region, the spirit of Zapata still lives. Currently, wall posters of Zapata are widely scattered in Tepoztlan and Cuernavaca. The spirit of defending the land against outside forces goes back well before the times of Zapata to at least the sixteenth century. The entire municipality of Tepoztlan is still composed of communally owned lands that the Tepozteco Indians have defended for centuries. In the sixteenth century, King Philip II of Spain recognized these communal land rights dating back to the Aztec empire (Weinberg 1996). Encroachment of ranches and plantations onto Tepoztlan's legally recognized communal lands was met with rebel activity in the Liberal Revolution against Santa Ana in the 1850s and again in the Zapata peasant insurrection of 1910. In 1929, Tepoztlan's communal lands were officially recognized in the new postrevolution constitution. In 1937, President Lazaro Cardenas declared Tepozteco National Park, an area that included the Tepozteco pyramid and its environs. By 1988, El Tepozteco and Lagunas de Zempoala National Parks were linked by the "Ajusco-Chichinautzin Ecological Corridor," transversing the Ajusco range connecting south to north and affording another layer of protection to many of Tepoztlan's forested communal lands. Here, in this heartland of Zapata and Quetzalcoatl, a community of wandering, free-spirited Mexican cultural workers decided to go back to the land to live in an intentional community.

Mexico's indigenous population is the largest in the hemisphere. It includes over ten million people in officially recognized ethnolinguistic groups. In much of indigenous Mexico, levels of social capital are reported to be high. Many of these communities reproduce ancient traditions of horizontal cooperation, reciprocity, and self-help. Thousands of villages make community decisions about resource allocation and justice by consensus, and they maintain powerful norms of accountability between leaders and community members. While there are increasing religious and class divisions within many communities, "the overall degree of horizontal organization and norms of reciprocity in indigenous Mexico is quite remarkable" (Fox 1996).

With its strong horizontal traditions of communal land ownership, village cooperation, indigenous languages, and peasant revolutions, the

Cuauhnahuac bioregion is no exception. The founding of Huehuecoyotl in the late 1960s occurred in the context of a society with relatively high levels of ecosocial capital.

The story begins with a group of people who eventually settled down in an intentional community in the Tepozteco hills of the Cuauhnahuac bioregion. It begins with Alberto Ruz Buenfil's story. Ruz was involved with a group of his friends in the 1968 university student movement in Mexico City. Ruz is the son of a well-respected archeologist who supported Castro's overthrow of Batista. As an archeologist, the elder Ruz had excavated the pyramid tomb of the ancient Mayan city of Palenque in the State of Chiapas.

The younger Ruz and his *companeros* were part of the libertarian movement of the 1960s that was already searching for a different way of life. On 2 October 1968, a student revolt at the Plaza de Las Tres Culturas of Tlateloco was put down by armed might, and a massacre ensued. This massacre contributed to an awakening of Mexicans to state brutality on the one hand and to an increased awareness of the need for people to have power on the other (Sanchez Navarro 1989).

As a result of these struggles and the search for an alternative, Ruz joined an intentional community, his first attempt to actually live in an alternative way. Too often, as a student and "left" activist, he had observed people espousing different political and social goals without trying to bring these ideals into daily life (Ruz 1988). He lived in this community for one year before getting together with some others in a group that began to travel around the world, visiting many different countries and cultures. Then, after spending one year in India, they became The Illuminated Elephants Travelling Theatre Ashram. In effect, the group was a travelling intentional community of self-proclaimed gypsy artists from eight different nationalities. They performed traditional songs of many different cultures. Drama, myth, music, ritual, and ceremony were combined in their wandering theatre performances. The community also investigated local traditional musical instruments, playing these instruments and showing local people how to make them and play them. For ten years, they travelled the world with these performances.

In 1981, they decided to settle down in Mexico, dreaming of "creating a village." At this time, the group met with another group, some Italian "revolutionary youth" of the 1970s who had formed "a loose form of community and a strong sense of bonding" among members (Ciarlo 1998, 1). The two groups became friendly and then united to "create a village that would apply the principles of art, ecology, spirituality and social justice" in a common effort to live sustainably (Ciarlo 1998, 1).

They chose a canyon in the Ajusco Mountains, an hour and a half by car from Mexico City, up against the mountains of Tepozteco National Park in the heart of Nahuatl-speaking people's traditional territory. The parcel of land they chose was small, fewer than ten acres. It was owned in common by a traditional indigenous village. However, deeds with rights to use the land could be held and sold by individuals. The newly formed group bought the deed in the name of one of the Mexican members. It was at this time too that they changed their name from The Illuminated Elephants to Huehuecoyotl, after the Nahuatl name for the place. Huehuecoyotl means "old, old coyote."

For three years, they lived in the canyon without any external power or energy supply, burning oil lamps for light. They built themselves a road in from the highway, and over time they constructed a comfortable place in which to live. At the bottom of the canyon, the land spreads out in front of their place. Here, at first, they attempted to grow much of their own food. The climate in the Cuauhnahuac bioregion has an extended eight-month dry season, so they built a small dam and cisterns underneath all the houses as a water catchment system. Initially, their storage capacity was not enough to furnish water over the entire eight months, so they had to import water by truck when their local water ran out (Lloyd 1989).

Designing and building their village were implemented through a learn-by-doing approach. One of the community members was also an architecture student at the Mexican National University. He involved some of his classmates and professors, as well as other members of Huehuecoyotl, in a project for the collective design of an "ecologically centred" village community on their land. They selected spaces for cisterns, houses, workshops, a theatre, and a community kitchen, and they lined a large open area with fruit trees and gardens. With minimum resources, they built their village. In the process, they learned about adobe making and building, ferro-cement construction, water capturing and filtering systems, organic gardening, road construction, and roofing with various materials (Ciarlo 1998).

The community operated by consensus and by dividing into several affinity groups. In all, there were about twenty-five people in the community at that time. In addition to growing food, affinity groups began a beekeeping operation. They also started a pasta-making business and a carpentry shop. The beekeeping operation functioned for about five years, when the group lost their bees to a wild African variety. Also, the pasta business did not do well. Eventually, it was sold to someone outside the community (King Cobos 1998).

After these experiences, the community members found that they were much better at cultural healing and performance, the work they'd been doing together for so long, than they were at beekeeping or gardening, so they began to barter their skills with local villagers, exchanging their skills at performance, communication, and instrument making for the skills of local people at growing food and constructing houses from local materials. In this way, they learned new skills and, at least as important, became more involved in local community projects. Huehuecoyotl people helped to set up a women's clothing cooperative in the village, bringing together and utilizing the skills of women from villages around the region. This was the beginning of building ongoing communications as well as economic and cultural linkages with local people. This work was then extended to the two nearest villages and the town of Tepoztlan, building familiarity, trust, economic exchange, and norms of cooperation with local people and organizations.

One affinity group of four continued the performance work of The Illuminated Elephants, travelling around Mexico, Central America, and the United States. Another affinity group founded an elementary "ecological" school in Tepoztlan. Within a relatively short period of time, a location was found, the school was built, and community people began to teach there. From the beginning, the curriculum combined learning to grow the community's own food with learning a diversity of spiritual understandings and practices. The school itself also engaged in outreach work to other schools. In 1989, the children at the ecological school went to all the other schools in Tepoztlan and invited them to go on a march "for the animals." Over 400 children participated in the march all over town in support of the animals and the environment. This was apparently the first such children's demonstration ever held in Mexico (Lloyd 1989). It is another example of success in building a web of horizontal linkages in civil society, this time undertaken by the children themselves. It also illustrates the potential for work by a small group of individuals (the affinity group) to be effectively and speedily leveraged in the context of relatively high levels of social and ecosocial capital in Cuauhnahuac.

Another affinity group began building a cultural centre/theatre at Huehuecoyotl. A stage was built first, and then pillars were erected for the roof, but the project stalled for lack of money. Eventually, after several years, the centre was built. It is now used as a site of cultural work. Artistic events, theatre, dance, music, and plastic arts workshops are held at the centre. It is also available for other groups to hold conferences, workshops, and retreats. In addition, a carpentry shop produces musical instruments that are marketed in several places in Mexico and the United States at fairs, in shops, and by mail. This business remains small-scale and controlled by the instrument makers (King Cobos 1998).

Several members are also busy writing books on the connections between spirituality and bioregionalism. Ruz has translated some of the works of Bill Devall, Peter Berg, and David Haenke into Spanish, and they have been circulated in the Mexican ecology movement. In 1989, Ruz edited and published a booklet entitled *Rainbow: A Nation without Borders*, a collection from different authors around the world of personal stories and tales of their own "rainbow" organizations, on which more later. In addition to this, Huehuecoyotl has produced a sporadic journal, *El Viejo Coyote*, which has

drawn on everything from 1960s LSD-guru Timothy Leary to the philosophy of the French Situationists. Ruz and Huehuecoyotl have also had their
input into the left in Mexico, in part through producing several editions of
"El Gallo Illustrado," a weekly insert of the left-leaning daily *El Dia*, exploring ecology and alternative community. In 1985, Huehuecoyotl was among
the groups participating in publishing a monthly called *Arcoredes*, or "Rainbow Network," an ecology-oriented journal (Weinberg 1989).

Although they are involved in print and electronic forms of communication and networking, Ruz and the Huehuecoyotl community place more
emphasis on face-to-face communication. They visit other places often,
experience and interact with other people in their places, and in turn encourage others to visit their community at Huehuecoyotl. Direct engagement, they have emphasized, is the way to build both personal and group
commitment, interlinking different communities through more intense levels of mutual commitment. For the past eight years, Ruz and some others
have been involved with several more ambitious itinerant projects, or "cara-
vans," travelling first to Central America and later to South America for
face-to-face networking, performance theatre, and solidarity building with
indigenous, ecological, and political groups. The work of the Caravana
Arcoiris Por La Paz (Rainbow Peace Caravan) soon intersected with ecovillage
networking and the rapidly spreading numbers of ecovillage communities
(see Conclusion). This face-to-face networking by the caravan has been an
important part of this community's horizontal strategy to spread bioregional
and permacultural ideas in civil society across interest and geography.

In the period after Huehuecoyotl established itself in the Morelos Mountains, the ecological movement burgeoned in Mexico. In 1984, there were
some fifteen to twenty groups and associations working independently. By
1988, those numbers had grown rapidly to between 200 and 300 throughout the country. The earthquake in Mexico City in 1985 actually contributed to the growth of local citizens' efforts and organizations. The ecological
crisis, especially in Mexico City, had grown to such proportions that the
government and state organizations were incapable of helping people at
the local level, devastated by the earthquake. The people began to realize
that only they themselves could really do anything to address the crisis.
Ruz observed that this situation spurred an awakening of ecological and
social consciousness from which Mexican civil society has not turned back
(1988).

In 1987, three organizations – Huehuecoyotl, Sobrevivencia, and Grupo
de Estudios Ambientales (Environmental Study Group) – organized a seminar on deep ecology, inviting John Milton, Bill Devall, Peter Berg, and David
Haenke to speak. Between 200 and 300 people from the ecology movement
in Mexico participated in conference workshops and seminars. It was out of
the work of this conference that Ruz translated bioregional and deep ecology

works into Spanish. Soon after, in 1988, three groups from Mexico sent representatives to the third North American Bioregional Congress: Sobrevivencia, Huehuecoyotl, and Red Alternativa de Ecomunicacion. This was the emergence in the bioregional movement of what were to become strong north-south direct links of solidarity in civil society.

The spiritual understanding of the Huehuecoyotl community is a primary root of its activity. The members spend a great deal of energy in helping to reclaim and/or strengthen indigenous Mexican spiritual traditions. In March 1989, several members of Huehuecoyotl took part in a journey to a southern bioregion of Mexico in order to ritually reopen several Mayan ceremonial centres. The Mexican government, while trying to preserve these ceremonial centres as tourist attractions, had forbidden their use as ceremonial centres. The journey began in Palenque on 12 March, with about 200 people. This group made their way to the sacred centre of Chichen Itza for the spring equinox, where over 40,000 people from all over the planet participated (Lloyd 1989). This strong emphasis on working with a wide diversity of indigenous groups and traditions has marked Mexican bioregionalism.

For Ruz and Huehuecoyotl, the effort to reclaim and revive older traditional ways of life is complemented by the search to birth new spiritual practices and understandings. In his message of greeting from the Anahuac bioregion in Mexico to the continental bioregional gathering in 1988, Ruz spoke of the currently awakening consciousness of Mexican people manifesting itself through "a movement that is ecological and bioregional, spiritual and political" (Zuckerman 1989, 47). Ruz eloquently described the reemergence of traditional indigenous consciousness such as the Mayans, the Aztecs, the Toltecs, and the Olmecs, this time in new forms within the alternative movement in Mexico. For Ruz, the rebirth of the old and the birth of the new are one and the same, a phenomenon of a "new age" rooted in the past. Quetzalcoatl, the Feathered Serpent of the Rainbow, symbolizes the voice of the emerging age, a rainbow of diversity, many colours, one symbol. Ruz points out that this symbolism is simultaneously spiritual and political, recognizing unity and diversity, the old and the new, all in one. It can be viewed both cosmologically and ecologically. When I spoke to Ruz at NABC III, he pointed out that the main reason he was at the congress was to search for and learn ways to deal with our differences so that we can all work for a society of equals in which we learn to respect the differences. This, he affirmed, is "the spirit of the rainbow": each colour band is entirely unique, yet all colours are part of an integrated whole (1988).

In the 1990s, working with other local groups and individuals, people from Huehuecoyotl built a local and regional network of groups that work together in their local communities in various ways. Laura Kuri and Fabio Manzini have worked closely with people from Huehuecoyotl and with other local groups. Kuri became acquainted with bioregional thought and practice in

1988 when she attended the third North American continental congress. She soon began local cultural, educational, and networking activity in the Cuauhnahuac bioregion in 1990. At first, she worked with Espacio Verde (Green Space), the most "activist" group of the bioregion. Kuri and her fellow bioregional activists also began working with "social" groups (not only green groups), women, political parties, other political groups, schools, and the University of Cuernavaca.

For Kuri, one of the most important projects that she worked on was with a group of very poor women: "Some of them don't know how to write or read, but they have a lot of heart, and they have a lot of sensibility, so we've been working with them. They became a very strong group, and they have already started a recycling centre ... And they go to schools to work on recycling" (1996).

Another locally important group that Kuri worked with was Luna Nueva (New Moon). This is a women's group in Tepoztlan. Luna Nueva works on issues of health, nutrition, community development, and environmental education. In their education workshops, Kuri works with them to host series about bioregionalism, using maps of the bioregion as a way to learn about their local ecological and human community. Kuri and her conet-workers also work with and support local traditional medicine and healing groups.

I spoke with Kuri about the local work of bioregionalists at the continental bioregional gathering in Tepoztlan in 1996. Kuri spoke passionately about the strength of local traditions in the region: "The people that live in this area are Native people but also people from everywhere else that have come here. So it's another 'border' [in the ecological sense of species-rich edge communities], and it's very rich in tradition. Still very rich in tradition, in this area we haven't lost tradition. So that's something that we have that's very beautiful, no? And it's very close to bioregionalism." This important observation connects bioregional philosophy and older, indigenous Mexican traditions of living with the land. This region has long traditions of indigenous communal use of the land, and even the current political borders correspond to the biogeographical borders of the Cuauhnahuac bioregion. In such a context, the vision of bioregionalism is merely common sense for many local people.

The intense bioregional education work with local groups integrates health, environmental, and community development issues with local traditional knowledge and modern ecological knowledge. From a social capital perspective, this outreach practice builds stronger social relations with local people, building trust, norms of cooperation, and civic solidarity, as well as actual horizontal networks between the diverse groups. This grassroots community involvement provides the space for Mexican bioregionalists to educate the community in Tepoztlan and its region about bioregional ideas. In this education outreach process, knowledge flows both ways. Others from Huehuecoyotl, such as Andres King Cobos, are also working closely with local traditional healers, learning medicinal herbs, healing techniques, and traditional ceremonial and ritual practice from local elders. This close, two-way education process is illustrative of Mexican bioregionalism, which has included and integrated traditional indigenous groups and knowledge from its inception in 1990. Again, the hands-on bioregional approach to education through common experiential learning facilitates the building of trust and norms of cooperation, solidarity, and reciprocity, all essential to the bioregional horizontal strategy in civil society.

One important form of public education work that Kuri speaks about is the *fiestas* ("parties") that her group periodically helps to organize in the *barrios* ("neighbourhood districts"). These *fiestas* employ street theatre, mime, clown shows, music, and drumming to illustrate ecological themes in popular form. In this, they also work with another movement called La Fiesta de la Planta Medicinale (Earth Medicine Party). Other local organizations that they have worked with include organic growers and alternative energy use and solar power groups.

Finally, Kuri spoke with me about the importance of sociopolitical support work: "We do a lot of political work. Support for social problems, no? And we also work in supporting political problems, such as the problem that Tepoztlan has now. Espacio Verde, the group in which I work, was one of the principal groups supporting that movement. So that's when we mixed up [integrated] the ecology and the social movement work" (1996).

The "political problem" that Kuri refers to is the struggle of the people of Tepoztlan against a giant golf course/entertainment development complex planned for the municipality that was defeated when the townspeople rejected it overwhelmingly. In the process of the struggle against the golf course, the town's citizens occupied the town hall. The mayor, a supporter of the federal ruling party and the golf course, fled to Cuernavaca, and the citizens began to govern themselves, declaring their town a Municipio Libre Constitutional or Constitutional Free Municipality (which they have a right to do under the constitution of the United States of Mexico). The townspeople immediately set up committees of citizens to implement their political action in the *barrios* and the political, municipality-wide Tepoztlan Committee of Unity. For this dramatic act of civic solidarity to be possible, high levels of social capital were required. From the perspective of democratic civil society theory, it is clear that the local bioregional back-to-the-land community was working in a much more favourable environment than their counterparts in the Mattole, operating in a civil society sphere where there were already strong horizontal bonds of cooperation, mutual aid, and reciprocity. Moreover, when it came to expanding organizing into the political sphere, strong horizontal bonds provided a context for effective vertical action that resulted in the removal of a corrupt local government official.

The educational, cultural, social, and political support demonstrated by the local network of bioregional and alternative groups for the political struggles of the townspeople against unjust and environmentally destructive development was returned in 1996 when over forty local leaders and elders of the Tepoztlan Committee of Unity, plus more than 150 local schoolchildren from fifteen schools in the municipal district, attended the weeklong continental bioregional gathering held in their town. Elders and town leaders took full part in the week's activities.

While the local bioregionalists and other alternative network groups in the region cannot claim credit for an important historical development such as the liberation of Tepoztlan, their work in support of local and democratic civil society, and in building horizontal networks and norms of cooperation and civic solidarity with local peoples, has contributed to advancing local understanding of the concept and practice of bioregionalism. For a relatively small number of people, they have done a lot of work in the neighbourhoods, the *barrios*, and among the townspeople and local villagers to raise local consciousness about ecology and Mexican bioregionalism. And, at least as important, they have created strong bonds of mutual respect and trust and helped to strengthen already strong norms of horizontal cooperation in a region with a long history of autonomous cooperative action and social revolution. In such contexts, efforts at effective local and regional action are leveraged by the relatively high existing levels of social capital, themselves a heritage of historical levels of social capital.

The intentional community at Huehuecoyotl, in spite of these intense horizontal outreach efforts in their own local context and in their Mexico-wide, face-to-face networking campaign, have also managed to keep developing their "village" on their small piece of land. Ciarlo (1998) reports that after sixteen years most of the original members remain. This is testimony to the existence of strong bonds of community developed over time. In addition, several children have been born there, and a handful of new members have joined.

Members of Huehuecoyotl have once again renamed their community. It is now the Ecoaldea Huehuecoyotl or Huehuecoyotl Eco-Village. With their hard-won experience at building their own intentional community of place, they now host permaculture workshops, Earth festivals, ecotours, and bioregional gatherings at their ecovillage to share their experience with a broader circle of people. In addition, Huehuecoyotl members played a key role on the Steering Council and Site Committee that organized the continental bioregional gathering in Tepoztlan in 1996. Huehuecoyotl has also joined another new network, the Ecovillage Network of the Americas, where Ciarlo (1998) works as a member of the steering committee.

The Yalakom River Community
The story of the Yalakom River community in southwestern British Columbia, Canada, is one with which I have been personally involved for over twenty years. Over much of this period, I have visited and/or lived for short stays with several different households in the Yalakom River community and in the nearby town of Lillooet. For several years, I was also a member of a cooperative house in Vancouver that served as an urban base for Camelsfoot, an intentional community within the larger Yalakom River community that took on an instrumental role in spreading bioregional ideas in the valley and beyond. This house, which we called Clark House, was also for several years the Vancouver base for the larger community of back-to-the-landers in the Yalakom watershed. During the years that I lived at Clark House from 1981 to 1985, individuals or groups from Camelsfoot and the larger Yalakom community would suddenly show up at Clark House for a city visit, or en route to visit relatives elsewhere in the world, and later attend green or bioregional gatherings sometimes in far-off places. Each visit, whether it was people coming from the valley or me going to the Yalakom, was usually an occasion for general philosophical discussion about the political or ecological state of the world, the back-to-the-land movement, culture, place, local gossip, and, in the case of the people from Camelsfoot, a certain method of inquiry that they were developing based, in part, on the work of John Dewey. Whenever they came to Clark House, some of the country came with them. One summer we even had goats from the valley boarding in the basement and a small home salmon-canning operation.

Philosophy, for the people from Camelsfoot, was not a casual activity. It was a daily practice, one that they said must grow out of the issues of everyday life and return to these issues to test and validate the concepts that they were developing as part of a transactional philosophy of daily inquiry into our habits, customs, and lived experiences. I joined in many of these discussions over nearly a five-year period. I came to understand that this method of inquiry was being developed by the people at Camelsfoot so that individuals from our fragmented, "free enterprise," monocultural society, broken off from communal ways of living in extended families, could actually learn to function again as cooperative members of a community, could begin to practise truly thinking together and living in what Camelsfoot people often referred to as "adaptive groups." In the Camelsfoot community, there was an ongoing discussion on culture as adaptive behaviour and a general understanding, well grounded in anthropological literature, that humans have lived this way for most of our time on the planet.

A good part of these ongoing discussions was focused on the importance of developing a "common story" together. There was a growing understanding that, if people could learn to think together and to live cooperatively together in community, then weaving a common story out of the separate threads of individual lives was essential. Story was seen as a common thread that was actually lived out or enacted together as a community. In this way, stories were not only tales that were told but also, more importantly, tales that were lived. Camelsfoot people often spoke of "having the story together." For them, this was key to the initiation of a process of building a new, cooperative culture. If people could have their story together through a process of inquiry that included learning by doing, conventional individualistic habits could be transformed into new norms of cooperation, mutual aid, and communal living. Camelsfoot members recognized that this goal would not be easy. They believed that it would take a minimum of three generations to truly establish cooperative cultural norms in an intentional community or in society.

The intentional community at Camelsfoot began in the mid-1970s out of a discussion group, originally a circle of friends in North Vancouver. Some of these people were students of Fred Brown, communications department chair and professor for a short while at Simon Fraser University. Philosophically, Brown had been strongly influenced by the thought of George Mead and John Dewey, with its emphasis on inquiry as learning by doing. Fred took Dewey's concept of social inquiry and gave it a grounded context. For Brown, social inquiry was best carried on by an inquiry group, one that lived and inquired together in a domestic setting. In this endeavour, Brown placed central importance on the concept of "home." Before teaching at SFU, Brown had been head of the philosophy department at the University of Havana, in the mid-1960s. During this time, he had come to know Fidel Castro personally and on occasion had carried on philosophical and political discussions with the Cuban leader. Earlier, Brown had been, among other things, a night watchman at a nuclear reactor at the University of Chicago, a cowboy, a mountain guide, and a teacher in a Native village in northern British Columbia. With his combined philosophical and practical life experience, he was an ideal person to lead a group of people into the wild mountains of the southern BC interior to build an intentional community centred on daily inquiry.

Glen Makepeace, another member of the Camelsfoot community, has written that it was Brown's philosophy of community that drew people to him. At a memorial for Fred at the third continental bioregional movement gathering, Glen recalled that Fred used to say that the central question in philosophy is "how shall we live"? For Makepeace, the essence of Brown's philosophy was "we once lived in communities. We lost them. And now we need to rebuild them if we're going to survive." Brown also believed that to regenerate sustainable, locally adapted communities we need to look at the original sustainable communities "not because we're trying to rebuild past cultures and communities, but because we can learn from them" (in Zuckerman 1989, 22).

In the mid-1970s, after a considerable time spent discussing culture, community, philosophy, and a method of inquiry while still at Simon Fraser, the group moved out of the university, left the city, and became a catalyst for the back-to-the-land, intentional community movement in the Yalakom valley.

The Yalakom River flows out of the coastal mountains east into the Bridge River, which flows into the Fraser River just north of the town of Lillooet. The Yalakom is also known as the north fork of the Bridge River. These rivers flow through a rugged, mountainous terrain with a dry interior climate, cold in winter and hot, sometimes very hot, in summer. This is ponderosa pine and big sagebrush country in the lower elevations, with interior Douglas-fir, Montane spruce, and Engleman spruce-subalpine fir and alpine tundra biogeoclimatic zones at higher elevations. The terrain is inhabited by mountain goats, bighorn sheep, beaver, deer, moose, grizzly bears, and cougars. It is wild country. In 1977, a few groups and some individuals scattered among the mountains began the work of community building in the Yalakom River valley "with little more in common than a love of good food and a love of the land" ("The Bridge River People" 1983).

In those early days, food was a force for community. The people in the valley bulk-ordered whatever food they were unable to grow through Fed-Up Co-Operative Wholesalers in east-end Vancouver. The semiannual load from the co-op was always the occasion for a social and musical get-together of the people. Over the years, a lasting interest developed in making music together. Music nights thus developed into a custom among the valley people. Music, bulk food orders, social gatherings and celebrations, construction bees, along with much gossip and philosophy all contributed to the creation of a strong sense of community and an emerging new identity as the Yalakom community. Yet it was only the beginning of a process that was envisioned to require generations to establish as a social norm.

In addition to building their own housing and independent energy systems, various groups and individuals in the valley grew vegetables and raised chickens, goats, pigs, horses, and cows. Some began cultivating fruit and nut trees. Susan Brown, wife of Fred Brown, and others began to develop a permaculture garden and to spread ideas about permaculture in the valley. Some picked wild berries in season as well as apricots in the town of Lillooet with a little cooperation from property owners uninterested in the harvest. Another form of income came from knapweed picking. This work was paid for by the provincial Ministry of Forests in an agreement reached with the community as an alternative to the ministry's plan of spraying the knap-weed with Tordon. Trade, mostly in the form of barter, and friendships de-veloped with some local Native people. An ideal, simple, and relatively peaceful life in the mountains seemed to be assured.

Then in 1981, BC Hydro, a provincial public utility, announced plans to develop yet another megaproject to produce power. The project was to be a $2.5 billion coal-fired thermoelectric power plant, a smoke-belching behe-moth at Hat Creek, just over the hill from the Yalakom River valley. Ini-tially, it was the food co-op organization that enabled people in the Yalakom to arouse the collective consciousness to attempt "to block Bonner's death wish for the earth," as a mimeographed leaflet of the time referred to the project. Robert Bonner was then chairman of BC Hydro. He was also an executive member of the powerful Rockefeller-organized Trilateral Commis-sion, whose activities have contributed so much to building the new global economic order through, among other things, many megaprojects designed to fuel "free" trade and the global corporate economy of economic man (Sklar 1980).

Extremely unpopular, this BC Hydro megaproject was the immediate, and potentially catastrophic, threat to the region that stimulated the first "Hat Creek Survival Gathering." The threat went far beyond the Yalakom and the local community. Salmon runs in the much larger Thompson-Fraser watershed would also be threatened. Some Yalakom people constructed a BC Hydro float that satirized the megaproject, BC Hydro, and its Trilateral Commission connections. The float travelled to parades and marches around the province with the message "Stop Hat Creek." Support groups sprang up, including a committee in Vancouver, the Hat Creek Action Committee, in which I participated. I still have a tattered "Stop Hat Creek" T-shirt from those days made by two members of the Action Committee. The following year a professional theatre company, the Caravan Theatre, put on a road show that toured the province with a very entertaining, cuttingly satirical play that revealed the social and ecological problems that the megaproject would create. The play, *Stranger in the Land*, also exposed and satirized BC Hydro's Trilateral Commission connections. The play thus became a power-ful symbolic representation of the globalization of Western monoculture and its political economic system. This road show acted to catalyze local opposition to the Hat Creek megaproject throughout southern British Columbia.

Members of the Yalakom opposition, in the meantime, were developing some theatre of their own. A papier-mâché, three-headed "Hydra," repre-senting acid rain, massive public debt, and a destructive BC Hydro bureau-cracy, helped to focus more parades and demonstrations on the effects of the megaproject. Opposition to BC Hydro's plan grew more widespread, and the focus broadened. It included opposition to all of the utility's mega-projects and to the policy of unsustainable growth manifested in them. Even as early as the 1982 Survival Gathering, the call went out from the gathering for "the creation of a cohesive alternative ... the power of a new vision ... the change from a technological society to an ecological society," as a leaflet for the gathering expressed it. Not long after this gathering, BC Hydro put its plan for the Hat Creek megaproject on the shelf. However, by this time, opposition to BC Hydro at the Survival Gatherings had begun to take on a much larger critique, focusing on the Western model of a global consumer civilization.

By 1983, bioregional literature had begun to influence the people at the Camelsfoot community. Peter Berg visited Clark House that year, meeting with people from "the Foot," as we fondly called it. An extended exchange of views took place with Berg around key issues such as the nature and meaning of human community, how to go about building community, and how to develop the kinds of extended community bonding that seem so peripheral to modern society. I remember the high spirit of that discussion, which I believe helped very much to enrich the thinking of those of us involved in this encounter, which went on for many hours. It was the beginning of a process in which Camelsfoot thought on community and social inquiry encountered bioregional thought about place and community.

That year, too, the first of three issues of a self-published journal, the *Catalyst*, about the philosophy of the Yalakom community, came out. Reflecting the influence of bioregional thought in the valley, it was entitled *Reinhabiting B.C.* This publication, originally the newspaper for the food co-op distributor, also became the vehicle for the people of the Yalakom community to disseminate their philosophy, their politics, and their poetry along with their regular food co-op business and catalogues. The *Catalyst* was the beginning of bioregional publishing in British Columbia (and, for that matter, in Canada).

In 1986, a publishing group, formed out of the *Catalyst* experience, founded the *New Catalyst*, also a bioregional publication. Much broader in scope, it addressed issues across the province and beyond. At first, the *New Catalyst*, like the old journal, was produced by community members in the Yalakom valley. It continued for four years until production of the *New Catalyst* moved to Gabriola Island with Chris and Judy Plant. Some valley people, missing the truly local character of the old *Catalyst*, began in 1988 to publish the *Yalakom Review*, retaining the local character of the old *Catalyst*.

In 1984, a number of people in the Yalakom watershed became involved in the BC Green Party, which had formed in 1983. Not surprisingly, given their emphasis on philosophy, they became involved in party philosophy and policy deliberations and in the education policy committee. They played a strong role in helping to formulate early BC Green Party policy, philosophy, and values. They began from the bioregional premise that, as the *Catalyst* put it, "an ecological society is impossible without starting with a responsibility to one's own community and place, and a respect for the community and place of others." In education, flowing from the understanding evolved at Camelsfoot that the communal experience must encompass at least three generations to constitute a truly transformed society with solid norms of mutual aid, they put forward – in the *Catalyst* – a philosophy of education as "an evolutionary process which allows humans to modify behaviours and adapt to ongoing changes in the environment, both biological and social ... Education as a continuous inquiry exposes us to established ways of doing things and mediates the changes from old ways to new ways peacefully" ("Green Movement" 1985).

To facilitate this community educational process, they proposed that the Green Party foster the creation of small community, neighbourhood, or home-based learning centres run by local residents. They also supported opening all existing school facilities to all community members. They thought that it was crucial to bridge the gap between teacher and student, school life and real life, work and play. Therefore, they recommended a more holistic approach to community education, including the encouragement of community participation in both academic and nonacademic activities; the sharing of knowledge, information, and skills with each other and with the children; the development of learning networks and exchanges both inside and outside the community; the founding of mixed-age groups; and the encouragement of learning as part of the daily functioning of a community, with everyone taking the roles of both teacher and student. While these recommendations to the Green Party were advanced as policy guidelines for the party, the Yalakom River people involved also began to organize more systematically to achieve these goals in their own community. With a long-term perspective on creation of a cooperative culture over a minimum of three generations, the first generation realized that it was essential to involve the second generation as much as possible in the work of evolving norms of mutual aid through lived experience. However, there was a growing awareness that the emergent valley-wide community's ability to remain sustainable over the long term would also require broader societal change.

At that time, Green Party activity was seen by some Yalakom River people as a way to begin to address the question of broader political, social, and cultural transformation. Reinhabitory practices and community building were viewed as a base out of which to work toward broader change through philosophical dialogue, communication, and networking via Green Party activity. As one philosopher from the valley who wanted to remain anonymous put it, "if you come from one of these communities and you come out to oppose something, you're better suited to survive if you can return to your community or work out of it, so the community in the bioregion is also a strategic unit for participation in the world at large." As can readily be seen, this model of cultural, social, and political transformation is based on the concept of a network or confederation of diverse, local, autonomous, place-appropriate communities, not only as the goal or end product of ecological society, but also as the very means to achieve it. In the Yalakom, people were coming to understand that local place-based communities were the basis of such a strategy.

In the Yalakom River community, there was also a rejection of history as "his story," the story of patriarchal civilization, of what some people began to call (after Mumford) the "power complex" and the "megamachine," also known as "industrial growth society." There was a growing feeling that the patriarchy had gone berserk, but in the Yalakom this understanding of patriarchy led not to the development of an exclusive "her story," as it did within separatist feminism, but to the creation of "our story," the story of an inclusive culture in embryo, the story of an emerging people. Nevertheless, feminism, an inclusive feminism, did begin to develop in the Yalakom River area, as elsewhere in the movement. Perhaps this was because, without an understanding of the patriarchy, without a critique of sexism and a practice or a process to deal with deeply ingrained habits, the Yalakom community, like any other, could not begin to move beyond dualistic, patriarchal culture. Initially, perhaps because the growing community at that time was relatively isolated from the influence of feminism in the wider movement for social change, there was resistance to feminist ideas and a fear among some men and women in the valley that feminism could lead to separatism. These fears were not totally unfounded since, in the more urban areas and particularly in Vancouver's east-end alternative community of the early 1980s, cultural feminism had a strong separatist tendency.

At the Hat Creek Survival Gatherings of 1982 and 1983, certain feminists from Vancouver perceived and began to critique surviving patriarchal and sexist relationships among the valley's people. These relationships, in part at least, were one source of feminist activity within the Yalakom community itself. Involvement in the broader green movement in British Columbia in the following years contributed to strengthening feminist activity. Having started later than in some urban communities, feminist consciousness grew rapidly, thanks in great measure to the work of Judith Plant and a number of other women in the valley. Due to the strength of community and ecological consciousness among the people, feminism did not take a separatist direction and soon developed into an inclusive form of ecological feminism. By 1989, the Bridge River people had hosted a Labour Day gathering on ecofeminism in conjunction with the BC Green Ecofeminist Caucus.

The people in the Yalakom community have been engaged over the past twenty years in various ways with the wider society in the region, helping to initiate and build cultural, political, economic, and social relations and networks in civil society. For example, community members from the Yalakom have initiated the Lillooet Peace and Ecology Group; helped to start the Lillooet Farmers' Market, where they promote organic produce and farming; founded the local International Women's Day annual gathering; helped to organize talent shows for all ages; and joined baseball and volleyball teams, reaching out for new friendships in the "wider community" (Wright 1997). These efforts at creating horizontal relationships with others in civil society included building links with Native peoples.

The Yalakom community is adjacent to the Bridge River (Xwisten) Reserve. The entire Yalakom watershed is on traditional Xwisten territory. The Yalakom community has worked with First Nations at the political level, supporting Native struggles for the Stein and the Lil'wat People's Struggle in Mount Currie. They have also partnered with the Lillooet Tribal Council of the St'at'imc Nation in a Forest Renewal of British Columbia grant application for restoration projects in the Yalakom. More fundamentally for the Yalakom community, they interact with Native people culturally in personal friendships and at feasts, pow-wows, sports events, music concerts, gatherings, Lillooet Friendship Centre events, and International Women's Day activities (Wright 1997).

Far from remaining an isolated enclave in the Yalakom, the emergent valley community spent a good deal of its time and energy pursuing horizontal links with other groups in civil society. This work is reflected in the diversity of networks created, from those with First Nations to peace, labour, ecofeminist, and farmer groups, including the ongoing sports teams and cultural activities. Like bioregional reinhabitants in the Mattole and Tepoztlan, the valley community in the Yalakom understands the necessity of such horizontal bridge building as an essential part of reinhabitation. Moreover, the creation of these social, cultural, and political links, as well as the ecological work demanded by living in place, set the framework for economic activity. This activity itself is primarily subsistence activity or, as Sahlins would say, an economics of livelihood. In other words, the economic sphere of activity – the permaculture gardens, independent energy systems, self-made housing, bartering, berry picking, and home schooling – is embedded in a cultural, political, and ecological praxis.

The central organizing body of the Yalakom community is the Yalakom Community Council (YCC), which has been meeting monthly since 1987. The YCC is held as a council circle to discuss community concerns. Consensus process is used in the planning and strategizing that take place around community business. Full discussion is held on questions such as land trusts, forestry and land use, how to better organize the informal economy in the valley, and when the next meeting of the food co-op, ecological society, or men's and women's circles will take place. The ecological society refers to the Yalakom Ecological Society (YES), formed in 1985. YCC and YES are used as the community's interface with other groups in civil society, with local Ministry of Forests and Environment personnel, and with the public (Wright 1997).

The community has also had to learn to defend the watershed against clear-cutting in the forests of the Yalakom. In the 1970s, community members fought to prevent large clear-cuts and road building in the Yalakom watershed planned by Evans Forest Products, a local mill. In 1982, a Coordinated Resource Management Plan (CRMP) was set up in Lillooet. After a year of frustration at the "inability" of the government-run body to address substantive issues or produce a management plan, the community dropped out of the process, as did some other local members of the public. CRMP eventually disappeared. However, the CRMP experience provided the Yalakom community with the opportunity to get to know local Forestry and Environment personnel, develop relationships with some of the forest workers in the Timber Supply Area, as well as network with the BC Watershed Alliance (Wright 1997). Here we see horizontal networking in civil society combined with emergent vertical bridge building with personnel in the political sphere and agencies of the state.

In the 1980s, the Yalakom community was also active in the successful fight to save the nearby Stein watershed. However, in 1989, the local mill (now Ainsworth Forest Products), in its five-year logging plan, proposed to log over half of the Yalakom watershed without adequate investigation into landscape-scale issues, with no forest cover information, and with no long-term plan. The Yalakom community held a series of special meetings and councils and reached consensus that maintaining biotic diversity and ecosystem integrity would be a "bottom-line goal" for the watershed. This was the beginning of a struggle for a long-term, ecosystem-based plan for the watershed that has not yet been resolved.

In the struggle to defend their watershed and develop some vertical forms of communication with government agencies, various Yalakom community members have been sent at the community's expense to Ministry of Forests and Environment courses on "forest ecosystem networks" and "biogeoclimatic zones." As well, certain community members have taken Silva Forest Foundation courses on, and ecological economics for, practical planning and landscape analysis. Some Yalakom reinhabitants have also learned to map ecosystem types in their own watershed, identify rare and special ecosystems, and carry out on-the-ground observations of wildlife habitat. They have learned to use aerial photos, topographic maps, biogeoclimatic maps, ecosystem classification data, and forest cover maps to create a map of the distribution and abundance of factors important to ecosystem function, such as plant community types, winter ranges, other habitat features, and the location of rare species (Wright 1997).

Yalakom members have also organized two public educational presentations by BC ecoforester Herb Hammond (1991) and another on the proposals for protected areas in the Timber Supply Area. They have also made presentations to all the forest land base commissions that have passed through the region and attended most of the conferences on forestry-related issues in the lower and central parts of British Columbia. Since 1996, three members of the community have participated on the Lillooet District Community Resources Board (CRB), part of the Lillooet Land Resource Management Plan. The Yalakom community views the CRB as a forum for local people to use consensus process to work out an acceptable land use plan that represents local interests, respects ecosystem integrity, and maintains biotic diversity (Wright 1997).

Far from remaining an isolated, parochial group, Yalakom members have built an impressive network of horizontal relationships in local and regional civil society. They have also developed extensive vertical bridges with local and regional government agencies and personnel. They are networked horizontally on a wider scale with other province-wide networks, such as the British Columbia Environmental Network. They participated in continental bioregional gatherings and were the main organizers of the third North American Bioregional Congress in Squamish. All of these broader links are based on the strength of their local community relationships. The Yalakom community has worked hard to build strong ties among members. Many years of living, working, struggling, cooperating, reaching consensus, and celebrating together have indeed produced strong bonds of friendship, mutual support, reciprocity, trust, and solidarity among the community members. This bonding work has not always been easy. The Yalakom community is no utopia, but it has established a real presence in the region.

Inevitably, problems and conflicts have arisen between people in the community, which has had to learn to deal with them. Like Helen Forsey, these community members recognize cultural barriers to cooperation. Van Andruss and Eleanor Wright have described some of the obstacles: "Of course, the way to tribal unity is hard, and difficulties persistently arise. We are in a period when North American consumer society seems to be reaching its highest peak. Many people have been hurt by the system; they feel bruised all over, and trust is not easy to come by. The acquisition of private property accentuates tendencies toward individualism. Titles of land ownership isolate us. Money, sex and male dominance are other possible stumbling blocks to genuine community" (Forsey 1993).

In the 1990s, the Yalakom community acted to deal with conflicts and tensions. Some members attended courses in conflict resolution methods, nonviolence, mediation, facilitation, and reevaluation and co-counselling methods to help individuals and the community as a whole better develop their consensus process and think, work, live, and build together. Despite their conflicts and tensions, people in the community learned that they could settle disputes and cooperate to organize themselves. They learned to value compassion, flexibility, and a sense of humour, while building the trust in each other necessary for community, as Andruss and Wright note: "Most of our life in common is founded on trust, goodwill, generosity and patience. The love underneath is what has held our little world together, and still does" (Forsey 1993).

The Yalakom community is learning to ground itself in place, in the rhythms of the land and the yearly cycle of the seasons. The circle, the organized form of their community council, is also the form used to celebrate their connection to place and the Earth, their ecological kinship with the land community. This embodied understanding of the use of ritual ceremony and story in their extended family circle is expressed simply and poetically by Andruss and Wright:

> Tomorrow night is full moon and Winter Solstice both. The old year is ending and the new year just beginning. Yes, there will be celebrations. The people of this valley will get together; there will be music, dancing, feasting – and beautiful desserts!
>
> At some point in the evening, we will form a circle and speak to each other, all of us together. We'll acknowledge the presence of elders and special guests. We'll remember friends who could not be present; we'll honour the household hosting the occasion. We'll mention the value of the food and the preparers of the food, and we'll thank the Earth that produced it.
>
> Gifts will be exchanged. These are not Christmas presents, they are Solstice presents, intended to celebrate the rhythms of our fruitful planet and our good friendships with each other.
>
> Ours is a community of place. It is composed not only of human partners, but of ponderosas and firs, bunchgrasses, birds and cold-running creeks. Within this web of beings we are attempting to make ourselves a home. (Forsey 1993)

Clearly, the use of ritual in seasonal celebrations by the Yalakom community is simple, uses the circle form, and celebrates the rhythms of the Earth, the nonhuman beings of their community of place, and the bonds between people that they have struggled hard to create in their effort to become indigenous to place.

In a civil society theoretical view, the use of these tools takes place within a strategy of reinhabitation that builds a local valley-wide community of place while networking horizontally with other groups in civil society beyond the local watershed. This strategy produced a certain amount of success in terms of creating lasting bonds between community members (an increase in trust and love) and a number of new networks both within and outside the community. Norms of cooperation, mutual aid, civic solidarity, and ecological kinship are being formed incrementally through daily practice, but from the evidence they are emergent norms. They have not been consolidated yet as established social norms, even within the Yalakom community. Clearly, building reinhabitory community is a slow process.

Reinhabiting Cities and Towns

Reinhabitation for urban regions presents a different dimension to efforts at living in place from what we have seen with the back-to-the-land movement. Peter Berg, speaking on green city issues at NABC II in 1986, emphasized the necessity of what he called "large-scale reinhabitory activity" in urban regions. Reinhabitation in cities confronts the daunting triple challenge of transforming the consciousness and behaviour of large numbers of urban residents, the necessity of implementing institutional/structural change, and the need for physical transformation of built environments. Anthropologist Roy Rappaport influenced early bioregional thought regarding the problem of reinhabiting cities. Over thirty years ago, Rappaport called for restructuring the ecology of cities but at the same time pointed out that this "restructuring" presented a problem not only for cities but also for society, its organizations, its general governance, and its values (1970). In this period, some bioregionalists often dismissed cities as hopeless relics of a corrupt and dying civilization. I encountered such attitudes myself at the Hat Creek gatherings throughout the 1980s.

For many in the bioregional movement, reinhabiting cities presented three other problems as well, according to Berg. He reports that, from the point of view of many back-to-the-landers in the 1970s and early 1980s, an attitude of "why bother with cities anyway?" existed. These people had abandoned cities because they realized that they were not healthy environments and wanted to try really different experiments of what truly cooperative community could be – but outside cities. However, Berg and other bioregionalists realized that, unless urban reinhabitation was seriously addressed, the bioregional movement would remain marginal to society. As Berg argued at the 1986 congress, if the bioregional movement did not integrate a green city orientation into its vision and work, it was in danger of remaining "a rural, sparsely populated, land-based phenomenon" that "could be destroyed by not being able to relate to urban populations." To avoid this unwelcome outcome, Berg and other urban bioregionalists were already making efforts to give green city organizing a greater priority in the bioregional movement and in society more generally.

The green city idea within bioregionalism has an immediate precursor in the concept of "reinhabiting cities and towns," developed in the early 1980s. In *Reinhabiting Cities and Towns: Designing for Sustainability*, John Todd and George Tukel (1981) discuss patterns and processes in nature and their relationship to urban and regional design. For them, biogeography, history, and community structures are understood as intertwined phenomena. They argue that knowing a place is the first step in the evolution of bioregionally based design practices. At this local scale, Todd and Tukel envision an approach to urban neighbourhood and district scale design based on forms of solar energy and community energy systems, a soil rebuilding program, solar aquaculture and stream daylighting, various forms of urban site and neighbourhood-/district-scale agriculture, passive and active solar building design, a diversity of forms of private and public transportation, and the use of a form of bioregional mapping that they called "place patterning."

In *Toward a Bioregional Model: Clearing Ground for Watershed Planning*, published in 1982 by Planet Drum, Tukel discusses a bioregional approach to planning. He cautions that a bioregional model is not a blueprint. Rather, what is essential for a bioregional model of planning is maintaining (or restoring) the health and diversity of the life place. Such an approach, Tukel argues, requires a cultural identity that locates humans within the membership of the "wider life-community." Tukel views a bioregional culture-nature relationship as symbiotic. He argues that, as the knowledge base of a bioregional model increasingly draws its content from the surrounding ecology, the accompanying cultural habits will grow adaptive in equal proportion: "No longer an invention by the heirs to and practitioners of the scientific revolution (engineering, design, communications), cultural behaviour comes to support and is supported by its native terrain" (1982, 5). At a site-planning and neighbourhood scale, urban built environments and open spaces can be designed (or redesigned) to be multifunctional and renewable over the course of time.

At the scale of the city and the bioregion, by taking their cue from shifting local successional patterns, design and planning can strive to accomplish discrete goals (within the overall transition to sustainability) and thereby maintain flexibility. Tukel's approach would allow for incremental change as part of a long-term comprehensive vision and process of transformation in accord with the natural patterns and processes of the bioregion. Furthermore, in place patterning on a regional scale, the synoptic vision achieved via mapping the long-term structural portrayal of the watershed and the bioregion can be keyed directly to the material, energetic, and informational elements that make up the region. Doing so enables one to picture – through multiple overlays – the aggregate effects of human activities within the bioregion. For Tukel, what is important is to reveal the "recognizable pattern that inheres in the watershed and connects human movements, ecological stress and functional degradation or possible disintegration" (1982, 13).

When working toward a bioregional model based on patterns in nature, Tukel emphasizes that it is crucial to base the model on the fact that natural succession is driven by solar energy. Conversion to the use of solar forms of power is not exclusively a bioregional idea, but it was seen as essential to a bioregional model by its founders. The early work of Berg, Tukel, and John and Nancy Todd on reinhabiting cities and towns points to the crucial link between renewable forms of solar energy and bioregional processes and patterns. The city is viewed in its bioregional context as one element within a bioregion. In this model, the life and health of the bioregion must come first. For Tukel, the design implications of a symbiotic model are that, over time, design requirements become part of a vernacular, part of the very memory of the human community. This view recognizes culture as a central factor in societal transformation and thus raises the problem of long-term generational change in a civil society dominated by both state and corporate spheres.

These early bioregional urban reinhabitory ideas were born out of the richness of interdisciplinary thought and experiment taking place in California in the late 1970s and early 1980s. One of the key events that contributed to early ecological city/green city thinking was held in 1980. Two architects and teachers from Sausalito, California, Sim Van der Ryn and Peter Calthorpe, organized a week-long intensive "Solar Cities Design Workshop" at the Westerbeke Ranch near Sonoma, California. This was an interdisciplinary group of forty-five leading innovators in ecology and community design, including architects, community organizers, transportation specialists, ecologists, biologists, agriculturists, planners, public officials, entrepreneurs, and others. The organizers of the workshop, including Van der Ryn and Calthorpe, hoped to develop a holistic perspective on sustainable cities. They called the approach that emerged from this early *charette* "a new design synthesis" in their book *Sustainable Communities: A New Design Synthesis for Cities, Suburbs, and Towns* (1986). Peter Berg participated in the week-long workshop. Later Van der Ryn and Calthorpe participated, in turn, in the Celebrate the Longest Night conference in 1985 organized by Planet Drum that launched green city organizing in the Bay Area.

The goal of the Van der Ryn and Calthorpe *charette* was to design ways in which three prototypical urban communities – an older, inner-city eastern neighbourhood; a postwar western suburb; and a piece of raw land within a growing metropolitan area – could be revisioned into places that, over a twenty-year period, reduced their dependence on fossil fuel and increased community self-reliance and livability. The design synthesis that emerged from these case studies included more compact, mixed-use communities; more efficient buildings; diverse transit systems; ecologically sound agriculture based on diverse crops; water and waste conservation; diversity in transportation over "auto monoculture" consistent with mixed-use zoning; solar passive architecture; and community-controlled energy and waste systems. A strong bioregional influence was evident in the importance given to design that amplifies the unique qualities of each place as well as a call to respect the uniqueness and integrity of each region. Also of key importance for bioregional reinhabitory urban design was the idea that the modern geographical separation of production and consumption could be reintegrated through a transformed "homeplace" that, according to Van der Ryn and Calthorpe, "rather than being merely the site of consumption, might, through its very design produce some of its own food and energy, as well as become the locus of work for its residents" (1986, xiii). Here was an important paradigm shift in thinking about the urban homeplace from its limited role in the globalized monoculture of consumerism toward becoming once again the hub of a decentralized mode of domestic production of extended families and more self-reliant communities and neighbourhoods.

Van der Ryn and Calthorpe cite the designs of the New Alchemy Ark in Massachusetts and the Farallones Institute Integral Urban House in Berkeley as examples of early experiments toward creating sustainable homeplaces that actually integrate food and energy production. However, in this context, they caution that urban self-reliance cannot be an individual affair since in the city survival is a collective enterprise and constructive action must necessarily be cooperative. Such cooperation presents a real challenge to global monoculture.

Van der Ryn and Calthorpe, influenced by bioregional thought, also point out that, while such proposals (higher density, mixed use, passive solar, urban agriculture, etc.) are becoming commonplace, what needs to become a priority – beyond material efficiencies and simple conservation – is a sense of reverence for the nature of a place that "bespeaks a greater everyday understanding of our region, its watershed, climate, geology, plants, animals, and most importantly, its activities – its life" (1986, xvi). Again we see the influence of bioregional thinking about the central importance of culture, place, and region in early concepts of sustainable urban communities.

Equally importantly, from the point of view of cultural shift and community building, Van der Ryn and Calthorpe argue that the imperative for compact urban design, energy efficiency through community energy and waste systems, and so on reintroduces the notion of "the commons." They point out that the old English commons not only gave village people access to productive land but also underlay "their common identity and therefore their power." Van der Ryn and Calthorpe then call for a new recognition of place and commons in the transition to sustainable cities: "We need to move towards a sense that our place is a habitat within, rather than a settlement beyond, the ecosystem. The other aspect missing is the notion of the commons, that the public domain must become richer as the private domain becomes more frugal; that success and well-being must be a shared, rather than a private affair. It is the missing sense of ecology and the commons that makes places real, turns 'housing' into dwelling, 'zones' into neighborhoods, 'municipalities' into communities, and ultimately, our natural environment into a home" (1986, xvi-xvii).

Here place and commons are brought together, the former a cultural concept, the latter a political one. In this integrated view, a common identity with place through sharing the same lands, the commons, can be very empowering. Moreover, it is a common empowerment in that the power is "their power," not merely empowerment for individuals. When place and commons coincide, bioregional community emerges.

Another key contribution to the emergence of urban reinhabitation and ecological or sustainable city thought and experiment in the Bay Area was the group in Berkeley that called itself Urban Ecology. It was founded in 1975 by Richard Register and others. Register recalls that a number of people interested in the ideas of Paolo Soleri on cities and what Soleri called "arcology" (architecture plus ecology) wanted to test some of his concepts (Canfield 1990, 98-100). Arcology envisions building cities as single composite structures that integrate density through vertical rather than horizontal growth. Such arcologies would, by design, virtually eliminate the automobile. The city, designed as a vast single structure linked by walkways and elevators, would allow people to walk and/or ride elevators to any location within the city in a few minutes. A model arcology called Arcosanti, designed to accommodate 5,000 people, is now being built in the Arizona high desert on the top of a basalt mesa near Phoenix. Soleri argues that "arcology is in clear opposition to suburban sprawl because it advocates a lean (frugal) but intense mode of life, the only one realistically implementable on planet Earth already host to 5 billion people on top of the vegetable and animal kingdoms" (Canfield 1990, 103-4).

Although admiring Soleri's visionary ideas, Register and the others in the fledgling Urban Ecology group soon turned to exploring the transformation of existing cities rather than building new towns from scratch. However, how to achieve "integrated density" remained a cardinal issue for Urban Ecology. In its view of integrated density, density (or proximity) and diversity are linked. Diversity at close proximity means "just about everything beneficial! Land conservation, pollution reduction, energy conservation, greater social vitality, cultural potential, and physical access of the city's benefits to a much wider range of people" (Canfield 1990, 98).

In the work of Urban Ecology, like that of Soleri, a strong link is made between integrated density and greater social vitality and cultural potential. For Soleri, as for the Urban Ecology group, the compression of many minds in cities, libraries, theatres, universities, forums for research, debate, and communication are all essential parts of the intense exchanges at many levels made possible by the proximity supplied by cities. That is, well-designed integrated density encourages social interaction and thus the likelihood of increased associational life, a key ingredient for strong webs of interaction, trust, and cooperation in civil society. Moreover, integrated density also means land conservation, pollution reduction, and energy conservation. Thus, integrated density is a promising strategy for implementing ecological cities because it links reduced aggregate consumption with increased opportunities for greater and richer social and community interchange and bonding. In other words, integrated density holds a huge potential for reducing aggregate natural capital throughput consumption while encouraging the formation of social and ecosocial capital. This potential raises the strategic question of how to realize such a vision given the dominance of corporate and state power over civil society in the globalizing cities of North America.

The people at Urban Ecology quickly realized that transforming existing cities would be enormously difficult and in opposition to the cultural and institutional barriers of property ownership and established land use patterns. As Register expressed it, putting a few more people on bicycles, increasing recycling efficiency, adding solar collectors, and planting a few trees on every block would be far from enough to end the tyranny of the automobile. The Urban Ecology group realized that working on local, often site-based, incremental reforms needed to be carried forward as partial steps and be complemented by direct political work on "the more basic strategies of changing land uses, urban design and architecture toward far more diversity at close proximity" (Canfield 1990, 98). Moreover, those at Urban Ecology saw that the complex and huge task of such an enormous change in established patterns would require a phased set of changes over many decades to shift people and built environments out of urban sprawl into "urban, neighbourhood and small town centers" (98). Given this understanding, a long-term vision of strategic and cultural change was needed to inspire and guide the transition to sustainable urban settlement.

Register describes the vision and strategy worked out by Urban Ecology along with a 140-year transitional policy plan for the city of Berkeley in *Ecocity Berkeley: Building Cities for a Healthy Future* (1987). In this visionary transitional plan, Register defines an ecocity as, simply, an ecologically healthy city. He points out the obvious, that no such city now exists, while also pointing to forerunners of the ecocity in some Medieval European cities and in the solar pueblos of the Indians of the American southwest. To begin the transition, Register promotes solar, wind, and recycling technologies; creek restoration projects; urban gardening and fruit tree planting; and foot, bike, and public modes of transportation in preference to the automobile as projects that reveal glimpses of and movement toward ecocities. Yet he strongly emphasizes the need to involve large numbers of people in a cultural-political process of transformation, a similarly broad restructuring of civilization called for by Rappaport.

Bioregional thinking, especially with regard to cultural change and the relationship of humans to place, has strongly informed the vision and work of Urban Ecology. Both emphasize the key importance of a long-term cultural transformation, the need for ecological city concepts to be firmly established and broadly understood and supported. These are key ingredients of a democratic transformation of and by civil society. Register gives full credit to activists in the bioregional movement for their influence on the thought of Urban Ecology, especially for rekindling the sense of place and alerting people to the extent of their impacts on nature: "You can't miss what you never knew. But by teaching us about the full richness of our biological environments, bioregionalists make it possible for people to know what they have had the misfortune never to have experienced personally, to miss it, want it back, and to become empowered to get it back" (1987, 7). More specifically, in Register's view, bioregional thinking about urban reinhabitation has contributed the fundamental green city concept of viewing the city dynamically as potentially able to contribute a great deal to the regeneration of its bioregion.

With respect to working toward the formation of a critical mass of actively involved people, Register admits that modern city dwellers are more familiar with technologies and built environments than with natural elements of the bioregion and biosphere. Consequently, he asserts, it is especially urgent for city dwellers to experience and learn as much as they can directly from nature: "We need to touch nature more intimately, let our children grow up knowing that vegetables don't just appear in the supermarket by magic, knowing instead the magic of sun, wind, rain, creeks, bees, butterflies, flowers, gardens, farms" (1987, 16).

Register cautions that ecocity planning and design must also take into account the extra-urban activities related to conventional urban forms: range and forest management, replacement of natural species with domestic ones, deforestation for agriculture, flooding of entire valleys for electricity and water for city and farm alike, and long-distance commuting, all contributing to the destruction of habitat and the diminution and extinction of species. Register firmly locates urban issues in the context of the bioregion, where urban, suburban, and rural dwellers are all responsible for the bioregion as a whole.

For Register and Urban Ecology, there are many ways for people in civil society to help build ecocities: from restoring creeks, rivers, shore fronts, and marshes right in the city to narrowing sidewalks and streets, reducing the number of cars, shrinking parking lots, new- and used-car lots, et cetera, and making serious food growing a conscious part of every urban person's experience by bringing agriculture into places where large numbers of people live and work.

Another essential concept developed by Urban Ecology is the use of proximity policies and proximity planning such as zoning regulations and tax incentives to "open up the city to nature while shifting urban activity to other, more focused and diverse areas" (Register 1987, 18). Proximity policies and planning mean that, if human development is concentrated in small areas of great diversity, public transportation will work best when moving people from one dense centre of activity to another. This dramatic change in land use releases extensive areas for habitat restoration within and around the city. It also means that horizontal networks of civically responsible and proactive urban dwellers need to be complemented by vertical political and economic campaigns to change public policy.

In advancing this ecologically informed land use model, Register argues that, through the application of urban ecology concepts and design processes, diversity, both natural habitat diversity and human cultural diversity, can be respected and integrated into a long-term design and planning approach that is community based and democratic. Through proximity planning, compact mixed-use urban areas (including horticulture and agriculture) would leave enough land area for humans and domestic species while allowing other lands to be restored or preserved for wildlife habitat, lands that are both large enough and interconnected via ecological corridors to support a diversity of wild populations.

Register and his coworkers have grounded their work in their own city, developing a transitional plan for Berkeley to be implemented in stages over the next 150 years. Moreover, the development of the plan was not dreamed up by the Urban Ecology group in some abstract ecocity think tank but informed by actual urban restoration work of several citizen groups in projects such as the restoration of Strawberry Creek or local efforts to prevent development on a waterfront marsh. Some citizens of Berkeley took an early lead in what Register and his cothinkers would eventually theorize as urban ecology. In Berkeley, there were groups working on introducing a "slow streets" (road narrowing) concept to curb auto traffic in the early 1980s and the initiation of a bicycle plan as early as the first half of the 1970s (Register 1987).

The Ecocity Berkeley concept developed by Urban Ecology considers several areas in Berkeley: the waterfront, the flats, and the hills; the neighbourhoods; the university; and the downtown. Specific strategies are developed for each area. Then a long-term plan for the entire city is developed and presented through a series of maps that depict Berkeley before Europeans arrived, in the present era, and in a series of four time periods or "stages" in the future. The plan is based on strategies such as gradually withdrawing from thinly populated, auto-dependent areas; incrementally building up dense, mixed-use centres of activity; bringing agricultural areas into places where large numbers of people live and work; making food growing a serious part of every urban person's experience; opening up and restoring Berkeley's nine creeks; and bringing ecological corridors into suburbia and sizable areas of restored habitat right into the city.

The thinking of Urban Ecology with respect to integrated density and proximity policies and planning is related to the work of Jane Jacobs. She uses the concepts of "diversity" and "intensity" in her discussion of urban form and design in *The Death and Life of Great American Cities* (1992), first published in 1961. Jacobs argued that "a city's very *structure* consists of a mixture of uses, and we get closer to its structural secrets when we deal with the conditions that generate diversity" (376). For Jacobs, there are four basic conditions that generate diversity:

1 The district, and indeed as many of its internal parts as possible, must serve more than one primary function: preferably more than two.
2 Most blocks must be short; that is, streets and opportunities to turn corners must be frequent.
3 The district must mingle buildings that vary in age and condition, including a good proportion of old ones so that they vary in the economic yield they must produce. This mingling must be fairly close grained.
4 There must be a sufficiently dense concentration of people, for whatever purposes they may be there. This includes dense concentration in the case of people who are there because of residence. (150-51)

When these four conditions were met, a city could manifest its true function as a favourable environment for the rich social-cultural-economic interaction of people. These multiple interactions illustrated the kind of vitality that Jacobs believed was the very definition of urban life. Indeed, for her, it was the intensity of mixed uses and the dense concentration of people that supplied the necessary conditions for this especially urban form of vitality. Streets, neighbourhoods, and districts "where diverse city uses and users give each other close-grained and lively support" were the various scales at which Jacobs identified the four generators of urban vitality (1992, 377). In her various case studies, Jacobs found that places where diversity and intensity could be observed were areas of vitality and rich interaction.

Her discussion of the conditions for vitality of urban neighbourhoods and districts and her concerns for the loss of community through what she called the "erosion" of the city by the automobile provided early groundwork for the later analysis of Urban Ecology. Jacobs's concerns regarding the relationship of urban form and design to urban vitality were primarily sociocultural and economic, not ecological. Nevertheless, without losing these social concerns of diversity and intensity, Urban Ecology brought an ecological dimension to the older discourse on diversity and density. Integrated density is one important basis for encouraging the buildup of a richer urban associational life, a greater density of networks of citizen involvement that favours the establishment of norms of trust and civic solidarity.

Indeed, Jacobs's special sense of urban vitality and community life is akin to the notion of social capital. This suggests a relationship between urban form, as it has been theorized by Jacobs, and social capital. Moreover, the integrated density concept of Urban Ecology, by opening up cities to urban ecological corridors, by daylighting and restoring urban creeks and streams, would encourage the generation of ecosocial capital. Ecocities, designed at the site, street, neighbourhood, district, and city-wide levels for intensity and diversity of uses and interactions in dense mixed-use areas, could arguably encourage and facilitate the building of communities where social capital and ecosocial capital flourish. But the strategic question remains, how would all this begin? How would sufficient social and ecosocial capital develop to begin the envisioned 140-year transformation of not only civil society but also the state and corporate spheres?

As the work and long-term plan of Urban Ecology have illustrated, the immense social effort to build ecocities is envisioned to take several generations to implement. This consideration bears directly on the issue of restructuring cities and urban regions and, as Rappaport argued, all of civilization. If restructuring is to be achieved democratically, high levels of social capital will be necessary for achievement of the strategy. However, democratic civil society theory also tells us that horizontal organizing and communication within the sphere of civil society are not enough. Policy changes as well as structural changes in state and corporate sectors will be necessary to support the cultural and socioeconomic shifts occurring in the civil society sphere.

The following two urban narrative accounts illustrate some ways and forms in which bioregionalists have attempted to address the challenge of restructuring in the San Francisco Bay Area and in Vancouver, British Columbia. In both cases, bioregionalists adopt a strategy of building local community action groups (the "seed" groups) complemented by horizontal community links and networks in civil society as a way to begin the long, difficult path to restructuring currently unsustainable cities. This is the horizontal dimension of the strategy on which are based various forms of public communication and vertical "bridging" with state and corporate sectors.

San Francisco

San Francisco Bay is the largest estuarine system on the west coast of North America with the largest complex of coastal marshes. The bay and estuary are composed of thirty-four distinct watersheds. The estuary is the place where freshwater and saltwater meet, a dynamic zone of overlapping eco-systems. Because of the estuary, the Bay Area has two to three times the bio-diversity of any single terrestrial or aquatic system. Combined with fertile soils, the region has a mild climate that allows year-round food production. The mild climate also means less energy for heating and cooling. The Bay Area from Sonoma County in the north to Santa Clara County in the south is over 100 miles long (see Figure 8).

Figure 8 This 1977 map, "Watershed Guide: A Map of the San Francisco Bay Area Watershed," was done for the Frisco Bay Mussel Group by artist Michael Moore, and is a good example of early bioregional mapping.

It includes the Silicon Valley. The Bay Area is a large urban region of 100 cities and nine counties with a total population of over six million people. The bay itself and the hills surrounding it do not provide a lot of room for urban sprawl, but sprawl has occurred nevertheless. Sprawl and pollution threaten the area's greenbelt.

Economic activity in the Bay Area is very diversified. Major industries in addition to agriculture include the high-tech industry in the Silicon Valley, a wine industry in the Napa Valley, several military bases, and a secondary materials industry. San Francisco Bay is degraded by pollution from long-time sewage and industrial discharges. The largest remaining tidal wetland in California is threatened by water diversion to quench the growing thirst of urban California and large-scale agriculture (Urban Ecology 1996).

It was in the Bay Area that the green city concept was conceived in the early 1980s. The notion began quite naively, according to Peter Berg, out of a brainstorming session at a rock concert in Golden Gate Park when Berg captured the crowd's attention by involving everyone in a participatory green city visioning session. His point about this beginning is that it was first and foremost a participatory activity involving many people. This initial act was both real and symbolic: real in that the burst of group chanting and energy at the rock concert eventually helped to move Berg and the Planet Drum people to more thought and action around green city initiatives, and symbolic in the sense that a transformation to green city policies and programs required change in consciousness and involvement of large numbers of people, a transformation that would require urban restructuring and involve more than one generation to accomplish.

The next part of the San Francisco story illustrates a different but complementary lesson: how to begin the transformation. Berg argues that a Green City Project does not have to begin by tackling the entire city. Victories can be won incrementally. Actions that authenticate, illustrate, and model more general propositions can be carried out at a neighbourhood scale. Berg recounts the story of the battle for the right to planting space on the sidewalk adjacent to his and his partner, Judy Goldhaft's, home at Planet Drum. This story begins when Berg was issued a ticket for having a sidewalk in ill repair. Planet Drum had deliberately left it in disrepair to allow the grass to grow up through it. After months of haggling with city hall, they finally won the right to rip up half their sidewalk to plant a garden with native plant species. The neighbours liked the garden and the plants. The story hit the newspapers and became a local cause célèbre.

The next phase of the story points once more to a broader scale of action. Planet Drum wanted to know how to fund an entire Green City Program. The effort to plan this program involved a good number of people, this time in a variety of more active roles. Planet Drum organized a winter solstice celebration to spread the idea of a green city far and wide and to involve more people in conceptualizing such a city. A major fund-raising event, Celebrate the Longest Night, took place in December 1985 on the winter solstice. Nearly 1,000 people, including poets, musicians, and theatre workers, attended the event. The celebration raised a lot of energy and some money. About $7,500 was raised to fund meetings toward developing a green city plan for the entire San Francisco Bay Area.

With this support, Planet Drum was able to implement the next phase. Nine community meetings, entitled Symposia on Urban Sustainability, were organized and held through the spring and summer of 1986. They addressed a range of topics on urban reinhabitation, based on the following themes: renewable energy, urban planting, urban wild habitat, transportation, recycling, cooperatives and collectives, sustainable planning, neighbourhood empowerment, and arts and communication. There was a broad range of participants at the nine meetings. For example, at the recycling and reuse meeting, there were representatives of some city and county recycling agencies, a range of private reuse businesses, citizen groups opposed to waste, youth employment agencies, and professional scavenger companies. At the urban wild habitat meeting, there were urban gardeners, defenders of open spaces, native plant experts, animal tenders, teachers, environmental writers, the founder of a citizen group that helped to secure Golden Gate National Recreation Area, and the director of Golden Gate Park. Although there were neighbourhood representatives at these meetings, the primary appeal of the series was to communities of interest based on the nine themes. Clearly, the strategic thinking included a recognition that, for an effective city-wide strategy, it was necessary to combine communities of both place and interest.

Each session began with a description of the current situation from each participant's point of view. For example, renewable energy advocates complained of no significant gains in using alternatives to fossil fuels since oil resumed a low price in the late 1970s. Neighbourhood representatives told how high-rise apartments and chain stores were crowding out the last remnants of unique small businesses and block-scale social and family life. Sustainable-planning proponents described the failure of residents' influence on growth-dominated municipal-planning processes. Transportation analysts forecast a doubling of the capacity of existing freeways and the addition of another deck to the Golden Gate Bridge unless people began using alternatives to automobiles.

Then participants were asked to envision alternatives. The broad range of suggestions and proposals was eventually condensed into a nine-part book: *A Green City Program for San Francisco Bay Area Cities and Towns,* published by Planet Drum (Berg, Magilavy, and Zuckerman 1989). The program is a full account of all the areas of sustainability covered in the community meetings. Berg, in his introduction to the book, frankly discusses some formidable barriers to such a shift, including a reference to the erosion of local community in the megalopolis of the Bay Area as well as to the vast scale of the ecological damage directly attributable to the ways in which cities currently function.

The program describes a list of benefits to be gained by cities from the implementation of the nine programs, along with both short-term and long-term strategies for municipal action, using the Bay Area as a model. For example, the report suggests that municipalities could create zoning policies that favour neighbourhood retailers over large shopping centres, establish small-business incubators where new businesses would pay low rent and share services and office equipment, and make significant improvements in public transit, public libraries, and low-income housing, favouring operators of socially responsible small businesses.

The report adopts a cumulative, holistic approach to the aggregation of many incremental changes across all nine areas of policy. For example, there are short sections linking each of the nine programs to other directly related program areas, carefully illustrating the interconnection of issues and weaving the overall program together. It was understood that, while single proposals may be modest, the cumulative effect of the implementation of all the proposals across all nine fronts would engender the beginning of a protracted transformation of urban areas into sustainable cities grounded in their bioregions.

The strategy holds out the promise that accumulated incremental reforms, guided by an overall program that sets a clear green city direction, would work to collectively shift our unsustainable urban patterns to more sustainable ones. That is, this strategy strongly implies the need for a shift in culture as well as a series of political reforms. Moreover, Berg specifically points out that the heart of the program lies in the sections headed "What Can Cities Do to Promote ... ?" The key is that these sections link cultural change with political change. Cultural change is the basis, but political change is also necessary to consolidate the shift in belief. As Berg expresses it, the values and practices of "a new kind of urban resident are matched with the needed alterations in municipal policies" to begin to implement the program (Berg, Magilavy, and Zuckerman 1989, xvi). Berg explains that green city programs can act as a catalyst to generate the popular will necessary to move governments and social institutions toward sustainable cities. Such programs, developed locally by green city activists for their particular city or town, can have a twofold effect. They can provide what Berg calls a "green city umbrella," under which individuals, neighbourhood organizations, labour groups, small businesses, and others, each involved with some aspects of urban sustainability, can begin to care about all of them. As well, once such a program is made public and developed into a "platform for change," Berg argues that it can become "a powerful tool for influencing boards of supervisors, town councils, elected officials and candidates for office" (xvi).

Small-scale economic activity is integrated, or embedded, into this incremental, but visionary, strategy. In the Green City Program, local small businesses are recognized as essential to an incremental strategy of cultural and political transformation. They keep money circulating in the neighbourhood, district, and local city. Locally owned businesses are concerned about the quality of their places and the local impacts of their decisions.

While not discussed explicitly in the Green City Program, there is nevertheless a clear strategy based on the creation and enhancement of a web of horizontal linkages of cooperation and collaboration within and among both communities of interest and geographical communities in the Bay Area, including neighbourhood organizations, small businesses, and labour groups. Action in the political sphere, developing vertical influence for municipal reforms in the state sector, is understood to be effective when supported by a strong web of cooperative relations and new cultural norms in the grassroots, the sphere of civil society. Creating a democratically derived "platform for change," a green city "umbrella" supports and enhances a common understanding of the interrelated characters of the diverse interests of the constituent communities of place and interest in civil society. That is, understanding is spread horizontally in the civil society sphere, enhanced by the development of a common program. Furthermore, this horizontal mix of interests expressed in the common Green City Program is understood to provide stronger support for developing vertical influence for policy reform in the political sphere among municipalities, town councils, boards of supervisors, and politicians. Clearly, this strategy is based on a complementary mix of dual horizontal and vertical strategies in the civil society and political spheres in the Bay Area. Note, however, that, while small business is viewed as essential to this strategy, there is no mention of the power and influence of finance capital or large corporate entities or of any strategy to deal with this sector.

Finally, the Planet Drum Green City Program sketches a vision of a green city that can be both an inspiration for transformation and a model against which to measure progress toward the green city. In this context, Berg spoke at NABC II in the summer of 1986 about the potential for a federation of green city constituencies in the Bay Area to become the urban component of a bioregional council: "I don't expect the people coming to these meetings to be bioregionalists, but, if we keep the framework bioregional, eventually they could see the validity of a federation of the nine Bay Area counties. Local governments could come together, sending representatives as the green city plank, or program, to a bioregional council/ congress/federation/whatever for northern Shasta/Alta California" (Hart et al. 1987).

For over a decade, the strategy of the Green City Program for the Bay Area has been communicated to many individuals and organizations, not only locally but internationally. Over that time, Planet Drum distributed 18,000 copies of its *Green City Program for San Francisco Bay Area Cities and Towns* (Goldhaft 1999).

The green city vision, for bioregionalists, contains several concepts that, taken together, offer a very different understanding of what an urban dweller, as opposed to an urban consumer, could be. This vision represents a definite cultural shift from the dominant *homo economicus* in what it means to be a human being, a cultural shift central to the bioregional strategy. However, it is not a shift to some abstract or unfounded notion of a human that has never existed. Rather, the notion of a "bioregional urbanite" contains a very familiar sense of the human being. For example, Berg compares this new urban dweller with the way that farmers used to live, knowing and practising many different skills, as a kind of handyman. He also speaks about the pride associated with such self-reliance.

Similarly, Todd and Tukel compare urban reinhabitation with bricolage, or enlightened tinkering with what is at hand:

> Designers like clean slates. The bricoleur is different. There is an assumption that the true potential of a house, a block, or a whole town has scarcely been tapped. The most humble objects, like a hundred feet of sidewalk, can be transformed. There is a human dimension to bricolage. The bricoleur tries to listen to the voice of a place as expressed through the history and inhabitants. There is a responsibility to maintain continuity. To transform is not to inoculate with misplaced status. If restoration leads to displacement it is failure. The benefits of restoration must accrue to residents and subsequently to others who are affected by the change (1981, 38).

The notion of a bioregional urban dweller as a bricoleur who, using a mixed kit of tools, cobbles together bits and pieces from her or his immediate surroundings to help redesign the neighbourhood supplies an apt metaphor to capture the sense of initial strategy involved in generating incremental cultural changes toward more general long-range urban transformation.

Moreover, in the Green City Program, cultural transformation for individuals and neighbourhoods is necessarily and integrally linked to broader social and political change. For example, neighbourhood character and empowerment, while they may be initiated through small, local, "doable" projects, simply cannot be fully implemented without broader political change. Neighbourhood empowerment is intricately linked to sustainable planning, which must involve larger numbers of people in the choices and policy shifts that could determine the ecological functioning of their urban bioregion. Sustainable planning, in turn, is related to all the other dimensions of a green city: transportation, urban planting, renewable energy, et cetera. In this approach, addressing transportation in a comprehensive Green City Program also means addressing land use and energy issues. Conserving energy and land use, as well as promoting the use of renewable energy, may mean great restrictions in the use of the private automobile. However, adopting energy-efficient forms of transportation such as walking, bicycling, and public transit is linked to proximity policies in land use planning toward integrated patterns of denser settlements whereby people live, work, shop, and play mostly in the same neighbourhood. In such an integrated context of change, local business too can thrive by supplying the needed goods and services at the smaller scales required for efficiency in dense mixed-use districts. This brings us back, of course, in a complete circle, to neighbourhood character, empowerment, and cultural change.

Planet Drum's Green City Program, then, is based on and promotes a holistic and comprehensive understanding of visionary long-term societal transformation rooted in incremental cultural, political, and economic change. It is a dual strategy, aimed at both horizontal democratic transformation in the civil society sphere and developing influence for policy reform in the political sphere. It suggests (implicitly) a general transformation not only of cities but also of all social, cultural, political, economic, and ecological relationships. This again recalls Rappaport's observation that to transform the structure of cities must mean a transformation in the structure of civilization itself.

The San Francisco Bay Area has been a laboratory for urban ecological thought and experiment for several decades. Planet Drum and Urban Ecology are just two of many different organizations in civil society working on melding issues of reform and transformation in the Bay Area. By the end of the 1980s, there were thirty-five citizen groups working on restoration of the bay's wetlands with names such as Save San Francisco Bay Association, San Francisco Bay Keepers, and the Bay Organization for Aquatic Transit. The Save San Francisco Bay Association was founded in 1960 when the bay was being used as a garbage dump. The Bay Keepers use 40 private boats, 3 airplanes, and as many as 250 volunteers to teach people about the ecology of the bay, how to collect evidence of pollution and water quality, and what they can do. Other urban activist groups in the Bay Area of the 1980s included several organizations for stream restoration, the San Francisco League of Urban Gardeners (founded in 1983 to protect community gardens jeopardized by the loss of government funding), Friends of the Urban Forest, Friends of the River, the Ecology Center, the Wild in the City Project, the Greenbelt Alliance, the San Francisco Conservation Corps, the California Coastal Conservancy, Youth in Action, social justice groups such as the Community Transformation Forum working on environmental justice issues, the Integral Urban House of the Farallones Institute, and the Earth Island Institute.

Various government agencies and small-business groups in the Bay Area bioregion were also involved with projects and new products to meet the growing demand for ecologically sustainable goods and services. These groups and many others came together to share experiences and ideas, to network, and to develop creative solutions toward ecologically healthy cities for four days in the spring of 1990 in the Bay Area at the first International Ecocity Conference (Canfield 1990).

By 1990, the San Francisco Bay Area was a cauldron of ecological thought and sociocultural experiment. The accumulation of these local, citizen-initiated efforts has produced a climate for political change, as the Green City Program envisioned. Politics was very much a part of the mix. The City of Berkeley took the lead in many of these efforts. Berkeley was an appropriate venue for such an international ecocity gathering. The conference was organized by Urban Ecology. Conference coplanning sponsors included the City of Berkeley and the Planet Drum Foundation. In all, over 750 people from around the world attended the conference, although most were from the United States. In the Bay Area, ferment and organization in civil society were beginning to produce some real vertical influence in the political sphere at the municipal level.

In his report on the conference evaluation by participants, Richard Register noted that many people appreciated the networking opportunities of having 130 speakers and some of the most important innovators in their field in the world. One participant dubbed it a "networking feast" (Canfield 1990, 112). Moreover, summing up the contribution of the conference, Register remarked that the process "gave a sense of the whole, a sense that cities can be whole, vital, healthy creations in which architecture, transportation, land use, food-growing, natural restoration, social and political arrangements can play their role connected in meaningful ways to all the other systems and subsystems of the city. And the city itself, seen in the context of its bioregion and planet, was portrayed as it should be understood: as a potentially responsible citizen of our Earth, a friend to all people and all other species" (5).

On the final day of the conference, subcommittees formed to represent women's interests, transportation issues, and issues of social justice, and the various interests joined to draft a conference summary statement. One of the most interesting proposals with respect to building community came from the women's group, which proposed that future ecocity conferences be structured to model the way in which participants would like to live in an actual ecocity. Their suggestions for this restructuring included having fewer speakers, more interaction, and more time for discussion and networking, and under the specific topic of "community building" the women proposed a place to breathe, sing, and be quiet together as well as more time for festivity and celebration. This feminist approach to organizing major international networking gatherings was closer to the way that continental bioregional gatherings have been held where the creation of community has been central (see Chapter 6).

A summary statement delivered by Afro-American architect Carl Anthony, a board member of both Urban Ecology and the Earth Island Institute, reported that Ecocity Conference participants embraced the interconnection between environmental justice and urban ecology and affirmed "a systems view of life which embraces the interconnectedness of everything on Earth" (Canfield 1990, 113). This linkage of social justice with urban ecology concerns provided a more holistic model of social change than had been the case in the environmental movement of the 1970s and 1980s. It reflected the strong participation of some people from the environmental justice movement in the United States.

The environmental justice movement began in the early 1980s. It emerged out of a situation whereby polluting industries had been exploiting the pro-growth and pro-jobs sentiments among poor, working-class, and minority communities. However, blacks and other minorities began to challenge the justice of the environment–jobs trade-off. The not-in-my-backyard (NIMBY) syndrome that originated in affluent neighbourhoods had finally "trickled down" to nearly all communities, even poor black communities. The environmental justice movement emerged in the deep southern United States, where marked ecological disparities exist between black and white communities. In fact, it has taken root in the segregated South just as the civil rights movement of the 1960s did a generation ago. Environmental groups in the black community often emerged out of established social action organizations, including the black church and other voluntary organizations that led the crusade against social injustice and racial discrimination in the earlier civil rights movement (Bullard and Wright 1990). In poor communities, especially poor minority communities on the front lines of toxic waste, disposal dumps, and concentrated petrochemical production facilities, it is not surprising that residents began to make the connection between racial discrimination, social justice, and habitat destruction. In some cases, the same civil rights leaders and activists have provided leadership for this "new" form of environmentalism. Not surprisingly, the environmental justice movement is employing the tactics of the older civil rights movement: protest, political pressure, lobbying, grassroots organizing, and litigation to address issues of environmental injustice. Black church leaders, community improvement workers, and civil rights activists planned and initiated local opposition strategies, helping to mobilize opposition to industrial polluters such as Union Carbide and hazardous waste dump operators such as Chemical

Waste Management, which sited its operations in black neighbourhoods (Bullard and Wright 1990).

In San Francisco, Carl Anthony helped to found and coedit *Race, Poverty, and the Environment*, a newsletter launched as a project of the Earth Island Institute in April 1990 as a networking tool for the growing environmental equity movement. Analyzing the situation of the US inner city after the International Ecocity Conference, Anthony drew some connections between suburban sprawl, destruction of forests, and abandonment of the inner city: "We chop down the trees to build suburban sprawl. Suburban sprawl eats up farmland on the metropolitan fringe, requires more freeways with attendant congestion, pollution and waste of fossil fuels. In order to pay for this new development ... whole neighborhoods, factory buildings, schools, stores and people must be abandoned. These abandoned neighborhoods become the waste dumps of industrial society, places where poor people and people of colour live" (in Linn 1990, 1).

With such strong participation, the International Ecocity Conference in Berkeley seemed to mark a turning point toward a more inclusive and holistic movement for sustainable cities and environmental justice. In addition to networking, sharing experiences and ideas, and forging a common sensibility among many different groups, another goal of the conference was to communicate their shared experiences and help to bring the ecocity message to a larger audience. The conference received good media coverage, and presenters generally benefited from public communication of their information and imagery. The conference was timed to take place just weeks before the globally successful Earth Day 1990, promoted by Denis Hayes of the Earth Day Foundation-1990 and the Global Cities Project in San Francisco and organized locally in 134 countries in the latter part of April. This example shows another key aspect of an emergent long-term societal change strategy: initiating forms of public communication with the political sphere based on the strength of horizontal networks in civil society. Moreover, the mere fact that local actions could be organized effectively in decentralized fashion in 134 countries spoke to the possibility of global networks in the civil society sphere and the potential meaning of a "global" civil society.

Hayes, also instrumental in organizing the first Earth Day in 1970, gave a keynote address to the Ecocity Conference. He spoke about the strength of the environmental movement in the early 1970s in the United States, reflected in legislative successes after Earth Day 1970 such as the Clean Air Act, the Clean Water Act, the Environmental Education Act, the Occupational Health and Safety Act, and the banning of DDT and lead in gasoline. He noted the large numbers of people and organizations taking part in Earth Day 1990 preparations, but he also noted that, in spite of the victories won, the problems that we now face are greater. Hayes called for building a stronger movement that has the necessary vision to work toward ecological cities.

The organizers of the conference were not naive about the extent of the ecological crisis or the need to work even harder to promote the ideas emerging from the convergence of so many different groups and interests.

Constantly throughout the four-day event, speakers pointed to the increasing list of global trends that had become worse over two decades even as the ecology movement had grown. By building a conference around a networking strategy embracing environmental justice issues, the importance of inner city community development, and a more vigorous recruitment of minorities, participants helped to advance the vision of the emergent ecological city movement beyond mere environmentalism. Urban ecology – combined with social justice – began to resemble a broader conceptual framework for full sociocultural and political economic transformation in order to effectively address the global restructuring problem that cities present.

From all of the above examples, it is clear that the strategy of structural change envisioned for urban regions is both incremental and visionary, short term and long term, cultural and political, economic and social and that it relies on the cumulative effect of many different local projects networked laterally across civil society, linking communities of place and communities of interest. Based on this strategy are forms of public communication and vertical "bridging" and influence building with the political sphere.

Back at Planet Drum, a continuing determination to advance the Green City Program for the Bay Area was marked by the initiation of a range of projects and actions. In 1990, Planet Drum began fund-raising and organizing to build a Green City Center. It envisioned a centre that would serve the city by highlighting existing green city events and activities and acting as a catalyst for green city work by promoting and coordinating the efforts of individuals, nonprofit organizations, municipal government agencies, and businesses.

The Green City Center would provide space to local groups for workshops, meetings, and talks as well as volunteer and staff support for cooperative projects. The goal of the centre, as Steven Lewis put it, was to "anticipate the extreme public interest and municipal need for a workable vision of urban transformation based on ecology and sustainability" (1990, 13). At this time, Planet Drum's *Raise the Stakes* journal began to publish a regular green city report based on its activities in the Bay Area. However, due to Planet Drum's inability to raise enough money for the Green City Center, the Green City Project began to shift focus from physically building the centre to implementing the projects that the centre was intended to house.

The first major project was to create a network for volunteers that Planet Drum called the Green City Volunteer Network. Although many participating groups are involved in activities such as habitat restoration, urban gardening, and green city policy initiatives, the network is not restricted to ecological/environmental organizations. Rather, the idea behind this network is that the green city concept is by definition about broad, interconnected realities, so horizontal networking on a broad civil society basis makes good, strategic sense. One long-term possibility of networking is that the relationships that are developed eventually form the basis for a broad horizontal coalition of communities of place and interest in the city with the vertical political clout to effectively promote policy change at the municipal level in a green city direction.

In the short term, the Volunteer Network met two important immediate needs: providing extra recruiting assistance for organizations that rely on volunteer support but do not have the time or resources to recruit them, and "producing incipient bioregionalists" (Gregory 1992, 22). This practical approach informs people who have begun to care for their homeplace/city and want to help protect and restore it but do not know what opportunities exist for doing so; the volunteer network informs people about what they can do and where they can go to do it. For example, in the Bay Area, many habitat restoration projects already existed but could never find enough volunteers. A volunteer network addresses this problem.

The Green City Volunteer Network was launched in July 1991. In a few months, the network made referrals for thirty-eight volunteers to twenty-seven ecological organizations. One year later the Volunteer Network was referring volunteers to over 110 ecological and environmental organizations in the Bay Area. The network continued to grow. By 1996, it was referring more than 200 persons per month to over 400 ecological and urban sustainability groups (Planet Drum Staff 1996). By 1998, the network served some 455 organizations in the Bay Area.

Soon after the network was up and running, Planet Drum's Green City Project launched a quarterly Green City Calendar to aid in the networking effort by highlighting volunteer opportunities around the Bay Area through publishing a volunteer directory. Funding was obtained from a private foundation to include a newsletter as part of the calendar. Activities of local groups could now be reported on. The calendar was becoming an especially valuable tool for youth and school groups. Publication of the calendar by the Volunteer Network helped to increase membership. Production of the calendar increased to 5,000 copies per issue. The calendar became a bimonthly publication. Distribution was increased as well to health food stores, outdoor supply stores, cafés, community centres, libraries, barbershops, schools, and bookstores throughout the Bay Area. Membership in the Green City Project increased from 5 people to 174 in the space of one year (Planet Drum Staff 1995-96). Volunteer network directories, such as the one in the Bay Area, are one tool to facilitate the involvement of new people in the movement. Given the huge size of the volunteer sector, this tool holds potential as an important key for building strong horizontal links in the civil society sphere.

A third dimension of the Green City Project – to hold regular "workshop workdays" – was launched in 1993. At workshop workdays (or "Green City Work Parties"), volunteers receive both educational talks and hands-on training while enjoying great food and fun. Each work party has at least two sponsoring organizations to encourage cooperation and communication between groups. At one of the early workshops, Planet Drum and the San Francisco League of Urban Gardeners joined with the Community Housing Partnership, a nonprofit, low-income housing developer, to finish the construction and planting of a rooftop garden at the Senator Hotel, a federally funded, low-income housing project. Other workshop workdays have included helping to daylight and restore Cordonicls Creek in Berkeley, installing a large terraced garden at a San Francisco high school, launching a storm drain stencilling (Save the Bay – Don't Dump) campaign, coordinating the participation of ecological organizations in the San Francisco Carnival (the largest multicultural celebration on the West Coast), building a community garden in San Francisco's Mission District, and restoring a Native American village site in Marin County.

In 1994, a fourth program was initiated, entitled Education Plus Action. This program coordinates hands-on bioregional education for Bay Area educators from Volunteer Network groups to Bay Area classrooms. Topics include urban forestry; endangered species; urban planting, gardening, and composting; green consumerism; air pollution; alternative energy; recycling; habitat restoration; creek restoration; environmental justice; alternative transportation; and bioregionalism. The program coordinator organizes both a classroom lesson and a hands-on activity for the day. Programs can be tailored to student and classroom needs. This program has grown in tandem with the Volunteer Network.

Taken as a whole, the Green City Project is viewed by its proponents as a long-term practical implementation of Planet Drum's Green City Program for San Francisco Bay Area Cities and Towns. An example of how this program works to build local community capacity through a combined application of bioregional tools is provided by a look at one East Oakland high school's Environmental Justice Project. This example, published in the Green City Calendar (Lanza 1998), also shows how a city-wide network can act to serve a neighbourhood community, strengthening both in the process.

The biology teacher at Castelmont High School, Marc Borbley, wanted to plan an environmental justice project for 150 of his students. He began by assigning his students to collect articles from the daily papers related to human health and the environment. He also encouraged his students to share their own stories of environmental health and social justice with the rest of the class. Meanwhile, he researched local environmental justice groups through Green City's Education Plus Action program as well as other neighbourhood organizations. He also met with community organizers from the Women's Cancer Resource Center, Chester Street Block Club, and the EPA's Environmental Justice Team.

Then Borbley began a community-mapping program with his students. He had the students work in small groups to map their neighbourhoods, including every detail of where they live: homes, recreation areas and parks, community centres, factories, businesses, drug alleys and crack houses, polluted places, scary places, places they liked to hang out, and places they weren't allowed to go. The students mapped all this and more, including dangerous intersections where drivers sped through stop signs. Next the maps were consolidated into a larger illustration of the district. Borbley and the community organizers then explained to the students the importance of understanding one's place in order to facilitate sufficient local empowerment to establish and protect health and safety.

The next step is for the students to learn to collect data from the community by interviewing friends, family, and neighbours about their personal health, including a history of respiratory diseases, chronic colds and flu, and cancer. Then the students will map the proximity of sick people to industrial areas and probably learn that there are more factories in communities of colour than in Euro-American or higher-income neighbourhoods. The final step planned in the mapping process will be to re-create the community map in an idealized green version, pointing to empty lots that could be greened as recreation spaces, where more business is needed, where a stoplight is needed to slow down traffic, which factories should be reported for air pollution, and so on. Borbley's classes hope to paint eventually a mural of their maps at the entrance to the school. In the meantime, they are learning how to work cooperatively as they educate themselves and their community. Finally, the students will give their findings to community organizations to assist in furthering the environmental justice movement.

This project illustrates the use of a community mapping and learning process that draws together a base of common experiential knowledge about the place in which the students live. Through their shared work, the students learn about their place and how to map, and they begin to develop norms of cooperation and civic solidarity. Through sharing their findings with other community organizations for environmental justice, they will begin to learn about networking as a resource for community groups and individuals.

In this narrative account of the San Francisco Bay Area, we have seen examples of the development and initial implementation of a long-term bioregional strategy for social, political, and economic restructuring. Clearly, this is a strategy that promotes cultural change in civil society through the cumulative effect of many small, doable projects that foster norms of cooperation, civic solidarity, and mutual aid. This strategy relies on creating small activist "seed" groups and horizontal networks in civil society at many different geographical scales up to and including the planetary scale. This democratic civil society strategy is combined with building public communication and "bridging" links to influence policy reform in the political sphere.

Vancouver

Vancouver is located, along with a number of smaller cities, in the lower Fraser River basin on British Columbia's southwest coast. Two mountain ranges, the Northern Cascades and the Canadian Coastal Range, meet to form the eastern end of the lower Fraser valley. Together with the other natural boundary, the saltwater of the Strait of Georgia, the mountains form a triangular delta and a valley that stretches inland for 160 kilometres to where the two ranges meet. The valley was sculpted by glaciers 15,000-20,000 years ago. The climate is characterized by cool, wet, long winters and fairly short, dry summers. The soils and the climate support a favourable growing season for agriculture, and there are extensive agricultural land reserves in the valley on both sides of the US-Canada border.

The total population of the region is over two million people, but most of the region is mountainous. So nearly all human settlement is in the valley bottom below the 200-metre level, putting pressure on space for agriculture as the human population continues to grow, especially in several suburban areas where the growth rate is high and the agricultural land reserve is primarily located. Most of the original forest cover has been stripped away for human settlement, agriculture, and industry. Concentrations of air pollutants can be as high as in Los Angeles (City of Vancouver 1990). Pollution that gets trapped in the airshed between the two mountain ranges (particularly in the narrower eastern portions of the valley when there is a temperature inversion) is a growing threat to the health of the region's population. The primary source of the air pollution is the one million motor vehicles in the valley (Greater Vancouver Regional District 1994). Land use, transportation, and health are thus major issues in the valley.

Vancouver is Canada's largest seaport. Trade, financial services, communications, banking, tourism, and the export of raw materials (particularly pulp, paper, and timber from the hinterlands of British Columbia) are the generators of the city's success. The economy is well diversified, with a substantial regional market and an educated workforce. Access to relatively cheap hydroelectric power, natural gas, and coal in the province has given the city a competitive edge compared with Toronto, Montreal, or Los Angeles (Greater Vancouver Regional District 1994).

While an ecological or green city vision for Vancouver and its region did not emerge publicly until the mid-1990s, the city and the region have a relatively rich history of civic action as well as a relatively strong awareness of environmental issues. In the early 1970s, a citizens' movement prevented the construction of an expressway into the heart of the city. At that time, too, the international Habitat Conference held in Vancouver's Jericho Park helped to inform and fuel environmental concerns among the region's residents. Traditionally, there has also been a relatively strong labour movement in Vancouver. Also, the city's clearly defined valley topography and its more limited land base have contributed to making the conservation and protection of land and air resources more compelling concerns to decision makers in Vancouver compared with Seattle or Portland (Reid 1994). These concerns have also helped to fuel citizens' involvement and mobilization in the planning process. Beginning with the Livable Region Planning Process initiated by Harry Lash in the early 1970s, the idea that citizens should be intimately involved in the planning process has become part of the accepted discourse about planning in this region (Reid 1994).

The end of the 1980s marked a near-global upswing in public concern over environmental issues. In Vancouver, the increase in awareness about environmental issues was accompanied by increased citizen involvement in planning processes and in self-organized activity. For example, the Forum for Planning Action, formed in 1989, sought increased citizen participation in planning for livable communities and sustainable resource management. In 1992, neighbourhood organizations all over the city were beginning to form coalitions concerned with having more effective input in decision making at city hall and to take the necessary steps to bring about better neighbourhood governance. Eventually, they formed a city-wide coalition called Neighbour to Neighbour (Lehan 1994). Another group, Community Steps to Regional Governance, formed in 1992 out of concern that proposed restructuring of the Greater Vancouver Regional District might render this regional body less accountable and democratic. Also in 1992, a number of organizations formed the Lower Mainland Drinking Water Coalition over the issue of logging in the North Shore watersheds used for the city's water supply. In 1993, the Vancouver Permaculture Network was formed to provide a forum for discussion and to coordinate permaculture training workshops. Also, many citizens' circles formed as part of the Vancouver City Plan process in which about 20,000 people actively took part by making submissions and attending events (City of Vancouver 1992). However, in spite of this burgeoning civic activity, there was no organization around a bioregional green city vision.

A comprehensive, explicitly green or ecological city vision and activity to promote it did not emerge in Vancouver until the Greening Our Cities conference in May 1994. This conference and the EcoCity Network conceived during it advanced an overall vision of ecological cities in the lower Fraser River valley for the first time. Following this, the EcoCity Network began to organize a number of activities in civil society to work toward raising awareness about and implementing ecocity principles and values in the region.

This is the story of how that work began and its relation to bioregional community building and networking in civil society.

The conference was organized by a small, self-appointed steering committee of social ecologists, ecofeminists, bioregionalists, and First Nations people, including me. Some came from organizations such as the Social Planning and Research Council of BC, the VanCity Savings Credit Union, the United Native Nations, and the Musqueam First Nation. Their long-term goal was to bring a broad spectrum of people together to build a green city movement in the Vancouver region. They hoped that the conference would act as a catalyst to enable the groups and individuals working in related areas to begin effective networking and coordination of already on-going local activities in order to have a bigger impact on public awareness and on local and regional government decision making.

Over 250 people attended the weekend conference at the Maritime Labour Centre. The conference included keynote speakers David Suzuki, Chief Leonard George of the Tsleil-Waututh Nation, Peter Berg, Nancy Skinner (municipal counsellor and green city activist from Berkeley), and Marcia Nozick (editor of *City Magazine*). Panel discussions focused on three major topics: "Living with the Land in the City" (transportation, land use, and urban ecology); "Community Well-Being"; and "Acting on Green City Visions" (Litke et al. 1994). The conference received a good deal of press coverage from small independent publications.

Small-group discussions focused on the overall theme of acting locally in the Vancouver region, while each dealt with a particular theme, including land use and housing, green spaces and restoration, transportation, food in the city, community economic development, decision-making processes, green city neighbourhood discussion circles, First Nations/green city issues, fair trade, spirituality, and the important question of the creation of a green city network. In addition to including the creation of a green city network topic in the discussion groups, there were long "networking" coffee and lunch breaks for informal get-togethers and a Saturday-evening cabaret that provided another occasion for informal networking and socializing.

At the conference, the small group discussions were key to success in planning ongoing actions and networking. In these groups, it was recognized that, in attempting to green built environments in the city, a comprehensive and diverse framework that enabled society to work with the physical flows of the city, such as energy use, water use, waste management, food production, and land use, was needed. Small groups recommended acting on the potential food production of the bioregion; an interconnected green spaces and restoration strategy for biodiversity protection based on a specific knowledge of this bioregion; and urban planning and development that adopted an integrated, multiple-use approach to resources and the environment, with a bioregional focus. It was also recognized that, for the protection and restoration of green spaces, greater public understanding of and familiarity with the bioregion were fundamental.

In addition to this bioregional focus, the conference produced a range of ecological or green city ideas similar to those already reviewed, including mixed-use urban densification, a strong policy on developing an urban forest, community economic development, the use of more equitable and inclusive decision-making processes such as consensus, and the use of the "ecological footprint" tool to assist in evaluating land use design and strategy.

In their evaluations, participants recognized successes in real networking among a diversity of people, the sharing of experiences, stories, and practical examples, and the action orientation of the conference. The two major goals of the steering committee – the emergence of an initial green city vision for the Vancouver region by a broad diversity of interests, and the creation of an intention and a momentum to form some kind of ongoing organization – had been achieved. First, the Conference Declaration agreed by consensus decision process to seek a green Vancouver region through linking ecological sustainability with social justice. The conference also declared a united commitment to create a more powerful sustainability movement to influence decision making in the region and to "promote an approach to community sustainability which links urban ecology, social justice, and healthy community-based economic development" (Litke et al. 1994, 1). Given the diversity of people and interests represented at the conference, the declaration marked an advance in consciousness away from mere environmentalism toward a more comprehensive understanding of the crisis of globalized civilization. The Conference Declaration recognized a "direct connection" between the global health of the planet and the greening of our cities and noted "the urgency and depth of change that is necessary" (1). Not only had the conference participants linked urban ecology to social justice, but they had also grounded these broader concerns in their commitment to pursue a long-term, community-focused strategy in the lower Fraser valley with a bioregional focus for urban restructuring.

Second, a process to create an ecocity network was initiated. Consensus process was used effectively in the small group of about twenty people who in two hours brainstormed and agreed on a common understanding of the goal of such a network. Six important functions or purposes of the network were identified: information, communication, education, advocacy, outreach/building constituency, and social interaction and fun. The network was viewed as a structure to help develop and support grassroots actions. Key to this role was the provision of a communication system to help "mobilize groups and projects beyond merely responding to government and business initiatives" (Litke et al. 1994, 29). Participatory process was seen as essential to bringing people together through an inclusive process that enables maximum participation, from agenda setting to carrying out actions. Other ideas discussed included a network/directory linking volunteers with groups (similar to that run by Planet Drum in San Francisco), suggested by Berg at the conference; a demonstration ecovillage; building a networking function into our various existing organizations; and, ultimately, building a green city coalition strong enough to affect decision making in the region.

Spirituality is often a controversial topic and is usually avoided at explicitly political conferences in civil society. This was not the case with the Greening Our Cities conference. Spirituality was acknowledged as a deep human need in the closing circle as well as in the small group that explicitly addressed spiritual concerns. In this group, spirituality was linked to both the acknowledgment of interconnection with all living beings and a sense of "wholeness, unity, a sense of meaning and purpose in our lives" (Litke et al. 1994, 37). It was recognized as well that spirituality, in the sense of regaining a sacred connection with the land, is less something new than a rediscovery. The group acknowledged that Western culture can learn vital lessons from the continuing spiritual connection and understanding of the natural world of "many traditional and contemporary First Nations communities" and the acknowledgment and respect of elders and their experience and wisdom. Finally, there was also an understanding that rituals, cultural celebrations, and seasonal rites of passage can help in two important ways: recognizing the sacredness of life, and as a tool to assist in building community.

With such positive sentiments among participants, it is not surprising that the last suggestion (to include a spiritual element in their own meetings) was immediately implemented in the closing ceremony of the conference. With spirits already high from the energy of the small groups, all the participants joined hands in a circle to celebrate the achievements of the conference, to commune together, and to lift spirits in mutual song, in this case a chant, one often sung at Earth gatherings and bioregional gatherings:

> We are the dance of the moon and sun,
> We are the power in everyone,
> We are the hope that will never die,
> We are the turning of the tide.

In the proceedings, this song was reprinted, accompanied by one of the graffiti posters done as part of the day's activities. In the poster, a childlike drawing depicts everyone standing in a circle holding hands. In the circle is a large, rooted tree, a big heart, two people connected by heart and mind, a flower mandala, and a yin-yang symbol. Both the song and the drawing reflected in some measure the feelings of bonding experienced by participants in the final circle. There were many hugs after that circle.

This circle ceremony done in light ritual style marked an active, spiritual beginning to ecocity network building in the Vancouver region. The use of consensus, small-group circles, ceremony, sharing experiences and stories, brainstorming, visioning, singing, and holding hands together in the closing circle facilitated the bonding of participants to each other. In one sense, the bonding was an initial, embodied experience of the benefits of networking among the participants themselves. Here we see another example of the initial formation of ecosocial capital through the combined effect of several community-building tools that facilitate spiritual, intellectual, emotional, and visceral dimensions of directly experienced bonds of community.

The first meeting of the EcoCity Network took place about six weeks later at the Society Promoting Environmental Conservation (SPEC) building. This and subsequent gatherings of the network were planned to encourage feelings of community for participants rather than the conventional "business" environment of so many social movement meetings. All the network gatherings integrated a social and/or cultural component, usually a potluck supper and an informal time for meeting and chatting with other people. The first four gatherings continued the consensus process initiated at the Greening Our Cities conference. Participants felt strongly that all who came to these gatherings should be fully included in the decision-making process. Moreover, every network meeting included a brief history of what had occurred to date in order to bring newcomers into the process. This approach allowed new people to join in the discussions intelligently from the beginning. In this way, the group as a whole more quickly consolidated past progress and made newcomers feel more a part of the process from the start. The first gathering at SPEC informed everyone of what had transpired at the conference and began exploring and deliberating the six functions identified at the conference. By the fourth gathering, consensus had been reached on the purpose of the network.

For the next year and a half, the EcoCity Network held four public forums, each beginning with a potluck dinner and social, on a variety of topics, from "What's Stopping Sustainability? Barriers to Change" to "Restoring the Urban Landscape in Greater Vancouver: Hands-on Restoration Ecology, Social Justice, and Community Development." Each forum was planned to explore the connections among issues and to bring together different interest groups working on the issues. Attendance at the forums varied from about fifty to seventy participants. However, by the end of this period, many of the ecocity activists became increasingly critical of the forum format. True, the forums had worked to assist face-to-face networking, and many new connections were being made. On the other hand, the circle of face-to-face networkers was no longer growing, and the forums were not getting much media coverage. Also, many of the activists involved as participants in the network wanted more direct action. Through another consensus process, participants decided to adopt a loose structure of more or less autonomous committees.

One committee took on a geographic focus, volunteering to work on creating and promoting a vision of sustainable development on the largely municipally owned industrial lands of Southeast False Creek in the older, inner city. Another committee coalesced around the issue of transportation. A third committee became centred on the importance of networking and soon focused on the project of creating an EcoCity Network volunteer directory and newsletter for the Vancouver region. A fourth committee was organized initially around housing and community-planning issues in the Downtown Eastside, a low-income district in the central city.

In addition to the creation of a network connected through the public forums and ongoing network meetings, the EcoCity Network – through the work of some of the committees – spawned several projects. One of these was the EcoCity Act Locally! Calendar, inspired by the Green City Calendar concept presented by Berg at the Greening Our Cities conference. This project was put together by the newsletter/volunteer directory committee, on which I served. The newsletter idea quickly metamorphosed into a calendar, designed as a free community service, that lists events and projects for any groups under the broad EcoCity Network interlinked themes of ecological sustainability, social justice, and community economic development. The bimonthly calendar includes a volunteer directory that assists active groups and prospective volunteers to connect to activities of their choice.

The volunteer coordinator of the Suzuki Foundation, Caterina Geuer, was recruited to the group. She, in turn, recruited three more, including two design and production people and a journalism school graduate. Shortly after, the woman who had organized the press outreach at the Greening Our Cities conference, Tonya Rehder, also joined the group. In a short space of time, a volunteer team had formed that had all the professional experience, training, and political savvy needed to produce a small, social movement calendar/newspaper. The first two issues were published bimonthly in *Common Ground* magazine, with a circulation of 65,000 in the Lower Mainland. Another 25,000 of the first issue also went out in the *Vancouver Echo*. There were also short articles featuring local groups and issues, a bioregional almanac, and a map of the bioregion of the lower Fraser basin named Salmonopolis by another group that had formed out of another EcoCity networking meeting, the Barefoot Cartographers.

The calendar group soon gelled into a solid editorial collective partly through using consensus well, partly through socializing together before meetings, partly through using humour during meetings, and partly because the skills among the collective were so well mixed for producing and promoting this type of publication. The group also began to have some social gatherings apart from meeting times, forming strong collegial bonds and soon thereafter some friendships. Individuals from a range of civic groups in Vancouver, including the David Suzuki Foundation, VanCity Savings Credit Union, Oxfam, the BC Women's Housing Coalition, the Northwest Wildlife Preservation Society, and others, praised the Act Locally! Calendar as a valuable tool for encouraging community participation and as a great service for community organizations. With such enthusiastic responses, the calendar group grew stronger together and more ambitious.

A sense had developed among the members that the calendar networking service and the EcoCity message should reach out more to the mainstream, the general public. They struck a subcommittee to begin negotiating with the *Georgia Straight*, a weekly newspaper with a news and entertainment format and a circulation of 110,000. After publishing and distributing a couple of issues independently, the subcommittee worked out an arrangement with the *Georgia Straight* for a bimonthly centre spread. The first issue in the *Georgia Straight* appeared in February 1998. Hundreds of groups used the calendar's service.

Another project that emerged from the EcoCity Network process was a bioregional mapping group that began when I called for volunteers at an EcoCity meeting. Six or seven people volunteered immediately. I also asked Doug Aberley to join us, and he readily agreed. At the first meeting, Don Alexander, one of the people on the steering committee of the Greening Our Cities conference, donated a map of the Puget Sound-Georgia Strait basin made specially for the conference to the budding cartographers, symbolically marking the beginning of the bioregional mapping group.

The group operated with a rough-and-ready style of informal consensus. After several more meetings, the group still had not decided precisely what area to map. There was much discussion about boundaries both cultural and natural. In the meantime, people chose themes to map and began to gather information for their respective thematic maps. In those early meetings, we also decided that, while our ultimate purpose was public education and consciousness raising, our first audience was ourselves. We all wanted to learn more about our home region and saw this project as the best way to do it. Finally, in January 1995, after much discussion over a nested series of maps, the group agreed to focus data-collecting efforts on the Lower Fraser and the Nooksack River watersheds, with which they felt the strongest identity (see Figure 9).

Bounded on the north by the Coastal Mountains, on the east and south by the Cascades, and on the west by the river mouth and the Strait of Georgia, this region formed an easily identifiable river delta and valley section framed by these two mountain ranges.

The whole group then spent most of one subsequent evening brainstorming and discussing names for the bioregion. Finally, we chose Salmonopolis, since all five species of salmon still spawn in the Fraser River system and

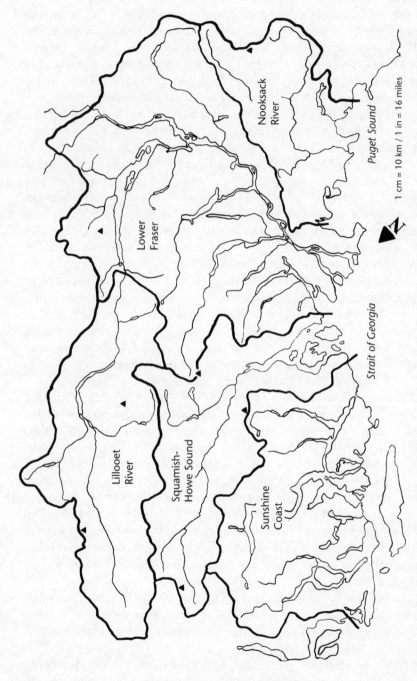

Nooksack
River

Puget Sound

1 cm = 10 km / 1 in = 16 miles

Lower
Fraser

Strait of Georgia

Lillooet
River

Squamish-
Howe Sound

Sunshine
Coast

Figure 9 A map of southwestern British Columbia bioregions, including the Lower Fraser and Nooksack River watersheds; taken from Aberley 1996.

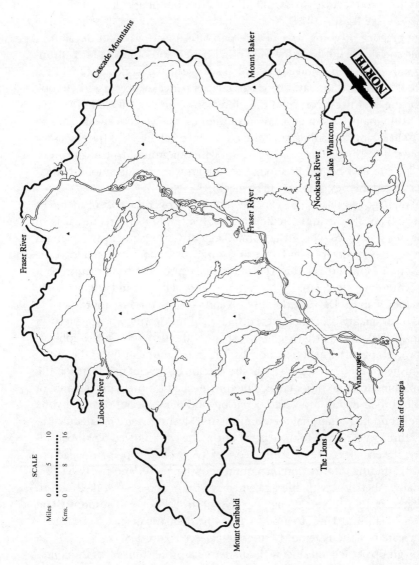

Figure 10 Salmonopolis – Watersheds of the Greater Fraser River Delta: A Bioregion Map; Barefoot Cartographers Group base map, 1995.

since the salmon is an indicator species for the health of the watershed. Salmonopolis was also the historical name for Steveston, originally a fishing village on the main arm of the Fraser. At the same time, the group began planning field trips to explore firsthand the boundaries of the bioregion as a way to "ground truth" our initial, tentative boundary decision for the bioregion (see Figure 10).

The practice of going to a nearby pub after meetings soon developed. People socialized, got to know each other better, and began to form stronger bonds. At first, map meetings took place every two weeks. The first field trip took place one Sunday. The group met for pancake breakfast, then took off for the southwest corner of the bioregion – the Lummi Nation reserve near Bellingham, Washington. We also went up the Nooksack watershed to Mount Baker, or Koma Kulshan ("the great white watcher"), as the Nooksack people call it. The field trip did help a lot with our ground-truthing process. The day trip also helped to strengthen the growing bonds among participants, as did a series of longer map meetings.

We managed to raise some expense money to cover the cost of materials through VanCity Savings Credit Union. This fund-raising required us to name our group. We chose the name Barefoot Cartographers as a play on China's barefoot doctors, and, by using grizzly bear footprints as a logo, we gave a nod to the grizzly, the "classic umbrella species of conservation biology" (Grumbine 1992, 66). Then Aberley was asked if we could produce some maps for Clean Air Day. Aberley and I volunteered to produce four thematic maps of air quality issues that were displayed at the downtown art gallery on Clean Air Day, the first public map display of the Barefoot Cartographers.

However, over the next few months, the initial momentum of the group diminished. Through their own life circumstances, several members left the group, some to go to other cities. The time needed for thematic research of a major urban region proved to be far beyond our expectations. Everyone in the group had other major commitments. Meetings were rescheduled to every three weeks, then to once per month. The work slowed down considerably. Nevertheless, the remaining core of five or six mappers struggled on, slowly gathering information on a number of themes for another two years.

Finally, Aberley – with the agreement of the mappers – worked out an arrangement for his bioregional map class at the School of Community and Regional Planning, UBC, to produce fifty-one thematic maps using the base map created by the Barefoot Cartographers (see Figure 11).

Map group participants met with Aberley's class three times over the course of the winter semester of 1998 to discuss the vision of Salmonopolis motivating the cartographers; to view, discuss, and give feedback on the progress of the maps; and to attend the final presentation at the end of term. Soon after the students finished the maps, through an arrangement between the Barefoot Cartographers and the organizers of Earth Day, the completed maps

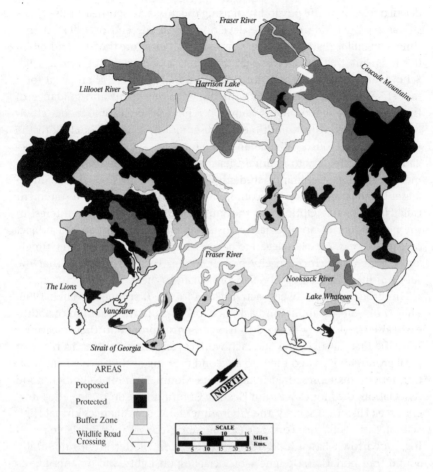

Figure 11 Salmonopolis – Watersheds of the Greater Fraser River Delta: A Bioregional Atlas. This is a map of protected areas and actual and proposed buffer zones, by the Barefoot Cartographers Group and the UBC School of Community and Regional Planning, 1998.

went on display for Earth Day at the new Vancouver Public Library downtown. As part of the day's activities, Aberley's students presented and explained their maps in a public workshop. Several of these maps were published in the EcoCity Act Locally! Calendar over a two-year period to help raise public consciousness about the bioregion.

A third autonomous subcommittee of the EcoCity Network formed around the geographically based issue of promoting the creation of an ecocity village (or model) in the downtown core on the city-owned former industrial lands of Southeast False Creek, a saltwater inlet. People's hopes for implementing a model ecovillage rose significantly when Vancouver City Council decided to explore the possibility of using the fifty-acre Southeast False Creek site as a model for sustainable development at the end of 1994. At that time, several local groups became motivated to promote the idea and mobilize to ensure that the city live up to its decision. Students at Virtual High School, an alternative educational institution, developed a proposal for a model sustainable community with the encouragement and guidance of the head of the school, Brent Cameron. They garnered some media attention for the idea with a multimedia presentation of their model. Both the Environmental Youth Alliance and Designers for Social Responsibility began to lobby the city to maintain its commitment to sustainable development in the area. Geography students of Professor Mark Roseland at Simon Fraser University developed a comprehensive and detailed vision statement called "Sustainable Options for the South East False Creek Site." Interest in the possibilities of an alternative sustainable development model project on the site grew. Activists began to believe that they could have some timely and effective influence on city hall. It was in this environment that the subcommittee of the EcoCity Network began to meet.

This group of about twelve activists met for the first time in March 1996. They spoke mostly about outreach, networking, and the situation of Southeast False Creek. They decided to use consensus process in their meetings. After the first meeting, the outreach work began. They contacted a range of local groups and invited them to a second meeting at the Native Education Centre. Groups represented included the Mount Pleasant Neighbourhood Association, the Mount Pleasant Healthy Community Committee, the Brewery Creek Historical Society, the Environmental Youth Alliance, Virtual High School, Farm Folk/City Folk, Lower Mainland Network for Affordable Housing, Downtown Eastside Residents' Association, Better Environmentally Sound Transportation, Designers for Social Responsibility, and Tenants' Rights Action Coalition. This was a larger meeting (forty to fifty people) at the Carnegie Community Centre in the Downtown Eastside. At that meeting, a decision was taken to form the Southeast False Creek Working Group. The Environmental Youth Alliance offered to contribute one half-time campaign coordinator from its paid staff time. This assistance promised to strengthen the volunteers' work. From this point on, the activists from the EcoCity Network interested in the geographically based struggle to implement an ecovillage model joined in the work of the Southeast False Creek Working Group. The responsibility for coordination of the work shifted from the EcoCity Network to the Environmental Youth Alliance.

The interests of the working group were quite diverse. Nevertheless, using consensus process, they agreed upon a vision statement and a joint strategy for action. However, few in the group trusted Vancouver City Council to live up to its promise of a model sustainable development project for the site. Council had hired Stanley Kwok, the architect responsible for Concord Pacific's expensive, super-high-density housing project on the north shore of False Creek, essentially a project of urban growth machine politics. This project contravened existing city policy documents such as the "City Plan," which called for the development of communities built around neighbourhood centres, not the automobile. The 20 percent affordable housing component of the Concord Pacific project was never built (Kong 1997). It soon became clear to the activists involved with Southeast False Creek that Kwok had no understanding of sustainable development or any sympathy for affordable housing. Kwok held a one-day workshop to discuss the concept of urban sustainability, but no knowledgeable people in the field or in related disciplines were invited (Blore 1998). Furthermore, Kwok refused to meet with the working group or any of its member groups. He claimed that he had no time to consult with people. This meant that there was to be no public input into the crucial early stage of the planning process. Kwok's only "bottom line" was the financial feasibility of the project, the only response that *homo economicus* would approve. A public outreach campaign was seen by the working group as imperative.

The working group's vision statement addressed eight major principles of a sustainable development model project for the site: affordable housing; mixed-use development to include neighbourhood centres, social services, retail, et cetera; safety; green space and shoreline restoration; alternative transportation; energy efficiency; water and waste; and social justice issues (Kong 1997). The statement emphasized the importance of an open public planning process and the need for social justice and affordable housing, given that the site was located in the midst of low-income, ethnically diverse districts. Having agreed on a joint strategy, the working group began to organize.

Much effort and time on the part of many volunteers resulted in a successful public event called Springfest, held in March 1997 at Creekside Park next to the Southeast False Creek site. Springfest included educational workshops and panels on the issues, site tours, public art displays, a giant puppet-making workshop, storytelling, a lantern-making workshop and lantern parade, and a chance to have public opinions recorded and sent to city hall. The event was well organized and received sympathetic media coverage. Pressure mounted on city hall to act.

At a meeting of city council in March filled with activists from many of the above-mentioned groups and others, the pressure was on for council to live up to its promise of having an open, public process. About thirty-five people made informed critiques of Kwok's concept plan, which lacked any definition of sustainable development. To its credit, council listened to the presenters, who asked that council consider sustainability more seriously.

Later, at another council meeting packed with activists, Councillor Price frankly admitted that what the city got for its $300,000 consultant fee for Kwok was "a lot of waste." Price added that Kwok may have to be, as he put it, "reined in from time to time."

Previously, the working group had been building bridges of vertical influence to city hall. This practice had also been an important part of the work of the EcoCity Network. City Councillor Sullivan had attended one or two EcoCity events, and at the May meeting Councillor Chiavario spoke strongly on behalf of moving beyond merely looking at dollars when it came to environmental issues such as Southeast False Creek. Sustainability seemed to be on council's agenda once again when it subsequently hired another consultant, Sheltair Scientific, to provide a definition of urban sustainable development. Since then, the city itself has taken a lead role through its planning department, producing a draft plan for Southeast False Creek after a series of public consultations.

Clearly, the strategy of the EcoCity Network in Vancouver is similar to that in the San Francisco Bay Area. Both are based on the creation of small, local action groups (rather than the intentional communities in two of the rural examples) that promote the formation of broader horizontal city-wide networks in civil society. The strategy is based on creating horizontal linkages among as large a number of groups as possible. It is a strategy that places cultural change at the centre of a long-term cumulative, incremental effort at societal transformation. In the case of Vancouver, community-building tools used were consensus process, small groups or affinity circles, bioregional mapping, story, and ceremony. In both cases, the horizontal networking in the civil society sphere supported a vertical strategy of developing influence in the political sphere at the level of the local state sector, the municipality. However, in Vancouver as in San Francisco, this strategy is merely at the initial stages of an envisioned process of transformation and restructuring that bioregionalist green city activists believe may take several generations to accomplish. Moreover, there has been little or no action to develop vertical influence for democratization in the corporate sector.

A new tool not illustrated in Chapter 4, the green or ecocity calendar and volunteer directory, has been used effectively for networking among organizations and for bringing in new volunteers to the groups in the networks. However, the urban narratives also show that the long-term strategy of societal transformation and restructuring over several generations is merely in its most initial stage. While norms of cooperation, mutual aid, and civic solidarity have been established among the seed groups and intentional communities, these norms have not been established in the broader society within which the groups operate.

Song of the People

People of the mountains
People of the plains
People of the oceans
   and the jungle rains
People of the savannahs
People of the steppes
People of the deserts
   of the Sonoran Southwest

People of the arctic
People of the Patagone
People of the continents
   of the heart/mind unknown
People of the cities
People of the towns
People of the farmlands
   and the wilderness around

There's love in the People
Who are struggling for the earth dance
The sooner we work together
The more we'll have a chance

For the love that sets us free
That gives us strength to work
For the love that sets us free
That gives us strength to live

For your education
   for your food
For your People
   for the nature of your place

For humanity
   for your soul
For the strength
   for the calm
One said "All ages are the same
Glorious and cruel
Only love makes a difference"

El amor que nos pone libre
Que da nos fuerza de vivir

El amor que nos pone libre
Que da nos fuerza de luchar

Para la education, para la comida
Par la gente, para la naturaleza
Para la humanidad, para el alma
Para la fuerza, para la calma

We see love in the people
Who are struggling for the Earth dance
The sooner we work together
The more we'll have a chance

(Repeat first verse)

– Chris Wells

6
Continental Movement: A Narrative Account of the Continental Bioregional Story

Introduction

The continental bioregional movement story originates in 1976 with Peter Berg's early call for a continental congress, which began as an event called the North American Bioregional Congress (NABC) in 1984. One important dimension of the story of these events is their evolution from a congress format to a ceremonial village format over the period of the first seven continental events that took place biannually from 1984 to 1996. An eighth gathering in 2002 held in Kansas is summarized in the conclusion.

This chapter presents a narrative account of the continental movement story posing several questions. Specifically, what does this story reveal about bioregionalists' efforts to organize and network beyond the local and bioregional scales at these continental events? How have bioregionalists attempted to build horizontal linkages and alliances with others in civil society at the broad geographical scale of the continent? What role have bioregional community-building tools played in this endeavour? And, finally, what is the record of vertical bridge-building efforts to develop democratic influence in state and corporate sectors?

The historical roots of the continental congress model can be found in the US revolutionary congressional tradition against British colonialism in the eighteenth century. Before the congress process was initiated, American bioregionalists in particular were initially inspired by – but also critical of – historical US revolutionary congressionalism. Berg's 1976 pamphlet, *Amble toward Continent Congress*, was originally written to protest the US bicentennial Declaration of Independence. It is an openly political pamphlet that denounces the Europeans who came as "invaders clearing terrain for an occupation civilization." Berg empathetically describes American indigenous peoples as "inhabitory peoples" who were ravaged by the European colonists.

By calling for a break with the US tradition of colonial conquest – in the name of the continent itself and supportive of inhabitory peoples – Berg proclaims the need for a cultural and political transformation of the dominant culture from a culture of occupation to a culture of inhabitation. His congress call is still within the US democratic congressional tradition, but it calls for radical change: "Continent congress isn't a simple exercise. It's an enormous effort to overcome the politics of extinction, the Earth-colonist globalism which exhausts whole continents, their peoples, and moves now to devastate deep floors of our planetary oceans" (1976).

While Berg is obviously deeply critical of the US tradition of colonial conquest, this is also a clarion call for the bioregional movement to locate itself in the struggle against global imperialism and for genuinely democratic politics. In this sense, Berg links the bioregional movement with democratic aspects of the original American revolutionary tradition, in particular with the participatory character of the revolutionary US congress tradition of the eighteenth and early nineteenth centuries. At the end of the twentieth century, however, the struggle was no longer against old-style colonialism but against the Earth-colonist globalism of economic man led by the United States. This initial inspiration for a continental bioregional movement is obviously informed by radical politics, ecological consciousness, civil society traditions, and an anti-imperialist global perspective.

Berg's call for a bioregional continental congress first found fertile ground not in San Francisco but in the Ozarks. In the late 1970s, David Haenke and others issued a call for a congress in the Ozarks. The Ozark Area Community Congress (OACC) attracted 150 people from fifteen US states. The congress model emerging from the Ozarks in the early 1980s was adopted by the first North American Bioregional Congress in 1984 (Henderson et al. 1984). Its core is based on forming "congressional committees" that meet for a week to discuss and eventually reach consensus on resolutions, mission statements, and action plans to be adopted (or not) by the plenary. Committee meeting time is also viewed as a space for networking, resource sharing, strategizing, and "just getting to know and learning to work with the other members" (1984, 7). At NABC I, committees included energy, agriculture/ permaculture, water, health, education, economics, political action, eco-defence, culture and arts, communities, ecofeminism, Native peoples, and spirituality.

The intent of this active "congressing" concept was to make the democratic process as participatory as possible and to avoid mere conference-style sessions, panel discussions, and workshops in which people passively "sit around and listen to keynote speakers, workshop leaders, and other entertainers" (1984, 61). In this congress model, overscheduling is discouraged in favour of leaving plenty of open time for "free-form networking and caucusing" (ibid.). Self-entertainment is encouraged (indeed, there are always plenty of experienced poets, singers, theatre arts people, dancers, drummers, and musicians among the participants at these events). Time is also left open in the evenings for culture-sharing programs. The "Ozarks Model" also discourages loading itself and its committees with all kinds of demands, goals, and objectives to be accomplished in a few months. On the contrary, a more relaxed, less workaholic style is encouraged, emphasizing sustained, committed effort over a lifetime. Two key goals of this model are to be a fully participatory event and to be an exercise in the creation of a "non-confrontive type shadow government," a "new kind of totality, run on ecological principles," that "represents all the necessary sectors of a functioning ecological society" (Haenke 1988).

Two important considerations for long-term cultural transformation strategy in civil society are evident. First, workaholic, stress-filled activity is not adequate for sustained lifetime efforts at social change. Stressed-out, overworked, frenetic individuals may not easily build trust among themselves, trust essential to horizontal bonding and to networking in civil society. Such organizing is simply not sustainable. In examining societies where high levels of social capital are the norm (Chapter 2), we saw that there is ample time for more relaxed social and working lives. Second, the creation of a nonconfrontive shadow government is a proposal to build an alternative political institutional network within the sphere of civil society. On a democratic civil society theoretical view, this concept is very properly a long-term strategic orientation for developing sustainable vertical influence for democratization in the formal political sphere of the state and its agencies. However, as we shall see, this second orientation reflects tensions in the movement that are still being played out.

The ceremonial village model, which evolved out of the congress model over several continental gatherings, is understood in the bioregional movement to be rooted in much older traditions than revolutionary US congressionalism. The village model concept comes directly from indigenous traditions of peoples in both North and South America and is described fully in the proceedings of the seventh continental gathering, the first to be held in Mexico (Briggs et al. 1997).

As bioregionalists understand the concept, traditional ceremonial villages were not meant to be lived in permanently. Rather, they were set up temporarily for nurture and educational and motivational purposes. Traditional ceremonial villages were a gathering of tribes and clans with multiple purposes: sharing ceremonies and celebrations, trading goods and knowledge, continuing ancient relations, settling disputes, meeting in council, engaging in friendly competition, finding partners, mating, and planning for the future (Briggs et al. 1997).

Taking its inspiration from these ancient traditions, the ceremonial village in the contemporary bioregional model is designed as an event that comprises all aspects of human life, including cultural and natural components, an event that takes charge of all our requirements – food, shelter, health, trade, ceremony, social interaction, and information sharing. In this model, the ceremonial village is itself the educational event and curriculum, comprising various kinds of educational activities, from formal workshops to impromptu "jamming" to large consensus decision-making plenaries. Informal discourse is given as much priority and regarded as an equally important part of the learning experience as any formal meetings. Proponents of this model admit that the process can often be chaotic, but they view such chaos as part of the experience of learning. However chaotic it appears, they argue that it works in various ways to broaden our lives: "The chaos of the ceremonial village is our constant reinvention of order. It is our richness. Those who experience it experience their own health, consciousness, and freedom to create ceremonial villages wherever they go" (1997, 8-9).

In the bioregional ceremonial village model, committees are replaced by councils. Councils function much as committees did, operating by consensus process. However, less time and emphasis are devoted to putting forward resolutions and statements for consideration by the plenary. This leaves more time for workshops (formal and informal), ceremonial and ritual activity, and a whole day devoted to support work in the local community where the gathering is held. As well, each day begins with a sunrise ceremony and ends with a sunset ceremony.

Both models place priority on participatory democracy, consensus decision making, and unscheduled time for informal networking, caucusing, and socializing. Both models encourage and include cultural-sharing programs in the evenings. Participants share as fully as possible in the work of making a week-long event work well without exhausting a small number of participants (often women) while most others participate only in the "important political work." Duties of food preparation and cooking, cleaning up, recycling, child care, latrines, et cetera are all shared in an organized manner that involves everyone. In both models, the number of participants (200-800) falls within estimates of appropriate human scale for a small village or neighbourhood community to work well. Indeed, the development of communal bonds is strongly encouraged.

Evolution of the North American Bioregional Congress
By the first NABC in May 1984, bioregionalists in the Ozarks had held four annual regional Ozark Area Community Congresses (OACC). In the early 1980s, OACC's energy drew people from twenty-five states. OACC also inspired the birth of other congresses. David Haenke recalled that in May 1982 the first Kansas Area Community Congress was held, the first of about fifteen bioregional congresses and councils to be inspired by OACC (Hart et al. 1987).

The idea of community congress was hatched in a series of meetings lasting through 1979, meetings that included "deep discussions about possibilities along spiritual, metaphysical and economic lines" (Hart et al. 1987, 38), discussions that sparked serious talk for a first OACC. This was the spark, but it had been preceded by other discussions and a broad concern of Ozark back-to-the-landers in the early and mid-1970s that the Ozarks were being trashed and polluted just like everywhere else. In the fall of 1976, as Haenke paced his cabin thinking about proposed Ozark area nuclear plants, forest devastation, and "a dozen other eco-cidal depredations," he struck upon the idea of an "Ozark Free State," the idea of creating "an unofficial, undeclared, parallel, ecological Ozark nation" (Hart et al. 1987, 38). For Haenke, OACC was to be a shadow government. In February 1977, the first Ozark "ecopolitics meeting" – attended by ten people – was held to discuss environmental defence, communications, and other problems. Two weeks later at New Life Farm, the idea for a congress of communities was born. These beginnings arose, in part, from concerns over both ecopolitical action and spiritual opposition to global corporate monoculture. We see again that, from its inception, bioregionalism is anything but a parochial philosophy. Indeed, here we see that Haenke and other founders of the movement in the Ozarks are concerned about global issues, but the inspiration is sparked by efforts to address global issues on the ground in one's home territory or region. Clearly, the "Ozark Nation" is to be created in the sphere of local civil society. This emergent idea requires long-term cultural change that incrementally builds its shadow government, rooted in a web of communities of place. In this view, effective bridges of political influence must have a solid, locally rooted foundation.

NABC I

NABC I drew heavily on the experiences of OACC and Kansas Area Watershed (KAW). The work was coordinated by New Life Farm's Bioregional Project set up by Haenke and other Ozarkians. NABC I was attended by 217 people from ten nations (including several First Nations) and thirty-nine states and provinces. Participants represented 130 organizations from bioregions across North America (Henderson et al. 1984). The five-day event was held at a rural camp in Excelsior Springs, north of Kansas City, Missouri. Most participants camped in tents. Child care and children's programs were provided by organizers and volunteers from among the participants. Moreover, the entire congress was run on volunteer energy, including a daily in-congress newsletter, called the *Voice of the Turtle*. Major goals of NABC I included bringing continental bioregionalists together along with those working in political ecology, sustainability, and the green movement; sharing the culture and history of the bioregions represented; helping to unify the bioregional movement; exploring the "great common ground" between bioregionalists and indigenous peoples; seeding new bioregional congresses and organizations; helping to focus green movement energies toward new coalitions and impacting on existing political/electoral systems; and, finally, determining whether NABC could become an ongoing organization.

These goals reflected an intent not only to begin networking continentally among local bioregional reinhabitants and organizations in a direct face-to-face manner but also to network more broadly with other social movements. Here we see another example of the bioregional strategy to connect local struggles to broader geographically dispersed networks as well as to other social sectors. In addition to the above goals, the organizers included a stated intention that the congress be a cooperative, fully participatory event, a "five day community, the nature of which we will create for ourselves ... We believe that an essential part of a strong Congress is that we become a cooperative community" (NABC/Bioregional Project Brochure 1984). Thus, the ambitious intent of the first congress was to help unify the bioregional movement and to build links to other movements while carrying out an experiment in living as an intentional community by people who were, for the most part, complete strangers to each other. Bioregional strategies of community building and networking were subjected to a trial by fire.

Indeed, few outside movement circles could have appreciated just how diverse a collection of individuals had gathered at this event. The facilitator, Caroline Estes, noted the "high degree of skepticism when we began as to whether such a widely diverse group of people could work in that degree of harmony and unity" (Henderson et al. 1984, 9). David Haenke described participants as "strong-minded, strong-willed, unshy, highly self-motivated people" (ibid.). Doug Aberley depicted them as "libertarians, 1930's decentralists, space colony prophets and utopian dreamers of many descriptions," all "happy to have an audience for their particular brand of snake oil" (1992, 3). Forging unity among such a collection of individuals seemed to be a daunting task.

The congress opened its first plenary session with a simple ritual, prayers, and a sweetgrass ceremony by Native Dineh (Navaho) elders from Big Mountain in the Four Corners area of the western United States. Two hundred people formed a circle in the dining hall for the opening. A round of introductions followed, with each participant giving his or her name, bioregion, and passion in life. The opening circle was reported in the *Voice of the Turtle* (the in-house newsletter of the North American Bioregional Congress) the following morning as an empowering experience: "Perhaps Lynn Stone from New York City spoke for us all when she said, 'We are here because we believe, and because we believe, we dare to offer an alternative vision for our nation, a new spirit among our leaders, and a true leadership for our global world.' We have taken our first steps toward empowerment" (1984a).

Alliance building was one key congress goal. How would this goal be pursued? The congress chose two initial paths. The first was to build bridges with indigenous peoples. The first resolution passed at the congress recognized and supported First Nations' treaty rights, land claims, and inherited rights. At least as important, the congress plenary also committed to developing and strengthening networks with indigenous and traditional peoples and encouraged NABC participants to do so in their own bioregions. As well, the congress adopted and published the statement of philosophy of the Native Peoples Committee that recognized and valued Native spirituality as a source of healing for all peoples and linked support for indigenous rights with support for all human rights and freedom.

The committee set up an information board at the congress, using a bioregional map to depict Native peoples' ongoing land-based struggles. A workshop on the struggle of Navajo and Hopi peoples for their lands was held at the congress and discussed in plenary. A letter-writing campaign was launched in support of Native peoples' struggles. These political solidarity actions, the active involvement of indigenous people at the congress, combined with the spiritual strength and shared meaning of the above philosophical affirmation initiated the bioregional movement's work toward building alliances with First Nations.

The second route to building horizontal links with other movements at NABC I was participants' work with the US green movement. NABC I made a strong start toward its stated goal of helping to focus green movement political energies toward new coalitions. The Green Movement Committee of NABC I, as Haenke observed, set the stage for the founding of the US green politics movement. In fact, four of the five convenors of the founding Committees of Correspondence meeting of the green politics movement in St. Paul three months later were NABC I Green Movement Committee members. At NABC I, the Green Movement Committee recognized "the need for bioregional principles and practices to be secured and protected, cooperatively and in a decentralized manner, through a green political organization" (Henderson et al. 1984, 24). The committee called for such an organization to "focus on open, democratic planning and political action supportive of local and regional autonomy and interdependence as reflected in the bioregional model" (1984, 24). Clearly, this was an important contribution by bioregionalists in founding the US green movement.

There remained the difficult task of building unity among the widely diverse assembly at the congress itself. How would this be achieved? Unity would have to be built through the active congressing of participants, the give and take of face-to-face horizontal communication. At this first congress, participants agreed by consensus on an overall mission statement (see Welcome Home! in Chapter 3); several reports and statements of principle; and over sixty resolutions on a wide variety of cultural, political, social, and economic issues, including agriculture, education, culture and arts, economics, forests, water, health, indigenous peoples and visible minorities, sovereignty and land rights, and public policy. Together the resolutions and statements formed the initial basis for a potential "green platform" of the congress, a fledgling program for Haenke's shadow government. In reaching consensus on a set of broadly conceived resolutions addressing a sizable spectrum of life issues, the diverse assembly began the long and difficult process of crafting some unity among the diversity.

A crucial part of building unity was the goal of creating a five-day intentional community among participants. As a concept, "community" was recognized by the congress plenary as the "basic unit of human habitation," the level of human interaction at which "we can reach our fullest potential and best effect social change" (Henderson et al. 1984, 16). At the same time, it was clearly recognized that human communities are "integral parts of the larger bioregional and planetary life communities" (ibid.). These were not to be parochial communities.

In the Community Empowerment Committee, participants discussed the idea that "the basic reason for the global crisis is that common people have no control over what is going on" (*Voice of the Turtle* 1984b). The mass society of our dominant consumerist system was seen as the cause of the decline of community life, since it makes personal relationships the least important factor. Then committee participants discussed and identified important factors in community empowerment, such as cultivating personal relationships and setting examples by personal lifestyle changes. In committee deliberations, Tom Berry pointed to the importance of "community story" as a unifying force and to the involvement of Native inhabitants/ elders as essential to the continuity of local communities. Finally, the committee put together a community empowerment "action list" endorsed by the congress plenary as a first step toward developing a general strategy for community empowerment.

On the evening of the last day, participants gathered in a silent circle outside the building where the final plenary had just dissolved. For the official close of the congress, South African Robert Mazibuko, founder of the African Tree Center, and Ron Rabin of Children of the Green Earth led the children of the congress in a tree-planting ceremony. Surrounded by congress participants in the final circle, the children planted a tree and sang "From our hearts, with our hands, for the Earth, all the world together." At the end of the ceremony, everyone was given a tree seedling to take and plant at their homes across the continent. Photos of the final circle in the published proceedings were accompanied by the following note: "Holding their seedlings high, those in the closing circle expressed their joy" (Henderson et al. 1984, 42).

A strong sense of unity of purpose and bonds of solidarity, trust, and love had evidently been forged among congress participants. What had been a scattering of individuals and groups in far-flung places across the continent now began to take more definite shape as a social movement with a specific mission and program. By the end of the congress, participants experienced a real sense of togetherness and accomplishment in forging their common program. Strangers got to know each other, exchange experiences, and build the necessary horizontal bonds among themselves. Congress facilitator Estes observed that "the level of love and trust amongst participants was tangible," and, to the surprise of "nearly everyone, we came away with a sense of unity and forward motion that was near miraculous, but believable" (Henderson et al. 1984, 10).

Estes attributed this success to an excellent process of consensus decision making. Aberley also recognized that consensus had worked to bring people together in democratic process: "At the end of the day, we all felt a well-earned sense of accomplishment, content that there was no more that could be done in the time allotted. For a brief time, I experienced the exhilaration of participation in a real democracy" (1992, 6). Many other similar comments were recorded in the evaluation section of the proceedings:

> Wonderful exercise of head and heart – I'm sorry to see it end ... It was a truly joyful experience to sit in the plenary on the last day and feel the strength of our mutual commitment ... The congress allowed a deep dialogue to take place, community was built, clarity was achieved ... The facilitation and use of consensus was excellent! ... A sincere effort was made to move away from hierarchical structures, to incorporate feminine principles and to accommodate each individual ... Elements that were effective were the opening and closing of plenary with song, poetry, and silence, the quality of food, the *Voice of the Turtle*, and the use of consensus. (Henderson et al. 1984, 59-60)

While consensus process was clearly a central factor in building trust, love, and unity in diversity, other factors were also at work. One important factor was the openness to exchanging views among participants themselves. Aberley notes the spirit of "a healthy anarchism" at the gathering that encouraged the sharing of viewpoints among participants (1992, 5). Some felt strongly that bioregional philosophy helped to bring people together. Author Kirkpatrick Sale commented that "What I and those I talked to felt was that the philosophy gave people a new way of seeing their lives, of involving friends and neighbours in the paramount task of rescuing the earth's communities – and our own" (Henderson et al. 1984, 1). Others believed that it was the process of sharing ideas and experiences that helped to unite the diverse assembly. Emily Stetson commented that the diverse conglomeration of individuals became united by discovering their inter-connectedness through sharing ideas and learning about each other's ef-forts: "Green politics, antinuclear efforts, and organic methods of agriculture, for example, all have a place within the larger picture of the bioregional movement" (2).

In addition to consensus process, specific tools such as storytelling and sharing, ceremony, cultural exchange and performance, song, and celebra-tion were used by bioregionalists in various situations during the congress. Songs and simple forms of ritual at NABC I performed in the plenary circle were effective in helping to create bonds of solidarity among participants. At the opening circle of NABC I, as noted, some 200 individuals introduced themselves as part of the exercise to get to know each other. Aberley, ini-tially skeptical about the strangely diverse "crowd" of participants, com-ments on what happened at the circle's closing: "After several hours of these introductions, an obvious spaceman suggested that we all join hands and hum together. My initial skepticism evaporated as a truly inspiring Tibetan harmony filled the hall. It was a long moment of unity born from diversity that I will never forget" (1992, 3).

Music (apart from ritual) was also used with great effect to help bond people. For some participants, one of the highlights of the first congress was the music of flutist Paul Winter and John Stokes played from a canoe on Lake Doniphan. Their music reverberated off the surrounding slopes of the lake for many participants to hear. Winter observed that "Making music brings all parts of the being together and reawakens a sense of connectedness to nature and to each other ... When we greet the world with music-making, as do the birds and the wolves, we're creating a ritual which can bring us whole again, and ground us for the entire day" (Henderson et al. 1984, 50).

When individuals feel fully alive and joyfully centred in their spirits, their energies are released, and they can work more cooperatively. Egopolitics, the alienated psychic space that many in our society all too often operate from, dissipates, making cooperation much easier. In other words, music making can contribute significantly to the building of bonds of trust and love essential for building community.

Another exercise that contributed to building unity was the making of a quilt. This project was started by one woman, Ella McDonald, in the hope that the quilt would provide a tangible, physical manifestation of NABC and help to transform "some of the verbal energy into peaceful, productive handwork" (Henderson et al. 1984, 47). The quilt project was initiated well before the congress began. One hundred bioregions and organizations were invited to participate. Seventeen squares were sent in. Another woman pieced them together so that they became the "plates" in a turtle shell. She embroidered the name and bioregion of each person beside the piece that the person had contributed. During the week of NABC I, people were invited and encouraged to participate by adding stitches to complete the quilt. Many did so, contributing new designs and patches. The process was discussed in the proceedings as "a visible way of 'weaving' the various threads of the NABC community together. For many, especially the men, it was their first opportunity to experience the craft, skill and camaraderie of working around a quilting frame" (47). The quilt would be displayed in a prominent place at future continental events as a symbol of this bonding process in community and movement building.

Judged in relation to its own goals, the congress was, in the view of musician Paul Winter, "an enormous networking success" (49). Indeed, the movement had succeeded in coming together to constitute itself as a movement beyond the level of the bioregion, creating the beginnings of a common vision for sustainable, bioregional society. NABC I produced a set of resolutions that participants had forged together in consensus process, resolutions that began the work of addressing as many different aspects and areas of life as an informal congress could produce in one week. Congressing, culture sharing, networking, working together, socializing, and getting to know one another all contributed to the bioregional community-bonding process that established the NABC as an ongoing event. By sharing cultural experiences from around the continent, NABC I participants had initiated a shared process of learning how to celebrate Turtle Island's continental linkages, both human and nonhuman. Continental networking was given flesh and bones. What NABC I did not do, of course, was have much impact on existing political/electoral systems, as the convenors had intended. In the early 1980s, bioregionalism was little known outside a small circle of practitioners and a few people in the green movement.

The experience of NABC I showed that, in such a closely shared cooperative context, levels of information and trust can build up quickly. Cooperation in daily activities of living also builds up norms of mutual aid. During the committee and plenary work, the new continental network was built with high levels of participation and cooperation. This too helps to create feelings of being included in the whole. Moreover, each participant can feel ownership of the process. As well, participants can feel positive about and take pride in their own contributions to the whole, to their new congress and network. Others who normally live far away are no longer disembodied telephone voices or e-mail data. On the contrary, participants bond with others on many different levels: intellectually, emotionally, spiritually, and viscerally. The network created is an embodied network.

One problem pointed out in the evaluations was that there was not enough participation from "minority groups." In the United States and Canada, the bioregional movement was underrepresented by members with other than European heritage. This failure to attract representative numbers of people of colour to the congresses would play an important role in future gatherings.

NABC II

The second continental congress took place at the end of August 1986 at Camp Innisfree on the shores of Lake Michigan in northwest Michigan near Traverse City. Unlike NABC I, it was held mostly outdoors. Residents of thirty-two US states, two Canadian provinces, and three other countries attended. However, there was no representation from Alaska, the Deep South, the Great Basin, or the Dakotas. Most of Canada and all of Mexico were still not represented. With just 200 participants, attendance was down slightly from NABC I. Again consensus process facilitated cooperation among a highly diverse collection of people, many of them new to NABC. The overall goal of this congress was to continue to engage in the process of networking and movement building, including building alliances across race and gender. More people of colour attended NABC II than NABC I.

For this second continental gathering, the congress model was further developed. Committees increased from fourteen to eighteen. A series of panels were organized to accommodate the number of people who wanted to make presentations. Panels included race and gender, community education, forestry, economics, spirituality, urban issues, and home ecology. These panels were used to introduce new people to bioregionalism, to assist participants in integrating into the congress process, and to address some potentially contentious issues such as race and gender.

Again the congress began with an Earth ritual. At the opening ceremony, Lewis Johnson, an Odawan elder from the host bioregion, led assembled participants in the Erecting the Centre of the Earth ceremony. A cedar pole was erected to represent the Centre of the Earth. This act also represented the joining of the spirit with the material, the joining of "Father Sky with Mother Earth" (Hart et al. 1987, 11). This ritual included tobacco offerings, prayers, and pipe sharing. Hanging from the branches of the "tree" were brightly coloured banners and bundles symbolic of the four directions and of Mother Earth and Father Sky. According to this tradition, all places on Earth are centres, but for any activity it is necessary to set the centre in balance, to give the centre form. The cedar pole was implanted to act as a centring and grounding force for the gathering.

For participants, this ceremony was charged with spiritual meaning. The editor of the proceedings, Alexandra Hart, observed that, for many participants, the cedar pole became "the center of our earth and our hearts for the week" (Hart et al. 1987, 11). For Haenke, exhausted after working long and hard to bring the event together, the opening prayer and assembly revived his spirit: "When NABC II finally comes to life, when we all assemble and pray together at Innisfree, the spirit comes pouring back in. I feel a torrent of it, like pure life water for parched bodies and souls" (Hart et al. 1987, 40). After the opening circle, Haenke presented a history of the movement to include newcomers and to help new and old participants integrate.

Movement building was a key theme. The Bioregional Movement Committee was specifically charged with thinking about, developing, and presenting proposals to the congress to build the movement across the continent. The committee asked to be given authority to identify bioregional organizations to carry out the following movement tasks and to monitor the success of these local groups to fulfill them: develop a directory of bioregional organizations in North America, initiate an information clearing house, start a skills exchange service, develop a bioregional literature list, and establish a book-selling service/mail order operation to offer a comprehensive list of bioregional titles. Local bioregional groups were also "strongly encouraged" to organize gatherings in their own bioregions and/ or among neighbouring bioregions. The decentralized organizational structure of the continental movement was confirmed and continued. In addition, the Bioregional Movement Committee recommended that the Steering Council identify bioregional groups from other continents and invite them to attend NABC III "as a first step in developing consciousness at a planetary level" (Hart et al. 1987, 15). The movement was already concerned about international and global networking problems and attempting to address such issues. It was hardly an international strategy, yet it was a small initial step toward planetary networking that recognized a need for global action.

Alliance building across race and gender was addressed as a key issue for the bioregional movement at this gathering. Social justice was very much part of bioregionalists' concerns. Between 70 and 80 people attended the race and gender panel, which opened the first workshop of NABC II. The increased presence of African-Americans and other people of colour at the gathering was viewed as "an important beginning to healing wounds between people" (Hart et al. 1987, 46). James McFadden and Nkenge Zola of the National Organization for an American Revolution (NOAR) both spoke about the cultural legacy of African-Americans on the land and their rhythmical and musical contributions to US culture. McFadden urged bioregionalists to reach out to African-Americans in their own bioregion to make use of their skills. He also stressed the importance of involving African-Americans at the beginning of any movement for truly building unity and a strong movement that could deal with racism and thus avoid being divided from without. Another crucial point made at this workshop was the need to develop a bioregional view of cities, especially devastated large US cities, if bioregionalism was to be relevant for the many people of colour in US inner cities. In reaching out to people of colour, the importance of communicating the bioregional vision in a language that most people could understand was articulated at this workshop and throughout the week.

Later in the week, the Native Peoples and People of Colour Committee proposed that NABC commit itself, through its steering committee, to actively work to involve people of colour at the national, regional, and local levels in both membership and leadership and that NABC help with financial assistance, so that people of colour could participate in local, regional, and continental meetings. The committee also proposed that "unlearning racism" workshops be initiated as a "stepping stone" to encourage more people of colour to participate in NABC events and bioregional activities. It was further proposed that NABC send a "racially, sexually, and bioregionally mixed delegation of representatives willing to follow the guidance of Indian elders" (Hart et al. 1987, 28) to the International Indian Treaty Council (IITC) in 1987 and that the delegates be committed to bringing the information back to NABC III and to their local bioregions. These resolutions were adopted by the plenary.

An ad hoc Mexico Committee was struck by several people concerned that there was no representation from Mexico at NABC II. They proposed that a concerted effort be made to network with "receptive and concerned people" (Hart et al. 1987, 28) to get involved with the congress movement. Efforts to contact and involve Mexican people in the movement were viewed as crucial to building a truly continental movement.

Gender too was a key issue at NABC II. At the race and gender workshop, Judith Plant described the links between ecofeminism and bioregionalism, including an ecofeminist view on place and home. The Ecofeminist Committee at NABC II (nine women and three men) proposed to deal with the difficult process of self-government at continental congresses by introducing some additional process tools to provide necessary emotional support: "Techniques exist to promote energy release, solidarity and empowerment to continue the work. We propose that we incorporate into our group work and meeting process, techniques such as conflict resolution, despair work and co-counseling" (Hart et al. 1987, 19). This process resolution was adopted by the plenary. Conflict resolution and co-counselling are sometimes referred to in social movements as feminist processes or tools. These "feminist" tools, little used in the first two continental gatherings, were to become more prominent in later gatherings. The Ecofeminist Committee also contributed a strong, principled, strategic statement on building community:

> Women have always been involved in building and sustaining community, and it is important to realize that qualities traditionally associated with

women reflect the values of bioregionalism. With this awareness we can insure that in creating new communities, we do not perpetuate oppressive social patterns. We affirm and support diverse forms of family life. Within bioregional community building, women and men can begin to articulate what it might mean to be females and males in the new society. The more we oppress each other and the planet, the less we are alive. As we learn to listen to the natural world and to each other, our perceptions are deepened, our intuition is reclaimed, our intelligence heightened, and all life is enhanced. (Hart et al. 1987, 18)

The newly proposed tools were then offered as a way to advance the praxis of the movement – at the continental gatherings – with respect to community building. Here we see that, although bioregional ecofeminists do not use the ecosocial capital concept, they understand the great need for "energy release, solidarity and empowerment" that tools that assist in dealing with rather than avoiding real conflicts within social movements might deliver.

At NABC II, green cities became an important dimension of the congress. Peter Berg spoke at length about green cities and described their conceptual genesis in San Francisco. As Stephanie Mills commented, the city was given voice at NABC II. However, in the next few years, a bioregional strategy for cities was not adopted by this gathering or by subsequent continental gatherings. There was no consensus at any of the congresses on this issue. Nevertheless, strategy was being conceived by bioregionalists out of a local practice toward urban reinhabitation in specific cities such as San Francisco, Chicago, Toronto, and New York.

Another key addition to the congress process at NABC II was the Mischief, Animism, Geomancy, and Interspecies Communication Committee (MAGIC). The birth of the MAGIC Committee brought all-species issues and practice into the open. Chris Wells (who had pioneered all-species festivals in Santa Fe) shared his vision, mask making, music, and stilt skills at NABC I (and again at NABC II), but now all-species work was taken up politically in committee. This new committee, with David Abrams as an important new participant at the congress, made a revolutionary proposal to the plenary that would help to transform the congress itself.

Wells, Abram, Muller, Hannon, and others proposed that NABC III recognize four participants "to represent the interests and perspectives of our non-human cousins: one for the four-legged and crawling cousins, one for those who swim in the waters, one for the winged beings, the birds of the air, and one very sensitive soul for all the plant people" (Hart et al. 1987, 26). This motion was adopted by the plenary. The MAGIC Committee also suggested that the four individuals (self-selected) not participate in any other capacity while they function as representatives of other species.

Of course, no one knew how this step toward interspecies communication, ecological kinship, and all-species democracy might work at future gatherings. But one thing was clear: this affirmation of animist philosophy was unanimously shared by the congress. From this point on, the continental congresses would include representation of other species. Unlike green city issues, there was full consensus on this turn toward a fuller form of democracy that bravely attempts to include other species' concerns and representation.

While there was consensus on all-species and animistic spirituality, the congress was unable to reach consensus on the statement about spirituality put forward by the Spirituality Committee. Although it was a nontheistic statement written in a similar animistic vein to the MAGIC Committee resolution, it was blocked by a few votes. Some participants believed that bioregionalism should not demand religious expression or participation, as Mills phrased it in her summary report of the congress. Mills and others thought that the "invocations, convocations and ritualization were contrived and subtly coercive of cynics, heretics, atheists and agnostics" (Hart et al. 1987, 9). This was the beginning of an open controversy on ritual practice within the bioregional movement. Haenke cautioned those who want to lead rituals for the group to recognize the huge responsibility that they take on and to explain to the group what they are going to do, getting approval and allowing anyone who feels uncomfortable to step aside.

Ritual and religion would again be controversial at future gatherings, but it is clear that the real controversy was not over animism as a belief system but over tools used to express and experience it, particularly over the use of ritual. Since these tools are also used to build community at the events themselves, this controversy opens up the question of what are legitimate tools for community building from a bioregional perspective.

It is important to recognize that resolutions passed at continental events do not presume to impose any policy on local or regional groups. Indeed, none of the networking organizations set up at NABC II was empowered to speak for NABC II between congresses. Participants at both NABC I and II also consistently refused to endorse products, events, movements, candidates, activities, or campaigns but did not try to prohibit local bioregional groups from doing so. For NABC participants, it is important, as Mills affirmed, that "NABC is strictly an event, a parliament of equals with no Kremlin lurking in the background" (Hart et al. 1987, 9).

Thus, NABC II continued the direction set at NABC I of building a decentralized continental network of autonomous local and (bio)regional groups linked by a common set of principles and a long-term strategy for societal transformation, a shadow government deeply embedded in the sphere of a geographically dispersed civil society.

NABC III

"From the opening circle of 300 people on a field, surrounded by glacier-capped peaks, on the land route from Asia, NABC III was different. Something about that opening cry stirred my blood. Then came the drumming." With this moving description, Katherine Adam recalled that NABC III struck a new chord for many participants (Dolcini et al. 1991, 6). NABC III was planned to be different from the previous congresses. First, the event was held in Canada in the summer of 1988, at the North Vancouver Outdoor School, in a place called Paradise Valley on the Cheakamus River, sixty-seven kilometres north of metropolitan Vancouver. Based on decisions made at the previous congress, NABC III would intentionally adopt a more cultural focus, urging bioregional groups to express their unique identities as people and places by telling their stories of place through presentations that expressed their bioregion to the rest of the congress, providing bioregional displays (including mapping projects) at the congress, and placing an accent on arts and culture (music, poetry, theatre, ceremonies, etc.). While cultural performance was not new to the congress, the cultural sharing during the evenings was now to be more comprehensive, with all participants encouraged to share their own culture with those of other bioregions.

NABC III attracted well over 300 participants, a larger number than either of the previous congresses. There were also more people of colour and more indigenous people. For the first time, there were representatives from Mexico. The congress model was stronger than ever. With seventeen working committees, there were more than at NABC I or II. The congressing dimension of the event remained central to the gathering. The new cultural emphasis did not alter the basic structure of the event. However, certain participants were beginning to ask more questions about it. Halfway through the gathering, Chris Plant gave voice to these concerns in the *Voice of the Turtle*. Some were asking how useful it was to continue refining resolutions already well thought out and adopted by the plenary. Other questions surfaced around the theme of just how "representative" the congress could be of bioregions across all of Turtle Island. In spite of these concerns, important new resolutions were put forward and adopted. Overall, the congress model remained strong, supported by most.

The opening circle began with the usual brief personal introductions, this time marked by the beat of a large, ceremonial host drum to affirm and seal the words of each person. Then Starhawk (attending her first bioregional gathering) led participants in a Wiccan "spiral dance" to the beat of a song honouring the Earth. Participants held hands and spiralled into and out of the centre, each passing by the other. After the dance, Eagle Star, a Cree singer and medicine man then living in the Yalakom/Bridge River watershed and one of the drummers, stepped into the centre of the circle to say that the traditional Native friendship dance had not been carried out and that this insulted the drum and the dance. Eagle Star explained that there is a great deal to learn from the rituals from which people of European descent borrow. He confessed that this oversight had caused him much pain. Several participants then immediately called for a traditional friendship dance. All readily agreed. Starhawk stepped into the circle to express her pain at causing Eagle Star pain while leading a dance that was part of her tradition. Eagle Star then asked Starhawk to lead the friendship dance, which enabled all participants to shake hands and greet each other eye to eye. As reported in the *Voice of the Turtle*, this painful conflict was resolved "with honesty and respect." However, the incident was symbolic of the potential for real difficulties to arise when attempting to build true "unity in diversity" across cultural borders and of the great care and respect required in the process of working together toward that goal. Of course, it also illustrated the importance of respect, honesty, and care needed when using any ritual. Although the incident ended positively, it showed clearly that, handled badly, ritual can undermine trust.

On Monday afternoon, after an orientation for people new to bioregionalism, a special panel of Native people, including representatives from Mexico, Argentina, the International Indian Treaty Council, and the Haida Nation, as well as a local Coast Salish woman, addressed the gathering in the Squamish Longhouse on the grounds of the outdoor school. The smell of burning sage filled the Longhouse as participants entered one by one through the low, arched door. Once assembled, all spoke of their long traditions living with the land and of the intense struggles to preserve their traditions in the face of European colonialism and settler encroachment and racism. Nilo Cayugeno of Argentina stated that his people, the Mapuche, have been bioregionalists for thousands of years. Two speakers challenged Eurobioregionalists to learn from their own traditions rather than emulating Native peoples' ways and stressed that it is only through respect that we can find a way to live together.

In the evening, the Longhouse, loaned to the bioregionalists by the Squamish Nation, was used for bioregional presentations and stories. The Longhouse (still used by the Squamish) was large, with an earth floor and five stone fire circles. For four nights in this ancient setting, stories of bioregions from the Cascades to the Yucatan Peninsula, enacted in theatre skits, songs, poetry, and performance art by congress participants, provided what one participant, Clifford Burke, called "a cultural map" of the continent (Zuckerman 1989, 8). For Burke, and for other veteran participants of previous congresses, this was an exciting advance in the practice of culture sharing through stories of place.

In addition to the evening Longhouse performances, there was late-evening poetry reading, singing, music making, stand-up comedy, light snacks, and informal conversation at the "Turtle Island Coffee House" set up by the Site Committee. Still later, for the high-energy people, there was drumming and dancing back at the Longhouse fire circle till the wee hours of the morning.

During the days, there were workshops offered on drumming and dancing, miming and folk ritual, and a "song swap" circle was held. Mask-making workshops were offered all week long by experienced people from the All-Species Project. A workshop on "nonhierarchical ritual" was led by Starhawk. There was also a traditional First Nations' sweat lodge held by Eagle Star. All week, he led daily sweats and, at the end of the gathering, announced that a total of 175 individuals had participated in the group sweats. For many, it was their first traditional First Nations sweat, and some participants spoke in glowing terms about the spiritual meaning of their experience.

For the first time at NABC, all-species pageantry was integrated into the week's activities. There was an ongoing salmon-mask workshop, a giant puppet show on old-growth forest issues, and an all-species workshop video presentation. There were all-species performances during dinner and an "All-Species Project Area" for participants to make masks and costumes in preparation for the All-Species Ball on the final evening. All-species resource people included children in this work. In addition, there was an all-species presentation and discussion at the panel on bioregional education. Finally, there was representation of all species – "the winged beings, the swimming beings, the plant beings, and the four-legged beings" – by four individuals during the congress plenary sessions (Zuckerman 1989, 38). The ancient community of beings worldview was reawakening within a population of humans raised in modern Western civilization. Moreover, the awakening was being called forth with the aid of an ancient face-to-face tool of community-building and communication: Earth ritual.

Green city issues and challenges were given more attention. A panel of Kirkpatrick Sale, Peter Berg, Debra Giannini (of Arcosanti), and John Papworth drew about seventy participants to an intense and lively discussion of positions and issues. The Green Cities Committee proposed that a green cities conference be convened in 1989, possibly in Chicago, to "help bring bioregional sensibilities to all urban dwellers of Turtle Island, to exchange skills and information serving to integrate cities with their bioregions, to strengthen minority and working class participation in the bioregional movement and to develop strategies for overcoming those unsound ecological practices which pollute our environment and poison our relationships with one another and with other species" (Zuckerman 1989, 71). That conference was organized and held in Chicago in July of 1989, with multiracial coalition building as a central focus (black American activist James Boggs gave the keynote speech). Berg spoke about Planet Drum's Green Cities Program as a model for the Bay Area. Other topics included progressive coalition building in cities and small-group caucusing.

Issues of race and gender were accorded greater priority than at NABC II. Increased involvement of people of colour and indigenous people was partly a result of the extra efforts of Steering Council and Site Committee members, many of whom were from the Yalakom River community. A panel discussion on sexism, racism, and the land held on the second day was attended by about eighty people. Margot Adair, Judith Plant, Gloria Yamato, Jacinta McCoy, and Dennis Jennings (of the International Indian Treaty Council) spoke.

In the later part of the workshop, small talking circles of four people or fewer engaged in an "unlearning racism" exercise. Participant Milo Guthrie's evaluation of these talking circles echoed those of some others, who thought that it was one of the most important workshops of NABC III: "This part of the workshop was very special to me and it was very important to hear people's personal stories and understand better who we are and how we see each other" (Zuckerman 1989, 17). Another participant, Alice Kidd from the Yalakom community, also commented that the small-group work of sharing experiences and stories was the most effective form for her for learning about racism as an obstacle to community and alliance building.

There were also workshops on Native land rights and multiracial alliances, a workshop led by a local Coast Salish woman, Kelly White, on Native peoples' issues, and a workshop on social ecology and traditional Native perspective. NABC II's mandate to involve more Native people, people of colour, and Mexicans was being implemented. Nevertheless, for the first time at NABC, problems of alliance building and friction across cultural and racial boundaries surfaced. At least some "people of colour" did not feel comfortable at the gathering, and they attributed their discomfort to ethnocentrism and/or racial bias. Some believed (erroneously) that Native people had been discouraged from attending the gathering. Jeffery Lewis, from Portland, Oregon, linked the problem to the "anti-urban bias of the movement" that alienated African-Americans living in the inner cities. Lewis suggested that bioregional gatherings be held in the cities, "where the contradictions that we're working to change are most apparent" (Zuckerman 1989, 27). A "people of colour" caucus was formed that did not include whites, but this caucus also participated in the Native Peoples and People of Colour Committee, which, of course, did.

The Native Peoples and People of Colour Committee, in its report to the plenary, outlined its concerns about the inability of NABC to fully involve people of colour and "a deeper concern" about perceived racism/sexism/classism within the consciousness of NABC. The committee proposed that a caucus for people of colour be established with an adequate share of the budgetary and organizational resources to meet its mandate, that a minimum of one-third of the Steering Council be people of colour, that this caucus be responsible for ensuring that people of colour be outreached, and that the Steering Council commit itself to participating in an "undoing racism" workshop in the next six months. The congress adopted these resolutions, with only one person standing aside (but not blocking). The committee additionally recommended that NABC IV adopt a multiracial, cultural, alliance-building theme; that a comprehensive sliding scale be adopted for NABC IV; and that an entire day at NABC IV be devoted to alliance building, including work on undoing racism/sexism/classism.

The Ecofeminism Committee also dealt with issues of race, gender, and class. In its report to the plenary were several recommendations on process to address the problem of "isms." The proposal included trained male and female facilitators for committees and plenary, alternate female and male speakers in plenary and committee meetings, and a presentation to be made to the entire congress on process and consensus, with simple guidelines distributed to all participants. The committee also proposed that "experiential workshops" be held on sexism, racism, classism, and ageism "and the interconnections between these attitudes and our relation with the Earth and all its species" (Zuckerman 1989, 56). Finally, the Ecofeminism Committee resolved that, while the congress does "wish to honour the North American native peoples without using their ceremonies and teachings inappropriately," the congress should "encourage people to ground themselves in the Earth from their own cultural heritage" (ibid.). Both the resolutions and the report were adopted by the congress.

By committing to ecofeminist concerns about process, the congress was committing to looking at changing itself. Thus, the Ecofeminist Committee strongly supported the process concerns of people of colour, and so, ultimately, did the congress plenary. Nevertheless, bioregionalists were discovering through direct experience that organizing across race was a difficult issue indeed, reflecting deep divisions in modern Canadian and American civil society. This experience confirms a fundamental theoretical understanding that the sphere of civil society is a terrain of struggle where genuine democracy must be created out of a diverse social mix through open discussions and horizontal forms of communication and exchange. Norms of co-operation and collaboration must be fostered and enhanced through praxis, not just assumed.

On Wednesday afternoon (day four), men and women met in separate circles. This too was a new feature of the congress. The women met in a large field and the men in the Longhouse. About eighty men sat inside the Longhouse in one large circle. Each explained why he was there. Many simply said "I'm here to learn." A suggestion to break into small groups to discuss "what it's like to be a man" or "what hurts to be a man" was followed (Zuckerman 1989, 32): that is, men were encouraged to talk about their emotions. Small groups were confidential by agreement in order to encourage a safe space for men to speak from the heart.

In the women's circle, seventy women were brought together by the beat of Alison Lang's great drum from the Yalakom. Then two women from the Olympic Peninsula shared a song from the time of the religious persecutions by the Inquisition, a song sung by women in Italy when they heard the Inquisitors were coming to their village. After that, women in the circle agreed to hold council. Constance Maytum spoke about her feelings leading up to the congress as she observed "many male/female dominant culture behaviour patterns" (Zuckerman 1989, 33). She also noted that, while most men and women in the congress community would be embarrassed to behave in the "gratuitous ways of the cultural paradigm," more subtle forms of sexism "still entangle us and leave us uncomfortable" (ibid.). After the council circle, the women joined in a ritual/theatre piece of "energy transformation," discussed social sewing projects, and watched a slide show of women artists' work. Both women's and men's circles were reconvened as one group for a ceremony to reintegrate the two circles. So, while diversity was recognized by separate circles, this ritual of reintegration honoured unity as well.

This congress was also the first to include Mexican participants who identified as bioregionalists. While there were only three Mexicans at this congress, their presence was well recognized and celebrated. They brought greetings from the three groups whom they represented and news of a dramatic awakening of ecological, spiritual, and political consciousness in Mexico over the past five years. For Alberto Ruz from Huehuecoyotl, this awakening was reflected by the dramatic increase in numbers of "independent associations, civil associations working to bring ecological awareness about environmental issues," from between 15 and 20 groups in 1984 to from between 200 and 300 organizations all over the country by NABC III (1988). In 1987, Huehuecoyotl, Sobrevivencia, and Grupo de Estudios Ambientales had invited David Haenke, Peter Berg, Bill Devall, and John Milton to a seminar on deep ecology in Mexico attended by up to 300 people. Ruz observed that, for the first time, issues of bioregionalism were discussed in Mexico. He himself translated pieces by Devall, Haenke, and Berg into Spanish that were published and circulated among a wide network of groups and individuals. At last, bioregionalism was beginning to move beyond its Euro-American cultural ghetto.

On Friday evening, the closing ceremony for NABC III culminated with the All-Species Costume Ball, for which people of all ages had been mask making and costume designing all week. Giant "bird-totem" puppets created by the All-Species Project "flew" into the circle of humans gathered in the large field for the closing circle. Then the band arrived for the costume ball. The band, Mama Coyote and the Boys, was entirely local, composed of bioregionalist "ecomusicians." It was a warm summer evening with a full moon. Dancing went on for many hours, congress participants dressed in wild animal costumes gyrating enthusiastically to wild polyrythmic beats till very late.

After the ball, up to eighty people – still dressed in full all-species costumes – gathered on the field for a Drawing down the Moon spiral dance. That night, with the full moon high in the sky, Starhawk, Eagle Star, Alberto Ruz, Arturo Pozo, and others began the carefully prepared "ecumenical" ritual incorporating several Earth traditions. A "sacred circle" was marked, drumming began, and chanting and dancing went on for two or three hours, during which the moon underwent a partial eclipse. For participants, the "old ways," the ancient Earth ways, were re-created that night, recalled to the present moment, and reenacted by the people themselves. One celebrant, Susan Meeker-Lowry, recalled her impressions: "A long, long time ago we were also at a gathering ... Then, as now, we were celebrating at a costume ball, under the full moon, preparing to dance with each other and all creatures of the Earth. It felt the same. It smelled the same. We are the same ones. Then as now" (Zuckerman 1989, 43).

What Meeker-Lowry was describing was her experience of "the Dreamtime" (after Australian Aboriginal traditional ecological knowledge), which rests just below the surface of being and is accessible in present time. By telling and reenacting the ancient stories in song and ritual, people can connect in some way not fully explicable to the linear rational mind to that "time out of time." Ritual reenactment calls forth that time of origins, and the ritual participant "in some sort becomes 'contemporary' with the events described" (Eliade 1968, 18).

The following morning was reserved for cleanup and good-byes. I too had been one of the dancers in the spiral dance ritual and had experienced something very similar to the Dreamtime, but at that time I had no name for it. However, I was in a state of elation: a joyful and peaceful energy centred in my chest but distributed throughout my body. This energy released or generated by the experience seemed to be boundless. I spoke with several other participants in the ritual dance who described similar experiences of this time out of time. For me, this state of elation and the expansive feeling of joyful energy in my heart lasted for several days after the event. Often I still feel this peaceful, joyful energy many years after the event. I feel it now as I recall the experience.

I also spoke with Glen Makepeace (who had attended all three continental congresses) about his impressions. He compared the event to Mayan ceremonial villages that he had read about, what he called "the making of a village for a week." Makepeace spoke of the excitement of coming together with people from far away who are also doing the same sort of work and of the "empowerment to just meet other people and see what wonderful people there are doing the work elsewhere" (1988).

Doug Aberley, also at his third continental gathering, expressed his reflections after the congress in his field notes. On the inclusion of all species in the congress plenary, he observed that "At first blush this seems hilarious. But it became quickly clear, by constantly seeing these mute sentinels, that the direction of dialogue was subtly shifted. To have an intellectual understanding that humans are only one species among several million is one thing, to have this understanding introduced into every minute of a meeting's events is another level of perception altogether" (1992). For Aberley, the best innovation was the nightly cultural evenings: "It was as if we were seeing for the first time the impact bioregionalism was having on the evolution of culture."

Don Alexander, attending his first bioregional event, had some criticisms of what he called "the tendency of some to impose pagan pomp and circumstance on gathering participants as a whole," but he also reflected on the strengths of the congress: the "rough-and-ready egalitarianism," with everyone chipping in to do support work, the consistency of practice and belief, and the integration of global and local, political and cultural. "At the congress, I felt that my whole being was involved serving food, caring for children, barbecuing salmon, listening to presentations, partying, going for walks, speaking up at plenaries, intervening in conflicts, and facilitating workshops. I bonded with people on an emotional as well as intellectual level" (Zuckerman 1989, 7).

Alberto Ruz also attended the congress for the first time. I spoke with him during the congress about the problems that surfaced with respect to race and cultural difference. He recognized that the path was not going to be easy. Ruz acknowledged the difficulties of outreach and reaching groups of Native people. He spoke about the suspicion of Native people and others of any movement "that has been started by white people," suspicion generated because they are just "tired of lip service, no?" But he also pointed out that "They are here, and they are learning just as we are learning, we are all learning from each other" (1988). Indeed, powerful horizontal webs of relations across gender, race, and geography were being formed. A new Earth culture was emerging in which true respect for difference was being built in spite of difficulties, tensions, and barriers.

If difference and diversity were at least an openly recognized problem within the movement, the problem of continuity at the congress events was not. Another key observation made by veteran participant Makepeace (1988) was that, by NABC III, there were only thirty individuals who had attended all three events. This fact points to a serious problem of continuity for the continental gatherings. This issue also contributed to the problems of race in that many of the new Afro-American and indigenous participants were unaware of the serious efforts and consensus decisions made at previous congresses for more inclusive gatherings.

NABC IV

NABC IV was held on the shore of Lake Cobbossecontee north of Portland, Maine, at a YMCA camp in August 1990. The event attracted more than 260 participants, somewhat fewer than NABC III. Participants came from North and South America and Japan. The committee and plenary work central to the congress model remained an important dimension of the event. At the outset, Susan Meeker-Lowry and Brian Tokar observed that, in spite of some feelings that committee work and resolutions had reached a culmination, there was still important work and further-reaching proposals for action needed (Dolcini et al. 1991, 5). In fact, there were nineteen committees operating at this congress, more than at any previous continental event. The congress continued to refine its own processes and tools and added some new features, such as a "children's congress" and "talking circles." As well, the new emphasis on cultural activities and sharing initiated at NABC III was enhanced, in part, by the strong, experienced cultural participation of six representatives from Mexico.

This time the congress was planned for a full seven days. The extra time meant that the ambitious schedule could be reasonably implemented without burnout. Two primary themes established by the Steering Council for the fourth congress were "Organizing Our Bioregions" and "Promoting Cultural Diversity – Building Alliances and Coalitions." The cultural diversity/ alliance-building theme was, of course, mandated by the previous congress. The theme "Organizing Our Bioregions" emerged from discussions within the Steering Council (and informally with various other individuals) on continental strategy. Structural changes outlined by the Steering Council were designed to accommodate continuing committee work and to provide time to seriously address alliance building in local bioregions as well as at the congress itself. Would the congress have room for both?

The fourth congress opened on Sunday evening with supper and an introductory circle. Participants introduced themselves by their bioregional places and their purposes at the gathering. Then participants were led in a guided meditation designed to take them to the "source roots of the bioregional energies they call home" (Dolcini et al. 1991, 2), after which everyone was invited to use the week to nourish stronger roots. In the final part of the evening, Roberto Mendoza, a Native American bioregionalist working on the Site Committee, recounted an indigenous legend about huge monsters that once terrorized the land until they were reduced to a manageable human scale. When the white settlers arrived and butchered the forests, they were seen as the monsters of the legend. Today, Mendoza suggested, these destructive giants are transnational corporations, and the bioregional challenge is to reduce these modern monsters to human scale. In the world at large (outside the magic circle of bioregional congresses), the corporate global agenda was advancing all too rapidly by the summer of

1990. Now, inside the full circle, for the first time, a profound concern about the corporate global megamachine was being raised.

Mendoza's talk was received enthusiastically by the assembly. Generally, corporate themes receive sympathetic hearing among bioregionalists in informal discussions. However, in focusing on the corporate monster before the plenary, Mendoza was tackling an issue that is key to the three-sphere model of civil society theory – the control of the formal economic sphere by the global corporate and financial oligarchy now attempting to consolidate its rule over the Earth through its neoliberal agenda. This issue had not been adequately addressed by the bioregional movement. What to do about neoliberal globalization remained hotly debated in the bioregional movement, as we shall see.

One important innovation at the Maine continental congress was the "children's congress," a program of games, crafts, music, dance, drama, and discussion to enable children to "celebrate the cultural diversity of Turtle Island." All participants were "encouraged to bring bioregional activities to share with the children," recognizing that it is "our collective responsibility to nurture the next generation" (Fourth North American Bioregional Conference 1990). Janice Walrafen spoke about this with me later when I asked her about her work with children at the congress. She replied enthusiastically: "The reason I work with children is because they are our future, and also, for me, they are the seeds of hope because they're not fixed in their behavioural patterns to the degree that they can't change ... So I'm there to help them keep that thread through, especially through puberty and adolescence. It's easy to let go of that animistic kind of reality that the children live with" (1990). The children were asked to explore the themes of NABC IV and put together a performance presentation to share with the entire congress on the final day.

Every morning after breakfast, a half hour was reserved for "talking circles" of four to six people. These circles were inspired by a ceremonial practice of Native Americans. During this time, participants were encouraged to share from the heart and spirit whatever may move him or her. These circles were intended to provide a confidential, non-judgmental container for whole-hearted listening. Participants in each talking circle stayed in the same group all week so that the circle might provide a support group for personal grounding. The circles also functioned as a way for new and old bioregionalists to share experiences and stories and another forum for individuals to get to know new people. These circles were popular with participants, and they became a permanent feature of continental gatherings, another important use of small groups as a tool for trust building and informal networking among virtual strangers at continental events.

After the talking circles, the rest of the first day of the congress was devoted to introducing bioregionalism, the history of the congress, and the use of consensus process for new and old participants in the morning, following up in the afternoon with a presentation of the story of the Upper Blackland Prairie group from Texas. The Texas presentation launched the theme of "Organizing Our Bioregions."

Monday evening was devoted to bioregional organizing. Six groups presented oral histories of their bioregional organizing efforts. At this session, Freeman House (who had been one of the strongest proponents of strictly local organizing) probably best articulated the necessity of local groups to form broader networks. He recounted the story of "Redwood Summer" in the Mattole Valley that year. Earth First! activists chose to focus on the Mattole in their campaign to save dwindling redwood forests. The attention of the US state was also drawn to the valley when the federal government decided to focus its "War on Drugs" campaign in the Mattole Valley, sending 600 troops to camp in the valley for six weeks. During this period, constant over-flights by army helicopters contributed to inducing fear in the valley's residents. This situation forced a reevaluation by some of the Mattole restorationists of their past successes. Clearly, for truly sustainable local success, House argued, broader networks were needed to consolidate the gains. The question – and challenge – for the movement that House posed, given a shared understanding that "bioregions could only be experienced and invoked by their inhabitants," was what NABC could actually do to assist and accelerate the process of local organizing: "To put our success in a bioregional context two things were needed that would not rise out of our own small area: the widespread availability of a body of bioregional literature and a forum for extra-regional discourse, and alliances and consolidations with like-minded communities in our own bioregion" (Dolcini et al. 1991, 9).

The necessity of a widely available body of bioregional literature was evident to many bioregionalists at this gathering. The publication of a collection of bioregional essays (formerly available mostly in obscure regional journals), *Home! A Bioregional Reader* (Andruss et al. 1990), provided the beginning of a solution, now available "hot off the press" at the congress. It was greeted with enthusiasm by many participants, and there was much talk at this congress of the need to reach out to mainstream society. *Home!* was the first of a series of bioregional books that would begin to bring this heretofore unknown literature to a wider public. Also, Gene Marshall had prepared a list of principles for bioregional organizing, part of a planned organizing handbook published in the proceedings to assist local organizers and activists. Still, the second half of House's proposed solution – alliance building across "isms" – would not be solved so easily.

Alliance building and, in particular, the tool chosen to deal with it at this congress, "undoing 'isms' workshops," were scheduled for both morning and afternoon the following day, Tuesday. On Tuesday morning, a large part of the congress assembled on a small grassy hill. The workshop was organized to address a plethora of "isms," including racism, sexism, ageism, and speciesism, all considered to be forms of oppressive behaviour. All NABC IV participants were encouraged to attend. The workshop was led by Margot Adair and Roberto Mendoza. Adair stressed the importance of both confronting our internal oppressions and transforming the institutions that keep "isms" in place. Mendoza argued that, when European immigrants came to this continent, they were promised socioeconomic privilege in return for denying their individual cultural heritage of place and being grouped under a broader category, "white." Colour thus became an effective tool for dividing people along racial lines. Adair pointed to the importance of "naming" different oppressive behaviours and attitudes as an aid to revealing and then altering behaviour. The assembled group then brainstormed a long list of oppressive behaviours.

One woman, Juana Gonzalez Paz (attending her first congress), identified herself as a lesbian feminist of colour to the assembly. She was concerned that she was the only person who openly identified as lesbian or gay and that there was only "a handful of people of colour" at the gathering. Gonzalez Paz was also concerned that there was "resistance, avoidance, denial and blatant racism" displayed by some participants at the undoing "isms" workshop. As an example, she referred to one white man who talked about feeling oppressed by the process and how the "man of colour" facilitator met with resistance when asking white people about their oppression. On the other hand, she also recognized that the consensus process did work: "I blocked any use of 'the human race' that didn't acknowledge power differentials and that concern seemed to be well-received" (Dolcini et al. 1991, 13).

This experience points to a number of problems with process at the workshop itself and with the effort at alliance building. First, NABC III had mandated the Steering Council to include people of colour, a minimum of one-third of its members, and to provide them with an adequate share of budgetary and organizational resources. This was done, and Jacinta McKoy (an African-American woman), who was hired as the staff person for the new Turtle Island Office, also became coordinator of the People of Colour Committee. Slightly less than one-third of the Steering Council were now people of colour. Their fares to Steering Council meetings were paid (others' fares were not). However, when funds dwindled, several of the people of colour representatives failed to attend the final Steering Council meeting before NABC IV. Moreover, although its specific mandate was to involve more people of colour, it did not manage to attract any new participants. As a result, there were not many people of colour at NABC IV from the United States or Canada. It was recognized – after the fact – that serious alliance building across race would not take place at the level of the Steering Council, which, after all, was merely a coordinating committee between gatherings with no power except that mandated by the congress itself. Alliance building across the racial barrier would first have to take place "in place" in the bioregions, a surprisingly "bioregional" lesson!

Second, there was the related problem of continuity at continental congresses. The process of informing and involving new participants in the congressing process did not seem to be adequate to the task. For example, people of colour new to the congress appeared to be unaware of past efforts at dealing with issues of race and gender, although, as this account has already shown, considerable effort had been spent on this issue. This problem raises an important consideration about social capital formation. Can social capital be raised effectively across geographical space merely through electronic or print forms of communication, as the organizers of both NABC III and IV tried to do? This consideration leads, of course, to a second related question. Can there be any such thing as a "global" civil society? Extensive efforts were made by print mail, telephone, and e-mail to involve people of colour, with little result. Or can social capital best be built locally through direct, "embodied," face-to-face communication? How much trust can be built between strangers through the telephone lines or via e-mail or the Internet? These are crucial questions for those concerned with broad social mobilization in "global" civil society.

Third, the particular application of the alliance-building tool, the undoing "isms" workshop at NABC IV, posed a problem. Adair recommends that a "safe space" be created for the honest and often painful admissions that "speaking from the heart" demands (see Chapter 4). As we have seen, small-group discussions proved to be useful in this respect for participants at NABC III. Yet the undoing "isms" workshop was not broken into small groups at NABC IV. The lesson here, then, is that small groups or "talking circles" may be essential to creating the safe space to build the quality of trust necessary for people to "come out" and speak frankly about their feelings regarding oppression.

Lack of participation by people of colour from the United States and Canada was very disappointing for members of the Steering Council and more generally for congress participants as a whole. However, a larger contingent of participants from Mexico supplied new energy to the People of Colour Committee and to the congress. During their cultural presentation Wednesday evening, the Mexican contingent included an update on Xochimilco bioregion, a slide presentation on the Cuauhnahuac bioregion, and a multimedia ceremony of music, poetry, and slides entitled the Return of Quetzalcoatl. The finale was performed by some members of the group The Illuminated Elephants from Huehuecoyotl who had many years of experience with cultural performance and ceremony (see Chapter 5). This ceremonial performance was, in fact, a participatory ritual that engaged everyone in the hall with warm southern energy and music, chant, drum, and dance. In this inclusive performance, sharing across cultures worked to generate good feelings and north-south bonds of solidarity, as several participants readily observed.

In the Native Peoples and People of Colour Committee meetings, the Mexicans put forward the proposition that the committee change its name to the Rainbow Peoples Committee, the rainbow being a symbol of all colours in their unity and difference. The plenary agreed. Other proposed changes included a resolution that the congress change its name to the Turtle Island Bioregional Congress (TIBC), since to Central America and Mexico North America means "Yankee" or "gringo," and that the Steering Council and Site Committee facilitate support for organizations composed of people of colour and poor people and make it a priority to facilitate their ability to attend meetings. These resolutions were adopted by the plenary. So, ironically, while NABC IV failed to develop any new links with people of colour within the United States and Canada, the north-south linkage across culture, race, and an even broader geography was growing stronger.

"Organizing Our Bioregions" was the second major theme of NABC IV. The Steering Council meeting, held during the congress, reviewed problems of bioregional organizing, education, and outreach since NABC III. Members of the council agreed that lack of leadership and funds prohibited gains between congresses and contributed to a failure to follow through on the plans laid at NABC III with respect to the Turtle Island Office, the NABC newsletter, and fund-raising. The Steering Council suggested that logistics for these projects be done through the Bioregional Movement Committee as well as at Steering Council meetings.

The solution to the continental networking problem expected to be presented to NABC V by the Steering Council was a proposal for a form of congress and steering committee representative of the "locally organized bioregional congresses." The resolution adopted by the plenary was that the process of selection of Steering Council members be approved by the plenary of NABC IV before it disbanded. This move seemed to hark back to Haenke's and OACC's shadow government congress of representatives.

The Steering Council, following the lead of the Rainbow Peoples Committee, also proposed that the name of the continental congress be changed to the Turtle Island Bioregional Congress. This name obviously represented a move to continue the congress model. So, on the one hand, the fourth congress continued to develop the congress model. However, within the congress and the Steering Council itself, increasing doubts about the wisdom of "resolutionary bioregionalism" continued to surface. Open comments from Steering Council members about passing more resolutions and the need to go into action reflected these doubts.

Furthermore, a talking circle held within the Green Cities Committee revealed a high level of frustration with the resolutionary process. Concerns that "we were going through the same motions as at the last two

NABC's" and that "some people were beginning to withdraw mentally" were voiced (Dolcini et al. 1991, 13). The Green Cities Committee decided to resign as a committee. Clearly, serious problems were developing with the congress resolutionary model.

Yet, as noted, there were more committees than at previous gatherings. Moreover, some committees added important new dimensions to their resolutionary work. For example, the Economics Committee (the largest one yet) completed its four-pronged conversion strategy (see Chapter 4). The Education Committee, having already established a set of fine principles, began to work on developing criteria to help people evaluate new "environmental" teaching material coming out on the market and on developing support for *Pollen*, the journal of bioregional education being published by Frank Traina at Sunrock Farm.

Another important example of ongoing committee work was that of the Forest Committee, which developed a proposal for a core-corridor system of biodiversity preservation two years before the groundbreaking core-corridor concept plan (for the United States) of Reed Noss and the Wildlands Project was published (Noss 1992). Moreover, the Forest Committee, in its preamble, linked the question of preserving habitats for all species to the issues of undoing "isms" within the human species: "In native ecosystems there is not the extent of power hierarchy – domination of the many by the few – which human cultures have created and are the basis of these 'isms'" (Dolcini et al. 1991, 45). This resolution was adopted by the congress. It was an important step forward for deep ecology, a move in the direction of integrating deep ecology concerns with those of social ecology.

While congress committee work remained strong, more "direct action" was a key plenary theme. First there was an intervention by "spider," an all-species representative, during the Education Committee's presentation. Spider objected to the proposal to have living creatures (spiders in particular) taken out of their natural habitats and brought into classrooms. Spider's discomfort was mimed (all-species representatives have no voice at the plenary). Then spider's objection was voiced by Caroline Estes, the congress facilitator, who argued that humans have a "very real responsibility to take Spider's message into the 'real world' to share with children, teachers – anyone involved with the kind of work that seems to involve the disruption of other species' lives to benefit us" (Dolcini et al. 1991, 4).

Other "direct action" interventions in the plenary occurred. These participatory forms of plenary presentation underlined congress participants' frustrations with "resolutionism" and signalled a shift in format.

Turtle Island Bioregional Congress (TIBC) V

The fifth congress was held in Texas Hill Country at Camp Stewart on the headwaters of the Guadalupe River in May 1992. Attendance was down from NABC IV to about 220 participants. This time there were more Mexicans than at any previous continental gathering. It was at this congress that a marked turn away from the congress model was implemented. In this sense, the hesitation of NABC IV was resolved. The Steering Council planned and presented for discussion and adoption the significant shifts in format and agenda.

The traditional committee structure was the major focus of the shift. The new agenda proposed was that committees meet at the beginning of the gathering "for a brief time" to study the work of the four previous congresses and to decide on their own future and relevance. The time previously taken by week-long committee work would then be spent in "Circles of Change." Circles of Change were offered by the Steering Council as a way to place specific committee concerns in a broader context and to "weave a strong fabric from the various committee threads" (Dubose 1992, 22).

These circles were focused specifically on bioregional practices or tools. The following five broad topic areas were suggested: (1) mapping and organizing, (2) continental links of communication, (3) the bioregional story, (4) living at home, and (5) ecosystem conservation and restoration. Ample space was created in the agenda for workshops offered by participants to share their special knowledge and skills, a feature established at NABC IV.

The opening circle of TIBC V began with drumming. Then Glen Makepeace read the "Welcome Home" statement drafted at NABC I. Participants joined hands, sang several songs and chants together, gave tribute to elders and children present, and introduced themselves to each other. The introductions were brief and different from previous years, affirming bioregionalism as a force in people's lives rather than "selling" other causes (Aberley 1992).

In the orientation session, both David Haenke and Stephanie Mills gave presentations on the history of the bioregional movement. Then the Steering Council presented its agenda for the congress. Immediately, it was met with concern that the committee structure had been abandoned for something that was unclear to participants. How could this Circles of Change structure, with many more people per group, allow the same level of work to be completed? A long discussion ensued. It was resolved to try out the new structure, but there was still what Aberley describes as "an ominous disapproval" among a significant group of congress participants (1992, 37). Worse, since the orientation session was pressed into the same morning as this important congress decision, many new people at the gathering did not get a very full historical introduction to either bioregionalism or the congress. Bioregionalists were not following their own prescriptions for involving people new to the movement. There simply was not enough emphasis on this crucial aspect of movement building, especially given the problem with continuity at congresses.

The next day after the morning talking circles, the committees met. Spanish translation was added to the day's events to accommodate the larger number of Mexican and other Spanish-speaking participants. Only thirteen committees actually assembled, fewer than at any previous congress. Moreover, several committees decided to dissolve.

Real difficulties with the transition arose. While the Bioregional Mapping Committee met and then moved easily into the Mapping Circle of Change, the Communities Committee, after unsuccessfully attempting to integrate into the Living at Home Circle of Change, continued to meet as a committee. The Ecofeminism Committee agreed to continue its work in the form of a committee, caucus, or affinity group. The Rainbow Peoples Committee was troubled by the fact that, of the six Circles of Change, none seemed to have been set up to deal with issues of social justice and racism or with "the wisdom, as well as the problems of indigenous peoples" (Dubose 1992, 16).

The MAGIC Committee simply chose to remain a working committee and to continue to represent other species at TIBC plenary meetings. It called upon all gathering participants to carry "a responsibility to be open to the 'voices' of the non-human world" (17). It recommended that it share responsibility for opening circle rituals and that other forms of MAGIC such as shamanic drumming and sacred circle dances with an all-species focus be utilized at the gatherings. Finally, the committee also recommended that it have an intermediary "protector," chosen from the MAGIC Committee, to act as a voice between the species' representatives (who do not have a voice) and the congress. This intermediary voice would communicate on behalf of the human participants at the plenary to the other species' representatives and vice versa. This addition to the all-species communication process put the protector in a role similar to that of a shaman who travels back and forth between human and nonhuman worlds.

The Spirituality Committee, before disbanding, pointed to and underlined the words of participant Luis Espinosa, a Bolivian shaman and spiritual leader of the Movimiento Pachamama (Mother Earth Movement), who pointed out in the opening plenary that "every part of our lives can be spiritual, including rational discussion of spirituality" (18). In the ensuing discussion, the Spirituality Committee was able to clarify "how embracing an Earthy form of spirituality means that every committee is a spiritual committee, that spirit is at the base of every effort to be and to build a sustainable society" (18). This was an echo of Haenke's position at NABC II. Based on this logic, the Spirituality Committee disbanded, the members joining the various Circles of Change.

A Permaculture Circle was added to the five Circles of Change. Another "proposal of marriage" between permaculture and bioregionalism was made by the Permaculture Circle of Change. This time, however, the marriage was to be embodied in action. A permaculture design was done for the Camp Stewart site. A topographic map of the site was made, and hundreds of plants were brought to the site, and seeds were distributed for planting. Plans for follow-up workdays and inspections were made as a hands-on work project and gift to Camp Stewart. This contribution of the congress was carried out to "embody the vision" of the congress by directly supporting the local community, setting a precedent for future continental events.

On the third full day of the congress, by which time participants had experienced one day of the old committee meetings and one day of the new Circles of Change, it became clear that some groups were wondering whether there should be any more continental gatherings. Some participants argued that these events were too time consuming, too expensive, and too draining of the energy of the organizers. Perhaps, they argued, it would be better to put the effort into local gatherings in the bioregions. Many seemed to agree. Another idea surfaced that a middle path would be to have a continental gathering every four years.

A discussion on continuity was also taking place in the Continental Links of Communication Circle of Change. This new debate underscored the magnitude of the continuity problem. Informal conversations at the congress revealed that at least 80 percent of participants were new to the congress process (Aberley 1998). The reply to whether there should be a gathering or not came forcefully from the "old guard" of the movement, one of whom was Stephanie Mills. She argued in that morning's *Voice of the Turtle* that "the congress is many things; party, reunion, week-long university of bioregionalism, healing community, summer camp. It is, perhaps most importantly, a council for considering and expressing bioregional values and strategies," and "a critical task we perform is detailing our vision of sustainable futures in our places" (*Voice of the Turtle* 1992).

In the end, the Continental Links of Communication Circle of Change, consisting of some of the old guard (Berg, Sale, Haenke, Goldhaft, and Adam), two key Mexican representatives (Ruz and Pozo), as well as some newcomers, reached consensus on continuing the congress every two years. They also emphasized strongly that orientation for newcomers be allocated one or two full days.

The Bioregional Story Circle of Change did its work in smaller breakout groups. Its vision of future gatherings also put strong emphasis on in-depth introduction to bioregional work and aspects of bioregional culture. Celebration and ritual were also stressed by this circle as ways to inspire, nurture and sustain us. The members also favoured a congress of representatives from bioregions as well as the formation of organizations based on biomes. Finally, they proposed that the congress change its name to the Turtle Island Bioregional Gathering (TIBG). This recommendation was adopted by the plenary, further shifting the continental gathering model.

Increased prominence of workshops also marked the transformation away from the pure congress model. The workshops were as diverse as the participants who offered them. Many were the "hands-on" variety, such as watershed planning, straw bale construction, and architectural design and planning. Others were more esoteric, such as Earth Literacy and Self-Esteem for Everyone Using Your "True Colours." The introduction of a number of workshops on tools for community building used by bioregionalists – including consensus and facilitation, conflict resolution, reevaluation counselling, and an all-species workshop – marked a shift in the congress toward increased awareness of the need to develop tools, processes, and skills for improved community building.

By the final plenary, it was clear that a marked change in the congress model was occurring. For future continental gatherings, there would be more space in the agenda for ceremonial, spiritual, and cultural activities. There would also be more emphasis on north-south networking and on opening continental gatherings to newcomers, as well as to children and elders. The children's and youth congresses were already a more integral part of the shifting congress model. As Aberley observed at the final plenary, "the goal here is for a holistic, not specialist, gathering where kids, elders, newcomers can feel welcome" (1992, 45). The shift in emphasis was not totally acceptable to all gathering participants. For some congress veterans, such as Kirkpatrick Sale and Doug Aberley, committees remained a useful way to focus the work of the gathering. There was a deep concern that too much emphasis on process was sacrificing the work of developing strategies for organizing and networking and for public education about the work and positions of the bioregional movement (Aberley 1992). This key strategic question of continental networking would remain a challenge for the movement and give rise to further tensions as the shift to the ceremonial village model continued.

Turtle Island Bioregional Gathering (TIBG) VI

The sixth continental gathering, Turtle Island Bioregional Gathering VI, was held on the bank of the Ohio River at the mouth of Otter Creek at a YMCA campsite, near Louisville, Kentucky, in August 1994. There were 200 participants. Certain elements of the event were carried forward as before: small talking circles, evening cultural presentations with bioregional story sharing, opening and closing circles, morning circles, and a children's congress. The intention of the gathering, expressed by the Steering Council and Site Committee, was to create a self-organizing cooperative community for a week.

For the first time, only the first two days (apart from meals, a group dance, and a barter fair and marketplace) were preplanned by the Steering Council. On the first two days, the agenda included a morning circle, small family circles, and "lodges." The lodges were similar to the Circles of Change of the Texas gathering, except that there were four instead of six, and they were intended as an orientation to bioregionalism and community building and as a history of the congress/gathering tradition.

In the opening circle of TIBG VI on Monday morning, after introductions, Haenke presented an overview of the history of the continental congresses, outlining the diversity of movements that had informed and contributed energy and ideas to bioregionalism, including deep ecology, social ecology, ecofeminism, creation spirituality, alternative technology, and so on.

On Monday afternoon, the lodges began. Although intended to provide more orientation to both bioregionalism and community building to better integrate newcomers, what actually happened in the lodges was quite different. None of the lodges spent time on further orientation to bioregionalism or community building. The mandate from TIBC V to put more emphasis on integrating newcomers was not followed. Moreover, given that the lodges were now responsible for the rest of the agenda of TIBG VI, it was not surprising that three of four lodges chose to address the immediate need to plan the gathering. The fourth lodge, the South lodge, chose instead to begin encouraging "communication, travel, and trade between bioregions in Mexico and the United States" by building a travel corridor that it called the Funnel. Its purpose was to help people from the United States and Canada attend the 1996 continental gathering proposed to be held in Mexico. The other three lodges presented separate proposals for an agenda to the plenary.

The following day, the plenary took two sessions (morning and afternoon) to come to consensus on the agenda for the rest of the gathering. The final proposal accepted was a compromise rather than a consensus. Mornings would be used for opening circle, family circles, and plenaries. After lunch, a block of time would be reserved for workshops, lodges, committees, and special interest groups or caucuses. The cultural sharing evenings would continue. This agenda appeared to give equal weight to workshops, committees, and lodges. However, the lodges didn't really meet again. Instead, workshops, certain committees, and interest groups (or circles) met. Since all were given the same time niche on the agenda, workshops now had at least equal priority with committee work, another significant change away from the congress model.

The Committee on Multicultural Representation (formerly the Rainbow Peoples Committee) recognized the lack of "cultural" diversity at TIBG VI. In view of the expectation that the next continental gathering would be held in Mexico, the committee recommended that efforts be made to work in local bioregions on outreach, developing ongoing relationships with other cultural groups and getting information to "other cultural groups and minority organizations well in advance of the 1996 gathering" (*Voice of the*

Turtle 1994a). In view of the great deal of effort (and similar resolutions) expended at previous gatherings and in between gatherings on multicultural representation at these events, this committee expressed its frustration at the possibility of going to Mexico without African-American, Native American, and other multicultural representation from the United States. Well thought out and based on previous experiences of the congresses, its recommendations for outreach strategies in local bioregions could only be carried out by local bioregionalists and others working in their own communities. How much effective local work had been done? Some good work was done in the San Francisco Bay Area, but it was not reflected in attendance at the continental gatherings. In spite of past experience, great effort and previous resolutions at the continental events, participation by African-Americans and other minority peoples remained very low.

With structure and agenda questions settled, the plenary was finally opened to discuss issues. Thursday's plenary began with the chant O-HI-O, celebrating the Ohio River's continuing beauty (in spite of multiple environmental threats to its health). The major issues for the remainder of the plenary were the request for help from local bioregionalists for support in the struggle to prevent development of a golf course in Otter Creek Park, the proposal of Mexican bioregionalists to host TIBG VII in 1996, and Planet Drum's proposal to establish a North American bioregional association. With respect to the golf course threat to Otter Creek, the decision of the plenary was to organize a letter-writing campaign before the end of the gathering. This was done.

On behalf of the recently established Mexican bioregional network, Guardians of the Earth Vision Council, Alberto Ruz officially extended an invitation to host the next continental gathering in 1996. This proposal was greeted with great enthusiasm by plenary participants. Congress participants had been looking forward to a continental gathering in Mexico since NABC IV. After careful explanation of the responsibilities involved, about fifteen persons stepped forward to the centre of the plenary circle to volunteer for the hard work of organizing a continental gathering (despite previous resolutions for a "representative" Steering Council, there was no mention of representation of bioregions this time). These self-selected volunteers were accepted warmly by the plenary participants. The new Steering Council was renamed the Continuity Committee.

Planet Drum's proposal to the plenary for a Bioregional Association of North America (BANA) was that it would be a membership organization with several purposes, including aid and assistance to bioregional member groups, a recognizable public presence and easily accessible source of information about the bioregional movement, an interface with the general public who want to be informed about local groups, and a forum for addressing issues and policies. It was also argued that BANA could provide a voice for bioregions against globalizing tendencies such as NAFTA and GATT and that it could be a first step toward creating planetary connections with similar organizations that Planet Drum thought likely to form on other continents. There was concern among some participants that an "official" permanent continental bioregional organization might be too susceptible to central-ized control. For its part, Planet Drum viewed the establishment of BANA as a change in strategy but not in values. Finally, TIBG VI reached consensus on the creation of a group to explore the potential of forming a bioregional association.

The Mexican contingent contributed an informative, dramatic, and in-spiring political education theatrical performance in the evening about the movement for democratization in Mexico. Some of the Mexican partici-pants had gone to the National Democratic Convention, Aguascalientes II, held in Chiapas, Mexico, only days before TIBG VI. This convention of 6,000 delegates from organizations of civil society all over Mexico was hosted by the Zapatista Liberation Army (EZLN) in the jungle in the territory under its control. Using its well-worn street theatre skills, the Mexican bioregional actors re-created the EZLN-hosted convention in the Chiapan jungle at TIBG VI, with the assembled bioregionalists as a participatory audience. Suddenly, TIBG VI bioregionalists were being addressed by a masked, pipe-smoking Subcommandante Marcos (played by Ruz), who welcomed the "delegates" to the gathering "in the jungle": "We welcome ... all those that do not come here to impose, manipulate or collect supposed debts that we should have with you. We welcome those that come from unorganized civil associa-tions, more than those that come from either small, medium or large politi-cal parties. We welcome transgressors of the unjust laws, the utopists, the poets, the visionaries ... those of you that come here to share, not to demand" (*Voice of the Turtle* 1994b).

"Marcos" talked on until he was interrupted by a "peasant woman" in the assembly who demanded that, in the honesty of real face-to-face dialogue, he remove his mask and speak with the people directly. "Marcos" agreed gallantly to throw her question to the democratic decision of the people assembled, explaining that, if he removed his mask, the Mexican security forces would be able to identify and kill him. The assembly cheered wildly for "Marcos" to keep his mask on.

After the theatrical performance, the assembled participants at TIBG VI joined the performers in a chanting and dancing celebration of Pachamama (Mother Earth) in Spanish. This theatrical/ritual re-creation of one event at another succeeded in creating an embodied, emotional identification for bioregional participants with the indigenous and popular struggle for de-mocracy in Mexican civil society.

The ritual/theatrical re-creation of the EZLN-hosted convention of Mexi-can civil society at a bioregional movement gathering was appropriately symbolic. There is a compelling argument to be made that the Zapatista movement is akin to bioregional movements. The EZLN lives in the forests of Chiapas, a bioregion still occupied by Mayan peoples, now joined by a variety of other indigenous people forced into the forest by racist ranchers and other oppressors of Mexican indigenous peoples. Moreover, the EZLN has not attempted to capture state power as did previous armed liberation movements. Rather, the Zapatistas defend their territory against the Mexican federal army, calling on Mexican civil society for the ultimate democratization of Mexico, only demanding autonomy and indigenous rights for themselves and all Mexican indigenous peoples (Marcos 2001; Ross 2000).

Mexican representatives at TIBG VI also informed gathering participants that they had made bioregional proposals in their presentation to the assembly of 6,000 in Chiapas. Bioregional ideas were thus communicated in an important forum of civil society in Mexico, from which they would be conveyed across the country among organizations of Mexican civil society. TIBG VI ended with much enthusiasm, looking forward to the next continental gathering in Mexico.

First Bioregional Gathering of the Americas

The seventh continental gathering was held in Tepoztlan in the State of Morelos, Mexico, in late November 1996 at Meztitla, a Boy Scout camp on the edge of town. This gathering stood out from all the others in several ways. First, the event was not only the seventh continental gathering of the North American bioregional movement, but it was also the sixth gathering of the Mexican bioregional movement, the Guardians of the Earth Vision Council (Consejo de Visiones, Guardianes de la Tierra) of Mexico, which had been meeting annually since 1991. The Mexican bioregional movement is an independent, autonomously organized movement inspired, in part, by the North American Bioregional Congresses. At its fifth council held in Jalisco, Mexico, in 1995, the Guardians of the Earth Vision Council decided by consensus to hold its next annual event in conjunction with TIBG VII. Sponsored by both movements, the overarching title of the continental gathering in Tepoztlan (agreed to by both movements through consensus process) was The First Bioregional Gathering of the Americas.

The idea for a Mexican network was born at a meeting in Huehuecoyotl in 1990 of ecologists, New Age leaders, Native spiritual guides, and scientists from several countries. The network was initially formed out of an "ecumenical" intention to "end the artificial separation that exists between scientific and spiritual thought" (Ruz 1996b). The Mexican bioregional network is a mix of three movements: the bioregional "ecology" movement, the rainbow network ("New Age" families, tribes, healers, and shamans), and representatives from a dozen indigenous peoples from Mexico and Central America (Ruz 1996a). As such, the Mexican bioregional movement has a very different base and starting point from the North American movement. It has its own history and distinct character, some of which is reflected in the Huehuecoyotl community and its particular face-to-face, village-to-village networking. At their annual gatherings, Guardians of the Earth Vision Council developed the practice of contributing both knowledge and hands-on support work for the local village community in which gatherings were held. Hands-on workshops were given in holistic health, nutrition, permaculture, bioregionalism, recycling and organic composting, consensus decision making, group facilitation, drums and shamanic songs, music and dance, puppet theatre, and mime.

The First Bioregional Gathering of the Americas was by far the largest of the bioregional continental events. Over 600 people were officially registered, but others who could not afford the registration fees were allowed to camp and cook their own food. Estimates of the total attendance ranged from 800 to 1,200 participants. One of the organizers, Bea Briggs, estimates that there were over 800 camped on the Meztitla campgrounds. Whatever the total, about 250 were from the United States, Canada, Europe, and Australia, the majority of these coming from the United States. Most participants were from Mexico, followed by Central America and then South America. There were about 70 indigenous participants, including elders, shamans, pipe carriers, dancers, and traditional healers. However, only three indigenous participants were from Canada and the United States.

This event was also marked by the strong participation of about forty townspeople from Tepoztlan, elders, and leaders in the successful struggle against the golf course development complex and for autonomy from the central government in Mexico City (see Chapter 5). Other local people from nearby Mexico City and elsewhere also visited the gathering at intervals throughout the week.

The greater size of this gathering, the participation of local townspeople, the greater diversity of cultures, the participation of significant numbers of indigenous people, the participation of greater numbers of rainbow or New Age types from both Mexico and the United States, plus the simple fact that the gathering was held in Mexico and conducted in both English and Spanish all contributed to making this gathering different in appearance and substance from previous continental gatherings. This was also the first bioregional gathering to be explicitly organized as a ceremonial village. The transformation over an eight-year period from bioregional congress model to a ceremonial village model was now completed. All aspects of the ceremonial village model were now in place.

The purpose of this ceremonial village was to create an event that borrowed from Native American traditions such as the Mayans, who set up temporary ceremonial villages for nurture, education, and motivation. The ceremonial village, in this contemporary context, was conceived to be more than a congress for political decision making, more than a gathering for cultural experimentation, although it was to preserve and contain both of these elements. The primary purpose was "to be a village of the 21st century social life we espouse ... We are attempting to live now, in spite of all our imperfections, the social life toward which we wish to move. Then, after the healing power of such seven day encampments, we return to our ordinary local places and invest ourselves in making elements of this ceremonial village become manifest in those places" (Briggs et al. 1997).

At the opening circle on Monday morning, Ruz, on behalf of the Steering Council, placed this gathering in the context of an ancient gathering of the tribes. The purpose of this ceremonial village was to bring different social movements across the Americas together in a "circle of equals" to live in community for a week. Within the greater village circle of the whole were the councils, or *consejos*, each of these a smaller circle of equals. Prior to the gathering, Ruz continued, the Steering Council set up seven councils: Spirituality, Children, Youth, Health, Ecology, Traditions (indigenous peoples), and Art and Culture. Councils took the place of the old committees. The councils were to be the core of the gathering. Participants set up an eighth council on education. Only one committee, the MAGIC Committee (with its special purpose), continued to meet.

Another difference at this gathering from all the others was the greatly increased number of workshops offered. Close to 100 workshops were held, over three times as many as at any other continental event. Many of these workshops were hands-on, learn-by-doing exercises on a wide variety of topics from various bioregional community-building tools to urban permaculture and to the peace process in Chiapas, including a workshop on Mexican cultural resistance. There were also a number of New Age-style workshops such as body and soul nutrition, exploring inner landscapes through authentic movement, and gypsy theatre and dance. The small talking/family circles of previous gatherings were retained, but they were now called clans, meeting daily in the morning after the opening circle. The clans functioned as both talking circle/support groups and work teams to assist with meal preparation, cleanup, child care, recycling, and so on.

Evenings were reserved for cultural presentations as at all gatherings since 1988. These included presentations of several songs and a salmon dance by bioregionalists from the Yalakom; a slide and musical presentation of the Rainbow Caravan from Huehuecoyotl illustrating their networking trip through Mexico and Central America; a series of folkloric Earth songs, *cantos a la Tierra*, by a musical family of reinhabitants from Michoacan called Tamu Tariaticha; a film and discussion about the Zapatista Liberation Army and the indigenous peoples' liberation struggle in Chiapas by Zapatistas and their supporters from Chiapas; and a song-sharing circle around the "sacred fire" facilitated by traditional elder Dona Margarita Nunez Garcia in which people from many cultures shared and led songs in their respective languages till late at night.

At the ceremonial village in Meztitla, the opening ceremony of the continental gathering was led by a traditional *curandera* (healer) in a huge white tent set up for plenaries. The *curandera* appeared suddenly, followed by two assistants, holding up a smoking goblet of incense. She uttered an incantation asking for a beam of the light of truth and understanding from the "centre of the universe." Then she approached the assembled participants, blessing each one with thanks to Madre Tonantzin, Aztec Earth goddess, while moving the still-smoking goblet up and down in front of each person's body as she moved slowly through the assembly. With well over 300 people in the tent, this took quite some time. Then assistants dipped large bouquets of small branches into water buckets and sprayed water into the air above participants, after which the three quickly departed. The First Bioregional Gathering of the Americas was officially opened.

Daily sunrise and sunset ceremonies were performed throughout the week, drawing on many different traditions. One of these was a conch-blowing ceremony to the four directions. There were also ceremonies to the sun, moon, and Venus and to the sacred fire kept by elder Dona Margarita. Some participants also held ceremonies in the surrounding wooded hills. There were Mayan ceremonies, Aztec ceremonies, Nahuatl ceremonies, a Nahuatl baptism, and a Nahuatl vigil. In addition, there were daily *temezcals* (sweat lodge or "house of vapours" in Nahuatl), organized especially for children, youth, women, and elders (as well as for men, of course). All this lent a much different appearance and feeling to this gathering, and, according to the report by the Council of Traditions, the ceremonies contributed to creating "an avenue of communication" with local *campesinos* and social activists (Briggs et al. 1997, 36).

Another element that made this gathering different from the others was the participation of the *chavos bandas* or urban youth gangs. Organized by Helen Samuels, a youth activist based in Mexico City, over twenty *chavos* from Mexico City, Monterey, Oaxaca, Las Angeles (Mexico), and Iztapalapa came to the Tepoztlan gathering to learn about bioregionalism and ecology. In return, they contributed to the gathering by providing a security force throughout the week (given tensions between the townspeople and the ruling central government party over the golf course debacle, security was necessary). These street youth also participated in the Youth Council, in initiation ceremonies, and in sweat lodges. A special pipe ceremony for these youth held in a teepee reported in the proceedings gives a sense of how a form of social capital – the street gang organization – can be transformed into an Earth-centred force for the community of beings:

With twenty youth pressed tightly against a teepee's canvas, a pipe passes around with a mix of herbs and sacred tobacco by a First Nation pipe carrier. As the pipe travels clockwise around the circle, each chavo makes a prayer, confession, or passes with silence. The pipe finally reaches Beatric, a gang youth from Iztapalapa about to make a journey as a representative to an international youth conference in Vienna. She asks for everyone to surround her with white light and to help her carry the intent of the circle overseas. With all the bad press that gangs get, this incident reveals how urban youth can take their warrior energy and channel it for Mother Earth. (Briggs et al. 1997, 38)

The Tepoztlan gathering also looked very different from all previous continental congresses. The broad diversity of people at the gathering was reflected, in part, by the colourful diversity of clothing and dress styles. New Age and rainbow family members in bright "hippie" garb, Mexican *campesinos* in their white shirts, dark pants, and sombreros, brilliantly feathered Aztec dancers, North Americans (and many Mexicans) in T-shirts and jeans, Middle Eastern costumes of New Age "gypsies," Mexican religious radicals dressed all in white or white with red sashes and headbands, clowns, jugglers, costumed stilt walkers, and others in various all-species costumes mixed together at intervals throughout the week. All this presented a brilliantly colourful picture of friendly chaos as *campesinos*, New Agers, gypsies, a variety of indigenous peoples in their traditional clothing, inner city Mexican youth, and Zapatista political representatives interacted with permaculturists, Mexican ecologists, North American back-to-the-landers, students, and green city activists.

The outward appearance of chaos at this gathering was reinforced by some serious logistical and organizational problems. Hundreds of unexpected participants put a severe strain on food, water, and latrine resources in a country and a region where good drinking water, in particular, was not easily available. Extra planning and effort were required to ensure an adequate supply (Ruz 1996a).

In addition to the logistical problems, there were some organizational mistakes made. Councils, intended to remain an essential part of the congressing aspect of the ceremonial village, were not sufficiently explained at the beginning to the many newcomers at the continental gathering. The orientation to bioregionalism was not done extensively enough and not given enough agenda time (only one morning, including translation time), particularly since several previous gatherings had left mandates to give orientation more attention. Finally, the clan system of talking circles/work groups was organized according to a rather complicated Mayan calendar/

astrology system that confused many people, who were unable to connect with their clans. These failings were recognized and openly discussed in the proceedings by several participants.

On Thursday, the community service work day, a crew of about sixty participants helped to build check dams on a creek that the local community wanted restored. Another group helped to start a permaculture garden at an alternative school in Tepoztlan. Meanwhile, at the gathering, other participants hosted the visit by 150 local schoolchildren and their teachers to the ceremonial village. The day's activities and educational events included a play, a puppet show for younger children about the creation of the universe and how to recycle the garbage, a clown show, song circles, and a "bioregional" workshop in which children voiced their ideas about how to save Tepoztlan from golf course development schemes.

Thursday was a dry, hot day. That afternoon I spoke with Laura Kuri, a key local organizer. She spoke at length about the years of work with local people and groups, with children and elders, that preceded this gathering. She said that the people of Tepoztlan are strong and that "they are already living in bioregionalism in their political way; they have their own government – the Municipio Libre y Constitucional de Tepoztlan" (1996). She spoke about the local people's courage in taking on federal forces, opposing an unjust and unsustainable golf course development, occupying the town hall, and finally deciding to run the municipality themselves: "What is happening here is a way to show the whole world that we can say 'this is it, ya basta! no mas! si, se puede! yes, we can!' This is a way to show the world that we can really take care of our places, that we can decide and in a peaceful way have a taking of the power of our place, no?"

On Friday, separate women's and men's circles were held. As well, local *campesinos* visited the gathering to discuss permaculture design and techniques with experienced permaculture design instructors from across the continent. Friday was also when the councils finally began to meet in preparation for Saturday's plenary presentations.

On Saturday, the presentation by the Ecology Council revealed an understanding of the continent of Turtle Island that was new to "North American" bioregionalists. Up to that point, bioregionalists from the United States and Canada understood that the term "Turtle Island" referred to conventional geographical definitions of the continent that comprised the United States, Canada, and Mexico. Now the Ecology Council was proposing that bioregionalists view both North and South America as part of one continent, "the Americas." The council explained that from Alaska to Chile one mountainous backbone united a single continent that had been artificially divided by the Panama Canal. This corresponded to a Mexican, Central, and South American view of North and South America as one continent. Mexican children are taught this view in school, according to participant

Sanchez Navarro. Furthermore, it was proposed that, since the year 2000 was when the United States was due to give back ownership of the Panama Canal to Panama, the Second Bioregional Gathering of the Americas be held in Panama in 2000. This was a rather large new concept to assimilate quickly for participants from *el norte* who had not previously considered the concept of a single hemispheric Turtle Island continent. The final decision was held over until Sunday.

Several brightly coloured, hand-painted maps of a single continent linked by a single mountainous "backbone" were on display for the week, as was a large placard with the slogan "one continent, one mountainous backbone, one people." This slogan was not to deny our differences but to recognize our common humanity as peoples of Turtle Island. Here was a potential antidote to the rigidly narrow identity politics that often dominated social movements in the United States and Canada in the last two decades of the twentieth century.

The final plenary was held early Saturday evening. It opened with a "gypsy caravan," a costumed parade (including some all-species pageantry) around the entire campgrounds to bring everyone – pied piper style – to the plenary under the big white tent. Then representatives from Tepoztlan's Committee of Unity addressed the assembly. To support the local townspeople in their political struggle, gathering participants raised $600. We listened intently as a Tepoztlan spokesperson declared that bioregionalists were supporting a struggle that was "one hundred percent ecological," a struggle of organized opposition to "neo-liberalism" in which townspeople "learned that the town can govern itself with our own representatives without repressive institutions."

Elder Nunez Garcia's opening blessing was followed by an elaborate and very beautiful pipe ceremony. Ruz explained to the hundreds in assembly – in Spanish and English – that eleven indigenous pipe carriers from South America to Canada would perform an "ecumenical" ceremony to symbolically unite the diversity of cultures, tribes, youth, and elders and to unite north and south. The pipe carriers were joined in the centre of the mass of people by youth and elders. Seven sacred pipes were slowly passed around in a series of concentric circles, ritually sealing the event by the "sharing of sacred smoke," honouring the land and the people of Tepoztlan. Antonio Lopez commented that it was an "unprecedented ceremony ... perhaps the first post-modern exchange of spiritual, indigenous traditions of the Americas" (Briggs et al. 1997, 71).

The pipe ceremony was followed by a "drawing down the moon" spiral dance led by Starhawk. Beating a drum, Starhawk asked that dancers focus on grounding the energy from the drawing down of the moon's energy and that the soft silvery power of the moon energy be given by the dancers to that land, to that place, and to the Tepoztlan people in their struggle for that place. The dancers (400-500 people) moved out from under the white tent to the surrounding field under the full moon, spiralling and chanting and singing the slogan of the Tepoztlan people's struggle for autonomy, "Si, se puede!" ("Yes, we can!"). This ritual of empowerment officially ended the First Bioregional Gathering of the Americas, leaving only Sunday morning (before cleanup) to decide on any future continental event.

On Sunday, the plenary was beset by tension over strong disagreement. On one side, David Haenke argued that "There was too much deference to traditions that don't come out of this movement. I truly believe that this was a wonderful event. The problem was calling it a bioregional congress. It was a rainbow thing, a gypsy thing, only in small part bioregional" (Briggs et al. 1997, 68). Haenke was not alone in this view. David Levine, a veteran of the movement from New York City who was at the Tepoztlan gathering, also saw the event as a rainbow gathering rather than a bioregional gathering (1996).

Later a long e-mail by Haenke addressed to "All Bioregional Folks" argued that rainbow people – as travelling gypsies – avow a placelessness and lack of any centre in ecologically defined space or belief that disqualifies them as bioregionalists. He feared that association with the rainbow/New Age movement would lead to marginalization of the bioregional movement. He believed that the sheer size of the event "tended to overwhelm our capacity to function consensually as peers" (1996).

Peter Berg replied that the event in Tepoztlan was very much a bioregional event, pointing out that native healing plants walks, bioregional mapping workshops, discussions of ecological philosophy and politics both local and international, as well as many other activities featured at previous bioregional gatherings were openly available to all participants. Berg argued that "worrying about whether people will accept us isn't as important as bringing in as many new people (whoever they are) into bioregionalism as we can. It's a broadly diverse movement that excludes fundamentalism by its very multiplicity" (1996a).

At the gathering in Tepoztlan, I asked Ruz about the need for more work in the bioregional movement at the international level. He replied that he thought the movement needed "translating" into a form that can be understood by other cultures and then applied to and blended with other cultures. Ruz then referred to certain "hard-core" bioregionalists who were saying that this was not a bioregional gathering. His reply to this reasoning was that he had been clear "from the beginning that it was not going to be a bioregional congress. It was going to be a blending of the best of your proposals with the best of the proposals coming from the south; otherwise, it would not be bioregionalism but bioregional imperialism" (1996a).

I also spoke to Chris Wells in Meztitla about his work in South America and about the bioregional movement. For Wells, the Tepoztlan gathering was very much a bioregional event. Wells, who has spent many years working in South America with various indigenous peoples, reported that, when indigenous peasants learn what bioregionalism is about, they relate to it right away because it reminds them of their own traditions: "Everywhere I go now, many different indigenous groups, they're picking up on this word [bioregional] immediately. It makes perfect sense to them in terms of their cultures" (1996).

From the perspective of building horizontal links with local community and cross-cultural north-south links in the civil society sphere, the gathering was viewed as a success even by those who criticized it for not being "bioregional" enough. Haenke, in spite of his hesitations and fears, recognized the strengths of the gathering.

Despite logistical and organizational problems and the ongoing problem of continuity, the First Bioregional Gathering of the Americas was quite successful in initiating cross-cultural north-south linkages. A permaculture institute in the Cuauhnahuac bioregion was founded as a result of the gathering. Green city groups continued to meet in Mexico City, inspired by the gathering and a pregathering green city event in Mexico City. Participants helped to initiate a north-south skills exchange database. Finally, Huehuecoyotl's Rainbow Peace Caravan continues its outreach journey, carrying and manifesting the bioregional message across South America.

Conclusion

My narrative account of the story of the continental gatherings has focused on bioregionalists' strategy of continental networking and alliance building. This narrative reveals, I think, several serious challenges for the movement. First, there is the problem of building alliances across race and culture in civil society. As this account shows, issues of race present a serious barrier to horizontal alliance building in the United States and Canada. In spite of much organizational effort, much time spent, with serious intentions and efforts to include people of colour in the congresses from the United States and Canada, US (and Canadian) bioregionalists have managed to achieve few lasting successes over a period of seven continental gatherings. This is a problem that will have to be tackled at a local level. Second, gender also remains a significant challenge to building horizontal links in civil society in the United States and Canada, one that sometimes requires separate men's and women's councils or events to address the issues. Third, the organization of continental networking events by bioregionalist activists (with few resources) has been a very difficult undertaking with many logistical and organizational problems, a lack of resources to effectively carry out ongoing linkage building between continental gatherings, and a serious problem with continuity of representation.

Nevertheless, I think that there is another important factor involved. From the mid-1980s to the mid-1990s, there was a strong influence of poststructuralist thought in most social movements. This influence took the form of a severe identity politics that put more emphasis on very defined group identities and politics (Saul 1995), to the detriment of building broader solidarity and unity. In short, "difference" was privileged over citizen responsibility for the whole of civil society. The privileging of difference to the near exclusion of solidarity in the sphere of civil society had serious ramifications for many social movements. The bioregional movement was no exception, as my narrative account has shown.

However, by the mid-1990s, many activists were simply getting fed up with overly narrow identity politics, this activist included. Moreover, as the global corporate megamachine moved into high gear with its global "free" trade agenda (e.g., MAI), many people in the mainstream (churches, trade unions, etc.) began to wake up to the "new" reality. Initiatives such as the Zapatistas' successful continental fora, In Defence of Humanity and Against Neoliberalism, in 1996 in Chiapas and in 1997 in Spain (dubbed by Marcos as "Intergalactica I and II"), raised consciousness around the extreme need for solidarity in the face of corporate globalization. The fact that Zapatistas themselves privileged the term "civil society" over "the working class" favoured inclusivity of all difference while simultaneously calling attention to the need for responsibility for the whole of civil society as well as all the parts. This movement toward unity in diversity was reflected at the 1996 bioregional continental gathering in Tepoztlan, as my narrative account has shown.

Which other benefits were produced by the "continentals"? First, and perhaps most important, was the creation of a common program of values, principles, and strategies covering a broad spectrum of many dimensions of life – ecological, philosophical, political, social, and cultural. This program provides a necessary unity in the still broad diversity of the movement. It also helps to provide a broadly conceived alternative to the dominant ideology of capitalist consumerism, one that is sorely needed to oppose globalism. Second, my account has indicated that face-to-face networking; sharing experiences, stories, songs, rituals, and politics; and helping with child care, cooking, cleanup, and recycling at these gatherings by everyone addresses the whole person to provide (in addition to intellectual and organizational solidarity) the embodied and emotional bonds of trust, joy, and love essential to community building. Third, in spite of the serious challenges to north-south cross-cultural networking, my account of the gathering in Tepoztlan illustrates that real advances were made in establishing horizontal north-south linkages across cultures in civil society. As we shall see in the next chapter, this strength was also evident in the eighth gathering in Kansas.

Verde

VERDE

La verde nervadura
en la piel de la palma
ha abierto mi corazón,
desatado los rios
de una canción antigua
de languidos tropicos
y cuñas felices,
en su joven espejo
la palma me encara
y me abraza verde.

...

GREEN

The green nervation
at the skin of palm
has opened my heart
unbound the rivers
of an ancient song
of languid tropics
and happy cradles,
in its youthful mirror
the palm faces me
and embraces me green

> – Andres King Cobos
> Huehuecoyotl
> Tepoztlan, Morelos, Mexico

Conclusion:
Civil Society Theory, Bioregionalism, and Global Order

Civil Society Theory Looks at Bioregionalism

As discussed in Chapter 1, Jean Cohen and Andrew Arato's (1992) theory of civil society recognizes and locates itself in the terrain of democratic cultural modernity. That is, it builds on the norms of democracy, egalitarianism, and universal human rights of the Enlightenment. Cohen and Arato recognize that those democratic norms have never been fully implemented, so there is a need to continue the democratic revolution. Furthermore, democratic societal transformation must base itself not solely on the working class as "the" agent of revolution but on the actions of civil society as a whole. Cohen and Arato's dual strategy, based in a democratically self-organized civil society, also aims at reforms in political and economic spheres toward more democratic institutions and processes. It is clear, however (see my introduction on corporate globalization), that even the limited democracy enjoyed in the major Western democracies is endangered under the neoliberal order of "the Washington Consensus." The question, then, is how can democracy best be defended? Cohen and Arato's approach is that democracy can best be defended through expanding or strengthening democracy in civil society and in democratic reform of both state and corporate sectors.

With respect to the civil society sphere, both "defensive" and "offensive" strategies are theorized by Cohen and Arato. The defence and expansion of democratic civil society through a horizontal strategy targeting norms, cultural identities, and models, as well as institutions of civil society, is a defensive strategy. It seeks to preserve and develop the communicative infrastructure of civil society through efforts to redefine identities, reinterpret norms, and develop egalitarian and democratic associational forms as widely as possible. In the political sphere, an offensive vertical strategy seeks to develop spaces within political society that could be democratized through a politics of bridging and building influence for institutional and legal reform. This dual strategy is key to meaningful, significant change, as the example of the feminist movement of the 1970s and 1980s in the United States shows. In the feminist movement, the horizontal spread of feminist consciousness helped to change cultural identities as well as gender norms and institutions of civil society, while also supporting a vertical strategy pursuing equal rights and the political and economic inclusion of women. These strategies reinforced each other, supporting "a wave of legislative action on feminist issues unequaled in U.S. history," increasing women's access to and influence on political elites, and electing and appointing more women to public office than ever before in American history (Cohen and Arato 1992, 552).

How has the bioregional movement fared with respect to this dual approach? Viewed from a civil society theoretical framework, it is clear that the bioregional movement has generally followed a dual strategy. With respect to horizontal strategy targeted at civil society, bioregionalists pursue a whole range of activities that fits into redefining identities, reinterpreting and reclaiming norms, and developing egalitarian, democratic associational forms. These range from bioregionalists' shared values of community, interdependence, respect for one another, and recognition of social justice in their sociocultural and economic strategies of building local intentional communities of place (composed of various levels of intensity and organization, as we have seen) and the bioregional and continental networks between them. Intensive and extensive efforts by bioregionalists to implement such a horizontal strategy are reflected in the accounts of the Mattole Restoration Society, the Yalakom River community, the Huehuecoyotl community, and green city activists in the San Francisco Bay Area and Vancouver/lower Fraser bioregion. All these local narratives also show that bioregionalists have made serious efforts at building horizontal alliances with groups and associations in civil society outside the bioregional movement. In addition, the narrative of the continental gatherings confirms the accounts from particular places and reveals the movement's vision, values, and intense efforts to live the vision of place-community in the very act of creating community at the gatherings themselves.

Bioregionalists have also pursued a similar and parallel vertical strategy of building influence for democratic and institutional change in the political sphere at the local level. In the Mattole River Valley, Mattole Restoration Council activists pursue a strategy of influencing the California Department of Fish and Game, the Bureau of Land Management, and the California Board of Forestry for regulatory reform supported by strong horizontal efforts to define new cultural watershed identities, develop norms of cooperation and civic solidarity, and build networks of restoration activists. In Tepoztlan, Mexico, in the Cuauhnahuac bioregion, Huehuecoyotl members work horizontally with a wide range of groups in civil society, where relatively high levels of social capital already exist, but they also work to create influence vertically with universities and political parties. In the Yalakom River valley in British Columbia, bioregional reinhabitants have worked vertically to influence personnel in the Ministries of Forestry and the Environment, campaign for reform in BC Hydro, and participate in government commissions and on the Lillooet District Community Resources Board. These actions are supported by many horizontal efforts to create community and place identity locally and regionally. Similarly, in urban regions such as the San Francisco Bay Area and the Vancouver/Salmonopolis bioregion, horizontal efforts directed at civil society to establish new cultural identities, to develop and model norms of cooperation and civic solidarity, and to build networks of citizen associations support vertical efforts in the political sphere to influence municipal politics and policies.

In addition, bioregionalists demonstrate explicit awareness of combining horizontal and vertical strategies. One good example of this is their discussions and actions with US greens at NABC I and II, recognizing that a green political organization could help to secure and protect bioregional principles and practice on the ground through focusing on democratic planning issues and political action supportive of local and regional autonomy.

These and other examples discussed in previous chapters show that bioregional movement strategy can be understood as a dual strategy similar to that of the feminist movement of the 1970s and 1980s in the United States. Although Cohen and Arato have not specifically considered the bioregional movement, this correspondence of strategies would not be surprising to them. Indeed, they argue that many social movements of the 1970s and 1980s (the so-called new social movements) demonstrated similar dual strategies (1992, 530-31). Moreover, bioregionalists have had some success in pursuing this dual strategy. Certainly in terms of the horizontal outreach strategy to others in civil society, a remarkable success can be observed. The number of groups and networks that identify with bioregionalism increased significantly over the period since its gestation, as did the number of bioregional publications and other publications that include material on bioregionalism (as we saw in Chapter 3). Additional outreach efforts have continued and expanded, most notably perhaps in Central and South America. The number of ecovillages (mentioned in Chapter 5) has been growing rapidly in Central and South America. The growth in the movement exploded particularly after 1995. Worldwide, the number of ecovillages has gone from 15 in 1989 to over 15,000 in 2002 (Bates 2002). In the experience of bioregionalist Albert Bates, who works with the Ecovillage Network, ecovillagers most often see their villages in the context of bioregions. Giovanni Ciarlo of the Ecovillage Network of the Americas and a member of Huehuecoyotl credits the work of the Caravan Acoiris Por La Paz from Huehuecoyotl for spreading bioregionalism and ecovillages. The Global Ecovillage Network defines an ecovillage as a small rural or urban community that integrates supportive social relations with ecological design practices, seeking to renew living systems, nurture the full development of each person, and explore a way of life that fosters harmony between people and nature. All of this, of course, is horizontal communication in civil society.

Most tellingly from a democratic civil society perspective (i.e., enhancing a culture of democracy), the lived experiences of bioregionalists show the existence of strong cultural identities with the communities and the places that bioregionalists attempt to reinhabit, identities that have kept them in these places for over two decades while patiently building their horizontal communities, networks, and alliances as well as their vertical lines of influence to the political sphere. Indeed, the sheer magnitude of all these efforts – horizontal and vertical – testifies to enormous motivation, conviction, and commitment to civic affairs on the part of bioregional actors. Finally, there is additional evidence of bioregional vertical influence in the political sphere. Two examples are the California Resource Agency's protocol for federal and state agencies for resource management of the "bioregions" of California and the Canadian federal government's Royal Commission on the Future of the Toronto Waterfront, which advanced a concept of the Greater Toronto Bioregion in text and map form (see Figure 3). This suggests the possibility of creating spaces within the political sphere for "bioregional" reforms, such as that in New Zealand, where fourteen major watershed boundaries were used to define administrative and political borders (Furuseth and Cocklin 1995).

All of the above evidence, including that of previous chapters, strongly suggests that, from the perspective of the theory of Cohen and Arato, bioregionalists are already pursuing a dual strategy akin to that identified and supported by their theory. So what is the problem? Why would bioregionalism pose any challenge to or offer any lesson for their civil society theory, other than to confirm it with another example of good civil society–based dual strategy? On one level, there is a serious or central problem with Cohen and Arato's theoretical model: it remains limited by the anthropocentric norms of the Enlightenment. Perhaps because they see the world with only modern eyes, Cohen and Arato appear to be unable to conceive of cultural traditions or norms more "universalist" than those of cultural modernity: "To opt for the preservation of traditions, if accompanied by a denial of the universalist tradition of cultural and political modernity, implies fundamentalism. Accordingly, the question that flows from our model becomes: Which traditions, which family form, which community, which solidarities are to be defended against disruptive intervention?" (1992, 24-25).

Here Cohen and Arato pose the problem of cultural relativism, the problem recognized by many postmodernists: since Western culture (modernity) is after all only one culture among many, how does one decide questions of justice between cultures? In attempting to answer their own question of which traditions to defend, Cohen and Arato further reveal their narrow cultural limitations:

> Even if cultural modernity itself is just one tradition among many, its universal thrust is the reflexive, nonauthoritarian relation toward tradition – an orientation that can be applied to itself and that implies autonomy rather than heteronomy. Indeed, traditions that have become problematic can be preserved only on the terrain of cultural modernity, i.e., through arguments that invoke principles. Such discussion does not mean the abolition of tradition, solidarity or meaning; rather, it is the only acceptable procedure for adjudicating between competing traditions, needs, or interests that are in conflict. Accordingly, our model points toward the *further* modernization of the culture and institutions of civil society as the only way to arrive at autonomy, self-reliance, and solidarity among peers. (1992, 25)

Although Cohen and Arato admit here that cultural modernity is only one tradition among many (therefore, by definition, *not* universal), they still conclude that only cultural modernity can adjudicate between competing "fundamentalist" traditions, interests, or needs because of its "universal thrust." This view implies that only modernity has a universal thrust. Moreover, further modernization is "the only way" to arrive at autonomy and self-reliance among peers. This suggests that modernity has nothing to learn from "fundamentalist traditions" in the search for more democratic forms of relations.

Given such a particular cultural (or social) construction, it is not surprising to find that Cohen and Arato are not open to cultures that could be conceived of as antimodern or premodern or fundamentalist: "Finally, we believe that programs of the 'great refusal,' whether directed against the state in the name of a civil society suspicious of all politics or against the modern economy in the name of some kind of socially reembedded nonmarket economy based on mutuality, reciprocity, and direct cooperation, are incompatible with modernity and with the presuppositions of modern democracy, despite the self-understanding of many of their proponents" (1992, 469).

It is clear from their discussion of the matter and from their citations of Habermas that Cohen and Arato derive their attitudes from Habermas's thesis on cultural modernity in which he condemns social movements that promote counterinstitutions in civil society as "particularist" and "reactive" as well as "tendentially antimodern communalist projects of dedifferentiation and withdrawal" (Cohen and Arato 1992, 529). "Dedifferentiation" is the term that Habermas uses to refer to the reembedding of the economic sphere into civil society. It is adopted without qualification and employed by Cohen and Arato in defence of their three-sphere model, which insists on the continued differentiation of the economic and political spheres from the civil society sphere (where continued differentiation of the spheres means the continued operation of the formal economy rather than its socialization). What is never really explained in Cohen and Arato is why embedded economies based on mutuality, reciprocity, and cooperation are by definition incompatible with modern civil society or why such embedded economies necessarily imply dedifferentiation and withdrawal. Rather, they present this argument as if it were self-evident. In the case of bioregionalism, on the contrary, the practice of community relations with embedded, mutualist forms of economic development has been accompanied (as we have seen throughout this book) by serious efforts to communicate and organize on a much wider basis, the very opposite of cultural withdrawal.

Habermas's thesis also states that cultural modernity carries with it an increased potential for self-reflection and for what he calls "decentered subjectivity" (which appears to be his expression for "social being") with regard to "all dimensions of action and world relations" (Cohen and Arato 1992, 524). It is difficult not to see this position as a form of Eurocentrism, as others already have (Gregory 1994, 175). Furthermore, Cohen and Arato approve of this claim even though, again, they offer no further reasons why cultural modernity is the best terrain for decentred subjects or increased self-reflection. On the contrary, many indigenous Earth-based cultures, the bioregional movement, and other Earth-centred social movements have essential lessons to contribute to civil society theory, lessons that bear on profound definitions and understandings of humans as truly social beings (see Chapter 2). Civil society theory has much to learn from such traditions if it wants to inspire a great social movement for a truly inclusive and much enhanced and strengthened postcolonial democracy.

Bioregionalism Informs Civil Society Theory

As we saw in Chapter 2, there was an internal dynamic, a harmony, between the way in which so-called natural resources, in the form of other beings, were regarded as both kin to humans and sacred in their own right and the indigenous domestic economy that stressed the careful, conservative use of natural systems and profound respect for all life. Indeed, there is no necessary contradiction between norms of cooperation, mutuality, reciprocity, and civic solidarity (identified as essential to social capital) and the formation of ecosocial capital. Rather, the evidence from both indigenous, Earth-based societies and contemporary bioregionalists' experiences supports the view that most often social capital norms, when informed by the community of beings form of ecosocial capital, are enhanced and deepened by the extension of kinship feelings to other species, rather than being undermined by such feelings. Another way to express this is that social capital is subsumed by ecosocial capital. Stories and ceremonies of indigenous peoples and bioregionalists, emerging from and informed by the places where people live, help to weave this more inclusive, relational, "all-species" meaning together. The evidence both from these societies and from the bioregional movement thus supports an argument for widening the ethical understanding of an anthropocentric cultural modernity to include other species as constitutive of both moral and practical importance for an ecologically sustainable use of natural resources (seeing the world as a warehouse of "resources" for humans makes it a problematic term from an all-species ethical framework). Informed by such an ecological ethic, the concept of universal human rights is thus more strongly guaranteed by additional rights for all species and for the matrix of life that all species depend upon for habitat and life support. At the same time, with respect to the use of natural resources, an ecological ethic tempers human rights with ethical responsibility for all species.

Reclaiming the community of beings ethic does not have to mean withdrawal or retreat into a particularistic, parochial, antimodern cultural morass, as Habermas and Cohen and Arato suppose. Indeed, bioregional vision, values, strategy, and lived experiences illustrate a common opening to both a broader, more diverse, and more democratic civil society and a more inclusive community of beings. Reclaiming a community of beings ethic can be understood as the basis of an essential theoretical contribution to a more holistic theory of civil society, one that provides an answer to the problem of cultural relativism posed by Cohen and Arato.

The problem here is that, in spite of the claims of Habermas and Cohen and Arato, cultural modernity really is just one more culture among the wide diversity of cultures, including many indigenous cultures that are still struggling for recognition and justice, often against a modernity imposed upon them by modern capitalistic consumerism as a form of cultural imperialism. Ethically speaking, there is no reason why cultural modernity should act as the arbiter for all cultures when it has not yet fully implemented its own Enlightenment program for human rights and self-determination.

A revised civil society theory that included the community of beings ethic, thus extending its moral concern to the whole of life, could supply a common inspiration for unity among the great diversity of cultures extant in the world today. Such an ethical stance should appeal to all cultures to search their own ancient roots for traces of the community of beings ethic as part of their evolutionary heritage and as part of a greater Earth-based understanding that all humans need to overcome alienation from the natural world. A broader identity with the community of beings does not mean an obliteration or even a weakening of human cultural difference; rather, it fosters the further flowering of difference linked by a greater affinity. As human ecologist Paul Shepard argues, identity is not only a "honing of personal singularity, but a compounding wealth of ever more refined relationships between the person and increasingly differentiated parts of the world ... The culmination of refined difference-with-affinity is a firm ground of personal confidence and membership in its largest sense" (1982, 12).

However, as we have seen, problems of cultural difference are not easily solved in practice (see Chapter 6). Racial difference and, perhaps to a lesser extent, gender difference are shown to be serious barriers to building unity in diversity, at least in the United States and Canada. Trust, a critical element of social capital, is not easily built between peoples in environments with a long history of racial and economic oppression, segregation, and political repression by one group over another. Within the bioregional movement, the Mexicans have indicated a possible way out of serious problems posed by the politics of difference. Their vision of a single continent of North and South American peoples, a single Turtle Island, united by a single mountainous backbone, while affirming the cultural diversity of all peoples in the hemisphere, supplies threads of common identity and affinity for the diverse peoples of Turtle Island. These linkages of common affinity and identity among peoples of place are enhanced and strengthened by the vision of a broader, more inclusive identity with Turtle Island. The creation of north-south linkages between indigenous, inhabitory peoples in South, Central, and North America and between indigenous peoples and bioregional reinhabitants of south and north is an important and encouraging beginning toward weaving affinity across the great diversity of cultures in the hemisphere.

The seventh continental gathering, in Mexico, had a "huge influence" on the sustainability and alternative networking culture of Mexico and the rest of Latin America (Ciarlo 2001). As mentioned earlier, the growth of ecovillages has blossomed particularly since 1995.

Another fundamental gap in Cohen and Arato's theory of civil society is its failure to address the crucial problem of the unsustainable consumption of natural capital. Given the magnitude of this problem, any theory of civil society relevant to the twenty-first century cannot ignore the depletion of natural capital and the growing rate of the extinction of species. Bioregionalism has an important contribution to make here as well. Bioregional design approaches supply strategies for reducing the aggregate ecological footprints of city dwellers and thus for reducing aggregate consumption of natural capital in urban areas. There is the important, groundbreaking work of George Tukel, the Todds, and Peter Berg on place patterning and living within solar incomes to support urban reinhabitation. Ecocity design for mixed-use, cluster development (or integrated density) promotes a diversity of urban land uses at close proximity, allowing additional land use to be opened up for urban agriculture, forestry, and ecological corridors, not just in the suburbs but in the inner city as well. In other words, bioregionalism addresses several design scales from the bioregional to watersheds within watersheds to the inner city, the district, and even the site, each fitting within the geographically larger-level scale. There is a striking resemblance between bioregional design and the work of Christopher Alexander and others (1977). At the site level is permaculture design with its "kinship gardens" and entropy strategies for reducing energy use as well as land use in support of an ethic that sees all life as allied associations.

Implementing urban integrated density means that housing, feeding, and moving people and goods will be done with much lower levels of material and energy throughput. Equally importantly, all of these integrated density design approaches include the development of a common urban bioregional cultural identity with place and home, bringing together the concepts of place and commons. Integrating cultural identities of place and commons encourages a unifying and empowering urban civic identity inclusive of a community of beings ethic, which lends great moral and philosophical support to individual as well as aggregate reductions in our ecological footprints. Thus, in bioregional vision and practice, a moral civic imperative to respect the community of beings through careful, conservative use of natural resources by individuals is linked to an urban region planning strategy to reduce aggregate consumption of natural capital.

Lived experiences of bioregionalists with ecosocial capital formation support the view that reducing individual consumption through voluntary simplicity need not be onerous. Indeed, for too long the dominant neoclassical cultural ideal of *homo economicus* has promoted a cultural view of the human individual as a selfish, economically calculating maximizer of utilities, an individual who meets his/her emotional as well as physical needs chiefly through the consumption of commodities. By contrast, bioregionalists' experiences support a view of humans as genuine social beings quite capable of discovering the joy of sharing common identities with other beings of place and the spiritual empowerment of emotional, embodied connection with the community of all beings in a particular place. As we have seen in previous chapters, these profound experiences of identity and empowerment supplant consumerist attempts at fulfilling emotional needs.

Bioregionalists live with long-term time frames – several generations – for social transformation. However, nowhere in Cohen and Arato's tome on civil society theory is there any consideration of a long-term generational time frame for their democratic revolution. For the immense societal changes demanded by bioregionalism, a long-term vision and a transitional strategy are essential. Theory for civil society that envisioned and integrated ecological sustainability would thematize a transition strategy of several generations. Such long-term approaches are no longer unthinkable. In fact, many long-term public planning processes and exercises envisioning sustainable places and cities have already been held in various urban regions in the United States and Canada (Beatley and Manning 1997).

Finally, Cohen and Arato's theory lacks any geographical dimension. Just as geographer David Harvey brought a geographical dimension to nongeographical Marxist theories of capitalist accumulation by locating the processes of concentration and centralization of capital in cities and urban regions of the most advanced capitalist countries (1989), so too post-Marxist civil society theory can benefit from the place-grounded ideas and experiences of the bioregional movement by thematizing the location of civil society strategies in particular places and bioregions. Given all of the above, what might an ecocentric civil society theory look like?

Toward an Ecocentric Civil Society Theory

An ecocentric civil society theory would begin by integrating the community of beings ethic into Enlightenment cultural capital. This would extend the domain of human morals to include ethical considerations for the rest of the family of all beings. In this ecological kinship ethic, the human family in all its rich diversity is understood as one member of a larger, much more diverse family or family of families that encompasses all life. Thus, the theoretical space of civil society would expand to conceptually include other species as part of a greater sphere of freedom. Human identity as a part of the community of beings would also expand so that identity and affinity would extend to other species and to the life process itself. A person's identity would thus include her or his local watershed and all its creatures, but this too would extend to an identity with and concern for the planetary ecosphere. Communicative action, thematized in Cohen and Arato (after Habermas) as essential to democratizing civil society, would not remain limited to human subjects, as in cultural modernism. Rather, communicative action would be theorized more holistically as an embodied process that should and can sometimes include other species, local landforms, and ecosystem processes. This broader field of communicative action would include the study of interspecies communication; various methods of communing with nature through story, ceremony, and ritualized circle journeys through and around local watersheds or landscapes; process experiments such as all-species representation at human councils; and ecological restoration as a process of healing watersheds, human communities, and individuals alike.

An ecocentric civil society theory would thematize overconsumption as a moral problem. Morally speaking, human overconsumption of natural capital would be regarded as seriously as exploitation and oppression of human subjects is under current Enlightenment ethics. For example, human action causing species extinction would be regarded as serious a crime as genocide and a crime that carried its own moral repugnance. Habitat rights would then apply to all species as a matter of fundamental principle. This is not to suggest that every microbe be given equal treatment with humans, but it does mean that profligate consumption in rich industrial countries that destroys species and their habitats should be regarded as a deeply serious criminal matter. The narrowly defined human "right" to unlimited consumption (*homo economicus* again!) should not be put ahead of vital habitat needs of other species. Of course, overconsumption by the rich would continue to be seen as an injustice to many human populations who are so desperately lacking even the basic necessities. Yet, in ecocentric civil society theory, a social ecological ethic would link overconsumption with both social and ecological justice.

A civil society theory that incorporated an ecological kinship ethic as one of its cultural norms along with cooperation, mutual aid, and reciprocity would thematize the spiritual energy, joy, and love in both social and ecosocial capital formation as a cultural capital resource for both individuals and communities. Motivational aspects of this formation process for reducing individual and aggregate consumption of natural capital and for committing to lifelong engagement in both personal and societal transformation would be a subject for intensive and extensive theorization and thematic exploration, linking these inquiries to praxis.

What would strategic considerations for defending and deepening democracy resemble from an ecocentric civil society theory perspective? A major strength of Cohen and Arato's civil society theory is its dual strategy with the interplay of vertical and horizontal strategies. This strategy would remain essential to a reconstructed ecocentric version of civil society theory. However, the new theory would contribute an important thematization of the relationship of generational time scales to civil society–based democratic transformation. Long-term strategic considerations over several generations may alter the emphasis between horizontally directed actions at the civil society sphere and vertically directed actions aimed at the economic or political sphere. However, it must be recognized that the dual strategy of Cohen and Arato, since it emphasizes the importance of horizontal actions aimed at identity and normative change in civil society, already contains a certain implicit, long-term perspective. None of these long-term themes need ignore the short-term urgency for reforms. Indeed, in an ecocentrically revised civil society theory, such urgency would be a priority for theoretical and practical reflection on the relationship of time scale to cultural transformation, particularly focusing on linking urgent, short-term vertical reforms with the long term.

Geography would become an important dimension of an ecocentric civil society theory. On the one hand, such a theory would thematize the interconnectedness of local places, bioregions, continents, and the entire planetary biosphere. Strong identity with place would not be seen to contradict any identity with bioregion, continent, and planet. Rather, they would be theorized as interconnected identities at broader and broader levels of identity and affinity. On the other hand, local watersheds and their encompassing bioregions would be thematized as the geographical scales most appropriate to reducing aggregate, or collective, ecological footprints of human populations. Without an effective transformation in local land use practices, no real sustainability can be achieved. Strong local and bioregional norms of democratic praxis in the civil society sphere are essential for supporting the decentralization of institutions in the political and economic spheres as well.

The self-limiting character of the democratic revolution and of self-limiting radicalism in social movements in Cohen and Arato's civil society theory would remain in a revised ecocentric theory. However, for those who think that only a totalizing revolution to abolish the state will liberate civil society, it is important to remember that Cohen and Arato stress that the self-limiting character of movements in civil society must be accompanied by deeply democratic reforms in the other two spheres to check the over-developed power of state and corporate structures if civil society is to have sufficient autonomy from both state and market forces to continue its de-mocratization process. That is, state and corporate structures must be held to a much greater social accountability through vertically aimed democratic reforms. The difference in an ecocentric version of the theory is that ecological responsibility and accountability are added to social responsibility/accountability, thus compounding the array of reforms to be sought and the urgency of seeking them.

Ecocentric Civil Society Theory Informs Bioregionalism

As we have seen, bioregionalists already pursue both a horizontal strategy aimed at civil society and, to a lesser extent, a strategy of developing vertical influence for reform in the political sphere. Yet bioregionalists generally do not take note of this fact. An ecocentric civil society theory would encourage the continuation of this dual approach by thematizing it to develop a conscious articulation of its strategic advantages. What was implicit in bioregional strategy would become explicitly recognized. The conscious application of this dual strategy would enable bioregional actors to better identify challenges and opportunities in specific strategic contexts. For example, awareness of the need for both horizontal and vertical strategies would alert activists to assess their own energies, capabilities, and numbers of people to carry out a dualistic strategy. Given the relatively low degree of community and associational life in the United States and Canada, the priority for horizontal strategies in civil society would be thematized. In certain specific situations, opportunities for reform in the political sphere may be identified that, if passed, might create a climate for increased horizontal activity. An example would be a campaign to decentralize certain government functions and jurisdictions to correspond with watershed boundaries, as has been done in California and New Zealand. In regions where there is already much horizontal associational activity, for example daylighting and restoring creeks and streams and their riparian zones, such reforms in the political sphere would support further consciousness raising and activity in civil society.

With respect to the question of the state and state power, the emphasis in an ecocentric civil society theory would shift from that of Cohen and Arato. The reflexive continuation of the welfare state would mean not only reforms in the political sphere for greater social and environmental controls but also incremental decentralization of the state. Currently, the bioregional movement does not have any consensus on the question of the state. Some would like to abolish it and others to reform it, but these remain personal opinions of individuals. Long-term bioregional thinking on the nation-state has suggested that nation-states may ultimately break down into smaller, regional (bioregional) configurations. One early influence in this respect is the work of Leopold Kohr (1978). However, in spite of its long-term vision of societal transformation, bioregional thought has not articulated any theoretically informed common vision with respect to any transformation of the state. An ecocentric civil society theory would contribute to bioregional thought by thematizing the long-term, incremental decentralization and democratization of the state rather than its abolition. In the short term, such a theoretically informed strategy could identify spaces for more immediate reforms that begin to move in the desired direction. For example, in Canada there is now a political space for increasing the power of municipalities and neighbourhoods in relation to provincial or federal jurisdictions. Several major Canadian cities and the Canadian Federation of Municipalities are pushing for the authority and funding to build effective, sustainable public transit, implement renewable energy plans, and create more public accountability, among other issues. Bioregional decentralists and others could take advantage of such situations, working to build alliances in civil society to strengthen and enhance local democracy.

There are some, for example Cholette, Alexander, and Tester (1996), who critique bioregionalists who would undermine state power by decentralizing at the risk of exposing both state and civil society to the unmitigated power of huge corporations under globalism. Given the enormous and growing power of global corporations (see Introduction), this is a well-founded fear. As Richard Swift, coeditor of the *New Internationalist Magazine,* has argued, powerful global corporations already often exercise effective "veto power" over democratically influenced decisions of even the most powerful nation states through capital strikes, the World Bank/IMF credit/debt squeeze, direct and indirect bribery, and their ability to influence public political debate through the corporate-owned media (2002, 62-69). Weakening the state even further opens the way for corporations to consolidate and strengthen their grip on decision making globally, nationally, regionally, and locally. However, such arguments ignore both the long-term nature of the societal transformation problem and the potential strength of a dual strategy pursued in both the political and the economic spheres. An incremental dualistic strategy, strengthening and building horizontal relations in civil society while pursuing short-term and long-term reforms to curb both the power of the state and the power of the corporations vis-à-vis civil society, would address these concerns. Limits on state power must be accompanied by equal (or perhaps greater) limits on corporate power. Neither can be achieved without the corresponding growth of democratic horizontal power in civil society as a prerequisite for and a basis of the democratization of state and corporate power. In such scenarios, the continued partial differentiation of state power (however decentralized) acts as a guarantee to protect individual rights against possible attacks from any rogue local civic majorities that may not respect human or all-species rights. A more democratic, decentralized state power could also provide a counterbalance against undue corporate power (especially if aligned with a reinvigorated democratic civil society). Nevertheless, in the economic sphere, as in the political sphere, the problem of unaccountable global corporate power has to be addressed.

The economic sphere represents the formal market economy. As we saw in Chapter 1, it includes collective bargaining and representation of workers on company boards. The reflexive continuation of the formal market, like the reflexive continuation of the welfare state, means that forms of democratic public control and accountability are necessary to ensure and enforce greater social and environmental responsibility/accountability of corporations. An ecocentric civil society approach to corporations would begin to address how they could be democratized to include in their decision making not only workers but also representatives of the communities where they operate, including the representation of all species. Cohen and Arato suggest that mediation between civil society and the economic sphere would involve strengthening the diversity of forms of property to enable civil society to gain a foothold in the formal economy. Such forms would include worker or employee ownership, nonprofit group ownership, community land trusts, et cetera. While based in civil society, these forms would mediate between civil and economic society, just as public political forms mediate between civil and political society. This strategy would begin a long-term shift toward industrial democracy without abolishing the formal market.

Bioregionalists have put almost all of their economic emphasis in developing and implementing horizontal strategies of community economic

development in the informal economy of civil society such as those suggested by Cohen and Arato. Ecocentric civil society theory would thematize
this realm as one of primary importance. Without a base in communities of
place and a democratic civil society, action for reform of state and corporate
institutions is merely oppositional. However, for most of the past two decades, bioregionalists have spent little or no effort working to develop vertical influence to curb the power of the corporate sector in theory or in practice.
An ecocentric civil society theory would thematize strategy in this overlooked dimension of the economic sphere. On the one hand, it would seek
to identify barriers or challenges for such a strategy. Perhaps the biggest
challenge here is to demystify neoclassical market theory and to identify its
narrowly conceived cultural underpinnings. This project is crucial to decon-
struct the concept of the formal market as a mechanism of liberation. On
the other hand, theoretical clarity in this realm would also assist in identifying cracks in the globalist, neoliberal (or neoconservative) paradigm. For
example, there is currently an opportunity for reform to assist in curbing
out-of-control speculation of international financial capital through a campaign to implement the Tobin Tax on international financial transactions.

Ecocentric civil society theory could also inform long-term bioregional
strategy by thematizing the relationship of civil and political spheres to the
economic sphere in the international arena, where transnational corporations and finance capital operate with virtually no social controls by either
civil society or the state (Korten 1995). Given the magnitude of this crisis,
theoretical work in this sphere is urgently needed to begin to identify strategies for action. For example, one potential strategy would promote some
combination of reinvigorated national corporate charter laws (e.g., those in
the United States and Canada) combined with the creation of international
regulations to enforce corporate social and environmental responsibility by
making corporations accountable. Some citizens are already beginning to
act to regain democratic authority over corporate charters. For example,
the townspeople of Arcata, California, have approved an initiative called
Measure F: The Arcata Initiative on Democracy and the Corporations, which
calls for town hall meetings to discuss the issue of democracy and corporations and the creation of a committee to establish "policies and programs
which ensure democratic control over corporations conducting business
within the city, in whatever ways are necessary to ensure the health and
well-being of our community and its environment" (Cienfuegos 1999). Other
examples of such local citizen municipal actions are multiplying. This expanding terrain of local citizen and municipal democratization "places the
fight for municipal self-governance directly in the path of the steamroller
of globalization" (Swift 2002, 107). The same thing can be said about the
ecovillage movement and the bioregional/green city movement.

Finally, when considering relations between the economic sphere dominated by the corporate sector and the political sphere dominated by the
state, we need to reflect on the ultimate danger posed by the integration of
economic and political spheres. This danger has been identified long ago.
The integration of corporate interests with the political interests of the state
is called corporatism. That is what Mussolini called it. It is a synonym for
fascism. I was reminded of this recently at a public talk given by Murray
Dobbin, involved in the movement against corporate globalization and
author of *The Myth of the Good Corporate Citizen: Democracy under the Rule of
Big Business*. In the context of the US military-industrial complex, President
Bush's new Homeland Security regime and the military tribunals set up after
9/11 are moves in the direction of consolidating corporate economic advances with state political power.

Bioregionalism Encounters Corporate Globalism
In the past two years (after the bulk of the research for this book was completed), people in the bioregional movement have begun to face up to issues of corporate power and globalization. This is partly because some
bioregionalists have become directly involved in the global peoples movement against corporate globalization. Others have begun to analyze and
write about issues of corporate rule. Indeed, the reality of neoliberal pushes
for more corporate control through favourable international agreements
on "free trade" such as NAFTA and the FTAA have caused many in society to
become concerned about the dangers of corporate rule. There is an obvious
link between actions in civil society to democratize the corporate sector in
the United States and Canada and the actions of the burgeoning global
citizen movement to address problems arising from the lack of accountability to citizens and governments the world over raised by the neoconservative/
neoliberal Washington Consensus of international finance capital and corporate global domination.

As I have argued, the bioregional movement does not have a worked-out
strategy on what to do about the corporate sector. Nevertheless, under the
pressure of growing concern about corporate globalization, some
bioregionalists have been discussing what to do about both corporate power
and globalization on the bioregional listserve over the past two years. These
discussions have generally coalesced around two positions. One position,
expressed most strongly by David Haenke, argues against joining or even
participating in the "antiglobalist" movement on the basis that such opposition draws necessary energy away from the more basic need to create
grounded, place-based, ongoing alternatives to the dominant system of
power. Haenke has also argued that antiglobalist protest demonstrations
actually end up supporting the corporate agenda since the demonstrators

are characterized in the corporate media as destructive crazies, thus discrediting the anticorporate position. The other position, put forward by Starhawk, Gene Marshall, Betsy Barnum, me, and others, is that it is necessary to oppose the global corporate agenda now since the implementation of trade agreements such as NAFTA and the FTAA will supersede the sovereignty of governments and citizens to institute laws, policies, and programs that do not conform to the neoliberal agenda. If bioregional visions and intentions are ever to become part of a democratic social reality, a broad social movement of civil society for the end of unaccountable corporate rule is essential. Starhawk, active in the antiglobalist movement since the protests in Seattle in 1999, also argues that the bioregional movement has some real gifts to offer activists in this movement, "especially in the area of articulating the visions, the new economic models, the sane and decentralized technologies" (2001). She also makes the point that, if bioregionalists want to have the moral authority to put forth these ideas to people who are risking their bodies and their freedom on a regular basis in the antiglobalization movement, then at least some bioregionalists need to take direct action by joining the work of resistance to corporate globalization.

These two positions need not be mutually exclusive. Indeed, those bioregionalists who argue for resistance to corporate rule also recognize the essential need for (and themselves engage in) local work on creating grounded, bioregional alternatives in civil society. And Haenke, on the other hand, with all his misgivings about the antiglobalization movement, recognizes the need for "appropriately-used (i.e., much more sparing, targeted, specific, contextualized) measures of protest and other opposition" (2001).

These Internet discussions provided an inspiration and impetus for the most recent continental gathering of bioregionalists, in Camp Wood, Kansas, the Eighth Continental Bioregional Congress. After a hiatus of six years with no continental gatherings, bioregionalists once again picked up the baton of continental networking in 2002 to renew the face-to-face exchange of local and bioregional experiences. Much had transpired since the 1996 gathering in Tepoztlan, Mexico. In Central and South America, the ongoing work of the Huehuecoyotl Caravan made substantial bioregionalist contributions to the explosive growth of the Ecovillage Network of the Americas. At the same time, the corporate neoliberal agenda was unfolding through elite and exclusive institutions such as NAFTA and the FTAA. Like others in the awakening antiglobalization movement of civil society, bioregionalists were beginning to face up to the stark reality of global economic and political corporatization. Issues of corporate rule, corporate abuse of democracy, resistance to the corporate agenda, renewal of civil society, and redistribution of wealth were important at the Kansas continental gathering.

Specific objectives and recommended actions were based on the principle that "citizens must set the rules for corporations." With respect to actions, the congress agreed that, "collectively, we can work to change the rules for corporate governance, prosecute and penalize corporate crime, and ultimately abolish corporate personhood. We must resist corporate globalization, privatization of the commons (water, air, land, airwaves, and gene pools), and GMO production and patents on life" (Continental Bioregional Congress Minutes 2002, 11).

In addition, congress participants fully agreed that we must get corporations out of public schools; create local representative economic justice councils; tax the rich instead of the poor; work to amend local ordinances, taxes, and codes that make it difficult to live sustainably; work toward ending agricultural and corporate subsidies; and establish the redistribution of wealth as a priority. It was understood that such initiatives should be advanced in the context of both political and economic actions, supported by the kinds of ongoing local efforts of education and organization examined throughout this book. Clearly, bioregionalists have begun to address problems of corporate rule and the crisis of democracy. Following a bioregional approach, these problems were to be addressed at the local level, in place.

The corporate global agenda was also examined and opposed by bioregionalists at Camp Wood. Broader networking initiatives were envisioned. The struggle against neoliberalism and for democracy, social justice, and ecological sustainability was given specific support at this gathering when participants reached consensus on adopting the Cochabamba Declaration, a networking effort of the global civil society movement for democracy. In December 2000, over 2,000 farmers, workers, indigenous people, students, professionals, environmentalists, educators, nongovernmental organizations, retired people, and an international delegation of water activists in Cochabamba put out this declaration in the defence of the vital right to water. This broad effort emerged from the struggle of Bolivians to get their public water system under civic control once again after the giant corporation Bechtel took it over and immediately raised the rates 200 percent, far beyond what families could afford. Widespread protests forced Bechtel to leave, but the corporation then sued the Bolivian government for $25 million. Bechtel brought its case before the World Bank's International Centre for the Settlement of Investment Disputes, a body that operates behind closed doors.

The Bechtel-Bolivia case threatens to be a prototype for the operation of secret trade courts in which transnational corporations can sue local, state/ provincial, and national governments to overturn laws or extract payment for actions that block their access to local markets. It was the World Bank that forced Cochabamba's water into Bechtel's hands in the first place by threatening to withhold $600 million in international debt relief if Bolivia didn't privatize Cochabamba's public water system (Shultz 2002). Such secret courts are proposed for the FTAA to be put in place by 2006. The

Cochabamba Declaration calls for the right to life, the respect of nature, and the uses and traditions of "our ancestors and our peoples," while declaring (among other things) that "water belongs to the earth and all species and is sacred to life and so must be conserved, reclaimed and protected for all future generations and its natural patterns respected." The declaration concludes by asserting that water is best protected by local communities and citizens and that the peoples of the Earth are the only vehicle to promote democracy and save water.

Another global issue discussed at Camp Wood was the lack of accountability of the United States to the world. Like a growing number of Americans recovering from the 9/11 terrorist attack and the climate of fear orchestrated by the Bush regime, US bioregionalists at the Kansas gathering were shocked and dismayed by the warlike actions and threats of their own federal government. Participants whom I spoke with informally at breakfast and over coffee readily agreed that the United States had become a "rogue state." During the very week of that bioregional event, the US Congress approved President Bush's war resolution against Iraq. The same day bioregionalists responded with a peace resolution that condemned the US government's war against Iraq and all war and called for a national referendum on war before any military actions against any country are taken.

At the Kansas gathering were many Mexicans, including Alberto Ruz and Liora Adler of the Caravan. From them and from Albert Bates, we received news of the rapid growth of ecovillages in Central and South America (as well as in Asia, Western Europe, and a few in the United States and Canada) and of the networks among them, including the Ecovillage Network of the Americas and the Global Ecovillage Network in Europe, Oceania/Asia and South Asia, and an International Secretariat in Denmark. The Huehuecoyotl Caravan proposed that the bioregional movement endorse and commit to participate in a hemispheric "gathering, congress or council of visions" (Ruz 2002) in Cuzco, Peru, in September 2003. The event in Cuzco focused on bringing together representatives from diverse ethnic, bioregional, and national networks from Mexico and Central and South America. This was agreed to by the plenary. Ruz commented shortly after the Kansas congress that with this decision "we open the possibility to create alliances with other networks, friendly organizations and movements working in the same direction our movement has been working for more than two decades, providing a unique experience for northern activists to meet, learn and share with people from the whole hemisphere" (2002). For Ruz, this was important good news for the expansion of the bioregional movement.

The Kansas congress was, in great part, a renewal of bioregional continental networking, a reinvigorated move to connect the local with the global, and a growing commitment to engage with issues of democracy and diversity vis-à-vis both corporate and state sectors at the local, bioregional, national, and global levels. Given that six years had gone by between bioregional "continentals," there was much discussion about how often North American bioregional gatherings should be held. Some suggested four years between gatherings to give local bioregional endeavours more priority and space. Ruz, in particular, argued strongly against this since the ecovillages and their networks were moving so fast. Enthusiasm built for holding a ninth continental bioregional congress in two years. Bioregional reinhabitants from EarthHaven, an ecovillage founded in 1994 in the Southern Appalachians in North Carolina, offered to host the next congress sometime in 2004. (Due to organizational problems this Congress was postponed to 2005.) This would be the first time the congress was hosted by a functioning ecovillage. Ruz stressed the importance of this precedent for hemispheric coherence with the burgeoning ecovillage movement and commented that it would help to support emerging or established intentional communities and ecovillages in the various bioregions of the north.

In conclusion, bioregionalists have at least begun to confront issues of corporate globalization. They have moved in the direction of identifying the corporate sector as a serious challenge to bioregional vision and praxis (or to any democratic citizens' initiatives). They have undertaken to begin opposing specific corporate actions such as Bechtel's case against Bolivia, while generally condemning privatization of the commons. Others have been directly involved in the global citizen movement against corporate rule and for democracy. What does all this mean? Bioregionalists, like millions of others around the globe, are starting to come to terms with the global corporate megamachine described and analyzed at the beginning of this book. From the perspective of building a democratic civil society, bioregionalist praxis has much to offer. Local/bioregional horizontal actions contribute to the strengthening of a consensus-building strategy for a democratic culture of cooperation and empowered citizen individual and collective responsibility. This represents an essential shift from the citizen as consumerist economic man toward the citizen as a genuine social being in a truly civil society where both individual and collective responsibility for the whole society – political, economic, and civil – and its ecological relationships with the natural world is everyone's business. A grounded culture of democracy in civil society is the only real and lasting basis for truly democratic reforms in both the political and the economic spheres, and it rightly remains a primary concern of bioregionalists. Around this fundamental vision, bioregionalists have patiently built a common program for long-term transformation through the work of consensus building at continental congresses. This alone has been a remarkable achievement, especially since this hard-won consensus is based on the direct experiences of bioregionalists living in very different circumstances in the United States, Mexico, and Canada. That is the strength of bioregional unity-in-diversity.

Bioregionalism presents a very logical (as well as eco-logical) and sensible alternative to globalism; rather, bioregionalism offers many bioregional alternatives to globalism, each made particular by the geography (biophysical and sociocultural), the history (natural and human), and the human capacity to reclaim, adapt, invent, and live indigenous and diverse bioregional solutions to globalism's one-world, monocultural, technological, neoconservative society. As John Drysek has argued (1997), and as I have shown, bioregionalism is informed by both a spiritual/romantic ethic and a practical, logical ethic. This is another strength of the movement. Bioregionalists have developed, borrowed, and adapted practical tools and methods to begin moving in the here and now toward real societal change. They have melded these practical tools with an emotionally and spiritually motivating ecocommunal ethic – also grounded in the here and now – of place, bioregion, and planet.

The outstanding problem is that this beautiful, long-term vision and the short- and long-term praxis to implement it are seriously endangered unless the global corporate agenda and global corporate power are addressed, not only in the long term but also in the immediate present. As the experience of the eighth continental congress showed, bioregionalists have begun to engage with the global megamachine, and some have become active in the global people's movement toward a democratic global order. Given the analysis in this book, much more needs to be done. First, much more can be done at the level of thinking through strategic questions. At the Kansas Continental Bioregional Congress, there was no consensus or even an attempt to reach consensus on a strategic approach to local-global organizing. Of course, the very size of the global power problem is daunting for anyone thinking about viable, sane, and democratic alternatives. It is doubtless too much to ask that quick consensus be reached about such a deeply crucial and vital question. Given the many voices and approaches within bioregionalism, and the fact that the peoples' movement for global democracy is young and emergent, more reflection and discussion may be the best initial approach. Real consensus process takes time, but it provides stronger commitment to action once true consensus is reached.

The problem of neoliberal globalization and the manic logic of the global megamachine are real world crises for anyone concerned about democracy, social justice, the right to self-determination for all peoples, and local and global ecological sustainability. Those who are starting to face up to corporate globalism need to envision real alternatives and discover real "places" (in the fullest sense of the word) to begin the transformation. The theoretical framework that I have employed throughout my exploration of bioregionalism is simply another tool to help think more clearly and strategically about democratic transformation of both corporate and state institutions as well as civil society in the age of global corporate rule.

References

Aberley, Doug. 1985. "Bioregionalism: A Territorial Approach to Governance and Development of Northwest British Columbia." MA thesis, University of British Columbia.
–. 1992. "Field Notes for Reclaiming the Commons: The History and Practice of Bioregionalism." Photocopy.
–, ed. 1993. *Boundaries of Home: Mapping for Local Empowerment*. Gabriola Island, BC: New Society Publishers.
–. 1998. Interview by author, 15 November, Vancouver, BC.
–. 1999. Interview by author, 20 October, Vancouver, BC.
Aberley, Doug, et al., eds. 1995. *Giving the Land a Voice: Mapping Our Home Places*. Salt Spring Island, BC: Salt Spring Island Community Services.
Abram, David. 1997. *The Spell of the Sensuous*. New York: Vintage Books.
Adair, Margot, and Sharon Howell. 1988. *The Subjective Side of Politics*. San Francisco: Tools for Change.
–. 1997. *Breaking Old Patterns, Weaving New Ties*. San Francisco: Tools for Change.
Adler, Margot. 1986. *Drawing down the Moon: Witches, Druids, Goddess-Worshippers, and Other Pagans in America Today*. Boston: Beacon Press.
Alexander, Christopher, et al. 1977. *A Pattern Language*. New York: Oxford University Press.
Amin, Samir. 1974. *Accumulation on a World Scale: A Critique of Underdevelopment Theory*. New York: Monthly Review Press.
Andruss, Van, Chris Plant, Judy Plant, and Eleanor Wright, eds. 1990. *Home! A Bioregional Reader*. Philadelphia: New Society Publishers.
Andruss, Van, and Eleanor Wright. 1984. "Culture Is the Missing Link." *Catalyst* April-May: 3.
Appleyard, Donald. 1981. *Livable Streets*. Berkeley: University of California Press.
Aulakh, Preet S., and Michael Schecter, eds. 2000. *Rethinking Globalization(s): From Corporate Transnationalism to Local Interventions*. East Lansing: Michigan State University.
Bates, Albert. 2002. Interview by author, 12 October, Camp Wood, Kansas.
Beatley, Timothy, and Kristy Manning. 1997. *The Ecology of Place: Planning for Environment, Economy, and Community*. Washington, DC: Island Press.
Beavis, Mary Ann. 1991. "Stewardship, Planning, and Public Policy." *Plan Canada* 31, 6: 75-82.
Bellah, Robert, et al. 1985. *Habits of the Heart*. Berkeley: University of California Press.
Berg, Peter, ed. 1976. *Amble toward Continent Congress*. San Francisco: Planet Drum Foundation.
–. 1978. *Reinhabiting a Separate Country: A Bioregional Anthology of Northern California*. San Francisco: Planet Drum Foundation.
–. 1983. "More than Just Saving What's Left." *Raise the Stakes* 8: 1-2.
–. 1986. "Growing a Life-Place Politics." *Raise the Stakes* 11: 5-8.
–. 1988a. Interview by author, 23 August, Paradise Valley, Squamish, BC. Tape recording.

–. 1988b. Green City Workshop, NABC III, 24 August, Paradise Valley, Squamish, BC. Tape recording.

–. 1989. Interview by author. 7 August, Planet Drum, San Francisco. Tape recording.

–. 1996a. "Gathering in Mexico." Bioregional Listserve, 1 December.

–. 1996b. Interview by author, 21 November, Tepoztlan, Mexico. Tape recording.

Berg, Peter, Beryl Magilavy, and Seth Zuckerman, eds. 1989. *A Green City Program for San Francisco Bay Area Cities and Towns*. San Francisco: Planet Drum Books.

Berger, John J. 1990. *Environmental Restoration: Science and Strategies for Restoring the Earth*. Washington, DC: Island Press.

Berkes, Fikret, and Carl Folke. 1994. "Investing in Cultural Capital for Sustainable Use of Natural Capital." In *Investing in Natural Capital,* ed. AnnMarie Jansson, Monica Hammer, Carl Folke, and Robert Costanza, 128-49. Washington, DC: Island Press.

Berman, Morris. 1981. *The Reenchantment of the World*. Ithaca, NY: Cornell University Press.

–. 1989. *Coming to Our Senses: Body and Spirit in the Hidden History of the West*. New York: Simon and Schuster.

Berman, Morris, Murray Bookchin, Ernest Callenbach, and Gary Snyder. 1981. "Cities: Salvaging the Parts." *Raise the Stakes* 1, 3: 12-14.

Berry, Tom. 1988. *The Dream of the Earth*. San Francisco: Sierra Club Books.

Bigwood, Carol. 1993. *Earth Muse: Feminism, Nature, and Art*. Philadelphia: Temple University Press.

Bird-David, Nurit. 1992. "Beyond the Original Affluent Society: A Culturalist Reformulation." *Current Anthropology* 33, 1: 25-47.

Block, Walter, ed. 1990. *Economics and the Environment: A Reconciliation*. Vancouver: Fraser Institute.

Blore, Sean. 1998. "The 'S' Word." *Georgia Straight* 25 June-2 July: 17.

Booth, Kelly. 1984. "How Humans Adapt." *Catalyst* April-May: 8.

Boothroyd, Peter, and Craig Davis. 1991. "The Meaning of Community Economic Development." UBC Planning Papers 25. Vancouver: School of Community and Regional Planning, University of British Columbia.

Bowers, C.A. 1993. *Education, Cultural Myths, and the Ecological Crisis*. Albany: State University of New York Press.

Brandt, Barbara. 1995. *Whole Life Economics: Revaluing Daily Life*. Philadelphia: New Society Publishers.

Brentamar, Olaf. 1997. "Kinship Gardening." E-mail communication.

"The Bridge River People." 1983. *Catalyst* April: 2.

Briggs, Beatrice, et al., eds. 1997. *The First Bioregional Gathering of the Americas Proceedings*. Blue Mounds, WI: Turtle Island Office.

Brody, Hugh. 1981. *Maps and Dreams*. New York: Penguin Books.

Brown, Lester, et al. 1996. *State of the World, 1996*. New York: W.W. Norton.

Brown, Lester, and Hal Kane. 1994. *Full House: Reassessing the Earth's Population Carrying Capacity*. New York: W.W. Norton.

Bullard, Robert, and Beverly Wright. 1990. "The Quest for Environmental Equity: Mobilizing the Black Community for Social Change." *Race, Poverty, and the Environment* 1, 2: 3.

Canfield, Christopher. 1990. *Ecocity Conference 1990: Report of the First International Ecocity Conference*. Berkeley: Urban Ecology.

Carr, Mike. 1990. "Place, Pattern, and Politics: The Bioregional Movement in Turtle Island." MA major paper, York University.

Castells, Manuel, and Peter Hall. 1997. *The Power of Identity*. London: Blackwell Publishers.

Cayley, David. 1986. *New Ideas in Ecology and Economics*. CBC Radio four-part series, 29 May-18 June.

Cheney, Jim. 1989. "Postmodern Environmental Ethics: Ethics as Bioregional Narrative." *Environmental Ethics* 11: 117-34.

Cholette, Kathryn, Don Alexander, and Frank Tester. 1996. "Centralism, De-Centralism, and Bioregionalism." *New City Magazine* 17: 35-38.

Chomsky, Noam. 1999. *Profit over People: Neoliberalism and Global Order.* New York: Seven Stories Press.

Ciarlo, Giovanni. 1998. "EcoAldea Huehuecoyotl A.C." *Ecovillages* 1, 1: 1.

–. 2001. Bioregional Listserve, 17 February.

Cienfuegos, Paul. 1999. "Arcata, CA's Measure F." E-mail communication.

City of Vancouver. 1990. *Clouds of Change: Final Report of the City of Vancouver Task Force on Atmospheric Change.* Vol. 1. Vancouver: City of Vancouver.

–. 1992. *City Plan* [draft]. Vancouver: City of Vancouver.

Clarkson, Linda, Vern Morisette, and Gabriel Regallet. 1992. *Our Responsibility to the Seventh Generation: Indigenous Peoples and Sustainable Development.* Winnipeg: International Institute for Sustainable Development.

Cohen, Jean, and Andrew Arato. 1992. *Civil Society and Political Theory.* Cambridge, MA: MIT Press.

Coleman, James. 1990. *Foundations of Social Theory.* Cambridge, MA: Harvard University Press.

Continental Bioregional Congress Minutes. 2002. 10 October, Camp Wood, Kansas.

Coover, Virginia, et al. 1977. *Resource Manual for a Living Revolution.* Philadelphia: New Society Press.

Cronon, William. 1983. *Changes in the Land: Indians, Colonists, and the Ecology of New England.* New York: Hill and Wang.

–, ed. 1996. *Uncommon Ground: Toward Reinventing Nature.* New York: W.W. Norton.

Daigle, Jean-Marc, and Donna Havinga. 1996. *Restoring Nature's Place.* Schomberg, ON: Ecological Outlook Consulting.

Dalton, George, ed. 1968. *Primitive, Archaic, and Modern Economies: Essays of Karl Polanyi.* New York: Anchor Books.

Daly, Herman, and John Cobb. 1989. *For the Common Good.* Boston: Beacon Press.

Davis, Mike. 1992. *City of Quartz: Excavating the Future in Los Angeles.* New York: Random House.

de Tocqueville, Alexis. 1969. *Democracy in America.* Garden City, NY: Anchor Books and Doubleday.

Diamond, Jared. 1992. *The Third Chimpanzee.* New York: HarperCollins.

Diamond, Stanley. 1974. *In Search of the Primitive: A Critique of Civilization.* New Brunswick, NJ: Transaction Books.

Dodd, Edwin Merrick. 1934. *American Business Corporations until 1860.* Cambridge, MA: Harvard University Press.

Dolcini, Marie, et al., eds. 1991. *North American Bioregional Congress Proceedings IV.* San Francisco: Planet Drum Foundation.

Douglas, Mike, and John Friedmann. 1998. *Cities for Citizens: Planning and the Rise of Civil Society in a Global Age.* Chichester, UK: John Wiley and Sons.

Drysek, John S. 1997. *The Politics of the Earth: Environmental Discourses.* Oxford: Oxford University Press.

Dubose, Pat, ed. 1992. *Turtle Island Bioregional Congress V Proceedings.* Blanco, Texas.

Dulas, Mikey, ed. 1996. "MRC Annual Statement." *Mattole Restoration Newsletter* winter: 11.

Eckersley, Robyn. 1992. *Environmentalism and Political Theory.* Albany: State University of New York Press.

Edwards, Bob, Michael Foley, and Mario Diani. 2001. *Beyond Tocqueville.* Hanover, NH: Tufts University.

Ehrlich, Paul R., and Anne Ehrlich. 1981. *Extinction: The Causes and Consequences of the Disappearance of the Species.* New York: Random House.

Eisler, Rianne. 1987. *The Chalice and the Blade: Our History, Our Future.* San Francisco: Harper and Row.

Eliade, Mircea. 1968. *Myth and Reality.* New York: Harper and Row.

Engwicht, David. 1993. *Reclaiming Our Cities and Towns: Better Living with Less Traffic.* Gabriola Island, BC: New Society Publishers.

Estes, Caroline. 1984. "Consensus." *In Context* autumn: 19.

Evernden, Neil. 1985. *The Natural Alien*. Toronto: University of Toronto Press.

Everton, Bob. 1996. "What Is the Relationship between Discourse Ethics and Civil Society?" Presented at the Learned Society, Canadian Communication Association Conference, 30 May-1 June, Brock University, Saint Catharines, ON.

Ewen, Stuart. 1976. *Captains of Consciousness: Advertising and the Social Roots of the Consumer Culture*. New York: McGraw-Hill.

Feit, Harvey. 1973. "The Ethno-Ecology of the Waswanipi Cree." In *Cultural Ecology*, ed. Bruce Cox, 115-25. Toronto: McClelland and Stewart.

Fine, Ben. 2001. *Social Capital versus Social Theory: Political Economy and Social Science at the Turn of the Millennium*. New York: Routledge.

Folke, Carl, et al. 1997. "Ecosystem Appropriations by Cities." *Ambio* 26: 167-72.

Forsey, Helen, ed. 1993. *Circles of Strength: Community Alternatives to Alienation*. Philadelphia: New Society Publishers.

Fourth North American Bioregional Congress. 1990. Pre-Congress brochure.

Fox, Jonathan. 1996. "How Does Civil Society Thicken? The Political Construction of Social Capital in Rural Mexico." Presented at the Workshop on Social Capital and Development: Implications for Policy and Program, 8-9 November, Harvard Center for Population and Development Studies, Boston.

Freund, Peter, and George Martin. 1993. *The Ecology of the Automobile*. Montreal: Black Rose Books.

Friedman, Milton. 1962. *Capitalism and Freedom*. Chicago: University of Chicago Press.

Friedmann, John. 1987. *Planning in the Public Domain*. Princeton: Princeton University Press.

–. 1990. *Empowerment: The Politics of Alternative Development*. Los Angeles: University of California.

–. 1998. "The New Political Economy of Planning: The Rise of Civil Society." In *Cities for Citizens: Planning and the Rise of Civil Society in a Global Age*, ed. Mike Douglas and John Friedmann, 19-35. New York: John Wiley and Sons.

Furuseth, O., and C. Cocklin. 1995. "Regional Perspectives on Resource Policy: Implementing Sustainable Management in New Zealand." *Journal of Environmental Planning and Management* 38, 2: 181-200.

Galbraith, J.K. 2000. "How the Economists Got It Wrong." *American Prospect* 11, 7, <http://www.prospect.org/print/vu/7/galbraith-j.html>.

Galtung, Johan. 1971. "A Structural Theory of Imperialism." *Journal of Peace Research* 8, 2: 437-81.

Goldhaft, Judy. 1989. Interview by author, 7 August, Planet Drum, San Francisco. Tape recording.

–. 1999. Telephone interview by author, 11 February.

Goodland, Robert. 1991. "The Case that the World Has Reached Limits." In *Environmentally Sustainable Economic Development: Building on Brundtland*, ed. Robert Goodland et al., 15-27. Paris: UNESCO.

Gowdy, John. 1998. *Limited Wants, Unlimited Means: A Reader on Hunter-Gatherer Economics and the Environment*. Washington, DC: Island Press.

Graeber, David. 2002. "The Globalization Movement: Some Points of Clarification." <gpm@listserver.jriver.com>.

Granovetter, Mark. 1985. "Economic Action, Social Structure, and Embeddedness." *American Journal of Sociology* 91: 481-510.

Greater Vancouver Regional District (GVRD). 1994. *Greater Vancouver Key Facts: A Statistical Profile of Greater Vancouver, Canada*. Vancouver: Strategic Planning Department, GVRD.

"Green Movement." 1985. *Catalyst* April: 19.

Gregory, Derek. 1994. *Geographical Imaginations*. Cambridge, MA: Blackwell Publishers.

Gregory, Lyman. 1992. "Green City Report." *Raise the Stakes* 18-19: 22.

Greider, William. 1997. *One World, Ready or Not: The Manic Logic of Global Capitalism*. New York: Simon and Schuster.

Grootaert, Christian. 1998. "Social Capital: The Missing Link?" Social Capital Initiative Working Paper No. 3, 1-24. Washington, DC: Social Development Department, World Bank.

Grossman, Richard, and Frank Adams. 1993. *Taking Care of Business: Citizenship and the Charter of Incorporation.* Cambridge, MA: Charter, Ink.

Grumbine, R. Edward. 1992. *Ghost Bears: Exploring the Biodiversity Crisis.* Washington, DC: Island Press.

Haenke, David. 1988. Interview by author, 20 August, Paradise Valley, Squamish, BC. Tape recording.

–. 1996. "Gathering in Mexico." Bioregional Listserve, 30 November.

–. 2001. Bioregional Listserve. 22 August.

Hammond, Herb. 1991. *Seeing the Forest among the Trees: The Case for Holistic Forest Use.* Vancouver: Polestar.

Hart, Alexandra, et al., eds. 1987. *North American Bioregional Congress Proceedings II.* Forestville, CA: Hart Publishing.

Harvard Center for Population and Development Studies. 1996. Workshop on Social Capital and Development: Implications for Policy and Program, Background Readings, 8-9 November, Harvard Center for Population and Development Studies, Cambridge, MA.

Harvey, David. 1989. *The Urban Experience.* Baltimore: Johns Hopkins University Press.

–. 2000. *Spaces of Hope.* Edinburgh: Edinburgh Univeristy Press.

Henderson, Denise, et al., eds. 1984. *North American Bioregional Congress Proceedings I.* Ozark Bioregion: New Life Farms.

Henderson, Hazel. 1991. *Paradigms in Progress: Life beyond Economics.* Indianapolis: Knowledge Systems.

hooks, bell. 1990. *Yearning: Race, Gender, and Cultural Politics.* Boston: South End Press.

House, Freeman. 1989. Interview by author, 3 August, Mattole Valley, CA. Tape recording.

–. 1994. "Why the Initiative Must Come from the Watersheds." Presented at President's Council for Sustainable Development, 4 October, Lake Tahoe. Photocopy.

–. 1995. "Reinhabitation and Ecological Restoration: A Marriage Proposal." Presented at the Society for Ecological Restoration meeting, Seattle. Photocopy.

–. 1996. "Forgetting and Remembering the Instructions of the Land." Rufus Putnam Lecture, 24 April, Ohio State University. Photocopy.

–. 1997a. "The Spirit of Restoration." Talk given at Shasta V, St. Patrick's Point Park, CA. Photocopy.

–. 1997b. Interview by author, 6 September, St. Patrick's Point Park, CA. Tape recording.

–. 1998. Telephone interview by author, 6 October, Vancouver, BC.

–. 1999. *Totem Salmon: Life Lessons from Another Species.* Boston: Beacon Press.

IIED. 1997. *Steps to Lighten Britain's Ecological Footprint.* London: International Institute for Environment and Development.

Independent Media Center. 2000. *This Is What Democracy Looks Like: A Documentary Film.* Seattle: Independent Media Center.

Jackins, Harvey. 1975. *Guidebook to Reevaluation Counseling.* Seattle: Rational Island Publishers.

Jacobs, Jane. 1992. *The Death and Life of Great American Cities.* New York: Vintage Books.

Jenks, Mike, and Rod Burgess. 2000. *Compact Cities: Sustainable Urban Forms for Developing Cities.* London: Spon Press.

Kaner, Sam. 1996. *Facilitator's Guide to Participatory Decision-Making.* Gabriola Island, BC: New Society Publishers.

Keane, John. 1988. *Civil Society and the State: New European Perspectives.* London: Verso.

Kelly, Marjorie. 1999. *Is Maximizing Returns to Shareholders a Legitimate Mandate?* San Francisco: Berrett-Koehler Communications.

King Cobos, Andres. 1998. Telephone interview by author, 24 September.

Klein, Naomi. 2000. *NO LOGO: Taking Aim at the Brand Bullies.* Toronto: Random House.

Kohr, Leopold. 1978. *The Breakdown of Nations.* New York: E.P. Dutton.

Kong, Ga-Ching. 1997. *Southeast False Creek: Council's Next Challenge.* Case Study Report 2. Vancouver: Social Change Institute.

Korten, David. 1995. *When Corporations Rule the World.* San Francisco: Berrett-Koehler Communications.

–. 1998. *Globalizing Civil Society: Reclaiming Our Right to Power.* New York: Seven Stories Press.

Kraft, Marty, et al. 1993. *Earth Day in Your School and Community*. Kansas City, MO: Heartland All Species Project.

Krupp, Edwin C. 1983. *Echoes of the Ancient Skies*. New York: New American Library.

Kuri, Laura. 1996. Interview by author, 21 November, Tepoztlan, Mexico. Tape recording.

LaChapelle, Dolores. 1978. *Earth Wisdom*. Silverton, CO: Finn Hill Arts.

–. 1988. *Sacred Land, Sacred Sex, Rapture of the Deep: Concerning Deep Ecology – and Celebrating Life*. Silverton, CO: Finn Hill Arts.

Lanza, Dana. 1998. "Environmental Justice: Teaching Links between Health and Environment." *Green City Newsletter and Calendar* 28: 3, 5.

Leacock, Eleanor, and Richard Lee, eds. 1987. *Politics and History in Band Societies*. New York: Cambridge University Press.

Leakey, Richard. 1994. *The Origin of Humankind*. New York: Basic Books.

Lee, Richard. 1992. "Art, Science, or Politics? The Crisis in Hunter-Gatherer Studies." *American Anthropologist* 94, 1: 31-54.

Lee, Richard, and Irvin Devore, eds. 1979. *Man the Hunter*. Hawthorn, NY: Adine Publishing.

Lehan, Mel. 1994. "Neighbour to Neighbour: A Brief History." *Forum for Planning Action Newsletter* fall: 6-7.

Leitner, Helga, and Mark Garner. 1993. "The Limits of Local Initiatives: A Reassessment of Urban Entrepreneurialism for Urban Development." *Urban Geography* 14, 1: 57-77.

Levine, David. 1996. Interview by author, 20 November, Tepoztlan, Mexico. Tape recording.

Lewis, Oscar. 1960. *Tepoztlán: Village in Mexico*. New York: Holt.

Lewis, Steven. 1990. "Green City Center Report." *Raise the Stakes* 16: 13.

Linn, Karl. 1990. "Inner Cities to Join Ecology Debate." *Race, Poverty, and the Environment* 1, 2: 1.

Lipschutz, Ronnie D. 1996. *Global Civil Society and Global Environmental Governance*. New York: SUNY Press.

Litke, Steve, et al. 1994. *Proceedings: Greening Our Cities Conference*. Vancouver: Social Planning and Research Council.

Lloyd, Steve. 1989. Interview by author, 18 June, Toronto. Tape recording.

Loury, Glen. 1977. "A Dynamic Theory of Racial Income Differences." In *Women, Minorities, and Employment Discrimination*, ed. P.A. Wallace and A. LaMond, 153-86. Lexington, MA: Lexington Books.

–. 1987. "Why Should We Care about Group Inequality?" *Social Philosophy and Policy* 5: 249-71.

MacPherson, C.B. 1973. *Democratic Theory: Essays in Retrieval*. Oxford: Clarendon Press.

Makepeace, Glen. 1988. Interview by author, 26 August, Paradise Valley, Squamish, BC. Tape recording.

–. 1997. Interview by author, 24 October, Vancouver, BC. Tape recording.

Mander, Jerry. 1991. *In the Absence of the Sacred: The Failure of Technology and the Survival of the Indian Nations*. San Francisco: Sierra Club Books.

Mann, Michael. 1986. *A History of Power from the Beginning to A.D. 1760*. Vol. 1 of *The Sources of Social Power*. Cambridge, UK: Cambridge University Press.

Marcos, Subcommandante. 2001. *Our Word Is Our Weapon: Selected Writings*. New York: Seven Stories Press.

Martinez, Dennis. 1993. "Managing a Precarious Balance: Wilderness versus Sustainable Forestry." *Winds of Change* summer: 23-28.

Marx, Karl, and Frederick Engels. 1975. *Selected Works*. Moscow: Progress Publishers.

Maser, Chris. 1988. *The Redesigned Forest*. San Pedro, CA: R. and E. Miles.

–. 1992. *Global Imperative*. Walpole, NH: Stillpoint Publishing.

McGinnis, Michael Vincent, ed. 1999. *Bioregionalism*. London: Routledge.

Medicine Eagle, Brooke. 1991. *Buffalo Woman Comes Singing*. New York: Ballantine Books.

Meeker-Lowry, Susan. 1988. *Economics as if the Earth Really Mattered*. Philadelphia: New Society Publishers.

Merchant, Carolyn. 1980. *The Death of Nature: Women, Ecology, and the Scientific Revolution*. New York: Harper and Row Publishers.

Mies, Maria. 1986. *Patriarchy and Accumulation on a World Scale: Women in the International Division of Labour.* London: Zed Books.

Mollison, Bill. 1990. *Permaculture: A Practical Guide for a Sustainable Future.* Washington, DC: Island Press.

Molotch, H. 1976. "The City as a Growth Machine: Toward a Political Economy of Place." *American Journal of Sociology* 82: 309-32.

–. 1993. "The Political Economy of Growth Machines." *Journal of Urban Affairs* 15, 1: 29-53.

Mumford, Lewis. 1970. *The Pentagon of Power.* New York: Harcourt Brace Jovanovich.

NABC/Bioregional Project Brochure. 1984.

Naess, Arne. 1990. *Ecology, Community, and Lifestyle.* New York: Cambridge University Press.

Nilsen, Richard. 1991. *Helping Nature Heal.* Berkeley: Whole Earth Catalogue and Ten Speed Press.

Noss, Reed. 1992. "The Wildlands Project Land Conservation Strategy." *Wild Earth* special issue: 10-26.

Permaculture Association of Western Australia. 1996. *Sixth International Permaculture Conference Proceedings, Sept. 27-Oct. 7.* Perth: Permaculture Association of Western Australia.

Pinkerton, Evelyn. 1998. "Integrated Management of a Temperate Montane Forest Ecosystem through Wholistic Forestry: A British Columbia Example." In *Linking Social and Ecological Systems: Management Practices and Social Mechanisms for Building Resilience,* ed. Fikret Berkes and Carl Folke, 363-89. Cambridge, UK: Cambridge University Press.

Plant, Judy, and Chris Plant, eds. 1990. *Turtle Talk.* Philadelphia: New Society Publishers.

Planet Drum Staff. 1995-96. "Green City Report." *Raise the Stakes* 25: 13.

–. 1996. "Green City Report." *Raise the Stakes* 26: 15.

Plumwood, Val. 1993. *Feminism and the Mastery of Nature.* New York: Routledge.

Polanyi, Karl. 1957. *The Great Transformation.* Boston: Beacon Press.

–. 1968. *Primitive, Archaic, and Modern Economies.* Garden City, NY: Anchor Books.

Pollock, Sarah. 1989. "The Charge of the Brook Brigades." *Sierra* 74, 6: 24-28.

Putnam, Robert. 1993a. *Making Democracy Work.* Princeton: Princeton University Press.

–. 1993b. "The Prosperous Community: Social Capital and Public Life." *American Prospect* spring: 35-42.

Pyne Addelson, Kathryn. 1991. *Impure Thoughts: Essays on Philosophy, Feminism, and Ethics.* Philadelphia: Temple University Press.

Rappaport, Roy. 1986. "Restructuring the Ecology of Cities." *Raise the Stakes* 11: 4-5.

Redmond, Layne. 1997. *When the Drummers Were Women: A Spiritual History of Rhythm.* New York: Three Rivers Press.

Rees, William. 1990. "Atmospheric Change: Human Ecology in Disequilibrium." *International Journal of Environmental Studies* 36: 103-24.

–. 1995. "Achieving Sustainability: Reform or Transformation?" *Journal of Planning Literature* 9, 4: 343-61.

–. 1996a. "The Footprints of Consumption: Tracking Ecosphere Decline." *Trumpeter* 14, 1: 2-4.

–. 1996b. "Revisiting Carrying Capacity: Area-Based Indicators of Sustainability." *Population and Environment* 17: 195-215.

–. 2002. "Globalization and Sustainability: Conflict or Convergence?" *Bulletin of Science, Techonology and Society* 22, 4: 249-68.

Rees, William, and Mathis Wackernagel. 1994. "Ecological Footprints and Appropriated Carrying Capacity: Measuring the Natural Capital Requirements of the Human Economy." In *Investing in Natural Capital: The Ecological Economics Approach to Sustainability,* ed. AnnMarie Jansson, Monica Hammer, Carl Folke, and Robert Costanza, 362-90. Washington, DC: Island Press.

Register, Richard. 1987. *Ecocity Berkeley.* Berkeley: North Atlantic Books.

Reid, Barton. 1994. "Regional Planning in Seattle and Vancouver: A Cross-Border Comparison." *Planning Action* April-May: 5.

Relph, Edward. 1987. *The Modern Urban Landscape.* Baltimore: Johns Hopkins University Press.

Ronfeldt, David, et al. 1998. *The Zapatista Social Netwar in Mexico.* Santa Monica: RAND.

Ross, John. 2000. *The War against Oblivion: Zapatista Chronicles*. Monroe, ME: Common Courage Press.

Rowan, John. 1988. *Ordinary Ecstasy: Humanistic Psychology in Action*. New York: Routledge Press.

Rowe, Stan. 1990. *Home Place: Essays on Ecology*. Edmonton: NeWest.

Royal Commission on the Future of the Toronto Waterfront. 1992. Regeneration: Toronto's Waterfront and the Sustainable City, final report.

Ruz, Alberto Buenfil. 1988. Interview by author, 24 August, Paradise Valley, Squamish, BC. Tape recording.

–. 1996a. Interview by author, 21 November, Tepoztlan, Mexico. Tape recording.

–. 1996b. *Guardians of the Earth Vision Council: Our Story*. Photocopy.

–. 2002. "Congress Report." Bioregional Listserve, 16 October.

Sahlins, Marshall. 1974. *Stone Age Economics*. London: Tavistock Publications.

Sale, Kirkpatrick. 1980. *Human Scale*. New York: Coward, McCann, and Geoghegan.

–. 1985. *Dwellers in the Land: The Bioregional Vision*. San Francisco: Sierra Club Books.

Sams, Jamie, and David Carson. 1988. *Medicine Cards: The Discovery of Power Through the Ways of Animals*. Santa Fe, NM: Bear and Co.

Sanchez Navarro, Virginia. 1989. "Remembering the Goddess: Ecofeminism in Mexico." *New Catalyst* 14: 7.

Sandercock, Leonie. 1998. *Toward Cosmopolis: Planning for Multicultural Cities*. Chichester, UK: John Wiley and Sons.

Saul, John Ralston. 1995. *The Unconscious Civilization*. Toronto: Anansi Press.

Schecter, Michael, ed. 1999. *The Revival of Civil Society: Global and Comparative Perspectives*. East Lansing: Michigan State University Press.

Schmookler, Andrew Bard. 1984. *The Parable of the Tribes: The Problem of Power in Social Evolution*. Boston: Houghton Mifflin.

Shapiro, Elan. 1993. "Bioregionalism: An Interview with Ecopsychologist Elan Shapiro." *Creation Spirituality* March-April: 17-19.

Shepard, Paul. 1982. *Nature and Madness*. San Francisco: Sierra Club Books.

Shultz, Jim. 2002. "Bechtel Stikes Back at Bolivia." Pacific News Service, 11 November.

Simpson, David. 1989. Interview by author, 4 August, Mattole Valley, CA. Tape recording.

Six Nations Confederacy. 1986. *A Basic Call to Consciousness*. Roosevelt Town, NY: Akwesasne Notes.

Sklar, Holly, ed. 1980. *Trilateralism: The Trilateral Commission and Elite Planning for World Management*. Montreal: Black Rose Books.

Solnit, Rebecca. 1992. "Up the River of Mercy." *Sierra Club Magazine* November-December: 50-57, 78-84.

Snyder, Gary. 1977. *The Old Ways: Six Essays*. San Francisco: City Light Books.

–. 1980. *The Real Work*. New York: New Directions Books.

–. 1990. *The Practice of the Wild*. New York: North Point Press.

Starhawk. 1987. *Truth or Dare: Encounters with Power, Authority, and Mystery*. San Francisco: Harper and Row.

–. 2001. Bioregional Listserve. 5 February.

Stemler, Randall. 1991. "Mattole Watershed Alliance Born." *Mattole Restoration Newsletter* winter: 4, 9.

Swift, Richard. 2002. *The No-Nonsense Guide to Democracy*. Oxford: New Internationalist Publications and Verso.

Tanner, Adrian. 1985. *Bringing Home Animals: Religious Ideology and Mode of Production of the Mistassini Cree Hunters*. St. John's: Institute of Social and Economic Research, Memorial University of Newfoundland.

Thomas, Keith. 1987. *Man and the Natural World: Changing Attitudes in England 1500-1800.* Harmondsworth, UK: Penguin Books.

Todd, John, and Nancy Todd. 1984. *Bioshelters, Ocean Arks, City Farming: Ecology as the Basis of Design*. San Francisco: Sierra Club Books.

Todd, John, and George Tukel. 1981. *Reinhabiting Cities and Towns: Designing for Sustainability*. San Francisco: Planet Drum Foundation.

Tourraine, Alain. 1979. *The Voice and the Eye*. Chicago: University of Chicago Press.

Traina, Frank. 1994. Interview by author, 22 August, Lake Cobbosseecontee, ME. Tape recording.

Traina, Frank, and Susan Darley-Hill, eds. 1995. *Perspectives in Bioregional Education*. Troy, OH: North American Association for Environmental Education.

Tukel, George. 1982. *Toward a Bioregional Model: Clearing Ground for Watershed Planning*. San Francisco: Planet Drum Foundation.

Turner, Frederick. 1983. *Beyond Geography: The Western Spirit against the Wilderness*. New Brunswick, NJ: Rutgers University Press.

United Nations Development Program (UNDP). 2001. Human Development Report. New York and Oxford: Oxford University Press.

Urban Ecology, Inc. 1996. *Blueprint for a Sustainable Bay Area*. San Francisco: Urban Ecology, Inc.

Van der Ryn, Sim, and Peter Calthorpe. 1986. *Sustainable Communities: A New Design Synthesis for Cities, Suburbs, and Towns*. San Francisco: Sierra Club Books.

Voice of the Turtle. 1984a. 22 May.

Voice of the Turtle. 1984b. 23 May.

Voice of the Turtle. 1992. 20 May.

Voice of the Turtle. 1994a. 19 August.

Voice of the Turtle. 1994b. 20 August.

Wackernagel, Mathis, and William Rees. 1996. *Our Ecological Footprint: Reducing Human Impact on the Earth*. Gabriola Island, BC: New Society Publishers.

Wackernagel, M., L. Onisto, P. Bello, A. Linares, I. Falfan, J. Garcia, A. Guerrero, and M. Guerrero. 1999. "National Natural Capital Accounting with the Ecological Footprint Concept." *Ecological Economics* 29: 375-90.

Wallerstein, Immanuel. 1979. *The Capitalist World Economy*. Cambridge, UK: Cambridge University Press.

Walrafen, Janice. 1990. Interview by author, 25 August, Lake Cobbosseecontee, ME. Tape recording.

Walzer, Michael, ed. 1995. *Toward a Global Civil Society*. Oxford: Berghahn Books.

Waring, Marilyn. 1988. *Counting for Nothing: What Men Value and What Women Are Worth*. Wellington, NZ: Allen and Unwin.

Warkentin, Craig. 2001. *Reshaping World Politics: NGOs, the Internet, and Global Civil Society*. Oxford: Rowman and Littlefield Publishers.

Weinberg, Bill. 1996. "The Golf War of Tepoztlan: Popular Defense and Ecological Struggle in the Heartland of Zapata." The First Bioregional Gathering of the Americas Proceedings. Photocopy.

–. 1989. "Alternative Print in Mexico." *New Catalyst* 13: 5-6.

Wells, Chris. 1996. Interview by author, 22 November, Tepoztlan, Mexico. Tape recording.

Wilmsen, Edwin, and James Denbow. 1990. "Paradigmatic History of San-Speaking Peoples and Current Attempts at Revision." *Current Anthropology* 31, 5: 489-522.

Wilson, Edward O. 1992. *The Diversity of Life*. New York: W.W. Norton.

Wood, John E. 1980. *Sun, Moon, and Standing Stones*. Oxford: Oxford University Press.

Woollard, Robert F., and Aleck Ostry, eds. 2000. *Fatal Consumption: Rethinking Sustainable Development*. Vancouver, BC: UBC Press.

World Commission on Environment and Development. 1987. *Our Common Future*. New York: Oxford University Press.

Worster, Donald. 1985. *Nature's Economy: A History of Ecological Ideas*. Cambridge, UK: Cambridge University Press.

Wright, Eleanor. 1997. Interview by author, 3 August, Yalakom Valley, BC.

Yaron, Gil. 2002. *The Corporation: Inside and Out*. Vancouver, BC: Aurora Institute.

Zuckerman, Seth, ed. 1989. *North American Bioregional Congress Proceedings III*. San Francisco: Planet Drum Foundation.

–. 1997. "Call for Public Input: What's Your Priority?" *Mattole Restoration Newsletter* 12: 6-7.

Index

156; values, 16-17, 98-99; vertical reform strategies, 17-18, 287; "Welcome Home!" mission statement, 79-80. *See also* bioregionalism; congresses, bioregional
Bioregional Movement Committee, at NABC congresses, 249, 266
Bioregional Story Circle of Change, at TIBC V, 270
bioregionalism: as alternative to globalism, 306; and civil society theory, 16, 18; contrast with globalization, 2, 3; core concepts, 73-85; definition, 2, 16; education values, 86-90; inclusion of community of beings ethic in revised civil society theory, 291-95; long time frames for social change, 294; premises of, 3; spread of, 2. *See also* bioregional movement
biotic shift, 76
Black Tuesday (9/11). *See* 9/11, 2001
Block, Walter, 22
Blumenfeld, Hans, 26
Boggs, James, 255
Bolivia, fight for ownership of water against Bechtel-Bolivia, 303, 305
Bonner, Robert, 187
Booth, Kelly, 83
Borbley, Marc, 218-19
Boundaries of Home: Mapping for Local Empowerment (Aberley), 141-42
brand names, and "global sweatshops," 3
Brandt, Barbara, 67
"Breaking Through Ritual," 124-25, 131, 157
Bretton Woods system, of international trade, 6
Brewery Creek Historical Society, 232
bricolage, 211
Bridge River people, 191
Bridge River (Xwisten) Reserve, 192
Briggs, Beatrice, 143, 276
British Columbia, bioregional vertical change strategies, 288
British Columbia Environmental Network, 194
Brown, Fred, 186
Brown, Susan, 187
Burke, Clifford, 254
Bush, George W., 301

California Coastal Conservancy, 212
California Resources Agency, 144, 289
Callenbach, Earnest, 71
Calliou, Sharilyn, 89, 90, 91, 154
Calthorpe, Peter, 198-99
Calvin Klein, 3

Camelsfoot (intentional community). *See* Yalakom River community
Cameron, Brent, 232
capitalism: and colonialism, 5; and consumption, 4-5, 21; and industrialization, 5; roots of, 37; three major periods, 5-6. *See also* cultural capital; ecosocial capital; manufactured capital; natural capital; social capital
Caravan Theatre, 188
Caravana Arcoiris Por La Paz (Rainbow Peace Caravan), 180, 288
Castro, Fidel, 186
Catalyst (journal), 188
Cayugeno, Nilo, 254
Celebrate the Longest Night (1985), 198, 208
celebration: as bioregional value, 96; as community-building tool, 97-98
ceremonial village: at First Bioregional Gathering of the Americas, 278; at NABC congresses, 259
ceremony. *See* celebration; ritual
chanting: and communication between conscious and older brains, 126-27; as means to move beyond economic man, 127; power of, 129-30
Chemical Waste Management, 214-15
Chiavario, Nancy, 234
Chichen Itza, 181
children: children's and youth congresses at TIBC V, 271; Huehuecoyotl, march for animals and environment, 179; involvement in salmonid enhancement, 165
Children of the Green Earth, 244
Children's Council, at First Bioregional Gathering of the Americas, 277
Chomsky, Noam, 4, 6, 8
Ciarlo, Giovanni, 288
cities. *See* ecocities; entries beginning with "urban"
civil society: colonization of, and loss of horizontal communication, 41; and concept of home, 79; definition, 12-13; dominated by economic society, 52; and "love" economy (women's unpaid labour), 66-68; as movement for global democracy, 12; and permaculture movement, 151; as pivotal dimension of transformational change, 48; post-9/11, emphasis on family and community, 10; preference of term over "working class" by Zapatistas, 284; removal of economy by free trade, 31-32; separation from formal economic and political spheres, 32; transformation, away from consum-

ecocentric civil society theory: and bioregionalism, 297-301; democratization of the state, 297-99; geography as important dimension, 296-97; horizontal and vertical strategies for change, 296; limits on power of corporations, 299-301; mediation between civil society and the economic sphere, 299-300; principles, 295-97

ecocentric social capital: and bioregional economics, 104; creation through story, 122; definition, 47; principles, 105; replacement of natural capital for sustainability, 52

ecocities: activities for creation of, 202; "bioregional urbanites," 211; as catalysts for political change, 209; definition, 201; democratization of municipalities and neighbourhoods, 298, 300; design, for diversity and mixed use, 293-94; diversity, and density, 200-1; diversity, and planning, 203; diversity and community, 205; formation of social and ecosocial capital, 201; historical examples, 201; history in bioregional movement, 70; horizontal linkages of cooperation and collaboration, 210; inner city community development, 216; integration of small-scale economic activity, 210; movement in Mexico, 283; at NABC II, 251; need for contact with nature, 202; proximity policies and planning for, 203; reciprocity between urban region and ecosystem, 103; "slow streets," 203; transformation of, 200; volunteer activities, 216-17; writings on, 196-97

EcoCity Act Locally! Calendar (Vancouver), 226, 227, 231

Ecocity Berkeley, 201, 203-4

Ecocity Berkeley: Building Cities for a Healthy Future (City of Berkeley), 201

ecocity conference (1990), 213-14

EcoCity Network (Vancouver), 221, 223-34

ecofeminism: and bioregionalism, 73; at Camelsfoot, 191; expansion of kinship values into civil society, 79; ideas for ecocity conference organization, 213-14; as part of radical planning tradition, 48; patchwork quilt as metaphor for diversity, 93-94; on redefinition of home, 78; revaluing of men's and women's roles, 80-81

Ecofeminist Committee, at bioregional congresses, 250-51, 257, 269

ecological economics: and ecocentric civil society theory, 299-300; integrated small-scale economic activities in green cities, 210; relationship of production and consumption, 51-52. *See also* bioregional economics

ecological footprint: calculation of, 23-24; definition, 23; of rich vs. poor countries, 2-4

ecological restoration. *See* restoration, ecological

ecological self, 127, 157

ecological worldview, 21, 22-23

ecologics. *See* ecological economics

Ecology Center (San Francisco), 212

Ecology Council, at First Bioregional Gathering of the Americas, 277, 280-81

economic liberalism, 31. *See also* neoliberalism

economic man: accumulation as replacement for community, 33-34; as artificially universalized, compared with relational human self, 127; challenged by bioregional movement, 16; challenged by ecofeminism, 81; definition, 17, 54; as disconnected from community, 33-34; and "fatal consumption" patterns, 21; as individualistic consumer, 34-35; and monoculture, by obliteration of race and ethnicity, 135; not challenged by Cohen-Arato civil society theory, 41; as selfish maximizer of utilities, 294; transformation from individualism to social embeddedness, 93

economic society: and civil society theory, 38, 39; domination of civil society, 52; low degree of public participation in, 41

economic theory, denial of biophysical limits to growth, 22

Economics Committee, at bioregional congresses, 267

Economics as if the Earth Really Mattered (Meeker-Lowry), 105

economy, informal, 67

ecoregion, as different from bioregion, 77

ecosocial capital: created through group participation, 157; created through permaculture, 153; definition, 17; formation by reducing consumption, 294; generated through drumming, 128; inclusion of community of beings ethic, 98, 291-93; realized by reduction of natural capital consumption in cities, 201; realized through chanting, 127-28; relation to social capital, 66; and spirituality, on All Species Day, 133-34

Printed and bound in Canada by Friesens
Set in Stone by Artegraphica Design Co. Ltd.
Copy editor: Dallas Harrison
Proofreader: Jillian Shoichet
Indexer: Annette Lorek